Lecture Notes in Computer Science 7904

Commenced Publication in 1973
Founding and Former Series Editors:
Gerhard Goos, Juris Hartmanis, and Jan van Leeuwen

Michael Huth   N. Asokan   Srdjan Čapkun
Ivan Flechais   Lizzie Coles-Kemp (Eds.)

Trust
and Trustworthy
Computing

6th International Conference, TRUST 2013
London, UK, June 17-19, 2013
Proceedings

 Springer

Volume Editors

Michael Huth
Imperial College London, UK
E-mail: m.huth@imperial.ac.uk

N. Asokan
University of Helsinki, Finland
E-mail: asokan@acm.org

Srdjan Čapkun
ETH Zurich, Switzerland
E-mail: srdjan.capkun@inf.ethz.ch

Ivan Flechais
University of Oxford, UK
E-mail: ivan.flechais@cs.ox.ac.uk

Lizzie Coles-Kemp
Royal Holloway University of London, Egham, UK
E-mail: lizzie.coles-kemp@rhul.ac.uk

ISSN 0302-9743   e-ISSN 1611-3349
ISBN 978-3-642-38907-8   e-ISBN 978-3-642-38908-5
DOI 10.1007/978-3-642-38908-5
Springer Heidelberg Dordrecht London New York

Library of Congress Control Number: 2013939781

CR Subject Classification (1998): C.2, K.6.5, E.3, D.4.6, J.1, H.4

LNCS Sublibrary: SL 4 – Security and Cryptology

Typesetting: Camera-ready by author, data conversion by Scientific Publishing Services, Chennai, India

Printed on acid-free paper

Springer is part of Springer Science+Business Media (www.springer.com)

Preface

This volume contains the proceedings of the 6th International Conference on Trust and Trustworthy Computing (TRUST), held in London, UK, during June 17–19 2013.

Continuing the tradition of the previous conferences, held in Villach (2008), Oxford (2009), Berlin (2010), Pittsburgh (2011), and Vienna (2012), TRUST 2013 featured both a technical and a socioeconomic track. Like its previous instances, TRUST 2013 provided a unique interdisciplinary forum for researchers, practitioners, and decision makers to explore and evaluate new ideas for designing, building, and using trustworthy computing systems.

The conference program of TRUST 2013 shows that research in trust and trustworthy computing is active, at a high level of competency, and that it spans a wide range of areas and topics. In the technical track, for example, papers dealt with issues such as key management, hypervisor usage, information flow analysis, trust in network measurements, random number generators, case studies that evaluate trust-based methods in practice, simulation environments for trusted platform modules, trust in applications running on mobile devices, trust across platforms, etc. Papers in the socioeconomic track investigated, for example, how trust is managed and perceived in online environments, and how the disclosure of personal data is perceived; and some papers probed trust issues across generations of users and for groups with special needs. It is also pleasing to report that some papers in the proceedings could be placed well in either of the two tracks, suggesting that research in both tracks is beginning to show genuine signs of convergence – an essential ingredient in building and validating the trustworthy systems of the future.

Paper submissions were received from 21 countries on four continents. The number of submitted papers was 39 in the technical track and 14 in the socioeconomic track. Of these 39 and 14 submissions, the Program Committees accepted 14 and 5 papers, respectively. This amounts to an acceptance rate of about 35% for both tracks, and overall. This year, we also encouraged people to report on work in progress by submitting 2-page abstracts describing ongoing research. A panel of experts reviewed these submitted abstracts. Five of these abstracts were selected to be included in these conference proceedings. We hope that these abstracts will convey a sense of the vibrancy and current themes of research in trusted and trustworthy computing. Authors of these abstracts also presented posters of their work at the conference. Furthermore, the conference program contained several keynotes by leaders in academia, industry, and government agencies.

We would like to express our gratitude to those people without whom TRUST 2013 would not have been this successful an event, and whom we mention now in no particular order: the Publicity Chairs, the members of the Steering

Committee (where Claire Vishik deserves a special mention for her continued and valuable advice during the preparation of this conference), the keynote speakers, and the panel (Androulaki Elli, Pouyan Sepehrdad, and Christian Wachsmann) who reviewed the 2-page abstracts. We also want to thank all Program Committee members and their sub-reviewers; their hard work made sure that the scientific program was of high quality and reflected both the depth and breadth of research in this area. Our special thanks goes to all those who submitted papers, and to all those who presented posters and papers at the conference. We thank SBA Research for assisting in the organization of this conference, notably Edgar Weippl and Yvonne Poul. Yvonne was instrumental in making sure that the planning and execution of the event went smoothly. Thomas Schneider helped with the planning of the conference program. Finally, we would like to acknowledge our sponsors Intel Corporation and Microsoft; their financial contribution was crucial for realizing the vision for TRUST 2013.

June 2013   Michael Huth
                                                                N. Asokan
                                                          Srdjan Capkun
                                                            Ivan Flechais
                                                      Lizzie Coles-Kemp

Organization

Steering Committee

Alessandro Acquisti	Carnegie Mellon University, USA
Boris Balacheff	Hewlett Packard, UK
Paul England	Microsoft, USA
Andrew Martin	University of Oxford, UK
Chris Mitchell	Royal Holloway University of London, UK
Sean Smith	Dartmouth College, USA
Ahmad-Reza Sadeghi	TU Darmstadt / Fraunhofer SIT, Germany
Claire Vishik	Intel, UK

General Chair

Michael Huth	Imperial College London, UK

Program Chairs (Technical Strand)

Srdjan Capkun	ETH Zurich, Switzerland
N. Asokan	University of Helsinki, Finland

Program Committee (Technical Strand)

Haibo Chen	Shanghai Jiao Tong University, China
Liqun Chen	HP Labs, UK
Xuhua Ding	Singapore Management University, Singapore
Jan-Erik Ekberg	Nokia Research Center, Finland
William Enck	NC State, USA
Michael Franz	UC Irvine, USA
Peter Gutman	University of Auckland, New Zealand
Trent Jaeger	Penn State University, USA
Limin Jia	CMU, USA
Apu Kapadia	Indiana University, USA
Ghassan Karame	NEC Laboratories, Germany
Engin Kirda	NorthEastern University, USA
Jiangtao Li	Intel Labs, USA
Mohammad Mannan	Concordia University, Canada
Ivan Martinovic	Oxford University, UK
Jonathan McCune	Google, USA

Program Chairs (Socioeconomic Track)

Program Committee (Socioeconomic Track)

Publicity Chairs (Technical Track)

Publicity Chairs (Socioeconomic Track)

John Vines   Newcastle University, UK
Shamal Faily   University of Oxford, UK

Table of Contents

Technical Strand

KISS: "Key It Simple and Secure" Corporate Key Management 1
Zongwei Zhou, Jun Han, Yue-Hsun Lin, Adrian Perrig, and
Virgil Gligor

Guardian: Hypervisor as Security Foothold for Personal Computers 19
Yueqiang Cheng and Xuhua Ding

Improving Trusted Tickets with State-Bound Keys 37
Jan Nordholz, Ronald Aigner, and Paul England

Group Signatures on Mobile Devices: Practical Experiences 47
Klaus Potzmader, Johannes Winter, Daniel Hein, Christian Hanser,
Peter Teufl, and Liqun Chen

Limiting Data Exposure in Monitoring Multi-domain Policy
Conformance 65
Mirko Montanari, Jun Ho Huh, Rakesh B. Bobba, and
Roy H. Campbell

Towards Trustworthy Network Measurements 83
Ghassan O. Karame

Stochastic Model of a Metastability-Based True Random Number
Generator 92
Molka Ben-Romdhane, Tarik Graba, and Jean-Luc Danger

Semi-automated Prototyping of a TPM v2 Software and Hardware
Simulation Platform 106
Martin Pirker and Johannes Winter

Tapping and Tripping with NFC 115
Sandeep Tamrakar and Jan-Erik Ekberg

TEEM: A User-Oriented Trusted Mobile Device for Multi-platform
Security Applications 133
Wei Feng, Dengguo Feng, Ge Wei, Yu Qin, Qianying Zhang, and
Dexian Chang

TRUMP: A Trusted Mobile Platform for Self-management of Chronic
Illness in Rural Areas 142
Chris Burnett, Peter Edwards, Timothy J. Norman,
Liang Chen, Yogachandran Rahulamathavan,
Mariesha Jaffray, and Edoardo Pignotti

First-Class Labels: Using Information Flow to Debug Security Holes 151
  Eric Hennigan, Christoph Kerschbaumer, Stefan Brunthaler,
  Per Larsen, and Michael Franz

A Framework for Evaluating Mobile App Repackaging Detection
Algorithms 169
  Heqing Huang, Sencun Zhu, Peng Liu, and Dinghao Wu

Towards Precise and Efficient Information Flow Control in Web
Browsers 187
  Christoph Kerschbaumer, Eric Hennigan, Per Larsen,
  Stefan Brunthaler, and Michael Franz

Socio-Economic Strand

Granddaughter Beware! An Intergenerational Case Study of Managing
Trust Issues in the Use of Facebook 196
  Ann Light and Lizzie Coles-Kemp

Contextualized Web Warnings, and How They Cause Distrust 205
  Steffen Bartsch, Melanie Volkamer, Heike Theuerling, and
  Fatih Karayumak

All In: Targeting Trustworthiness for Special Needs User Groups
in the Internet of Things 223
  Marc Busch, Christina Hochleitner, Mario Lorenz, Trenton Schulz,
  Manfred Tscheligi, and Eckhart Wittstock

Trust Domains: An Algebraic, Logical, and Utility-Theoretic
Approach 232
  Gabrielle Anderson, Matthew Collinson, and David Pym

"Fairly Truthful": The Impact of Perceived Effort, Fairness, Relevance,
and Sensitivity on Personal Data Disclosure 250
  Miguel Malheiros, Sören Preibusch, and M. Angela Sasse

Poster Abstracts

Formal Evaluation of Persona Trustworthiness with EUSTACE 267
  Shamal Faily, David Power, Philip Armstrong, and Ivan Fléchais

Identity Implies Trust in Distributed Systems – A Novel Approach 269
  Lyzgeo Merin Koshy, Marc Conrad, Mitul Shukla, and Tim French

Non-intrusive and Transparent Authentication on Smart Phones 271
  Nicholas Micallef, Mike Just, Lynne Baillie, and Gunes Kayacik

Quaestio-it.com: From Debates Towards Trustworthy Answers 273
  Valentinos Evripidou and Francesca Toni

Towards Verifiable Trust Management for Software Execution 275
    Michael Huth and Jim Huan-Pu Kuo

Author Index... 277

KISS: "Key It Simple and Secure" Corporate Key Management

Zongwei Zhou, Jun Han, Yue-Hsun Lin, Adrian Perrig, and Virgil Gligor

Carnegie Mellon University and CyLab, Pittsburgh, Pennsylvania, United States
{stephenzhou,junhan,tenma,perrig,gligor}@cmu.edu

Abstract. Deploying a corporate key management system faces fundamental challenges, such as fine-grained key usage control and secure system administration. None of the current commercial systems (either based on software or hardware security modules) or research proposals adequately address both challenges with small and simple Trusted Computing Base (TCB). This paper presents a new key management architecture, called KISS, to enable comprehensive, trustworthy, user-verifiable, and cost-effective key management. KISS protects the entire life cycle of cryptographic keys. In particular, KISS allows only authorized applications and/or users to use the keys. Using simple devices, administrators can remotely issue authenticated commands to KISS and verify system output. KISS leverages readily available commodity hardware and trusted computing primitives to design system bootstrap protocols and management mechanisms, which protects the system from malware attacks and insider attacks.

Keywords: Key Management, Trusted Computing, Isolation, Trusted Path.

1 Introduction

As consumers and corporations are increasingly concerned about security, deployments of cryptographic systems and protocols have grown from securing online banking and e-commerce to web email, search, social networking and sensitive data protection. However, the security guarantees diminish with inadequate key management practices, as exemplified by numerous real-world incidents. For example, in 2010 Stuxnet targeted Iranian uranium centrifuges, installing device drivers signed with private keys *stolen* from two high-tech companies [11]. In another incident, the private keys of DigiNotar, a Dutch certificate authority, were maliciously *misused* to issue fraudulent certificates for Gmail and other services [23]. Even high-profile, security-savvy institutions fall prey to inadequate key security, let alone companies with a lower priority for security.

Despite its indisputable significance, *none* of the current corporate key management systems (KMS) – either industrial solutions based on software, or hardware security modules (HSM), or research proposals known to us – provide comprehensive key management *with small and simple trusted computing base (TCB)*. There are at least two significant challenges that lead to the insufficiency of the KMS, as shown in Table 1.

Fine-grained Key Usage Control. A comprehensive life-cycle KMS should enforce *fine-grained key usage control* (i.e., whether an application operated by a user has the permission to access a specific cryptographic key). This problem is exacerbated with

M. Huth et al. (Eds.): TRUST 2013, LNCS 7904, pp. 1–18, 2013.

Table 1. A comparison between KISS and current key management systems. "HSM", "SW", and "TPM" represent the KMS that are based on HSM, software packages, and TPM seal storage, respectively. "ROT" denotes the root of trust of the systems.

Systems	Key Usage Control	Administration Interfaces	TCB	ROT
HSM [18,20,7,16,17]	coarse-grained (application or machine control)	HSM & complex admin dev, non-verifiable	large	HSM, admin dev
SW [15,19,9]	insecure (rely on OS)	keyboard/display, non-verifiable	large	OS
TPM [5,11,2,13,14]	coarse-grained (only application control)	keyboard/display, non-verifiable	large	TPM
KISS	fine-grained (both application and user control)	trusted path & simple admin dev, verifiable	small	TPM, admin dev

the current trend of Bring Your Own Device (BYOD), which allows client devices (e.g., tablets and laptops) to increasingly host both personal and security-sensitive corporate applications and data.

Although commercial HSMs [18, 20, 7, 15, 17] provide high-profile physical protection of cryptographic keys and algorithms, they fail to control key usage requests from outside their physical protection boundary (e.g., the users and applications on other client computers). The attackers can cause key misuse [23] by compromising client computers and submitting fake key usage requests to the HSMs. Some HSMs enable porting key usage applications to an in-module secure execution environment [18, 20]. This method only provides application-level key usage control, and is not scalable due to the limited resources of the dedicated environment. Some HSMs enforce key usage control by accepting requests from client machines that deploy special hardware tokens only. This mechanism is insecure because it cannot block requests from a compromised operating system (OS) or an application on an authenticated machine.

Cost-sensitive companies commonly deploy *key management software* [14, 19, 8] on commodity servers, and rely heavily on the underlying OS services to protect cryptographic keys and management operations. These systems are untrustworthy because modern OSes are large and routinely compromised by malware.

Research proposals (e.g., credential protection systems [5, 10, 2] and hypervisor-based solutions [12, 13]) leverage Trusted Platform Modules (TPM) sealed storage. It assures that the cryptographic keys sealed by an application can only be accessed by the same software. However, this approach is coarse-grained; it does not enforce any user authentication of the sealed keys.

Secure System Administration. A trustworthy KMS should allow benign administrators to securely manage the system and defend against attacks from malicious insiders. It must guarantee the authenticity of the communication between the administrators and the KMS. Otherwise, an adversary can cause unintended key management operations by stealing administrator login credentials, modifying or spoofing the administrator command input or the KMS output (e.g., operation result, system status).

The HSMs usually mandate the administrators to perform management operations via the I/O devices (e.g., keyboard and display) that are physically attached to the modules. For remote administration, they need complicated management software running on a commodity OS or a dedicated administrator device. Both mechanisms significantly increase system TCB and thus exposes larger attack surface. For software-based KMS, the I/O interfaces and authentication-relevant devices are controlled directly by the underlying OS, which means that the administrator credentials, input commands, and KMS output can easily be compromised by malware in the OS. Similarly, research proposals [5, 2, 10] do not support trustworthy remote management mechanisms. More importantly, none of KMS solutions provide intuitive ways for administrators to verify the status of the administration interfaces. Without such verification, administrators cannot trust any displayed system output and may mistakenly perform operations.

Contributions. To address the above challenges, this paper presents KISS (short for "Key it Simple and Secure"), a comprehensive, trustworthy, user-verifiable, and cost-effective enterprise key management architecture. Table 1 compares KISS with mainstream KMS and research proposals. Among them, KISS is the first KMS that supports *fine-grained key usage control* based on users, applications, and configurable access-control policies. To do this, KISS isolates authorized corporate applications from the untrusted OS and measures the code identities (cryptographic hash) of the protected applications. KISS also directly accepts user authentication by isolating user-interface devices and authentication relevant devices from the OS. Moreover, KISS enables *secure system administration*, leveraging a simple external device with minimal software/hardware settings. The KISS administrators execute thin terminal software on commodity machines. The thin terminal accepts administrator input via trusted paths, remotely transfers the input to and receives system output from the KISS system. The administrators use the external devices to *verify* the execution of the thin terminal and trusted paths and guarantee the *authenticity* of the input/output.

KISS leverages hypervisor-based isolation to protect the key management softwa e and cryptographic keys from the large untrusted OS, applications, and periphera] devices. The administrators securely bootstrap the KISS system using the simple *e*dministrator devices and lightweight protocols, regardless of malware attacks an*d* insider attacks from malicious administrators. These mechanisms together significantly reduce and simplify the KISS TCB, enabling higher security assurance. Because KISS leverages commodity hardware and trusted computing techniques, it is *cost-effective* and makes the wide adoption of KISS in small- and medium-sized business possible, in addition to financial or governmental institutions. KISS showcases how trusted computing technologies achieve tangible benefits when used to design trustworthy KMS.

Paper Organization. First, we describe the KISS attacker model and introduce the background in Sections 2 and 3, respectively. Section 4 describes in detail the KISS system model and administrative policies. In Section 5, we illustrate the KISS hypervisor-based architecture and the simplicity of the external administrator devices. Sections 6, 7, and 8 introduce the detailed mechanisms for system bootstrap, secure administration, and fine-grained key usage control, respectively. We analyze potential attacks on KISS and our defense mechanisms in Section 9. Section 10 discusses KISS extensions with stronger security properties or address real-world application issues. We then compare our solution with related work (Section 11) and conclude the paper.

2   Attacker Model

We consider an adversary that remotely exploits the *software vulnerabilities* of the OS and applications on KMS machines. The adversary can then access any system resources managed by the OS (e.g., memory, chip-set hardware, peripheral devices) and subvert any security services provided (e.g., process isolation or file system access-control). However, we trust the correctness of the key management software, and assume that it cannot be exploited by the adversary. The mechanisms to guarantee the correctness is out of the scope of this paper.

We also consider *insider attacks* from malicious administrators that attempt to leak, compromise, or misuse the cryptographic keys. They can actively issue unauthorized key management operations, intentionally misconfigure the KMS and corporate applications, or steal the administrator devices or credentials (e.g., password, smart cards) of benign administrators. However, benign administrators are trusted to protect their administrator devices and credentials and comply with the KISS protocols.

We do *not* address the following three types of attacks in this paper: (1) physical attacks to the hardware that KISS relies on (e.g., TPM), (2) side-channel attacks to cryptographic keys and algorithms, and (3) denial-of-service attacks. Countermeasures against these attacks are complementary to KISS.

3   Background

This section introduces the technical building blocks of KISS: program isolation [12, 13] and trusted paths [25, 3]. They are implemented based on readily available trusted computing primitives, such as dynamic root of trust for measurement (or *Late Launch*) [1, 9], *remote attestation*, and *sealed storage* [21].

Program Isolation. Recent research contributions [12, 13] demonstrate the capability of removing large commodity OS from the TCB of small program modules. These systems isolate program modules by leveraging a small and trustworthy hypervisor with higher privilege level than the OS. The hypervisor guarantees that the OS, applications, and DMA-capable devices cannot compromise the execution integrity, data integrity, and secrecy of the isolated program modules. The protected code modules are self-contained, and they should not rely on OS services.

Trusted Path. A Trusted Path (TP) is a protected channel providing secrecy and authenticity of data transfers between a user's I/O devices (e.g., keyboard, display, USB devices) and an isolated program trusted by the user. Recent research advances demonstrate the usage of a small, dedicated hypervisor to establish trusted paths, completely bypassing the commodity OS [25, 3]. The hypervisor exclusively redirects the I/O communications (e.g., memory-mapped I/O, DMA, interrupts) of the trusted-path devices to the isolated software module. The TP device drivers are included in the isolated software module and redesigned to communicate with the devices via the hypervisor.

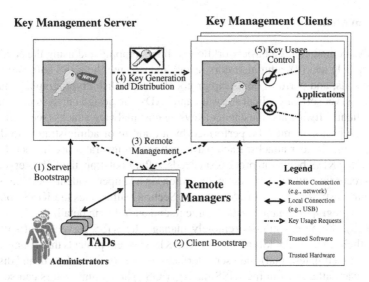

Fig. 1. KISS system model

4 Overview

Corporate key management in this paper refers to the establishment and usage of cryptographic keys in corporate and distributed environments. In this section, we provide a high-level overview of KISS system entities and model, and demonstrate how this model enables scalable and hierarchical enterprise key management.

4.1 System Entities

Figure 1 shows the four major entities in the KISS system.

Key Management Server (KISS Server). A commodity server machine that executes the key management software to perform server-side key life-cycle operations (e.g., key generation, registration, backup, revocation, de-registration, and destruction).

Key Management Clients (KISS Clients). Distributed machines (e.g., employees' desktops or corporate web servers) that install the KISS client software to receive cryptographic keys from the KISS server and use the keys to provide services to corporate applications. For example, On employees' desktops, the cryptographic keys stored in the KISS client software can be used to encrypt confidential documents. For a corporate web server, the keys are used to authenticate the outgoing network traffic.

Remote Managers (KISS Managers). Commodity machines used by KISS administrators to perform remote management. These machines install the KISS manager software to securely transfer administrative commands to and receive system output from the KISS server or clients.

Trusted Administrator Devices (KISS TAD). Small, dedicated devices that are directly connected (e.g., via USB) to the KISS server or clients for local administration, or connected with the KISS managers for remote management.

4.2   System Model

Figure 1 also demonstrates a basic workflow of bootstrapping and using the KISS system. In Steps (1) and (2), administrators install and execute the KISS software on the server or clients, and perform bootstrap protocols to establish cryptographic channels between the server software, client software and TADs. We design our system to protect the server/client software and the channel keys against malware attacks (see Section 5). The bootstrap protocols must be performed by a quorum of administrators to defend against malicious insider attacks. Each participating administrator use his/her TAD to confirm that the KISS bootstrap process succeeds. After bootstrap, the KISS server software starts recording subsequent system operations in a tamper-evident audit log, which helps the administrators detect insider attacks. Section 6 illustrates the KISS bootstrap protocols, cryptographic channel establishment, and audit log in detail.

In Step (3), the administrators remotely manage the KISS server/client software, leveraging their TADs and KISS managers. The KISS system protects the manager software (acting as a thin terminal) and user-interfaces devices (e.g., keyboard, and display) against malware attacks from the KISS manager OS. The administrators can securely input commands and review system output via the KISS manager user interfaces. The administrators use their TADs to authenticate the outgoing commands, and verify the authenticity of the operation results back from the KISS server/client software. Section 7 describes the remote management process and how our design significantly reduces KISS TCB.

In Step (4), new cryptographic keys (which are our key management products) are generated in the KISS server and securely distributed to the clients via the cryptographic channels established in step (2). In Step (5), the KISS client software protects the distributed keys, and handles key usage requests from various applications. KISS enables more fine-grained control of key usage than previous key management systems and proposals. It isolates the applications (similar to the isolation of KISS server software from the server OS) and measures their code identities. It also provides protected channels between authentication devices and the KISS client software, so that the KISS client software can directly authenticate the users of the applications. If the requests are from authorized users (e.g., company employees) and corporate applications (e.g., corporate document editors), the KISS client software uses the corresponding cryptographic keys to process the requests (e.g., decrypt confidential documents). The KISS client software rejects any key usage request from unauthorized users (e.g., visitors that are not allowed to read any confidential document) or applications (e.g., personal web browsers, media players). Section 8 describes the detailed mechanisms of our fine-grained key usage control.

The KISS client is necessary for collecting application and user information to perform key usage control. By receiving keys from the server, it also supports offline key usage, which reduces the key access latency and allows key usage when network connections are unavailable (e.g., while traveling on flights). However, offline key usage increases the risk of key abuse (e.g., when client machines are stolen). Companies might enforce special key usage policies to reduce this risk, such as requiring client machines to periodically obtain key usage permissions from the KISS server. Note that KISS can easily be modified to serve as the key usage control front end of the HSM.

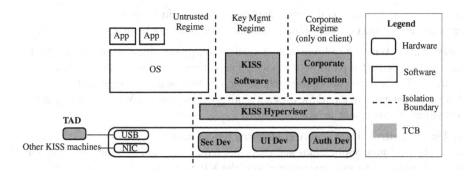

Fig. 2. System architecture for KISS client, server, and manager. Sec Dev is the hardware (e.g., TPM) that provides trusted computing primitives. UI Dev denotes the user-interface devices, such as a keyboard and a display. Auth Dev is the device used for authentication (e.g., fingerprint scanner, and keypad). The KISS machines communicate via the network interface cards (NIC), and connects with TADs via USB interfaces.

The KISS server software receives approved key usage requests from the clients, and securely transfers them to the HSM on the server machines via trusted paths. Both the cryptographic keys and algorithms are always protected inside HSM.

5   System Architecture

In this section, we introduce the unified hypervisor-based architecture for the KISS server, client, and manager, and the hardware/software settings of TAD. We demonstrate how our architectural design significantly reduces and simplifies the TCB of the whole system, which is necessary for achieving high security assurance.

5.1   KISS Server, Client, and Manager

KISS server, client, and manager share the same architecture, hence we only illustrate the KISS client in detail here. As shown in Figure 2, the KISS hypervisor is a thin layer of software running in a higher privilege than the commodity OS of the client. Unlike commercial hypervisors/virtual machine monitors (VMM) (e.g., VMware Workstation, Xen), the KISS hypervisor does not virtualize all hardware resources or support the concurrent execution of multiple OSes. Thus, the code base of the KISS hypervisor is orders of magnitude smaller and demonstrably simpler than an OS or a full-functioning hypervisor/VMM. The TCB of a KISS client is only the hypervisor, the client software, the corporate applications that utilize the keys, and some commodity hardware (e.g., Sec, Auth, and UI Dev in Fig. 2). The KISS hypervisor is dedicated to three main tasks:

Isolation. The KISS hypervisor divides the client to three isolated software regimes, which are lightweight "virtual machines" as described in Section 3. The key management regime runs the KISS client software and stores all cryptographic keys during its run time. We also leverage TPM sealed storage to protect the cryptographic keys at rest.

Each authorized application that uses the keys is isolated in its own corporate regime. The untrusted regime consists of the commodity OS, other applications, and devices.

Trusted Paths. When the administrators locally manage the client machine, the hypervisor establishes trusted paths between the client software and the UI Dev or Auth Dev (Figure 2). The trusted paths protect the administrator command input and the client software output and safeguard the user authentication credentials. We defer the detailed explanation to subsequent sections.

Key Usage Control. The hypervisor helps the KISS client software to collect the identifier of the corporate applications and users that request key usage. When isolating the corporate applications in corporate regimes, the KISS hypervisor computes a cryptographic hash of the corporate application code and static data, and transfers the hash value as application identifiers to the KISS client software. The hypervisor also establishes trusted paths between the authentication-relevant devices and the KISS client software, for user authentication. Section 8 describes the key usage control procedure.

5.2 TAD

TAD is a small, dedicated, embedded device that assists system administration, both locally and remotely. TAD employs much simpler software/hardware than the typical administrator devices in current KMS. TAD does not need a full user-interface hardware for the key management command input and system output. Instead, the administrator can leverage the trusted paths provided by the KISS hypervisor on the server, client or manager. TAD does not implement complicated key management software to interpret operation input/output. These are directly handled by the KISS server/client software. During remote management, the KISS manager software only collects and transfers administrator input to server/client, and receives returning operation results.

TAD implements software for the KISS bootstrap protocol, standard cryptographic primitives, remote attestation protocol, and necessary hardware drivers (note that the USB driver code is included, but not in the TCB). The TAD software is responsible for three tasks: (1) performing server/client bootstrap; (2) remotely attesting to the KISS server, client, and manager software; and (3) authenticating the administrator input and verifying the authenticity of the server/client output. To meet these functional requirements, TAD includes only a low-end CPU, small on-chip RAM and flash storage, a USB controller, a few buttons, a minimal display to show hexadecimal values, and a physical out-of-band channel receiver (e.g., QR code scanner).

6 System Bootstrap

In this section, we introduce the lightweight KISS bootstrap protocols. These protocols allow a quorum of administrators to verify that the "known good" KISS software is executing on the server/clients, and to establish cryptographic channels between their TADs, the server software and the client software. These channels (depicted in Figure 3) are used in secure system administration and key life-cycle operations. The bootstrap protocols are resilient against malware and insider attacks.

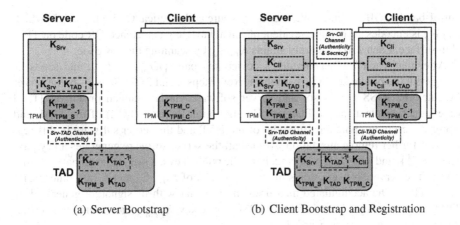

(a) Server Bootstrap   (b) Client Bootstrap and Registration

Fig. 3. Cryptographic channels established during KISS bootstrap. Before the bootstrap, the server and clients only have their TPM keys, and TADs has no pre-injected keys.

---

1. TPM $\xrightarrow{OOB}$ TAD_i : K_{TPM_S}
2. TAD_i : Generates device key pair $\{K_{TAD_i}, K_{TAD_i}^{-1}\}$
3. $TAD_i \to$ Server : $\{C_i, K_{TAD_i}\}$, where C_i lists the configurations of the Server,
                    e.g., # of involved administrators N, and quorum threshold t.
4. Server   : Gathers N messages from TAD_i before timeout,
                    late launches HYP and Server (their measurement is stored in TPM).
5. Server   : Checks that all C_i are consistent, and $N \geq t$,
                    generates Server key pair $\{K_{Srv}, K_{Srv}^{-1}\}$
6. Server $\to$ TPM : Stores the measurement of $\{K_{Srv}, C_i, \Lambda = \{K_1, \cdots, K_N\}\}$
7. $TAD_i \to$ TPM : Nonce R_i
8. TPM $\to$ Server : Signature $S_i = \{R_i, M\}_{K_{TPM\_S}^{-1}}$,
                    where M is the measurement of $\{HYP, Server, K_{Srv}, C_i, \Lambda\}$.
9. Server $\to TAD_i$: ID_i, S_i, Λ, K_{Srv}, where ID_i is a unique identifier for TAD_i
10. TAD_i : Verifies S_i and M, checks $K_{TAD_i} \in \Lambda$, $\#(\Lambda) = N$, and stores K_{Srv}

Fig. 4. KISS Server Bootstrap Protocol. Each administrator possesses a TAD_i.

6.1 Server Bootstrap

During the KISS server bootstrap, a quorum of administrators execute authentic KISS server software and establish the Srv-TAD cryptographic channel (Figure 3(a)). Our lightweight server bootstrap protocol needs minimal administrator involvement. It does not require pre-sharing secrets in TAD (e.g., vendor-injected device private keys). After the bootstrap, the server software starts recording subsequent system operations in a tamper-evident audit log, which help the administrators detect insider attacks.

Bootstrap Protocol. Figure 4 illustrates the server bootstrap protocol. Before the protocol begins, we assume that the administrators creates the necessary configuration file, C_i, of the KISS server software independently and store them in TADs. The C_i includes the number of participating administrators, N, a quorum threshold, t, and other necessary server parameters. In Step 1, each administrator gathers the information of the hardware root of trust, i.e., the TPM public key K_{TPM_S} of the server, via a trusted out-of-band (OOB) channel. We suggest a secure and practical OOB channel, in which K_{TPM_S} is encodes as a tamper-evident physical label, e.g., an etched QR code on TPM chip surface. Each TAD_i securely attains K_{TPM_S} by scanning the QR code.

After that, each TAD_i generates a device key pair, $\{K_{TAD_i}, K_{TAD_i}^{-1}\}$, and sends C_i along with the public key, K_{TAD_i}, to the server (Steps 2 and 3). In Steps 4–6, the server executes the KISS hypervisor and server software via late launch primitives [1, 9] Late launch resets a special Platform Configuration Register (PCR) of the TPM, and stores the cryptographic measurement of the HYP and the server software in this register for further remote attestation. After that, the server software generates a key pair, $\{K_{Srv}, K_{Srv}^{-1}\}$, and a key list, Λ, by receiving the public keys, K_{TAD_i}, from all participating TADs. The server software stores the measurement of K_{Srv}, C_i, and Λ into other PCRs of the TPM. The accumulated measurement, together with its signature generated by TPM attestation keys (linked with the TPM private key, $K_{TPM\_S}^{-1}$), are sent to the verifier during remote attestation (Step2 7– 9).

Upon receiving the attestation response, TAD verifies the signature using K_{TPM_S}, and trusts the authenticity of the accumulated measurement, M (Step 10). TAD re-computes M using its pre-installed knowledge (e.g., cryptographic hash of HYP and server software, configuration file C_i), the received K_{Srv} and Λ. If the verification succeeds, TAD trusts that an authentic hypervisor/server instance is executing on the KISS server with the appropriate configurations, and that the server instance has the server private key and a correct list of TAD public keys. TAD also verifies that its own public key is included in the public key list, Λ, and the number of keys in Λ equals to the number of participating administrators. If all verification passes, TAD notifies its administrator via the display. The only task that each administrator needs to perform is to visually check that all TADs display verification success messages. KISS introduces an additional computational overhead (e.g., remote attestation and quorum checking) compared to traditional system bootstrapping. However, we argue that this cost is acceptable, considering the security guarantees it achieves.

Audit Log. During the server bootstrap, malicious administrators may inject spurious configuration files with a small quorum threshold, or even forge administrator public keys. These administrators are then capable of passing the quorum check that is necessary for any key management operations. In KISS, the server software maintains an operation log to record all of the system administration operations, including bootstrap operations. This helps legitimate administrators/auditors detect any insider attacks during the server bootstrap. In addition, the audit log helps relaxes the quorum control and improves system usability. Becasue all key management operations are held accountable, KISS may allowing a smaller number of administrators or even merely one to perform operations.

The audit log is stored in the untrusted regime. The KISS server software maintains an aggregated hash of the log entries in the TPM non-volatile memory (NVRAM). The TPM NVRAM access-control (similar to sealed storage) ensures that only KISS server software can access/update that hash, Note that frequent NVRAM updates are impractical on TPM. To minimize NVRAM updates, we leverage an update mechanism that is similar to the PCR-NVRAM two stage update technique presented in [16]. During the audit procedure, the auditor verifies the integrity of the log by recomputing the aggregated hash and comparing it with the hash stored in TPM NVRAM.

6.2   Client Bootstrap and Registration

Bootstrapping a KISS client is similar to the server bootstrap. A quorum of administrators verifies the authenticity of the KISS hypervisor, client software, and its configuration file. The client software securely sends its public key, K_{Cli}, to each of the participating TADs, and collects the device public keys K_{TAD_i} (generated during the server bootstrap). The configuration file sent to the client software differs from the one established during the server bootstrap. It contains the server public key, K_{Srv}, and the client-side system parameters (e.g., access-control policies of key usage, user authentication information, and the corporate application information). These client-side configurations are used in the fine-grained key usage control (See Section 8). Upon a successful client bootstrap, TADs establish Cli-TAD cryptographic channels with the KISS client, which allows subsequent client administration.

The administrators then register the client to the server by sending the client software public key, K_{Cli}, to the server software, via Srv-TAD cryptographic channels. This establishes the Srv-Cli cryptographic channel (see Figure 3(b)). This channel diffs from the Srv-/Cli-TAD channel in that it provides both secrecy and integrity protection to the data transferred between the server and the clients (e.g., KISS product keys).

7   Secure System Administration

This section describes how the KISS administrators perform local and remote operations using their TADs and remote managers. Unlike traditional KMS, our remote management mechanism introduces a very small TCB that consists of a thin terminal, the KISS hypervisor, the user-interface devices on KISS manager, and the simple TADs. In addition, it enables flexible administrative policies for better usability.

Secure Local Management. Administrators physically present at the KISS server or client connect the TADs directly with the machines to perform management. TADs first perform remote attestation to verify that the connected KISS machine is executing the desired hypervisor, software, and trusted paths. Thus, any command input (or KISS system output) is securely directed to (or displayed by) the KISS server/client software. The administrators also use the TADs to authenticate their command input, by allowing the KISS server/client to display the command input with its digest (a cryptographic hash, $H(input)$) to the administrators. The alleged digest $H(input)$ is sent to the TADs via untrusted USB connection. The administrator confirms that the digest value displayed on his/her TAD is identical to the one on the server/client display. Then, the administrator press a button on the TAD to generate an authentication blob (digital signature) on digest $H(input)$ with the Srv-/Cli-TAD channel keys. The KISS server/client software verifies this blob to ensure the authenticity of launched commands.

Secure Remote Management. Administrators not physically present at the KISS server or client leverage the KISS managers and the TADs to perform maintenance tasks. The KISS manager software is isolated from the untrusted regime, and connects with the

Table 2. KISS System Operation Categorization

Category	Operations	Local or remote?	Quorum or any?	Manual or automatic?
1	server bootstrap, adding administrators	local	quorum	manual
2	server software and config update, removing administrators	either	quorum	manual
3	client bootstrap	local	either	manual
4	client registration, software and config update (e.g., change key usage control policy)	either	either	manual
5	server/client key life-cycle operations (e.g., key generation, distribution, usage)	either	either	either

user-interface devices via hypervisor-established trusted paths. The administrators not only use their TADs to authenticate the command input (the same as in local management), but also to verify the authenticity of the system output returning from the KISS server or client software. The KISS server/client generate similar authentication blobs for each of their responses, using the Srv-/Cli-TAD channel keys. The KISS manager software recomputes the digest $H(response)$, and displays it to the administrators via the trusted paths. It also forwards the digest and the authentication blob to the TADs. The TADs verify the authenticity of the blobs, and display the digest on the screen. If the two digests are identical, the administrators trust that the response indeed originated from the KISS server/clients. Note that our remote management mechanism can be extended to protect the secrecy of the command input and system output, and avoid the hash computation overhead and comparison efforts (Section 10).

Administrative Policies. KISS fully considers the balance between security and usability when making administrative policies. We categorize different system operations according to their administrative requirements, as is shown in Table 2.

In KISS, only three operations require the physical presence of administrators at the KISS server/client; the majority of operations can be performed remotely. In Category 1, server bootstrap and adding new administrators require the physical presence of a quorum of administrators. These two operations bootstrap cryptographic channels between TADs and the KISS server software and require our server bootstrap protocol (Section 6.1). Client bootstrap also mandates the physical presence of administrators, because administrators scan the TPM public key to their TADs.

In KISS, only a few operations mandate a quorum of administrators. We require all server-side administrative operations in Category 1 and 2 to be performed by an administrator quorum in an attempt to *prevent* malicious insider attacks on the KISS server. However, once the server audit log is bootstrapped, all subsequent client-side administrative operations in Categories 3 and 4 and server/client key life-cycle operations in Category 5 could possibly relax the quorum requirement, because we can always *detect* insider attacks by analyzing the audit log.

In addition, for efficiency and usability, all Category 5 operations can be automatically performed by the KISS server/client software, without the involvement of administrators. For example, once an authorized corporate application requests a new key, the

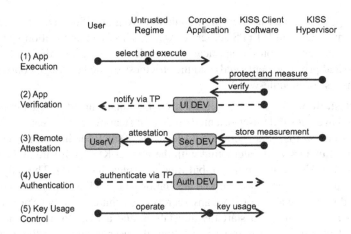

Fig. 5. Work flow of key usage control on KISS client. Dashed lines are interactions via trusted paths. UI, Sec, and Auth Dev are identical to those in Fig. 2. UserV denotes the users' dedicated verifier that can remotely attest to the KISS client.

KISS client software can immediately contact the server for the new key. These automatic operations are controlled by the administrator-configured key usage policies (see Section 8), and can be recorded in the server audit log (or similar audit logs on clients).

8 Fine-Grained Key Usage Control

This section explains how the KISS client software and hypervisor performs fine-grained control of key usage. Figure 5 presents a typical workflow where a user executes a KISS-capable application that uses the cryptographic key generated by KISS.

Application Verification. The user selects the corporate application he/she intends to run via the untrusted regime (e.g., via a pop-up dialog by the OS). The OS loads and executes the selected corporation application and notifies the KISS hypervisor of the application execution. The hypervisor creates a corporate regime and protects the executed application in this regime. The hypervisor then measures that application and sends the measurement as the application identifier to the KISS client software. The software compares the received measurement with the known-good value in its application database and notifies the result to the user via trusted paths. Recall that the authorized application database in the KISS client software was configured during the client bootstrap and can be updated by the administrators via remote management.

The KISS-capable corporate applications are not legacy applications. They are developed to execute in corporate regimes, communicating with the hypervisor instead of the OS [12, 13]. Note that recent research [6] eases this development effort by allowing protected applications to securely use OS services. The corporate application should also be modified to communicate with the KISS client software for key usage. While allowing key usage control, this introduces context switch overhead between the application and the KISS client software. A corporate application can be a stand-alone application (e.g., a KISS-capable document editor) or the security-sensitive modules of a legacy application that uses cryptographic keys (e.g., the ServerKeyExchange authentication module in an HTTPS server software). This is an application-specific design choice that depends on the application complexity (e.g., how the application is modularized and privilege-separated) and the strictness of the key usage control policy (application-wise or module-wise).

Remote Attestation. To trust the application verification results displayed in last step, and to defend against subtle user-oriented credential stealing attacks (e.g., tricking the user to input passwords), the users should leverage a small, dedicated device, called UserV, to attest that they are interacting with the correct KISS software and corporate applications. The UserV is similar to, but much simpler than TAD. The only task of the UserV is to perform standard remote attestation to the KISS hypervisor and client software. It does not generate or store any secrets (e.g., shared secrets or private keys). It merely needs one button to start the attestation, and a LED to display attestation results [25]. Upon successful remote attestation, the user verifies that the application displayed is the one that he/she intends to run. Otherwise, the user should stop interacting with the corporate applications to prevent any sensitive information leakage.

User Authentication. In order to use the corporate application, the user needs to authenticate to the KISS client software. If the authentication fails, the KISS hypervisor immediately teminates the corporate application. KISS can support all types of common authentication methods (knowledge, inherence, and ownership-based) and multi-factors authentication. For knowledge-based authentication (e.g., password, PIN) or inherence-based methods (e.g., fingerprint scanning, voice pattern recognition), the users should leverage the trusted paths between the authentication-relevant devices (e.g., keyboard, fingerprint reader) and the KISS client software. With the trusted paths, malware in the untrusted regime cannot intercept the users' credentials [1]. For ownership-based authentication, users usually carry certain authenticators (e.g., smart cards, security tokens) and rely on the embedded secrets to respond to the challenges of the KISS client software. No trusted path is needed between the authentication devices (e.g., smart card reader) and KISS client software. For all the authentication methods above, the KISS client software should be configured with necessary authentication information (e.g., password hash, fingerprint database, and keys to verify smart cards' responses) by the administrators during client bootstrap or remote management.

Key Usage Control. During execution, the corporate applications trigger key usage requests to the KISS client software via KISS hypervisor. The key usage requests can be driven by the users (e.g., the user wants to encrypt a confidential document) or by the application itself (e.g., the HTTPS web server software digitally signs its ServerKeyExchange messages). Upon receiving the key usage requests, the KISS client software knows the identifiers of the requesting application and the user. The KISS client software leverages the pre-configured access control policies to decide whether to approve or deny the requests. KISS supports flexible access-control policies with different granularity. It can perform simple ON/OFF key usage control. For example, KISS allows

---

[1] Even if the attackers have the users' credentials, they still need to physically be present at the KISS client to input the credentials. The KISS client software takes inputs directly from the hardware devices via trusted-paths, not from any software.

user Alice to use the authorized document editor to decrypt her own documents, but restricts other users who are using the same editor or Alice using different software (e.g., an email client, or a compromised document editor) from accessing the documents. It can also support more complicated policies, such as rate limiting, access time restriction, and role-based access control. The administrators decide the access control policies, configure them in the client software during bootstrap, and update the policies via remote management.

9   Security Analysis

This section analyzes potential attacks on KISS and our defense mechanisms.

System Bootstrap. During the system bootstrap, malicious administrators or malware on KISS server/clients may tamper with the code or configurations of the hypervisor and the KISS software. The benign administrators can detect this attack via TAD remote attestation. Malicious administrators may also launch Sybil attacks by creating bogus administrator accounts during the bootstrap process. As described in Section 6, the administrators visually check that all TADs display success messages. This confirms that the server/client software receives only the public keys of the participating TADs, not any bogus key.

Key Life-Cycle Operations. Malware in the server/client untrusted regime may try to modify the KISS software code, interfere with its execution, or access the cryptographic keys generated or stored by the software. The KISS hypervisor prevents these attacks by protecting the code and data memory of the KISS software from the untrusted regime. When the KISS software is at rest, the cryptographic keys are protected by the TPM sealed storage. Only the same KISS software can unseal the keys; the malware or the compromised KISS software cannot. Malware attacks that compromise the client software to trigger unintended KISS server operations also fail, because the client private key for authenticating operation requests is sealed by the TPM.

System Administration. Any manual administrative operation requires at least one authorized TAD. The malware cannot steal the private keys in TADs, nor can it intercept other administrator credentials, such as bio-metric information or passwords, which are transferred to the KISS software via trusted paths, and/or Srv-/Cli-TAD authentic channels (Section 7). Similarly, the administration commands and system output are also transferred via trusted paths or Srv-/Cli-TAD channels. The attackers cannot modify any command or forge any system output. Though malicious administrators may use their TADs to execute operations that do not require the quorum, those operations are recorded in the server/client audit log and held accountable.

Key Usage Control. As described in Section 8, unauthorized applications and users cannot bypass the KISS hypervisor and the client software to use any cryptographic key. A malicious administrator may intentionally update the application and user database in the KISS client software to allow key mis-uses. However, this administrative operation is recorded in the client audit log and held accountable. The malware cannot steal users' authentication credentials, because those credentials are delivered to the KISS client software via trusted paths. The users also verify that they are communicating with the authentic KISS client software before inputting their authentication credentials.

10   Discussion

This section discusses the KISS system extensions that provide higher security guarantees and address some real-world application issues (e.g., cloud computing).

Administrative Operation Secrecy. Section 7 describes how KISS protects the authenticity of administrative inputs and system outputs. We could extend KISS to protect input/output secrecy by establishing encryption keys for Srv-/Cli-TAD channels, and an extra trusted path on KISS manager between the manager software and the USB controllers that connects the TAD. Note that this trusted path also avoids the hash computation overhead and comparison efforts described in Section 7, because it protects the authenticity of data between the TAD and the manager software.

TPM 2.0 Enhanced Authorization. The TPM 2.0 library specification [22] is currently under public review. It supports enhanced authorization by allowing the construction of complex authorization policies using multiple authorization qualifiers (e.g., password, command HMAC, PCR values, NVRAM index values, and TPM time information). KISS can reduce its TCB by offloading some authorization checking to TPM 2.0, given that it can securely collect the authorization information, deliver it to the TPM, and protect it from the untrusted OS. However, it is not clear how the performance of TPM authorization checking compares to that of the KISS software.

Compatibility to Cloud Computing. The KISS hypervisor is a small, dedicated hypervisor that runs on bare metal. If the KISS servers and clients are deployed on an enterprise private cloud, we could consider (1) integrating KISS hypervisor with the full-functioning the hypervisor/VMM or (2) adding nested virtualization support [24] to KISS hypervisor and running the full-functioning hypervisor/VMM upon it. Option (1) has much larger TCB, but has better compatibility and performance than option (2).

11   Related Work

We review the state-of-the-art key management systems and related technologies. The first category of KMS solutions are **software-based solutions**, such as OpenSolaris Crypto KMS Agent Toolkit [14], IBM Tivoli Key Manager [8], and StrongKey opensource KMS software [19]. These rely on process isolation, user privilege control, and file permissions provided by the OS to protect cryptographic keys and control the applications' access to them. Their implementation of trusted paths for administrators is based on the OS services (e.g., Ctrl+Alt+Del command or trusted window manager). Compared with KISS, the software-only approaches are more cost-effective and easier to deploy on commodity computers (e.g., no hypervisor, work with legacy corporate applications, no security hardware requirement). However, they rely heavily on the large OS and thus fail to provide the same level of security assurance as KISS.

An alternative is leveraging high profile **HSMs** [20, 18, 15, 7, 17]. An HSM provides hardware-level tamper-resistant protection to cryptographic keys and algorithms for both run-time and at rest, while KISS provides hypervisor-based software isolation for keys and algorithm during run-time, and TPM level hardware protection for keys at rest. For performance, an HSM may employ customized hardware engine to accelerate cryptographic algorithms. It is more efficient than KISS and the software-only solutions. The downside of the HSM is that it fails to provide the same secure level of key usage control as in KISS, as we have explained in Section 1. Indeed, the KISS system can be extended to serve as the key usage control front end of the HSM, which may achieve the benefits of both systems. For system administration, some high-end HSMs [20, 18] achieve the same level of security guarantees as KISS (e.g., quorum control, trusted paths using on-HSM I/O devices, remote management using administrator devices). However, their administrator devices introduce larger TCB than KISS (e.g., complicated key management software stack for interpreting commands and operation results). The HSM administrators usually blindly trust the devices, and have no intuitive way to verify their software status.

There are research proposals that seek to offer similar protections for user credentials in the key management systems. Wallet-based web authentication systems (e.g., [5]) isolate user credentials in an isolated domain (e.g., a L4 process upon L4 Micro-kernel) during run-time and protect the credentials at rest by TPM-based sealed storage. They only allow authenticated websites to access their own credentials. These systems have a reasonable TCB size, but do not provide fine-grained and flexible key usage control as in KISS (e.g., user-based control). Bugiel and Ekberg [2] propose a system that only allows the application to access its own credentials (protected in mobile trusted module). The On-board Credentials (ObC) [10] approach enables an isolation environment (like KISS) for both third-party credential algorithms/applications and credentials, on smartphones and conventional computers. However, one faces multiple challenges extending these systems for corporate key management. For example, ObC approach lacks protection mechanisms against malicious administrators and do not support trusted paths for administrator management. PinUP [4] binds files to the applications that are authorized to use them by leveraging the SELinux capability mechanisms. This suggests that PinUP introduces a larger TCB to provide security assurance on par with KISS.

12   Conclusion

In this paper, we leverage widely-deployed trusted computing techniques to design a trustworthy key management system architecture. KISS aims to reduce cost by relying solely on commodity computer hardware, and minimize the system TCB by the thin-hypervisor-based design and lightweight administrator devices. KISS is the first key management system to support fine-grained control of key usage. KISS is bootstrapped and operated in the face of software attacks from malware in the OS and insider attacks from malicious administrators. KISS provides user-verifiable trusted paths and simple dedicated external devices for secure system administration. KISS showcases the benefits of applying trusted computing techniques to designing trustworthy systems. KISS offers trustworthy key management systems at a price point that enables wide-spread adoption beyond the security-sensitive financial or governmental institutions.

Acknowledgments. We are grateful to the reviewers and Aziz Mohaisen for their insightful suggestions. We also want to thank Geoffrey Hasker, Yueqiang Cheng, and Miao Yu for stimulating conversations and valuable feedback.

References

[1] AMD. AMD64 architecture programmer's manual. No. 24594 rev. 3.19 (2012)
[2] Bugiel, S., Ekberg, J.: Implementing an application-specific credential platform using late-launched mobile trusted module. In: Proc. ACM STC (2010)
[3] Cheng, Y., Ding, X., Deng, R.H.: DriverGuard: A fine-grained protection on I/O flows. In: Atluri, V., Diaz, C. (eds.) ESORICS 2011. LNCS, vol. 6879, pp. 227–244. Springer, Heidelberg (2011)
[4] Enck, W., McDaniel, P., Jaeger, T.: Pinup: Pinning user files to known applications. In: Proc. ACSAC (2008)
[5] Gajek, S., Löhr, H., Sadeghi, A., Winandy, M.: Truwallet: trustworthy and migratable wallet-based web authentication. In: Proc. ACM STC (2009)
[6] Hofmann, O.S., Kim, S., Dunn, A.M., Lee, M.Z., Witchel, E.: Inktag: secure applications on an untrusted operating system. In: Proc. ASPLOS (2013)
[7] HP. Enterprise Secure Key Manager, http://h18006.www1.hp.com/products/quickspecs/13978_div/13978_div.PDF
[8] IBM. Tivoli Key Lifecycle Manager, http://www-01.ibm.com/software/tivoli/products/key-lifecycle-mgr
[9] Intel. Intel trusted execution techonology. No. 315168-008 (2011)
[10] Kostiainen, K.: On-board Credentials: An Open Credential Platform for Mobile Devices. PhD thesis, Aalto University (2012)
[11] Matrosov, A., Rodionov, E., Harley, D., Malch, J.: Stuxnet Under the Microscope, http://www.eset.com/us/resources/white-papers/Stuxnet_Under_the_Microscope.pdf
[12] McCune, J., Li, Y., Qu, N., Zhou, Z., Datta, A., Gligor, V., Perrig, A.: TrustVisor: Efficient TCB reduction and attestation. In: Proc. IEEE Symp. on Security and Privacy (2010)
[13] McCune, J.M., Parno, B., Perrig, A., Reiter, M.K., Isozaki, H.: Flicker: An execution infrastructure for TCB minimization. In: Proc. EuroSys (2008)
[14] Oracle. Opensolaris project: Crypto kms agent toolkit, http://hub.opensolaris.org/bin/view/Project+kmsagenttoolkit/WebHome
[15] Oracle. Oracle Key Manager, http://www.oracle.com/us/products/servers-storage/storage/tape-storage/034335.pdf
[16] Parno, B., Lorch, J.R., Douceur, J.R., Mickens, J., McCune, J.M.: Memoir: Practical state continuity for protected modules. In: Proc. IEEE Symp. on Security and Privacy (2011)
[17] RSA. RSA Data Protection Manager, http://www.emc.com/security/rsa-data-protection-manager.html
[18] SafeNet. SafeNet hardware security modules, http://www.safenet-inc.com/products/data-protection/hardware-security-modules-hsms/
[19] StrongAuth. StrongKey SKMS, http://www.strongkey.org
[20] Thales. Thales hardware security modules, http://www.thales-esecurity.com/en/Products/Hardware%20Security%20Modules.aspx
[21] Trusted Computing Group. TPM specification version 1.2 (2009)
[22] Trusted Computing Group. Trusted platform module library family "2.0" (2011)
[23] VASCO. Diginotar reports security incident (2011), http://www.vasco.com/company/about_vasco/press_room/news_archive/2011/news_diginotar_reports_security_incident.aspx
[24] Zhang, F., Chen, J., Chen, H., Zang, B.: Cloudvisor: retrofitting protection of virtual machines in multi-tenant cloud with nested virtualization. In: Proc. ACM SOSP (2011)
[25] Zhou, Z., Gligor, V., Newsome, J., McCune, J.: Building verifiable trusted path on commodity x86 computers. In: Proc. IEEE Symp. on Security and Privacy (2012)

Guardian: Hypervisor as Security Foothold
for Personal Computers

Yueqiang Cheng and Xuhua Ding

School of Information Systems
Singapore Management University
{yqcheng.2008,xhding}@smu.edu.sg

Abstract. Personal computers lack of a security foothold to allow the end-users to protect their systems or to mitigate the damage. Existing candidates either rely on a large Trusted Computing Base (TCB) or are too costly to widely deploy for commodity use. To fill this gap, we propose a hypervisor-based security foothold, named as *Guardian*, for commodity personal computers. We innovate a bootup and shutdown mechanism to achieve both *integrity* and *availability* of Guardian. We also propose two security utilities based on Guardian. One is a device monitor which detects malicious manipulation on camera and network adaptors. The other is hyper-firewall whereby Guardian expects incoming and outgoing network packets based on policies specified by the user. We have implemented Guardian ($\approx$ 25K SLOC) and the two utilities ($\approx$ 2.1K SLOC) on a PC with an Intel processor. Our experiments show that Guardian is practical and incurs insignificant overhead to the system.

1 Introduction

The operating system is the cornerstone of all security applications such as anti-virus and firewall. Once the OS is compromised, the adversary has the ability to disable all security services and access all sensitive data in the system. Even if a security-conscious end-user is aware of the attack, she still can not get a reliable security foothold to mitigate the damage. It is challenging to seek a feasible and secure solution. Rewriting commodity OS, e.g., splitting the OS into low- and high-assurance portions, is too costly to be practical. Adopting new security-capable devices (e.g., secure co-processors) usually requires substantial modifications to hardware, OS and/or applications, which makes these solutions difficult to widely deploy in the near future.

A usable security foothold should meet the following requirements. Firstly, it should be secure against attacks from rootkits which can subvert the operating system. Secondly, it should allow the human user to use it, e.g., to issue a command. Last but not the least, it should be always available throughout the life cycle even when the OS is corrupted. By virtue of the virtualization, a hypervisor is widely deemed as a software which can resists attacks from an untrusted guest OS. However, almost no hypervisor can simultaneously satisfy all the above requirements, especially for the availability requirement.

M. Huth et al. (Eds.): TRUST 2013, LNCS 7904, pp. 19–36, 2013.
© Springer-Verlag Berlin Heidelberg 2013

In this paper, we harness the fast-growing hardware-assisted virtualization techniques to build a tiny but reliable hypervisor as the security foothold for personal computers. The hypervisor we propose is named as *Guardian*. Guardian has two prominent new features which are the enabling techniques for the hypervisor to become a security foothold. The first is a new secure bootup and shutdown mechanism, which enhances the existing hardware-based security boot up by offering integrity and availability protection of the TCB image and critical information. The other feature is a secure user-hypervisor interface which allows the end-user to issue commands to and receive responses from Guardian at runtime. The interface is secure in the sense that the channel between the human end-user and the hypervisor is authentic and the exchanged information is not exposed to the guest. We also propose two practical security utilities based on Guardian. The first is a device monitor utility, whereby the user can instruct Guardian to monitor the state of peripheral devices, e.g., a camera. The second is a hyper-firewall whereby Guardian inspects inbound/outbound network traffic and drops illegal packets. We have implemented Guardian on a desktop with a Linux guest. Guardian consists of around $25K$ SLOC, and the utilities consist of around $2.1K$ SLOC. Our experiments show that Guardian inflicts an insignificant workload to the whole system.

The growing hardware support for virtualization will continue to empower the hypervisor with more effective and stronger security control over commodity platforms with smaller code size and better performance. We envisage that using a hypervisor as a generic security foothold is a promising direction to greatly boost up the security for commodity platforms. Our work presented in this paper is an important step towards this ultimate goal. We summarize our contributions as follows:

1. We design and implement Guardian which is the first system to provide both *integrity* and *availability* guarantees. Note that all existing hypervisors do *not* achieve the availability guarantee.
2. We design and build a device monitor and a hyper-firewall as two security utilities on top of Guardian.

In the next section, we present our research objectives and threat model. Then we present the design of Guardian and the security utilities in Section 3 and Section 4. In Section 5, we describe the implementation and the evaluation. Finally, we discuss the related work in Section 6 and conclude the paper in Section 7.

2   Problem Definition

We aim to provide a tiny and reliable hypervisor as a security foothold for personal computers. Namely, we undertake to furnish the end-user with a reliable security basis when the conventional one (typically the operating system) fails. Though the security foothold, the human user can configure security policies and manage resources in the platform. It not only boosts up the system security, but also facilitates the end-user to determine the trustworthiness of her system. Note that we do *not* attempt to detect and remove malicious software from the platform, nor is to protect the operating system or a user application.

2.1 Threat Model

Since our goal is to assist the end-user, we assume that they are security- conscious users, who are happy and intended to use our system to protect their systems. We do not consider any human adversary who may have physical access to the system. For instance, the adversary can issue malicious DMA accesses by inserting extra physical devices (e.g., a firewire device). A malicious human user can always remove the hypervisor from the platform.

The adversary in our threat model is malware residing in the operating system which can subvert the operating system and launch arbitrary attacks. However, we assume that they can not compromise the hypervisor. Note that the hypervisor makes use of hardware-assisted virtualization techniques to defend against malicious software accesses and illicit DMA accesses. This assumption can be more reasonably held if the hypervisor has a tiny code size and simple logic so that only a small attack interface is exposed to the adversary. Existing techniques [4, 24, 39, 40] can also be applied to enhance hypervisor security.

We assume that the adversary can not compromise the hardware devices whose behavior always exactly follow their specifications. We also assume the system firmware is trusted. In fact, the modern BIOS has a built-in hardware lock mechanism [17, 35] to set itself as read-only so that the OS cannot tamper with it. Furthermore, the modern BIOS only accepts signed updates [36, 38]. Due to the complexity of the x86 platform (e.g., optional ROM), this assumption may not always true. Nonetheless, it is still possible to validate the system firmware by the proposed attestation approach [20] or by a trusted system integrator.

3 Design of Guardian

In this section, we introduce the techniques for establishing Guardian as a security foothold, and describe the functionalities of the two secure user interfaces.

3.1 Establishing Guardian as a Security Foothold

To establish Guardian as a security foothold, it is necessary but not sufficient to ensure a secure boot. The secure boot alone can only validate the integrity of the system's TCB image during booting up, while a reliable security foothold needs both integrity and availability guarantee, so that the system still boots up into a trusted state even if the TCB image on the hard drive are modified by attackers. We do not elaborate the details of secure boot (e.g., TPM-based secure boot [37]) to avoid verbosity as it has been widely used in the literature. Our focus is to explain how to ensure that the intact TCB image is always available for the boot up. The TCB of our system consists of the BIOS, the bootloader-core and the Guardian image. Recall that the BIOS is protected by the hardware and is trusted in our threat model. Therefore, we intend to protect the bootloader core and the Guardian image against runtime attacks.

A straightforward approach is for Guardian to intercept and validate every disk I/O, such that any access to the security critical image residing on the disk is blocked.

Obviously, this solution is costly due to the high overhead and complexity of a disk I/O interception multiplied by the huge number of disk operations.

We devise a novel scheme without interposing on disk operations. The basic idea (visualized in Figure 1) is that once Guardian is launched, it immediately relocates its image and the bootloader core from the disk into a protected memory region *prior to* launching the guest. Then, Guardian intercepts all power off events, and writes the protected image back to the disk before cleaning up the memory. In the following, we describe the details of secure boot up and secure shutdown, which in tandem with runtime protection bolster the availability of Guardian throughout its whole life cycle.

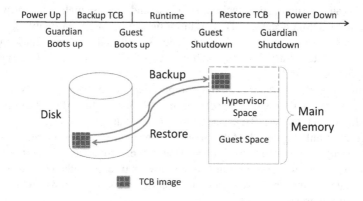

Fig. 1. Protection of the TCB (from power up to power down). The TCB consists of the Guardian image and the bootloader core. The protected memory for the TCB image is reserved by Guardian and inaccessible for the guest OS.

Secure Bootup. Figure 2 illustrates the disk layout for Guardian, where a special partition, referred to as the *hypervisor-partition*, is created during installation to avoid being trespassed by normal file systems. To allow for a secure boot without increasing the TCB size and complexity, we make slight changes on the bootloader (e.g., Grub 2). The BIOS passes the control to the bootloader core in the boot track. The bootloader core includes the Master Boot Record (MBR), the diskboot image and the basic-function image, which provides all basic functions and usually has to load other modules and configuration files such as *grub.cfg* to launch an operating system due to the limited size of the boot track (32KB in maximum).

Our modification is on the basic-function image only, such that it always launches Guardian *before* loading other components including the OS. In specific, once the core is loaded to the CPU by the BIOS (illustrated by Step 1 in Figure 3), it checks a bit flag in main memory (referred to as VMM_flag) which indicates Guardian's presence. If VMM_flag is not set, i.e., the core immediately passes the control to Guardian whose image is placed at a *fixed* disk address upon installation (Step 2 in Figure 3). The address of Guardian is hard-coded into the core, such that it loads Guardian directly using disk I/O without involving any file system.

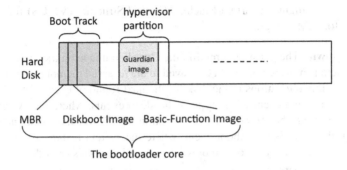

Fig. 2. An illustration of the disk layout

After occupying the CPU, Guardian loads the TCB image into a reserved memory region. It then configures the hypervisor page table, the EPT and IOMMU to ensure that the reserved region is not in the hypervisor or the guest's space and not accessible by DMA devices either. Separating the reserved region from the hypervisor space ensures no accidental accesses to the region. (As shown later, Guardian must map the region into its space by re-configuring the page table in order to access it.)

Finally, Guardian sets VMM_flag indicating its presence, and passes the control back to the bootloader core (Step 3). After asserting the flag is set, the core loads other modules and configuration files (Step 4) and proceeds to boot up the guest in the normal way (Step 5).

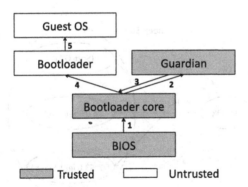

Fig. 3. The sequence of secure bootup

Device Configuration Space Protection. A rootkit may manipulate the device config-uration space (e.g., the space-overlapping attack [44]) to thwart Guardian to intercept certain I/O events or access to I/O data. In order to defeat the configuration space ma-nipulations and conflicts/overlapping between different devices, Guardian is poised to intercept and validate any update to the device configuration registers after its boot up. Note that these registers are located in the northbridge chipset [11]. The interception are realized via configuring Virtual-Machine Control Structure (VMCS) for I/O ports and the EPT for MMIO regions.

Secure Shutdown. The guest may modify the Guardian image on the disk. Therefore, when the system is powered off, the TCB saved in the reserved memory must be written back to their original locations in the disk for the next round of execution. There exist two types of shutdown events. One type is the sleep events, where the system enters a sleep state through the Advanced Configuration and Power-management Interface (ACPI) [14]; the other is the reboot event, where the system restarts from the BIOS. Guardian intercepts both types of shutdown events and responds accordingly.

ACPI Sleep. The ACPI sleep event is managed by the Operating System Power Management (OSPM) subsystem on the modern ACPI-compatible system. Receiving commands from software (e.g., system call) or external interrupts (e.g., the System Control Interrupt triggered by pressing the power/sleep button or closing the laptop lid), the OSPM subsystem sets the PM1a_CNT register to force the system entering the corresponding sleep state. Note that Guardian prohibits the ACPI sleep event to be triggered by the optional sleep control and PM1b_CNT registers. Specifically, there is a 32-bit pointer in the Fixed ACPI Table (FADT) pointing to the PM1b_CNT block. Guardian clears this pointer and intercepts accesses to the PM1b_CNT register. The same method is used on the control sleep register.

Guardian intercepts the guest's sleep command issued to the PM1a_CNT register. Note that the actual interception method depends on whether the register is accessed by PIO or MMIO. The former involves VMCS configuration whereas the latter requires the EPT.

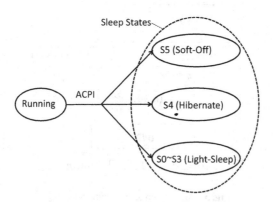

Fig. 4. ACPI sleep states

Among the six Sleep states ($S0$ to $S5$) defined in the ACPI specification (in Figure 4), the light-sleep ($S0$ to $S3$) states are not of concern, because the main memory remains powered and Guardian remains alive. Therefore, Guardian performs no action. For the soft-off state ($S5$) where the system will be powered off, Guardian restores the TCB image back to the respective disk locations by using direct disk I/O operations. Note that Guardian needs to re-activate the disk which has been closed (but remains powered) before the ACIP sleep command is issued. In the end, Guardian clears VMM_flag and resumes the intercepted ACPI command which turns the platform off.

It is slightly more complicated to deal with the hibernation state $S4$ due to the need for platform context saving. Guardian needs to save its context into the hypervisor partition, in addition to the restoration work done for $S5$. For the guest context, Guardian disables and prohibits the ACPI S4BIOS Transition [1], which bypasses Guardian as the BIOS directly saves *all* memory content into the hard disk including Guardian's context. Therefore, only the OS-assisted hibernation method is supported and the OS must write its own context into the disk before hibernation.

Note that after the PM1a_CNT register is set, the platform passes the point of no return, because the ACPI hardware will force the platform to enter $S4$ or $S5$ state and no software will be loaded to the CPU. In other words, Guardian is the last piece of code executed before shutdown, which guarantees the security of the TCB and critical data resting on the disk.

System Reboot. There are three possible ways to reboot a system. One is ACPI reset, which is activated by the ACPI reset register. Note that the system will immediately reboot once the reset register is set. The ACPI reset register can be accessed by port I/O or memory-mapped I/O, which can be intercepted by Guardian through configuring the VMCS or EPT, respectively. The second way is essentially triggered by the CPU INIT signal. Guardian intercepts the event through configuring the VMCS.

In the third way, an attacker can switch the CPU to the real mode and jump to the BIOS entry to reboot the system. The tricky part is that it can bypass the INIT and ACPI reset mechanisms, meaning that the previous two interception methods will fail to intercept this one. To intercept it, a straightforward solution is to intercept the CPU switch from protected mode to real mode. However, the cost will significantly rise up when legitimate CPU-mode switches take place frequently, e.g., in Windows. Our solution is to prevent jumping to the BIOS reboot-routine from the guest by configuring the EPT. Any attempts from the guest OS to reboot the system will be intercepted by Guardian whose response is to repeat Step 3-5 in secure bootup without rebooting the whole platform.

Recovery. Guardian provides an alternative secure boot mechanism, where the system is able to boot up from a trusted-storage, such as a live CD or a read-only USB token. The bootup sequence is the same as the one described in Section 3.1. For convenience, the end-user can configure the system always boot up from a trusted storage, such that the system still can boot up into a trusted state.

The secure shutdown procedure may not be triggered due to some unexpected and irresistible events, e.g., power failure or system crash. Given that such unexpected system failure events may lead to the untrustworthiness of the TCB image, we need the TPM-based secure boot [37] to guarantee that only the trusted image can be booted.

---

[1] It clears the F bit in the Firmware ACPI Control Structure (FACS) and intercepts accesses to the SMI_CMD command register, which is S4BIOS service activation.

In such cases, the system can not boot up, and the security-conscious end-users need the recovery mechanism to restore Guardian image. Specifically, the bootloader in the trusted storage is extended to restore TCB image into the hard drive. Note that the boot-loader originally has the capabilities to read/write the hard drive, the trusted storage and the main memory. Therefore, we can easily combine these functions to do the recovery.

3.2   Secure User-Hypervisor Interface

The secure interface is a duplex channel between the end-user and Guardian without involving the guest OS. Guardian shields the channel against any access from the guest. With the interface, the end-user can configure Guardian during its boot-up, and issue commands during runtime. For the sake of usability and simplicity, we do not rely on any external device such as a USB token. The user inputs are through the keyboard while the outputs are via the display in VGA mode.

Guardian provides two secure UIs. One is the Boot Up Secure User Interface (BUSUI), which is used in the secure boot phase before the guest starts to run. Since the platform then is in a trustworthy state, the implementation of BUSUI is straightforward. Guardian utilizes the BIOS services (i.e. INT 0x16 and 0x10) for input and output. The end-user activates it by holding a special key for a few seconds. In our current design, a user can deposit a text message to Guardian as a shared secret and can also input policies.

The other interface is the Run Time Secure User Interface (RTSUI), which is used after the guest boots up. The RTSUI can be dynamically launched by the end-user. RTSUI extends the secure user interface in KGuard [8]. Namely, Guardian securely receive inputs of a human user through a keyboard while it securely produces outputs through the display. Both the input and output paths are inaccessible to the guest OS. Since the interface in KGuard is only for password input, we extend it to a command-line interface such that the user can conveniently input commands and read responses.

4   Security Utilities

When designing security utilities based on Guardian, we endeavor to deal with threats plaguing normal end-users and system administrators. To this end, we propose a device monitor and a hyper-firewall.

4.1   Device Monitoring

A rootkit can misuse a peripheral device without the user's consent. For instance, it can quickly turn on the camera of a laptop to take a picture of the user and then turn it off. In a stealthy manner, it can also turn a network adaptor into the promiscuous mode so as to sniff the entire LAN traffic. We develop a Guardian utility to monitor the states of the camera and the network interface. In case of risky device usage, the end-user is alerted via the hypervisor-user interface or a beep sound. Note that the beep cannot be stopped by the adversary, because Guardian is able to intercept all accesses to that device.

Camera Control. Our design considers an external camera attached to the platform through a USB interface. (It can also be extended for a built-in camera.) The USB port is controlled by an EHCI [16] or UHCI [15] controller. In either case, a *frame list*, with its base address specified by the *PERIODICLISTBASE* register, is used to queue I/O commands. To enable the camera, the driver must insert a *transfer descriptor* or TD to the frame list. The host controller automatically fetches it from the queue and responds properly.

Upon the user's activation command, the camera control utility makes use of the interception primitive to set read-only on the region for the base register, the frame list and the TD queue. If it detects a new TD with the open command UVC_SET_CUR for the camera, it alerts the user through a beep sound.

NIC Promiscuous Mode Control. The control on the network interface is simpler than EHCI. The Unicast Promiscuous Enabled (UPE) bit and the Multicast Promiscuous Enabled (MPE) in the Receive ConTroL Register (RCTL) are the flags that turns on the NIC's promiscuous mode. The monitoring utility intercepts the accesses to RCTL. Once the UPE bit or the MPE bit is set, an alert is raised to the user.

Note that Guardian and its utilities are not burdened with the complicated task of device management, for instance, to block illegal operations. This is to keep the hypervisor size small and more reliable.

4.2   Hyper-firewall

Recent attacks have shown that both application-level and OS-level firewalls can be disabled by rootkits. One solution proposed recently is the VMwall [32], which isolates the firewall in a separated domain (i.e., the Dom0 in the Xen setting). However, this approach dramatically increases the TCB size and requires the user to run two domains concurrently.

We propose in this section a more elegant and stronger solution called *hyper-firewall* as the firewall functions in the hypervisor space. The basic idea is that a Guardian utility interposes on network I/O. It drops illegal packets if their TCP/IP headers are not compliant to the firewall policies set by the end-user through the secure UI. Since Guardian does not comprise any NIC driver, this utility does not significantly increase Guardian's code size. The main challenge is how to intercept network packets in an efficient way. Before presenting the details, we briefly explain the network I/O mechanism.

The packet transmission mechanism is illustrated in Figure 5. The NIC makes use of a ring buffer (essentially a circular queue) to store *transmit descriptors* which point to the packets to transmit. The ring buffer has its base address saved in the TDBAL and TDBAH registers, has its size saved in the TDLENL and TDLENH registers, and has a head register and a tail register pointing to the queue head and tail respectively. The NIC always dequeues the descriptor pointed by the head register, and then fetches the corresponding packet. After retrieval, it advances the head pointer. The tail pointer is maintained by the device driver. To send a new packet, the driver enqueues one or multiple descriptors. Then, the tail pointer is also advanced. The NIC only uses the descriptors between the head and the tail. It stops transmission when the two pointers collide.

The packet receiving mechanism is analogous to the transmission mechanism. It also has a ring buffer storing *receive descriptors*, and has its own base address registers, length registers, and the head and tail registers. Initially, the driver allocates a set of fixed

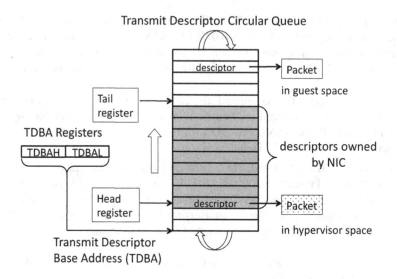

Fig. 5. The transmit descriptor circular queue used by the NIC

length DMA buffers, and enqueues the corresponding descriptors into the ring queue. When receiving packets, the NIC stores them into those pre-allocated DMA buffers, updates the corresponding descriptors, and advances the head pointer accordingly. Finally, it throws out an interrupt to notify the driver to fetch the packets according to the descriptors. Since the packet sending and receiving mechanisms are different, we design two interposition schemes, respectively. Note that the registers used by NICs may be different. To support all NICs, we can provide a profile which can provide necessary information for Guardian to understand register meanings.

Outbound Packet Filter. Guardian uses the EPT to intercept all write accesses the TDBAL, TDBAH, TDLENL and TDLENH registers so that Guardian can always locate the legitimate ring buffer. Similarly, it sets up the EPT and IOMMU tables, such that the head register can only be updated by the NIC[2], and all accesses to the tail register are intercepted by Guardian. Lastly, it sets the entire ring buffer as read-only.

When a write access to the ring buffer is intercepted by Guardian, it checks whether the write overwrites an existing descriptor which has not been fetched by the NIC. If so, the access is blocked; otherwise, Guardian emulates the write. When a write access to the tail register is intercepted, Guardian performs the following. (1) It checks whether the packets pointed by the descriptors between the present tail and the new tail are compliant with the firewall policies; (2) It copies all legal packets to the hypervisor space and updates those descriptors accordingly so that the NIC can fetch them from their new locations; for illegal packets, it sets the packet-length field in their descriptors as zero; (3) It emulates the tail update.

---

[2] In the current hardware specification, the driver is not able to instruct the NIC to update the header register.

Once the packets are moved to the hypervisor space, their descriptors are not allowed to be changed. Note that packets are much smaller than a memory page. Therefore, relocating them into the hypervisor space avoids undesirable page faults as compared to protecting them in the guest space.

Inbound Packet Filter. The inbound packet filter mechanism is similar to its outbound counterpart. By enforcing access control on those control registers and the ring buffer for the receiving descriptor, Guardian locates the DMA buffers allocated by the driver. To retrieve a packet, the driver first fetches the receive descriptor which triggers a page fault. Guardian then performs the packet inspection according to the firewall policies, and drops illegal ones.

5   Implementation

We have built a prototype of Guardian on a Dell OptiPlex 990 MT desktop with an Intel(R) Core(TM) i7-2600 CPU @ 3.40GHz processor[3] and 4GB main memory. Guardian consists of around 25K SLOC for its core functions, which is much smaller than Xen (263K SLOC for Xen-4.1.2) and Linux (8,143k SLOC for Linux-2.6.33.20). A comprehensive comparison between Guardian and other hypervisors is listed in Figure 6.

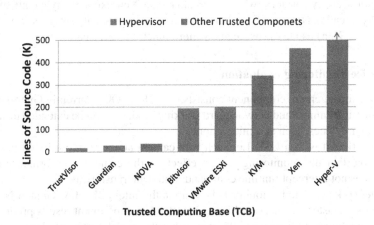

Trusted Computing Base (TCB)

Fig. 6. Comparison of the TCB size. TrustVisor itself is around 17K SLOC. NOVA [33] consists of the microhypervisor (9K SLOC), and several trusted components, i.e., a thin user level environment (7K SLOC), and the VMM (20K SLOC). BitVisor [31] and VMware ESXi are 194K and 200K SLOC, respectively. KVM is around 200K SLOC, as well as a customized QEMU (140K SLOC). Xen is around 263K SLOC with Dom0 that can be customized to 200K SLOC [19]. Microsoft Hyper-V uses a Xen-like architecture with a hypervisor (around 100K SLOC) and Windows Server 2008 (larger than 400K SLOC).

---

[3] The Hyper-threading mode is disabled since our current hypervisor does not support the multiprocessor mechanism.

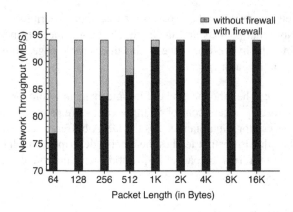

Fig. 7. The benchmark results with and without hyper-firewall

The binary size of Guardian is around $223KB$, which is much smaller than Xen (around 1,264KB for Xen-4.1.2) and Linux (around 134,134KB for Linux-2.6.33.20) image, and the bootloader core is around $30KB$. Guardian reserves 512KB memory space for TCB images and other critical information. Guardian also provides 11 hypercalls for security services, which is smaller than Xen exported hypercall surfaces (i.e., 46 hypercalls). Note that Guardian only focus on the security services, while these systems (e.g., Xen) usually provide many more functional services.

5.1 Device Monitoring Evaluation

The device management component consists of 1.2K SLOC. Currently Guardian supports to monitor camera and network card working modes. It can be extended to support other similar devices, such as a microphone.

We experiment with a USB Logitech web camera attached on an EHCI host controller. Note that the monitoring has no effect on the camera's performance as the scheme does not intercept runtime commands and data transferring.

The network card mode monitor is built upon the Intel 82579LM Gigabit Network Card, whose registers are accessed using MMIO. The experiment results produced by network benchmark tool *netperf* [25] prove that the monitor service almost does not affect the network I/O throughout. Note that the device management service does not require any modifications in the guest kernel or device drivers.

5.2 Hyper-firewall Evaluation

The packet filter service is built on the Intel Corporation 82579LM Gigabit Network Card, and does not add any code into the guest OS. Current hyper-firewall supports adding policies on inbound and outbound packets. For the outbound packets, hyper-firewall restricts the region of the target destination (e.g., external IP addresses), and for the inbound packets, hyper-firewall restricts the connection ports (e.g., SSH port 22).

All hyper-firewall policies can be enabled and disabled through the RTSUI. All experiments show the hyper-firewall works well. We tested the network I/O performance with benchmark tool *netperf* [25]. When we only enable outbound policy, the performance results show that our hyper-firewall only introduces (0.096% - 0.064%) performance overhead; when we enable inbound and outbound policies, the hyper-firewall introduces (18.29% - 0.26%) performance overhead. Note that the short packet setting generates more interceptions. Thus its performance is relatively low. Note that the monitoring of NIC does not affect the I/O speed of other derives. The packet filter service only adds $0.9K$ SLOC into Guardian.

5.3 System Benchmark

We first measure the overhead on the OS operations using the LmBench suite. Figure 8 shows the results: socket (local connection), memory operations (i.e., read, write and bcopy) and some system calls (i.e., mmap, fork+exec and fork+exit). However, fork+exec and fork+exit incur higher performance penalties of 39% and 38%, which are heavily dependent on the Intel EPT performance. We do believe that this could be improved with the performance enhancing of memory virtualization.

We also measure computation performance with Guardian. The results generated by the benchmark tool SPEC CPU 2006 (see Figure 9) show that Guardian usually only introduces 0.2% - 10.3% performance loss, and may lead to 38.2% performance overhead in some extreme cases (i.e., memory intensive operations with extreme low cache hit rate), which is also dependent on the page operations of current Intel EPT. Again, we believe that it can be improved in the further.

For I/O-bound benchmark test, we select a range of benchmark tools, including Bonnie, Postmark, netperf and Linux kernel. For Bonnie, we use a 1GB file and perform sequential read/write (fread/fwrite) and random access (frandom). For Postmark, we choose 20,000 files, 100,000 transactions and 100 subdirectories, as well as all other default parameters. For netperf, we use another local machine as the netperf server, and

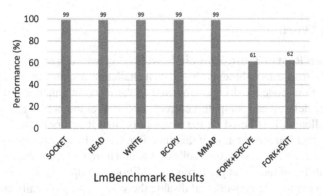

Fig. 8. The LmBench results on OS operations

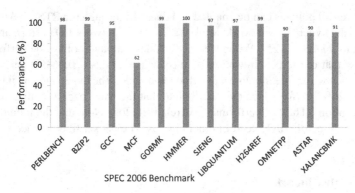

Fig. 9. The system benchmark comparison results generated by *SPEC CPU 2006*

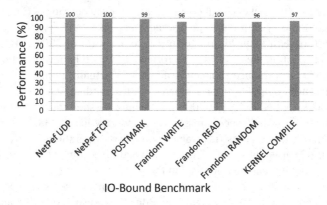

Fig. 10. The I/O-bound benchmark results

run both TCP STREAM and UDP STREAM benchmarks to measure basic network performance. For Linux kernel, we compile the Linux-2.6.33.20 with default configuration. Figure 10 shows the results.

6   Related Work

Software-Based Root of Trust. Software-based ROTs have been proposed and used in [27,29,30]. The trust establishment is based on a challenge-response protocol. A speed-optimized function (code block) is established as the ROT on a platform if, within an acceptable time delay, it can compute a correct checksum of memory regions according to a given challenge. It is based on the assumption that it incurs a noticeably longer delay for any other implementation of this function. It also has a restriction on both the adversary's capability, for instance no collusion with a third party, as mentioned in [10]) and the capabilities of the target platforms. In addition, to stop the proxy attack, it may even require to unplug the network and disable the wireless to physically cut down the connection with outside. These limitations and requirements lead to inconvenience or even to impracticability. Thus, software ROTs are unqualified to be a security foothold for normal users' computers.

Hardware-Based Root of Trust. The hardware-based ROT can be categorized into static ROTs and dynamic ROTs. A static ROT is a built-in platform component. When the platform boots up, a trust chain can be established from the ROT up to the operating system. The TPM chip [37] is a typical example of static hardware ROT. As a chip on the motherboard, it is secure against all software attacks. Secure (or authenticated) boot up, remote attestation and sealed storage are the main security services provided by the TPM framework. The main disadvantages of TPM are its low speed, inflexibility and passiveness. Therefore, to support various security services, it usually requires assistance from certain secure software routine (e.g., hypervisor). IBM's secure co-processor [2] is a strong hardware root of trust with such a high price tag that it is not feasible for the mass market. SMART [10] is a hardware-software co-designed scheme, where a piece of code works on a modified *low-end* microcontroller units (MCU) to function as a dynamic ROT. The SwitchBlade architecture [5] can prevent persistent rootkits from infecting security-critical files (e.g., kernel image) with an ROT residing on the disk controller. These ROTs may be integrated with Guardian though carefully design and implementation.

AMD Secure Virtual Machine (SVM) [1] and Intel Trusted Execution Technology (TXT) [18] are dynamic ROTs. These new processor features allow a piece of code to be securely executed in an isolated environment enforced by the hardware. Despite of their easiness of use, they incur high latency as showed in the Flicker system [22]. Fortunately, the high latency may be tolerable for the end-users, since it only required once when the system as well as Guardian boots up. The boot mechanism of Guardian is compatible with dynamic ROT techniques.

Hypervisor Related Security Systems. Many hypervisor-based security systems have been designed and reported in the literature. For instance, a hypervisor can be applied for I/O related protection [9,31], for kernel integrity protection [3,13,23,26,28,41,42], and for user space protection [6,7,12,21,34,43]. By studying these systems, we identify cryptographic engine, measurement, emulation, interception and manipulation as the fundamental security primitives which are adopted in Guardian as well.

Our work has remarkable differences with the aforementioned systems. Guardian aims to be a versatile hypervisor. By bring together a number of fundamental security primitives, Guardian facilitates the design and implementation of virtualization-based security systems, rather than focusing only on a single security problem. In addition, Guardian caters to the security needs of the end-user, which demands Guardian to be highly efficient, easy-to-use and compatible with the operating system and applications

Note that those schemes [4,24,39,40] that enhance the hypervisor security are complimentary to our work. The security of Guardian will be further improved if these techniques are applied in its implementation.

7   Conclusion

In this paper, we have proposed Guardian as a security foothold on the end-user systems to enhance their security. Specifically, we introduced Guardian whose integrity and availability were guaranteed by the novel bootup and shutdown technique. Guardian also provided a secure user interface, through which the end-user could update the configurations of Guardian or dynamically activate/deactivate a dedicated security service for the security needs. We also proposed two security utilities based on Guardian: a device monitor which detects malicious device operations and a hyper-firewall which inspects the incoming and outgoing network packets from the hypervisor space. We have implemented Guardian and the two utilities. The experiment results show that they are efficient and easy to use. Our work demonstrates that computer security can be significantly boosted up by using a tiny and reliable hypervisor.

Acknowledgement. We thank the reviewers and especially Mohammad Mannan for their constructive comments. This research/project is supported by the Singapore National Research Foundation under its International Research Centre@ Singapore Funding Initiative and administered by the IDM Programme Office.

References

1. AMD. Secure virtual machine architecture reference manual. Technical report (2005)
2. Arnold, T.W., Van Doom, L.P.: The IBM PCIXCC: a new cryptographic coprocessor for the IBM eserver. IBM J. Res. Dev. 48(3-4), 475–487 (2004)
3. Azab, A.M., Ning, P., Sezer, E.C., Zhang, X.: HIMA: A hypervisor-based integrity measurement agent. In: Proceedings of the 2009 Annual Computer Security Applications Conference, ACSAC 2009, pp. 461–470. IEEE Computer Society, Washington, DC (2009)
4. Azab, A.M., Ning, P., Wang, Z., Jiang, X., Zhang, X., Skalsky, N.C.: Hypersentry: enabling stealthy in-context measurement of hypervisor integrity. In: Proceedings of the 17th ACM Conference on Computer and Communications Security, CCS 2010, pp. 38–49. ACM, New York (2010)
5. Butler, K.R.B., McLaughlin, S., Moyer, T., McDaniel, P.D.: New security architectures based on emerging disk functionality. IEEE Security and Privacy Magazine (September 2010)
6. Champagne, D., Lee, R.B.: Scalable architectural support for trusted software. In: Jacob, M.T., Das, C.R., Bose, P. (eds.) HPCA, pp. 1–12. IEEE Computer Society (2010)
7. Chen, X., Garfinkel, T., Christopher Lewis, E., Subrahmanyam, P., Waldspurger, C.A., Boneh, D., Dwoskin, J., Ports, D.R.K.: Overshadow: A virtualization-based approach to retrofitting protection in commodity operating systems. In: Proceedings of the 13th International Conference on Architectural Support for Programming Languages and Operating Systems, ASPLOS 2008, Seattle, WA, USA (March 2008)
8. Cheng, Y., Ding, X.: Virtualization based password protection against malware in untrusted operating systems. In: Katzenbeisser, S., Weippl, E., Camp, L.J., Volkamer, M., Reiter, M., Zhang, X. (eds.) Trust 2012. LNCS, vol. 7344, pp. 201–218. Springer, Heidelberg (2012)
9. Cheng, Y., Ding, X., Deng, R.H.: Driverguard: a fine-grained protection on I/O flows. In: Atluri, V., Diaz, C. (eds.) ESORICS 2011. LNCS, vol. 6879, pp. 227–244. Springer, Heidelberg (2011)
10. Eldefrawy, K., Francillon, A., Perito, D., Tsudik, G.: SMART: Secure and Minimal Architecture for (Establishing a Dynamic) Root of Trust. In: Proceedings of the 19th Annual Network and Distributed System Security Symposium, San Diego, USA, February 5-8 (2012)
11. Fleming, S.: Accessing pci express configuration registers using intel chipsets. otechnical report (2008)
12. Garfinkel, T., Pfaff, B., Chow, J., Rosenblum, M., Boneh, D.: Terra: a virtual machine-based platform for trusted computing. In: Proceedings of the 9th ACM Symposium on Operating Systems Principles, pp. 193–206. ACM, New York (2003)

13. Grace, M., Wang, Z., Srinivasan, D., Li, J., Jiang, X., Liang, Z., Liakh, S.: Transparent protection of commodity OS kernels using hardware virtualization. In: Jajodia, S., Zhou, J. (eds.) SecureComm 2010. LNICST, vol. 50, pp. 162–180. Springer, Heidelberg (2010)
14. Hewleet-Packard, Intel, Microsoft, Phoenix, and Toshiba. Advanced configuration and power interface specification. (Revision 3.0b) (October 2006)
15. Intel. Universal host controller interface (UHCI) design guide (March 1996)
16. Intel. Enhanced host controller interface specification for universal serial bus (March 2002)
17. Intel. Intel I/O controller hub 9 (ICH9) family datasheet (2008)
18. Intel. Intel Trusted Execution Technology (Intel TXT) software development guide (December 2009)
19. Keller, E., Szefer, J., Rexford, J., Lee, R.B.: Nohype: virtualized cloud infrastructure without the virtualization. In: Proceedings of the 37th Annual International Symposium on Computer Architecture, ISCA 2010, pp. 350–361. ACM, New York (2010)
20. Li, Y., McCune, J.M., Perrig, A.: Viper: verifying the integrity of peripherals' firmware. In: Proceedings of the 18th ACM Conference on Computer and Communications Security, CCS 2011, pp. 3–16. ACM, New York (2011)
21. McCune, J.M., Li, Y., Qu, N., Zhou, Z., Datta, A., Gligor, V., Perrig, A.: Trustvisor: Efficient TCB reduction and attestation. In: Proceedings of the 2010 IEEE Symposium on Security and Privacy, pp. 143–158. IEEE Computer Society, Washington, DC (2010)
22. McCune, J.M., Parno, B., Perrig, A., Reiter, M.K., Isozaki, H.: Flicker: An execution infrastructure for TCB minimization. In: Proceedings of the ACM European Conference in Computer Systems (EuroSys) (April 2008)
23. de Oliveira, D.A.S., Felix Wu, S.: Protecting kernel code and data with a virtualization-aware collaborative operating system. In: Proceedings of the 2009 Annual Computer Security Applications Conference, ACSAC 2009, pp. 451–460. IEEE Computer Society, Washington, DC (2009)
24. Rafal, W., Joanna, R., Alexander, T.: Xen 0wning trilogy, Black Hat conference (2008)
25. Rick, J.: Network Performance Benchmark Tool - Netpref,
http://www.netperf.org/netperf/
26. Riley, R., Jiang, X., Xu, D.: Guest-transparent prevention of kernel rootkits with VMM-based memory shadowing. In: Lippmann, R., Kirda, E., Trachtenberg, A. (eds.) RAID 2008. LNCS, vol. 5230, pp. 1–20. Springer, Heidelberg (2008)
27. Seshadri, A., Luk, M., Perrig, A., van Doorn, L., Khosla, P.: Scuba: Secure code update by attestation in sensor networks. In: Proceedings of the 5th ACM Workshop on Wireless Security, WiSe 2006, pp. 85–94. ACM, New York (2006)
28. Seshadri, A., Luk, M., Qu, N., Perrig, A.: Secvisor: a tiny hypervisor to provide lifetime kernel code integrity for commodity OSes. In: Proceedings of Twenty-First ACM SIGOPS Symposium on Operating Systems Principles, SOSP 2007, pp. 335–350. ACM, New York (2007)
29. Seshadri, A., Luk, M., Shi, E., Perrig, A., van Doorn, L., Khosla, P.: Pioneer: verifying code integrity and enforcing untampered code execution on legacy systems. In: Proceedings of the Twentieth ACM Symposium on Operating Systems Principles, SOSP 2005, pp. 1–16. ACM, New York (2005)
30. Seshadri, A., Perrig, A., van Doorn, L., Khosla, P.K.: SWATT: Software-based attestation for embedded devices. In: IEEE Symposium on Security and Privacy (2004)
31. Shinagawa, T., Eiraku, H., Tanimoto, K., Omote, K., Hasegawa, S., Horie, T., Hirano, M., Kourai, K., Oyama, Y., Kawai, E., Kono, K., Chiba, S., Shinjo, Y., Kato, K.: Bitvisor: a thin hypervisor for enforcing I/O device security. In: Proceedings of the 2009 ACM SIGPLAN/SIGOPS International Conference on Virtual Execution Environments, VEE 2009, pp. 121–130. ACM, New York (2009)

32. Srivastava, A., Giffin, J.: Tamper-resistant, application-aware blocking of malicious network connections. In: Lippmann, R., Kirda, E., Trachtenberg, A. (eds.) RAID 2008. LNCS, vol. 5230, pp. 39–58. Springer, Heidelberg (2008)
33. Steinberg, U., Kauer, B.: Nova: A microhypervisor-based secure virtualization architecture. In: Proceedings of the European Conference on Computer Systems (2010)
34. Strackx, R., Piessens, F.: Fides: selectively hardening software application components against kernel-level or process-level malware. In: Proceedings of the 2012 ACM Conference on Computer and Communications Security, CCS 2012, pp. 2–13. ACM, New York (2012)
35. Sun, K., Wang, J., Zhang, F., Stavrou, A.: SecureSwitch: BIOS-assisted isolation and switch between trusted and untrusted commodity OSes. In: Proceedings of the 19th Annual Network and Distributed System Security Symposium, San Diego, California, USA (2012)
36. Phoenix Technologies: Trustedcore: Foundation for secure CRTM and BIOS implementation (2006), https://forms.phoenix.com/whitepaperdownload-/docs/trustedcore_wp.pdf
37. Trusted Computing Group: TPM main specification. Main Specification Version 1.2 rev. 85 (February 2005)
38. Vasudevan, A., Parno, B., Qu, N., Gligor, V.D., Perrig, A.: Lockdown: A safe and practical environment for security applications (CMU-Cylab-09-011) (2009)
39. Wang, J., Stavrou, A., Ghosh, A.: HyperCheck: A hardware-assisted integrity monitor. In: Jha, S., Sommer, R., Kreibich, C. (eds.) RAID 2010. LNCS, vol. 6307, pp. 158–177. Springer, Heidelberg (2010)
40. Wang, Z., Jiang, X.: Hypersafe: A lightweight approach to provide lifetime hypervisor control-flow integrity. In: Proceedings of the 2010 IEEE Symposium on Security and Privacy, SP 2010, pp. 380–395. IEEE Computer Society, Washington, DC (2010)
41. Wang, Z., Jiang, X., Cui, W., Wang, X.: Countering persistent kernel rootkits through systematic hook discovery. In: Lippmann, R., Kirda, E., Trachtenberg, A. (eds.) RAID 2008. LNCS, vol. 5230, pp. 21–38. Springer, Heidelberg (2008)
42. Xiong, X., Tian, D., Liu, P.: Practical protection of kernel integrity for commodity os from untrusted extensions. NDSS (2011)
43. Yang, J., Shin, K.G.: Using hypervisor to provide data secrecy for user applications on a per-page basis. In: Proceedings of the Fourth ACM SIGPLAN/SIGOPS International Conference on Virtual Execution Environments, VEE 2008, pp. 71–80. ACM, New York (2008)
44. Zhou, Z., Gligor, V.D., Newsome, J., McCune, J.M.: Building verifiable trusted path on commodity x86 computers. In: Proceedings of the IEEE Symposium on Security and Privacy (May 2012)

Improving Trusted Tickets
with State-Bound Keys

Jan Nordholz[1], Ronald Aigner[2], and Paul England[2]

[1] TU Berlin, Germany
jnordholz@sec.t-labs.tu-berlin.de
[2] Extreme Computing Group, Microsoft Research
{ronald.aigner,paul.england}@microsoft.com

Abstract. Traditional network authentication systems like Windows'
Active Directory or MIT's Kerberos only provide for mutual authentication of communicating entities, e.g. a user's email client interacting
with an IMAP server, while the user's machine is inherently assumed to
be trusted. While there have been first attempts to explicitly establish
this trust relationship by leveraging the Trusted Platform Module, these
provide no means to directly react to potentially relevant changes in the
client's system state. We expand previous designs by binding keys to the
current platform state and involving these in the network authentication
process, thereby guaranteeing the continued validity of the attestee.

1 Introduction

As by now a TPM can be found in almost every contemporary desktop computer,
so has its adoption in security software become widespread. Chipset firmware,
OS loader programs and finally the OS kernel itself use it to log the respective
subsequent components of the boot chain into a verifiable log buffer, harddisk
encryption solutions like BitLocker[3] use it to seal their cryptographic material
once the booting process has finished, and remote attestation protocols use the
recorded system events and the platform state represented by the TPM's registers to judge the trust to place into that system according to a certain policy.

Network authentication services, on the other hand, usually do not bother
with establishing a trust relationship with the system a client logs on from; in
fact – although this is an orthogonal observation and neither of the two features
strictly requires the other – most do not even identify the client host[1]. While
identifying the host may be undesirable or just unnecessary, garnering trust can
only be beneficial.

Especially in a corporate setting, where the IT department can exert tight
control over the tolerated configurations, trust in a client can be defined as the
combination of two assertions: first, that the client host is running an uncom-
promised operating system, and second, that the configuration of the system
remains inside a predefined subset of the configuration state space theoretically

---

[1] Except for logging its purported identity, represented e. g. by its IP address.

M. Huth et al. (Eds.): TRUST 2013, LNCS 7904, pp. 37–46, 2013.
© Springer-Verlag Berlin Heidelberg 2013

allowed by the OS. Our approach presents a TPM-assisted solution that allows a service instance to gain reliable insights to both of these questions, while at the same time integrating nicely into the well-known Kerberos network authentication framework. We also elaborate on viable techniques for withdrawing credentials given out based on these observations.

2   Background

The Trusted Platform Module was conceived as a vessel for placing trust into a running system. Part of that trust relationship is that private parts of asymmetric encryption keys never leave the TPM. A special asymmetric key is the so-called Endorsement Key (EK), because it is endorsed by the manufacturer of the TPM or the platform manufacturer. The endorsement comes in the form of a certificate containing the public portion of the EK signed by the manufacturer. For TPM 2.0 devices the EK is generated from a unique seed using a key template. This process will always generate the same EK on a TPM, if the seed stays the same. This EK itself, accompanied by its EK certificate, would suffice to sign data and prove its uniqueness. However, on TPM 1.2 devices an EK cannot be used to create signatures. Our solution should target the broadest set of TPMs, so we used this limitations as a prerequisite. The one-to-one mapping between EKs and hardware platforms has several benefits, e.g., it allows for the revocation of individual keys if their factorization becomes known. However, it comes with the drawback of making platforms exposing their EK easily identifiable and thus traceable.

To ameliorate this problem, the EK is used to establish trust in an additional "pseudonymous" key, which is also non-exportable and therefore tied to the platform it was generated on, but does not share the privacy concerns and usage limitations of EKs. These Attestation Identity Keys (AIKs) are certified by a certification authority (CA) based on the EK certificate presented together with the AIK. The CA can inspect the EK certificate and the AIK public portion and generate an activation challenge for the TPM. Only a TPM which possesses both keys can decrypt the challenge. Part of the challenge is a secret, which can be a symmetric key to decrypt the certificate for the AIK issued by the CA. The AIK certificate can then be used to identify the AIK as originating from a TPM[7]. The concept of AIKs allows to use different keys for different services, which further protects users from cross referencing keys.

With this technique the exposure of the EK can be limited to a single trusted service. As we are chiefly discussing corporate settings in our approach, this seems like a reasonable assumption. For scenarios where this might not be desirable, there is also the option of engaging in a zero-knowledge protocol to prove a platform's authenticity[2]. Whichever protocol is used, further communication partners of the platform can then trust a given AIK by virtue of a matching signature by a "privacy CA" instead of relying on the EK.

Another important property of a TPM are non-resettable Platform Configuration Registers (PCR). A PCR can be extended through a trapdoor function, which takes as input the PCR's previous value and a new value to incorporate into the new PCR value. Because these non-resettable PCRs take a well-known value only when the TPM is powered on and can only be extended after that, the value of a PCR cannot be rolled back, only forward. The TCG defines 16 non-resettable PCRs for PC architectures. Most of these contain well defined values, as specified in [8]. The BIOS of a PC will extend hashes of boot events into the PCRs. The operating system loader and the operating system itself continue these measurements throughout the boot process. Such boot events include hashes of all the binaries loaded and executed. In parallel the system keeps a log of these events containing additional information, such as name of binary, size, etc. Because the PCRs are non-resettable, they can be used to verify the integrity of the TCG event log. Under the assumption that every stage of the boot chain checks the validity (cryptographic signatures, soundness of configuration, etc.) of the subsequent stage and writes the resulting measurement into the event log and a hash into the PCRs, there is reliable proof that a certain boot chain has been traversed. This ensures that even if a component of the chain is later found to be malicious (due to a zero-day vulnerability), it cannot erase its presence or alter its image to appear benign without creating a mismatch between log and PCR values. Using a TPM-held asymmetric key (e. g. an AIK), the TPM can then create and sign a "quote" of the PCR values. This way trust in the AIK certificate can be extended to the TCG event log.

A TPM may also create a key bound to the values of a selection of PCRs. That key can only be used as long as the selected PCRs have the same values used at the time of the creation of the key. Should one of the selected PCRs change its value, the key is rendered useless. We call these keys PCR bound keys or state bound keys.

3   Design

3.1   TPM-Based Protocol

Using the AIK signed PCR quote together with a TCG event log and AIK certificate allows an attestor to successfully verify the integrity of the TCG event log, tracing back the AIK to a cryptographic root of trust. However, the result of this attestation process only applies to the very moment in time when the quote was generated on the attestee – even while the examination of the attestor is running, new entries might be added to the attestee's event log. This would alter the system state and possibly also its conformance level to the attestor's standards. Therefore the basic AIK based variant of this protocol (as described in [11]) applies only to systems where there is little change in system state and/or this problem is negligible.

While the pragmatic approach to this problem might be to simply reduce the attack window by keeping the validity period of (possibly stale) attestation certificates at a minimum, there is also a systematic solution using state bound keys. At the cost of the generation of the state bound key, a platform can prove at any time whether its state still matches the one which has been examined at the time of the creation of the PCR quote.

The common remote attestation protocol can be easily extended to include a new TPM-shielded state bound – ephemeral – key (EPH). Congruently to the EK $\rightarrow$ AIK trust transition above, the TPM can issue a creation certificate, which proves the basic characteristics of the EPH and is signed by the AIK. If this data is supplied to the attestation service, it can compare the quoted set of PCRs with the system state to which the EPH has been bound. If the two match, the EPH can then serve as an unforgeable proof of the client's system state.

This approach completely eliminates the need for an explicit validity period on the attestation certificate – it is valid as long as the EPH bound to it can be used and as the attestor trusts the components running on the system. However, the chosen method is of course unable to protect against unknown vulnerabilities and the ensuing possibility of memory-resident malware; however once the vulnerable component is identified, systems which have loaded (and therefore executed) a vulnerable version of this specific component can be denied attestation, effectively forcing them to upgrade to a safe version and to reboot.

All this requires that every significant change in system state actually renders the EPH unusable. Changes on the OS layer, such as subsequent loading of additional code modules is discussed in detail in related work[12,5]. Depending on the scenario there can be other forms of system state changes which should be considered significant, e. g., changes to the system code libraries. If an attestor trusts a system configuration it can also establish trust in the policy enforced on the attestee, which will change the PCRs if a known significant event occurs. This policy enforcement is technically trivial, as all necessary API elements[2] are available on today's major operating systems. The attestee can run a "watchdog" service, which enforces the requirements of the attestor.

Due to this scenario-dependent definition of the system state space, we have expanded the basic remote attestation protocol to allow the attestation service to push a list of state inspection requests to the client. These checks can be instantaneous, meaning that the results should be transmitted as part of the system quote, or continuous, i. e. changes to the requested property should be constantly monitored by the watchdog and EPH should be revoked (by extending a PCR and logging the event) if a property leaves the defined "safe state space".

These additional checks allow for easy determination of system configuration like the version of the operating system, the patchlevel of core libraries or the state of vital system services. As a side effect this also defeats the common "proxy" attack: the possibility for an attacker to have all TPM operations executed on a third, clean machine in order to make his own compromised machine appear innocuous can be thwarted by simply including a check that asks for the attestee's hostname or network interface configuration. If an attacker is acting

---

[2] This includes registering file system directories for kernel notifications, communicating with the TPM from userland – on Windows monitoring the System Registry is advisable, too.

as man-in-the-middle, the answer will not match the client address as seen by the attestation daemon.

3.2   Kerberos Integration

The Kerberos authentication framework and its surrounding ecosystem of glue libraries (libsasl, libgssapi etc.) have become the de-facto standard for large-scale authentication settings in Unix-based networks. While its definition, conventions and API designs span more than a dozen RFC documents, its basic messages are comparatively simple and easily extensible. At the heart of the protocol lie the message exchanges between client and Authentication Service (AS) and between client and Ticket Granting Service (TGS). The former establishes the client's identity by issuing a long-lived Ticket Granting Ticket (TGT) encrypted to the user's pre-shared key (more commonly the "password"), the latter can be requested to hand out tickets for individual services, provided that an appropriate permitting TGT can be presented.

The flow of information in both directions can be extended by supplying optional data in generic holes of the protocol which have been designed explicitly for this purpose. Requests allow for additional "preauthentication" data to be supplied, and returned tickets can be constrained to specific use cases or circumstances by filling in the so-called (and somewhat mis-named) "authorization" element.

The idea of integrating the additional trust gained by a remote attestation certificate into the Kerberos protocol leads to the fundamental question at which point the additional information should be fed into the protocol. Theoretically all three entry points (AS / TGS / kerberized service) would lead to a valid combination – we have consciously chosen the second approach in our design for the following reasons:

– As the attestation certificate includes EPH, including it into the request to the AS would mean that the TGT was bound to EPH, too. This breaks the Single Sign-On property of the Kerberos protocol, as the AS exchange would have to be repeated (and therefor the user's password reentered) whenever EPH expires.
– Establishing the TPM-based trust into the client includes many checks which do not actually involve the client interactively: verifying the RSA signature on the attestation certificate against the well-known attestation service key, parsing of contained policy compliance statements, unpacking of EPH modulus etc. These could be performed by each kerberized service individually – we deemed it more suitable to keep these operations inside the KDC instead of the server-side Kerberos libraries.

The only part of the proof which still has to be performed by the actual kerberized service is then a signature by the key EPH on a nonce chosen by the server. In order to keep the protocol backwards-compatible with standard Kerberos implementations, this requires an additional pair of messages to be exchanged after the service ticket itself has been presented and validated.

4   Implementation

The network service components of our scenario do not depend on a specific hardware configuration or feature set and they implement little new functionality beyond the well-established roles in the Remote Attestation protocol. We have therefore opted to build the Privacy CA and the Attestation Service as small standalone C♯ applications with only several hundred lines of code each.

The attestation client has been implemented on top of the TSS API as specified by the TCG[9]. Our Windows implementation uses the primitive operations provided by the recent `tpm.sys` kernel driver[4], whereas our Linux implementation uses the full TSS interface as provided by the TrouSerS `tcsd` daemon[1].

Finally, we have made small changes to the MIT Kerberos implementation and the GSS-API library to add our attestation components, thereby replacing about 200 lines and adding another 350, spread out over 12 files. The changes consist of the following logical items:

- inclusion of attestation certificate in TGS request
- inclusion of certificate in returned TGT
- introduction of a new GSSAPI context flag representing TPM-based trust
- protocol extension: extra message pair containing EPH signature
- creation and verification of extra message pair
- implementation of above concepts in GSS sample applications[3]

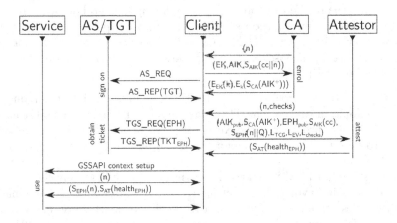

Fig. 1. Protocol visualization. Note that the AS exchange and the remote attestation can be completed in arbitrary order, as they do not depend on each other

We will now describe each part of the protocol (cf. also figure 1). TPM operations as defined in version 1.2 of the TPM Specification[10] are typeset in italics.

---

[3] This alone accounts for nearly 50% of the whole patch set.

1 communication with Privacy CA

1a The client connects to the Privacy CA, creates an AIK bound to a nonce chosen by the CA (*TPM_CreateIdentity*), and transmits the activation request.

1b The PCA validates the properties of the AIK, the soundness of the EK and the signature, and replies with an activation blob which is decrypted by the client using *TPM_ActivateIdentity* and stored for later use.

2 remote attestation

2a The client connects to the attestation service and receives a nonce and a list of system checks.

2b The client determines the current system state by repeatedly calling *TPM_PCRRead* and finally generates an ephemeral key EPH bound to the determined set of PCR values by executing *TPM_CreateWrapKey*. In the rare case of a change in PCR state during this operation, the step is repeated.

2c The client links EPH to AIK by executing *TPM_CertifyKey2*.

2d The client performs the requested checks on its state.

2e The client generates a quote on the current system state through *TPM_Quote2*, using EPH as the signing key and the combination of the TCG bootup event log, the log of accumulated system state change events and the results of the requested instantaneous system checks as "external quote data".

2f The client transmits the quote, the actual log data and check results, the required public key material to verify the signatures and the PCA certificate from step 1 back to the attestation daemon.

2g The attestation daemon verifies the trust chain, assesses the client's bootup chain, its history of monitored events and its responses to the requested checks and determines its compliance to a set of pre-defined policies (e. g. "Win8 patchlevel 2013/01/01" or "Ubuntu Lucid").

2h The daemon issues an attestation certificate that ties EPH to the determined list of fulfilled policies and transmits it to the client.

3 Kerberos protocol

3a During sign-on, the client obtains a regular TGT from the AS.

3b While trying to obtain a ticket for a particular kerberized service, the client checks for the presence of a valid attestation certificate. If one is found, the client includes it as preauthentication in its request to the TGS.

3c The TGS performs validity checks on the included certificate and stores a parsed version (which still includes the list of policies and the public part of EPH) as an authorization element in the resulting service ticket.

3d The client connects to the kerberized service, presents its ticket and indicates that additional operations to establish TPM-based trust are desired.

3e The service issues a nonce.

3f The client executes *TPM_Sign* on the nonce, thus producing an SS_INFO signature of it using EPH as the key, and transmits the result. Note that the attestation service has to verify that EPH's key properties specify the TPM_SS_RSASSAPKCS1v15_INFO signature scheme. Otherwise it would be possible to create and sign a message with EPH which is indistinguishable from a system quote – a problem particular to this specific protocol, as AIKs are explicitly forbidden to engage in *TPM_Sign* operations.

3g The service verifies the signature using the public part of EPH and is then able to grant additional privileges according to the set of policies the client is now proven to fulfil.

Several parts of this protocol can be easily optimized. Step 1 does not have to be repeated at all if the AIK is persistently stored on the client – it may only be desirable in order to change the platform's pseudonym for the later stages, and doing so is possible at all times because a change in AIK does not invalidate already issued attestation certificates.

EPH on the other hand has to be generated at least once per bootup due to its dependency on the PCR values. As *TPM_Sign* is the only primitive cryptographic operation exposed by the TPM interface, it is impossible to tie the key closer into the establishment of the TLS context. If the system state changes and EPH becomes unavailable, existing connections which have been created through the above protocol will continue to work if they are not torn down explicitly. This is no technical challenge however, as the expiration of EPH has been caused by an extension of a PCR value, which can only have been issued by the OS or the userland component of our aforementioned policy watchdog: this daemon can also communicate this event to all processes which have running EPH-based network connections.

5   Evaluation

Our protocol incurs only modest overhead and has almost no surprising factors compared to regular incarnations of remote attestation. Measurements of boot components vary between 10 and 60 ms each (mainly dependent on the TPM model), so assuming a number of about 100 components – which represents a typical Windows7 installation; typical Linux installations tend to have less – yields a total slowdown for a cold boot of just a few seconds.

Due to the infrequent need for fresh RSA key pairs, these requests are usually satisfied by the key pregeneration cache of the TPM and thus do not incur an additional delay. The remote attestation protocol therefore completes in about 4 seconds (privacy CA) and 5 to 7 seconds (attestation service), depending on the length of the transmitted TCG log and the list of requested system checks. Our experiments indicate further that, once a system has performed its initial boot up and loading of additional driver modules has completed, the configuration of the system remains stable if a few basic optimizations are applied (e. g. the generation of additional PCR events for repeated loading and unloading of identical instances of the same driver module is suppressed). This holds true even if additional aspects of system configuration are being monitored, like watching core keys of the Windows Registry or the contents of /lib on a Linux installation. These only change during system upgrade procedures or deliberate system reconfiguration by an administrator, in which cases the penalty of regenerating a TPM RSA keypair and repeating the attestation process seems admissible.

The only unique delay introduced by our protocol is the *TPM_Sign* operation on the nonce during the initialization of the GSSAPI session. Our measurements indicate an average duration of about 2.5 seconds per connection attempt – however this operation is only executed after the service ticket has been presented and both parties have agreed to engage in the "upgraded" handshake method, so this time is never wasted.

6   Conclusion, Future Work

The designed protocol extensions to the Kerberos framework allow for a convenient integration of hardware-based trust certificates, thus allowing network services to include this new trust dimension into the authentication process. Next steps may include extending the scenario to support mutual authentication, or to integrate TPM-shielded RSA keys into an adaptation of the Kerberos PKINIT extension (cf. [13]). Finally, the use of state-bound keys is not restricted to Kerberos, e. g. Goldman et al.[6] describe an approach to link TPM based attestation to SSL certificates. Their implementation differs in the reversed model (the service attempts to prove its validity to a client) and their reliance on short certificate expiration times and instantaneous certificate revocation by the watchdog, but is quite similar with respect to melding the current system properties into a TPM-bound health certificate. Combining and further exploring these techniques may provide valuable insights.

References

1. TrouSerS - the open-source software stack, http://trousers.sourceforge.net
2. Brickell, E., Camenisch, J., Chen, L.: Direct anonymous attestation. In: Proceedings of the 11th ACM Conference on Computer and Communications Security, CCS 2004, pp. 132–145. ACM, New York (2004),
   http://doi.acm.org/10.1145/1030083.1030103
3. Corporation, M.: TPM and BitLocker drive encryption,
   http://msdn.microsoft.com/en-us/library/windows/hardware/gg487306.aspx
4. Corporation, M.: TPM platform crypto-provider toolkit,
   http://research.microsoft.com/en-us/downloads/
   74c45746-24ad-4cb7-ba4b-0c6df2f92d5d/default.aspx
5. Corporation, M.: Secured Boot and Measured Boot: Hardening Early Boot components against malware. Tech. rep., Microsoft Corporation (2012)
6. Goldman, K.A., Perez, R., Sailer, R.: Linking Remote Attestation to Secure Tunnel Endpoints. IBM Technical Paper (2006),
   http://domino.research.ibm.com/library/cyberdig.nsf/1e4115aea78b6e7c
   ......85256b360066f0d4/fb0d5a04296a0bee852571ff0054f9fb
7. Group, T.I.W.: A CMC profile for AIK certificate enrollment. Tech. rep., Trusted Computing Group (2011)
8. Group, T.P.C.W.: TCG PC client specific implementation specification for conventional BIOS. Tech. rep., Trusted Computing Group (2012)

9. Group, T.C.: TCG Software Stack (TSS) Specification Version 1.2 level 1. Tech. rep., Trusted Computing Group (2007),
http://www.trustedcomputinggroup.org/files/resource_files/
6479CD77-1D09-3519-AD89EAD1BC8C97F0/TSS_1_2_Errata_A-final.pdf

10. Group, T.C.: TPM main specification level 2 version 1.2 revision 116. Tech. rep., Trusted Computing Group (2011),
http://www.trustedcomputinggroup.org/resources/tpm_main_specification

11. Leicher, A., Kuntze, N., Schmidt, A.U.: Implementation of a trusted ticket system. In: Gritzalis, D., Lopez, J. (eds.) SEC 2009. IFIP AICT, vol. 297, pp. 152–163. Springer, Heidelberg (2009),
http://dx.doi.org/10.1007/978-3-642-01244-0_14

12. Sailer, R., Zhang, X., Jaeger, T., van Doorn, L.: Design and implementation of a TCG-based integrity measurement architecture. In: Proceedings of the 13th USENIX Security Symposium, pp. 223–238. ACM (2004)

13. Zhu, L., Tung, B.: Rfc4556: Public key cryptography for initial authentication in kerberos (PKINIT) (2006),
http://tools.ietf.org/html/rfc4556

Group Signatures on Mobile Devices: Practical Experiences

Klaus Potzmader[1], Johannes Winter[1], Daniel Hein[1], Christian Hanser[1], Peter Teufl[1], and Liqun Chen[2]

[1] Institute for Applied Information Processing and Communications,
Inffeldgasse 16a,
8010 Graz,
Austria
klaus.potzmader@student.tugraz.at,
{johannes.winter,daniel.hein,chanser,peter.teufl}@iaik.tugraz.at
[2] Hewlett-Packard Laboratories,
Long Down Avenue, Stoke Gifford,
Bristol, BS34 8QZ,
United Kingdom
liqun.chen@hp.com

Abstract. Group signature schemes enable participants to sign on behalf of a group in an anonymous manner. The upcoming ISO20008-2 standard defines seven such schemes, which differ in terms of capabilities, used crypto systems and revocation approaches. Further information about practical considerations, such as runtime performance or implementation overhead is considered useful when deciding for a certain scheme. We present a Java framework that allows for a detailed comparison of the mechanisms, of which three are already implemented. For these implemented mechanisms, a detailed performance evaluation is shown for both a notebook and Android-based mobile devices. Furthermore, significant experiences during implementing and evaluating the schemes as well as crucial bottlenecks are pointed out. We remain in the flexible Java environment, without special platform-specific optimizations. Using precomputation, we already achieve acceptable online signing timings. Signing times are considered most important given proposed application scenarios.

Keywords: Group signatures, performance evaluation, mobile devices, list signature scheme, DAA, e-voting, attestation, e-payment, Android, Java.

1 Introduction

Group signature schemes as first introduced by Chaum and van Heyst [17] allow participants to sign messages on behalf of a group in an anonymous manner. The signature scheme ensures to a verifier by cryptographic means that the signer is indeed a valid member of such a group, but does not reveal the specific signer's

M. Huth et al. (Eds.): TRUST 2013, LNCS 7904, pp. 47–64, 2013.
© Springer-Verlag Berlin Heidelberg 2013

identity. The anonymity resides in the verifier not knowing what exact member actually signed the document. The degree of anonymity thus strongly depends on the group size.

Group signatures have many interesting applications, such as e-voting [16], e-bidding [21], online payment [29] or anonymous attestation [9]. Many of the above use-cases would additionally benefit from mobile usage. Mobile usage requires efficient implementations on mobile devices, such as mobile phones. Even with the advent of computationally powerful smartphones, implementing group signature schemes with reasonable security and response times is still a challenge. Group signatures are based on cryptographic algorithms which are considerably more complex than schemes that use a single public key per entity. The problem is only exacerbated by the sheer number and variety of different group signature schemes that have been proposed. Often these schemes are based on different cryptographic approaches, such as RSA or elliptic curve cryptography (ECC). In an effort to alleviate the above problems, ISO/IEC have proposed the ISO20008-2 [24,25] standard, which is currently a *Draft International Standard (DIS)* and undergoing public review.

In this paper, we present an evaluation of three different group signature schemes. All three mechanisms are part of the ISO20008-2 standard [25]. The first mechanism is a scheme for e-voting, proposed by Canard et al. [16]. It is designed to enable anonymous ballots, whilst still being capable of detecting double-voting without de-anonymizing the voter. ECC-DAA, the second mechanism we analyze, was originally introduced by Chen et al. [20] and is designed for the upcoming Trusted Platform Module (TPM) 2.0[1] specification. Used in conjunction with a TPM, ECC-DAA allows users to prove a specific load-time software state to a remote entity, called attestation. The remote verifier is thereby not able to identify the user, but can be sure that the platform report originates from a valid TPM. The final mechanism, the scheme by Isshiki et al. [23] gears towards using group signatures for identity management. Labels which uniquely define a specific group member shall be masqueraded behind a credential that represents the group as a whole. Therefore, a verifier does not learn any specifics about an enquiring member, only whether it is a valid member of a group or not.

The goal of our evaluation is to determine the applicability of those schemes for use on mobile devices. To achieve this, we have implemented a Java based framework for evaluating group signature schemes. We have designed the framework to be flexible enough to encompass the different cryptographic approaches of the three mechanisms, while also providing the common cryptographic primitives used by some of the three mechanisms. We have chosen Java because of its wide use in mobile phones based on Google's Android[2] operating system. Furthermore, it allows for detailed comparisons without platform-specific optimizations, thus providing a generalized overview.

---

[1] http://www.trustedcomputinggroup.org/resources/
trusted_platform_module_specifications_in_public_review

[2] http://www.android.com/

Our framework can be extended to implement more than the three mechanisms we compare in this paper. Additionally, we have organized the framework to abstract cryptographic primitives from existing implementations in the Java runtime. The reason for this abstraction is ability to replace cryptographic primitives with different implementations both in Java and C and thus to evaluate their efficiency. Finally, we make most of the framework publicly available under an open source license[3].

In addition to just evaluating the schemes against each other, we also consider aspects such as optimization for a specific use case. For example, all steps for ECC-DAA can be precomputed if the use case requires total anonymity.

The paper is organized as follows. In Section 2, the properties, components and revocation approaches of group signature schemes are discussed in general. Moreover, the implemented schemes are summarized and compared. Section 3 provides a detailed comparison regarding runtime and memory usage of the schemes, both on a notebook and on mobile devices. In Section 4, these results are put into the context of other evaluations by merging them in a table. A summary of the results and future work aspects are given in Section 5.

2   Background

In the following, group signature schemes are discussed in a broader view, incorporating the related concepts of so-called list signature schemes and attestation.

Group signature schemes strive to fulfill the properties *Soundness and Completeness, Anonymity, Unforgeability, Traceability, Coalition Resistance, Non-Frameability* and *Unlinkability* as defined by Chaum and van Heyst [17] and extended by Bellare et al. [5, 6]. Note that opening is generally considered a mandatory feature for group signature schemes and linking is usually undesirable [17]. However, scenarios such as electronic voting have shown uses for types of schemes where opening is less critical and conditional linking is desirable to detect double usage. Canard et al. label these schemata as *list signature schemes* [16]. Therefore, traceability and unlinkability are considered optional features in this case to incorporate both attestation and list signature schemes. List signature schemes additionally require that adversaries can at most produce one valid signature per linking indicator and corrupted member. Any additional signature would cause the adversary to be either detected or to reveal the identity of the corrupted member.

Scheme Processes. Group signature schemes are comprised of the following individual processes:

- **Group Establishment.** The group is initially set up. That is, its public key and the corresponding group membership issuing key are created. The creating instance, now holding the membership issuing key, is called *issuing authority.*

---

[3] Available at https://github.com/klapm/group-signature-scheme-eval

- **Joining.** New members get added to the group. This is done by a joint computation of the applicant and the issuing authority in a way that the private key of the applicant remains secret. The issuing authority issues a membership credential to complete the join process.
- **Signing.** Valid members are able to sign documents. Signatures depend on both the private key and the membership credential, but do not reveal any of them in a computationally feasible way.
- **Verification.** Using the group public key, a verifier is able to tell whether a given signature was issued by a valid member of the group.
- **Revocation.** Existing members are being excluded from the group. Revoked members can no longer sign on behalf of the group. This can be achieved in several ways, which are discussed below.
- **Opening.** Optional, depending on whether the scheme supports opening. A separate authority, the so-called *opening authority* is installed, able to open signatures and thus reveal the specific identity of a signature's author.
- **Linking.** Optional, only applicable if linking is supported and enabled. Given two signatures, any stakeholder is able to tell apart whether these signatures were created by the same author.

Revocation. A challenging task for group signature schemes is to remove existing members without affecting the workings of the group as a whole. Several approaches appear throughout the literature [19, 24], all of which have advantages and disadvantages:

- **Private Key Revocation.** A compromised private key of a group member is added to a list of no longer valid keys. Verifiers, given a signature, are able to determine whether the signature was created using such a key. If the revocation list stores both the private key and the associated member id, a revocation check might immediately reveal the identity of the otherwise anonymous signer if her key was revoked before. Depending on where this list is stored and who has access to it, revocation can either be *global*, that is affecting all verifiers or *local*, per verifier [9].
- **Blacklist Revocation.** Blacklist revocation is typically a local revocation, in which a verifier stores a list of no longer valid signatures. Given a new signature, the verifier is then able to determine whether this new signature was created by either a blacklisted or still valid author [9].
- **Signature Revocation.** Signature revocation has the same effect as blacklist revocation, but uses a different approach to achieve it. With signature revocation, revoked signatures are kept in a list as well. A verifier then requires additional proof from the signer, showing that she is not the one who created any signatures on that list to accept her signature. Naturally, this approach impacts the overall verification performance. Signature revocation can be a local or global revocation, depending on where the list is stored and who has access to it [10].
- **Credential Revocation.** In this scenario, the membership credentials of revoked members are stored in a list. Signers might then be required to prove

that their credential is not on that list. This proof is typically done implicitly, such that non-revoked signers prove their credibility by being able to still produce valid signatures. This mechanism is also referred to as credential update or re-keying and usually involves an update of the public key and membership credentials. Existing signers who are supposed to keep their membership are notified with means to update their membership credential when another member is about to be dismissed. Since the credential of the leaving member gets outdated, she is no longer able to participate. Credential revocation is a global revocation. Note that credential update invalidates existing signatures, as existing signatures will no longer verify when using the newly created public key [8, 14].

The implemented schemes are briefly explained in the following subsections, and their relevant properties are summarized for comparison in a table below.

2.1 Canard et al.

The first implemented scheme is the list signature scheme proposed by Canard et al. [16]. We will refer to it using its authors as name. List signature schemes support linking signatures as long as they are *tagged* with the same value. Following the author's original description, a tag is typically a time frame in which no two signatures are allowed, e.g., a voting period. Linking two signatures can be done by every stakeholder, without the need for any secret, called *public detection* by the authors. If two signatures were created using different tags, linkability is computationally infeasible.

The author's proposed scheme is based on work by Ateniese et al. [2] and supports multiple revocation processes, namely private key revocation, both locally and globally, and blacklisting. The scheme's security is based on both the strong RSA and the decisional Diffie Hellman (DDH) assumptions (cf. Section 2 in [16]).

2.2 Direct Anonymous Attestation

Direct Anonymous Attestation (DAA) was originally introduced by Brickell et al. [9] as a mechanism to remotely authenticate a trusted platform in a privacy-preserving way. It is intended to be used in conjunction with a Trusted Platform Module[4] (TPM) and, therefore, strictly splits the signing party into a computationally powerful *assistant signer* and a less powerful *principal signer*, the smaller TPM chip. While it differs in its purpose, it is similar to the previously described list signature scheme when comparing at a property level. DAA also supports linking, given the signatures were crafted using the same *linking base*, a generalization of what has previously been called *tag*.

For this work, the pairing-based ECC-DAA variant, as proposed by Chen et al. [20], was implemented using Barreto-Naehrig [3] curves. It was designed for the Trusted Computing Group[5] (TCG) and is now included in the TPM 2.0

---

[4] http://www.trustedcomputinggroup.org/developers/trusted_platform_module
[5] http://www.trustedcomputinggroup.org

specification. As we do not utilize a TPM in this setting, the strict split-up between assistant and principal signer was omitted and both components are merged into one signing party.

The ECC-DAA variant is most flexible in terms of revocation, supporting private key revocation, signature revocation, both either locally or globally, blacklisting and credential update. It is provably secure under the DDH, Lysyanskaya-Rivest-Sahai-Wolf (LRSW) and static Diffie-Hellman (SDH) assumptions, see Section 1 in [20].

2.3 Isshiki et al.

The third implemented scheme was introduced by Isshiki et al. [23] and is an adaption of the Camenisch-Groth scheme [13], enabling faster revocation. The scheme is RSA-based and supports opening, with the opening capability built on top of an additional elliptic curve group.

In this scheme, the opening authority is entirely separated from the issuing authority. The issuing authority holds the secret membership issuing key, which corresponds to the group's public key. The opening authority holds another secret, called *group membership opening key*. Its counterpart is the so-called *group opening key* and yet another public key for the group. To achieve this setup, both authorities are involved during the initial group establishment. The scheme supports credential update as revocation mechanism and is secure under the strong RSA and DDH assumptions, see Section 4.2 in [23].

2.4 Comparison Summary

The properties of the three implemented schemes are summarized in Table 1. The reason for choosing these three schemes is that they vary in both their goals and their construction. The intention is to gain a principal overview of the three schemes, and measurements that are roughly mappable to related schemes based on similar principles. For example, schemes such as the one's described in [2,13].

Table 1. Scheme comparison

Scheme	Optional Linkability	Openable	Crypto-System(s)	Intractability Assumptions	Revocation Support CU	PKR	BL	SR
Canard et al.	✓		RSA	Strong RSA, DDH	✓	✓		
ECC-DAA	✓		ECC, Pairings	DDH, LRSW, SDH	✓	✓	✓	✓
Isshiki et al.		✓	RSA, ECC	Strong RSA, DDH	✓			

CU: Credential Update, PKR: Private Key Revocation, BL: Blacklisting, SR: Signature Revocation

3   Results and Evaluation

Performance measurements regarding both runtime and memory were gathered on an off-the-shelf notebook as well as on multiple mobile devices. Concerning the mobile scenario, especially signing is critical. Signing and verifying denote regular tasks, whereas group creation and joining are sporadic, if not one-time events. In mobile scenarios, these two operations have to perform sufficiently fast in time-constrained settings, for example when placing an order using the mobile phone. Therefore, the presented analysis concentrates on these two operations.

Before presenting concrete measurements, the framework and test setup are described. Furthermore, we emphasize that we conducted all tests without active revocation, even though the framework supports it. After discussing the actual results, we conclude this section with the key lessons we learned.

3.1   Framework

All evaluated group signature schemes are embedded in a common framework and use the same implementation of cryptographic primitives. The framework's purpose is to provide a flexible environment for performance measurement and future extension, but it is limited to the task of comparing individual schemes. Therefore, we did not implement standalone components and message passing is done entirely locally by simple method invocations. Hence, the measurements do not include network communication overhead.

The framework is written in pure Java and does not rely on any external libraries. The same code base runs on both Java Standard Edition and Android without requiring any special adjustments. The group signature schemes are unified under a common interface and the surrounding evaluation code is the same for all concrete implementations. The implementation supports all necessary operations, including revocation mechanisms, but focus was put on measurements for signing and verification. As a consequence, sub-protocols such as proving the knowledge of a discrete logarithm in the scheme of Isshiki et al. were omitted.

The pairing map, as required by ECC-DAA, is essentially a Java port of the Optimal Ate Pairing C implementation[6] provided by Beuchat et al. [4]. We ported the version of January 2013 from Beuchat et al., which in turn benefited from insights gained by Aranha et al. [1]. Porting from an assembler-optimized C implementation to an interpreted language, such as Java, has various drawbacks regarding runtime performance. Some of the optimizations have to be abandoned and choosing Java comes with further performance impacts, such as just-in-time compilation and garbage collection. These circumstances leave us at considerably slower timings of about 7ms for a single pairing evaluation, compared to about 0.5ms of the original C version, measured on the same notebook. Nevertheless, Java was chosen to allow for general comparability of the schemes by disregarding platform-specific optimizations and to allow easy portability.

---

[6] Available at `http://homepage1.nifty.com/herumi/crypt/ate-pairing.html`

3.2   Test Setup

The notebook case tests were performed on a Lenovo ThinkPad T420s notebook, equipped with an Intel i7-2620M CPU at 2x2.7GHz and 8GB of RAM using Windows 8 x64 and Java 1.7.0_11, 64 bit. For the mobile case, different devices were used during the evaluation. The devices and their relevant specifications are listed in Table 2.

Table 2. Devices used for the evaluation

Device	Galaxy Nexus i9250	Galaxy S Plus i9001	Galaxy S3 GT-I9300
Manufacturer	Samsung	Samsung	Samsung
Operating System	Android 4.2	Android 2.3.6	Android 4.0.4
CPU	2x1.2GHz ARM Cortex-A9	1.4GHz ARM Cortex-A9	4x1.4GHz ARM Cortex-A9
System-on-Chip	Texas Instruments OMAP 4460	Qualcomm Snap-dragon S2 MSM8255	Samsung Exynos 4412
Memory	1024MB	1024MB	1024MB

The shown evaluations are not always directly comparable due to the different crypto-systems. In fact, a key length of 256 bit in ECC-DAA implies 128 bit security strength. The schemes by Canard et al. and Isshiki et al. evaluate to 112 bit security strength at a parameterization with a modulus length of 2048 bit. *Security strength* in this context denotes the number of operations required to break a cryptographic algorithm, specified in bits; so 80 bit security strength means at least 2^{80} required operations. Table 3 summarizes the evaluated parameterizations, of which all except the 80 bit setup of Canard et al. are recommended choices by the ISO20008-2.2 draft standard. Note that the value l_p at the scheme by Canard et al. refers to a single factor of the composite modulus. For details on these parameters, we refer the reader to the ISO20008-2 draft [25] or the original sources [16, 20, 23]. The following results will refer to these setups using the modulus length as indicator.

All measurements were conducted without a revocation mechanism in place. Enabling revocation when evaluating the schemes adds numerous additional parameters, such as the group size or the specific revocation approach used. The different revocation approaches are hardly comparable, with strong dependencies on either the group size or the number of already-revoked members. Furthermore, the introduced revocation approaches are not always influencing the verification time. For example, signature revocation might influence signing, and credential update is an entirely separate process. Considering these differences, we decided to exclude revocation from the evaluation, despite its impact for practical purposes. However, the framework supports revocation, so revocation experiments can be carried out as well.

Table 3. Scheme security comparison

Scheme	Canard et al.		ECC-DAA	Isshiki et al.	
Parameterization	$l_p = 512$	$l_p = 1024$	$t = 256$	$K_n = 1024$	$K_n = 2048$
	$k = 160$	$k = 160$	$p = \lvert 256 \rvert$	$K = 160$	$K = 224$
	$l_x = 160$	$l_x = 160$		$K_c = 160$	$K_c = 224$
	$l_e = 170$	$l_e = 170$		$K_s = 60$	$K_s = 112$
	$l_E = 420$	$l_E = 420$		$K_e = 504$	$K_e = 736$
	$l_X = 410$	$l_X = 410$		$K'_e = 60$	$K'_e = 60$
	$\epsilon = 5/4$	$\epsilon = 5/4$			
Security Strength	80 bit	112 bit	128 bit	80 bit	112 bit

3.3 Runtime

The following data was gathered by averaging the single processes over 100 iterations. The mean values are explicitly shown, whereas the standard deviation is only indicated using error bars. Signing was computed using a different message per sign operation, though within the same group. Verification was also varied in terms of message and signature.

Runtimes are split into the notebook and mobile cases. The mobile case is discussed in more detail, including precomputation. Parts of the signature, which do not depend on the message can be precomputed, such that the online signing time is further decreased. Additionally, if optional linkability is disabled in ECC-DAA and in the scheme by Canard et al., then most of the signature attributes are precomputable. We will leverage this ability by shifting workload to a precomputation phase.

Furthermore, we measured the runtimes with two different primitive arithmetic implementations for elliptic curve cryptography, namely the default `java.math.BigInteger`, denoted *BigInteger* from now on, and a custom implementation, denoted *custom*. There were particular reasons for choosing another underlying implementation, which will be discussed later on.

Notebook. Runtimes for signing and verifying on a notebook-like environment are given in Figure 1. We can see that the parameter length and, thus, the length of the internally used values roughly dictates the runtimes. In this setting, ECC-DAA outperforms the schemes by Canard et al. and Isshiki et al. It is faster in both signing and verifying and provides higher security strength at the same time. Indeed, all schemes are fast enough to be used out of the box, with no measurement exceeding 335ms. There are only small differences between the two used arithmetic implementations, with the custom one being marginally slower.

Mobile Device. On Android, a different picture emerges. The same implementation, deployed as an app, results in the signing times as depicted in Figure 2. We can see that there is not just simple upscaling in place, resulting from the

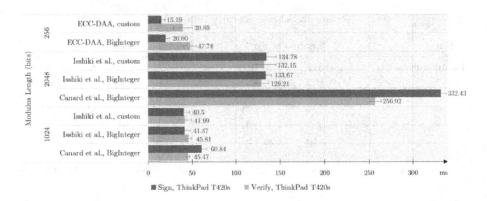

Fig. 1. Signing and verifying, notebook case

limited computational power of the devices. Contrary to the notebook case, the non-ECC scheme by Canard et al. does no longer exceed the runtimes of the other two schemes that much. Furthermore, we see stronger differences between using Java's default BigInteger and the custom implementation.

Before discussing the reasons of these runtime effects, we show the achieved online times when utilizing the fact that certain parts of the signatures are precomputable.

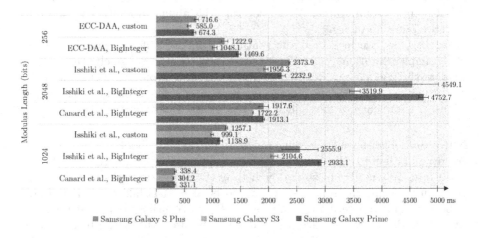

Fig. 2. Signing without precomputation, mobile case

Precomputation. ECC-DAA and the scheme by Canard et al. support optional linkability by computing a linking base into the signature, given that linkability is desired and the verifier shall be able to provide the linking-base at sign time. In this scenario, only those parts of the signature not depending on either the message or the linking base can be precomputed. We refer to this case using the term *partial precomputation.*

If linkability is not required in a certain use case, it can be disabled by setting the linking base to a constant value. Here, almost the whole signature is precomputable, thus vastly decreasing the online signing time. This will be called *full precomputation* from now on.

The scheme by Isshiki et al. does not support linking, but allows for extensive precomputation as well, referred to as plain *precomputation.* Figure 3 is a comparison of the evaluated schemes using partial (PPC) as well as full (FPC) precomputation for ECC-DAA and the scheme by Canard et al., and precomputation (PC) for the scheme by Isshiki et al.

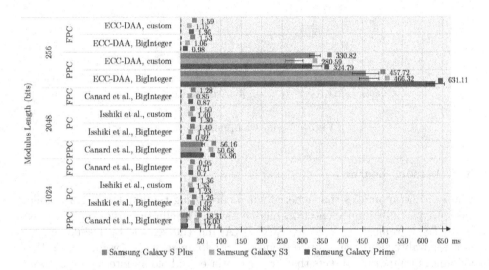

Fig. 3. Signing with precomputation, mobile case

ECC-DAA with partial precomputation leaves three point multiplications for the online signing phase, whereas seven out of seven can be precomputed in case linkability is not needed. The gap between precomputations is smaller for the scheme by Canard et al., where the difference is essentially one hash computation and three modular exponentiations. Precomputing the signature for Isshiki et al. reduces the needed operations at signing time to one hash computation as well as five additions, multiplications and reductions. Given the differing complexity in the remaining operations, the shown gap in runtime is reasonable. With full precomputation, the ECC-DAA workload is reduced to a single hash computation as well as one plain additon, multiplication and reduction.

Verification. As depicted in Figure 4, the notebook results are almost inverted. As in the mobile signing setting, ECC-DAA and the scheme by Isshiki et al. are considerably slower than the scheme by Canard et al. Again, this partially stems from implementation issues when using elliptic curve cryptography. However, verification is a less critical factor regarding mobile device performance when considering typical application scenarios for group signature schemes. Commonly, verification can take place at more powerful devices [9, 16, 21, 30].

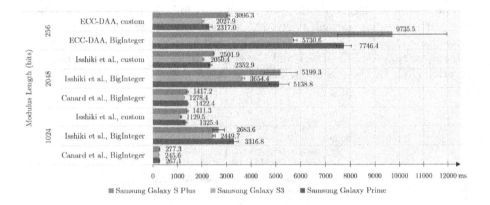

Fig. 4. Verification, mobile case

3.4 Lessons Learned

The runtime anomalies that emerge when comparing the notebook and mobile cases are partially implementation-related issues. The elliptic curve cryptography part of the framework, used by ECC-DAA and the scheme by Isshiki et al., is comparably slower on mobile devices. The dominating factor for this is the amount of temporary objects that are instantiated to hold an intermediate value for a short amount of time and are then of no use anymore. Thus, a lot of runtime and memory is wasted on instantiating, copying and then garbage collecting these objects.

The main reason for this is Java's immutable `BigInteger` implementation. Each operation on a BigInteger leads to the allocation of a new object, storing the result. Considering that BigIntegers are the most basic element, used by all prime and extension field operations, this has a major impact on runtime. These temporary instances are less of a problem with operations, such as modular exponentiation, as used by the schemes by Canard et al. and Isshiki et al. Modular exponentiation is provided by Java's BigInteger and uses a mutable variant internally. The problem becomes apparent for operations built on top of BigIntegers, such as point multiplication or pairings. Therefore, the scheme by Canard et al. was only tested with BigIntegers, as the expected gain from using the custom implementation is very low.

While this is generally a non-issue in the notebook case, it has noticeable impact when the algorithms are run on an Android based mobile device. The reason for this is much slower garbage collection in combination with a strict collection enforcement policy.

The garbage collection overhead is severe enough that point multiplication is faster using affine coordinates than a mix of Jacobian and affine coordinates, to give an example. Using mixed coordinates in point multiplication allows to omit expensive modular inversions during point addition and doubling within the double-and-add cycle and is thus usually the faster variant [12,30]. However, using Java's BigInteger, point multiplication in affine coordinates turned out to be faster, since it requires less intermediate instances.

Android garbage collection is triggered as soon as there are enough collectable objects, regardless of the overall free heap. Therefore, the small overall memory footprint of our implementation poses no advantage in that regard. Originally, our implementation was developed to give an overview of the different schemes. It turned out that there is a strong indication that such a portable implementation is almost powerful enough to be used already, without the need to resort to highly optimized, but device dependent implementations. In light of this and also to decouple this platform dependent implementation factor, we aimed at alleviating the problem by reducing the amount of intermediate instances.

We decided to use a custom integer arithmetic implementation and plug it underneath the field operations. Since this custom implementation is designed to enforce in-place operations wherever possible, lots of instantiations are spared. Furthermore, fixed-width integer arithmetic is used, allowing for easier recycling of no longer used objects. Taming the garbage collector this way reduces runtimes dramatically. The problem is ameliorated, but there are still a few garbage collection runs that cost considerable runtime. Nevertheless, the attempt to decrease runtimes is successful, considering the visible runtime drops in the measurements.

3.5 Memory

The exact amount of memory consumed by the schemes alone is difficult to pinpoint in a managed, garbage-collected environment such as Java. On the notebook, we approximated a heap consumption of below 5.5 megabytes and a permanent generation space of about 4MB. Lower artificially introduced memory limits were just ignored by the JVM. Therefore, these values are a loose upper bar. As we see from experiments on the mobile devices themselves, the schemes run with less than that. For example, on the Samsung Galaxy S3 device we used, the initial free heap memory per app is as low as one megabyte, since the remaining heap is already filled with preloaded Android elements. The implementation ran under these circumstances without further heap growth, thus having only one megabyte of heap available seems to be enough.

Code Size. The code size was determined by the resulting size of the `classes` `.dex` file when exporting an APK package. ProGuard[7] was enabled when doing

---

[7] http://developer.android.com/tools/help/proguard.html

Table 4. Code size comparison

Complete Set	Canard et al.	ECC-DAA	Isshiki et al.	Framework
349KB	163KB	249KB	257KB	273KB

these tests, which reduces the size by renaming variable names to commonly short identifiers. Table 4 lists the code size for each module.

Complete set refers to the whole functionality, including ECC/Pairing code and all schemes. *Framework* on the other hand is infrastructure material only. The separate scheme sizes denote the code size of both the specified scheme itself and the required framework code for it to work, hence the overlaps.

Since the scheme by Canard et al. does not use any elliptic curve cryptography, its code size is naturally smaller, as the ECC part of the framework can be dropped. More than half of the overall code size is consumed by underlying primitive functionality. ECC-DAA and the scheme by Isshiki et al. are almost equal in size. Generally, code size is low enough to be run on mobile devices with the whole package having a size of less than 350KB.

4   Related Work

Group signatures have become an extensive field of research with many different proposed schemes and suggested approaches. For surveys on group signature schemes themselves, we refer the reader to [26, 31].

Implementational aspects of group signatures were evaluated in various related publications. In Table 5, several publications are put into context to allow for a rough overview of current advances. Unfortunately, a direct comparison is not possible, since all approaches differ in terms of the test setup, used cryptosystem and the scheme itself. Furthermore, vital details such as the used pairing map are omitted as well. The intention is to give a brief overview on how a Java-based implementation fits into this picture, both in the mobile and the notebook case. Still, these values have to be taken with a grain of salt, especially when comparing individual results. Most shown implementations are C-based and use the pairing-based cryptography library PBC[8]. A high-level implementation in Java typically cannot compete with low-level C implementations using partial assembler optimizations, not to mention hardware solutions based on Application-Specific Integrated Circuits (ASICs) or Field-Programmable Gate Arrays (FPGAs). However, the enhanced flexibility of platform indepence might be worth the longer runtimes. The additional runtimes seem acceptable, especially when comparing our results with the native code estimations from Manulis et al. [26].

---

[8] See https://crypto.stanford.edu/pbc/

Table 5. Comparison of other published results

	Source	Remarks	Scheme	Setup	Strength	Sign	Verify
Hardware	Morioka et al. [27]		Isshiki et al. [23]	ASIC	80 bit	135ms	135ms
	Manulis et al. [26]	C/ASM, PBC, estimations	Boneh-Shacham [8]	FPGA	128 bit	128.7ms	144.76ms
			Bichsel et al. [7]	FPGA	128 bit	58.3ms	52.3ms
Mixed	Chen, Page, Smart [20]	C/ASM	RSA-DAA [9]	TPM	128 bit	33700ms	194ms
			ECC-DAA [20]			3400ms	48.31ms
	Canard et al. [15]	C, PBC	XSGS [22], online signing	WSN	80 bit	< 200ms	55ms
			XSGS [22], offline signing		80 bit	3995-6596ms	55ms
Smartphone	Manulis et al. [26]	Android NDK, PBC, estimations	Camenisch-Groth [13]			431.5ms	431.5ms
			Boneh-Shacham [8]	PHONE	128 bit	1211.7ms	2118ms
			Bichsel et al. [7]			1002.3ms	1577.4ms
PC	Manulis et al. [26]	C/ASM, PBC, estimations	Camenisch-Groth [13]	MPC		170.4ms	170.4ms
			Boneh-Shacham [8]	MPC	128 bit	402.4ms	691.6ms
				MPC*		131.4ms	150.1ms
			Bichsel et al. [7]	MPC		332ms	508ms
				MPC*		61ms	56.8ms
	Bringer and Patey [11]	C++	Boneh-Shacham [8]			1000ms	1170ms
			Chen-Li (patched) [11,18]	BPPC	80 bit	450ms	400ms

Legend:

ASIC	0.25um ASIC Implementation, 100MHz clock frequency, by Morioka et al. [27]
BPPC	Intel Core2Duo, 2.93GHz
FPGA	Xilinx Virtex-6 FPGA prototype, assumptions based on [32]
MPC	Intel Core Duo LV L2400, 1.66GHz
MPC*	Same as MPC, but assuming the pairing measurements as shown by Naehrig et al. [28]
PHONE	HTC Desire, 1 GHz Qualcomm ARMv7 Scorpion CPU
TPM	33MHz ARMv7, emulated TPM; 2.4 GHz Intel Core2-6600 host platform
WSN	MICAz/TelosB wireless sensor node platforms; 1.4 GHz Intel Core2Duo CPU host platform, see [15]

5 Conclusion and Future Work

Implementing group signature schemes in plain Java for the Android operating system yielded various interesting insights. Group signature schemes are considered ready for scenarios, where signature creation is performed on mobile devices and verification is done on a more powerful device. The shown schemes by Canard et al., Chen et al. and Isshiki et al. allow for precomputing parts of the signature, enabling tolerable online signature timings. The concrete timings are differing between the schemes and use cases, but are generally considered acceptable. The worst case scenario runtime we measured averages at about 330ms for online signing, with a huge gap to the second longest run of about 56ms. Newer smartphone generations seem to improve these results significantly. Verification runtimes are in part noticeably slower, but common scenarios only require signing to be performed on low-power end user devices. Therefore, we consider the technology ready to be used on mobile devices. A partial native code implementation might even allow for omitting the precomputation step whilst still delivering acceptable runtimes.

The framework did not only enable detailed comparisons of the schemes, it also revealed factors of considerable impact regarding the runtime environment. The Android garbage collector turned out to be the main bottleneck. Therefore, having less intermediates and recycling instances is of great importance on Android. The runtimes of individual operations tend to be tightly coupled with the amount of required intermediate instances. Cumulative effects, such as the garbage collector kicking in after a certain threshold of objects to collect might also hinder runtime estimations based on the timings of individual operations.

The accompanying framework is open source and allows further extension with the remaining schemes defined in ISO20008-2 [25] or other, similar schemes.

Subsequent anticipated steps are to loosen the platform independence a bit and to implement parts of the framework using the Android Native Development Kit. Given the unmanaged memory environment, this is expected to result in further acceleration.

References

1. Aranha, D.F., Karabina, K., Longa, P., Gebotys, C.H., López, J.: Faster Explicit Formulas for Computing Pairings over Ordinary Curves. In: Paterson, K.G. (ed.) EUROCRYPT 2011. LNCS, vol. 6632, pp. 48–68. Springer, Heidelberg (2011)
2. Ateniese, G., Camenisch, J., Joye, M., Tsudik, G.: A Practical and Provably Secure Coalition-Resistant Group Signature Scheme. In: Bellare, M. (ed.) CRYPTO 2000. LNCS, vol. 1880, pp. 255–270. Springer, Heidelberg (2000)
3. Barreto, P.S.L.M., Naehrig, M.: Pairing-Friendly Elliptic Curves of Prime Order. In: Preneel, B., Tavares, S. (eds.) SAC 2005. LNCS, vol. 3897, pp. 319–331. Springer, Heidelberg (2006)
4. Beuchat, J.-L., González-Díaz, J.E., Mitsunari, S., Okamoto, E., Rodríguez-Henríquez, F., Teruya, T.: High-Speed Software Implementation of the Optimal Ate Pairing over Barreto Naehrig Curves. In: Joye, M., Miyaji, A., Otsuka, A. (eds.) Pairing 2010. LNCS, vol. 6487, pp. 21–39. Springer, Heidelberg (2010)

5. Bellare, M., Micciancio, D., Warinischi, B.: Foundations of Group Signatures: Formal Definitions, Simplified Requirements, and a Construction Based on General Assumptions. In: Biham, E. (ed.) EUROCRYPT 2003. LNCS, vol. 2656, pp. 614–629. Springer, Heidelberg (2003)

6. Bellare, M., Shi, H., Zhang, C.: Foundations of Group Signatures: The Case of Dynamic Groups. In: Menezes, A.J. (ed.) CT-RSA 2005. LNCS, vol. 3376, pp. 136–153. Springer, Heidelberg (2005)

7. Bichsel, P., Camenisch, J., Neven, G., Smart, N.P., Warinschi, B.: Get Shorty via Group Signatures without Encryption. In: Garay, J.A., De Prisco, R. (eds.) SCN 2010. LNCS, vol. 6280, pp. 381–398. Springer, Heidelberg (2010)

8. Boneh, D., Shacham, H.: Group Signatures with Verifier-local Revocation. In: 11th ACM Conference on Computer and Communications Security, pp. 168–177. ACM Press, New York (2004)

9. Brickell, E., Camenisch, J., Chen, L.: Direct Anonymous Attestation. In: 11th ACM Conference on Computer and Communications Security, pp. 132–145. ACM Press, New York (2004)

10. Brickell, E., Li, J.: Enhanced Privacy ID: A Direct Anonymous Attestation Scheme with Enhanced Revocation Capabilities. In: 6th ACM Workshop on Privacy in the Electronic Society, pp. 21–30. ACM Press, New York (2007)

11. Bringer, J., Patey, A.: Backward Unlinkability for a VLR Group Signature Scheme with Efficient Revocation Check. Cryptology ePrint Archive, Report 2011/376 (2011), http://eprint.iacr.org/2011/376

12. Brown, M., Hankerson, D., López, J., Menezes, A.: Software Implementation of the NIST Elliptic Curves over Prime Fields. In: Naccache, D. (ed.) CT-RSA 2001. LNCS, vol. 2020, pp. 250–265. Springer, Heidelberg (2001)

13. Camenisch, J., Groth, J.: Group Signatures: Better Efficiency and New Theoretical Aspects. In: Blundo, C., Cimato, S. (eds.) SCN 2004. LNCS, vol. 3352, pp. 120–133. Springer, Heidelberg (2005)

14. Camenisch, J., Lysyanskaya, A.: Dynamic Accumulators and Application to Efficient Revocation of Anonymous Credentials. In: Yung, M. (ed.) CRYPTO 2002. LNCS, vol. 2442, pp. 61–76. Springer, Heidelberg (2002)

15. Canard, S., Coisel, I., De Meulenaer, G., Pereira, O.: Group Signatures are Suitable for Constrained Devices. In: Rhee, K.-H., Nyang, D. (eds.) ICISC 2010. LNCS, vol. 6829, pp. 133–150. Springer, Heidelberg (2011)

16. Canard, S., Schoenmakers, B., Stam, M., Traoré, J.: List Signature Schemes. J. Discrete Applied Mathematics 154(2), 189–201 (2006)

17. Chaum, D., van Heyst, E.: Group Signatures. In: Davies, D.W. (ed.) EUROCRYPT 1991. LNCS, vol. 547, pp. 257–265. Springer, Heidelberg (1991)

18. Chen, L., Li, J.: VLR Group Signatures with Indisputable Exculpability and Efficient Revocation. In: 2nd IEEE International Conference on Social Computing, pp. 727–734. IEEE Press, New York (2010)

19. Chen, L., Li, J.: Revocation of Direct Anonymous Attestation. In: Chen, L., Yung, M. (eds.) INTRUST 2010. LNCS, vol. 6802, pp. 128–147. Springer, Heidelberg (2011)

20. Chen, L., Page, D., Smart, N.P.: On the Design and Implementation of an Efficient DAA Scheme. In: Gollmann, D., Lanet, J.-L., Iguchi-Cartigny, J. (eds.) CARDIS 2010. LNCS, vol. 6035, pp. 223–237. Springer, Heidelberg (2010)

21. Chen, L., Pedersen, T.P.: New group signature schemes. In: De Santis, A. (ed.) EUROCRYPT 1994. LNCS, vol. 950, pp. 171–181. Springer, Heidelberg (1995)

22. Delerablée, C., Pointcheval, D.: Dynamic Fully Anonymous Short Group Signatures. In: Nguyen, P.Q. (ed.) VIETCRYPT 2006. LNCS, vol. 4341, pp. 193–210. Springer, Heidelberg (2006)
23. Isshiki, T., Mori, K., Sako, K., Teranishi, I., Yonezawa, S.: Using Group Signatures for Identity Management and its Implementation. In: 2nd ACM workshop on Digital Identity Management, pp. 73–78. ACM Press, New York (2006)
24. ISO/IEC 20008-1: Information technology - Security techniques - Anonymous digital signatures - Part 1: General. Stage 40.20. International Organization for Standardization. Geneva, Switzerland (2012)
25. ISO/IEC 20008-2: Information technology - Security techniques - Anonymous digital signatures - Part 2: Mechanisms using a group public key. Stage 40.20. International Organization for Standardization. Geneva, Switzerland (2012)
26. Manulis, M., Fleischhacker, N., Günther, F., Kiefer, F., Poettering, B.: Group Signatures - Authentication with Privacy, a study issued by the German Federal Office for Information Security (BSI) (2012),
    https://www.bsi.bund.de/ContentBSI/Publikationen/
    Studien/GroupSignatures/GruPA.html
27. Morioka, S., Isshiki, T., Obana, S., Nakamura, Y., Sako, K.: Flexible Architecture Optimization and ASIC Implementation of Group Signature Algorithm using a Customized HLS Methodology. In: 2011 IEEE International Symposium on Hardware-Oriented Security and Trust (HOST), pp. 57–62. IEEE Press, New York (2011)
28. Naehrig, M., Niederhagen, R., Schwabe, P.: New Software Speed Records for Cryptographic Pairings. In: Abdalla, M., Barreto, P.S.L.M. (eds.) LATINCRYPT 2010. LNCS, vol. 6212, pp. 109–123. Springer, Heidelberg (2010)
29. Popescu, C.: An Electronic Cash System Based on Group Blind Signatures. J. Informatica 17(4), 551–564 (2006)
30. Rivain, M.: Fast and Regular Algorithms for Scalar Multiplication over Elliptic Curves. Cryptology ePrint Archive, Report 2011/338 (2011),
    http://eprint.iacr.org/2011/338
31. Wang, G.: Security Analysis of Several Group Signature Schemes. In: Johansson, T., Maitra, S. (eds.) INDOCRYPT 2003. LNCS, vol. 2904, pp. 252–265. Springer, Heidelberg (2003)
32. Yao, G.X., Junfeng, F., Cheung, R.C.C., Verbauwhede, I.: A High Speed Pairing Coprocessor Using RNS and Lazy Reduction. Cryptology ePrint Archive, Report 2011/258 (2011), http://eprint.iacr.org/2011/258

Limiting Data Exposure in Monitoring Multi-domain Policy Conformance*

Mirko Montanari, Jun Ho Huh, Rakesh B. Bobba, and Roy H. Campbell

University of Illinois at Urbana-Champaign
{mmontan2,jhhuh,rbobba,rhc}@illinois.edu

Abstract. In hybrid- or multi-cloud systems, security information and event management systems often work with abstract level information provided by the service providers. Privacy and confidentiality requirements discourage sharing of the raw data. With access to only the partial information, detecting anomalies and policy violations becomes much more difficult in those environments.

This paper proposes a mechanism for detecting undesirable events over the composition of multiple independent systems that have constraints in sharing information because of security and privacy concerns. Our approach complements other privacy-preserving event-sharing methods by focusing on discrete events such as system and network configuration changes. We use *logic-based policies* to define undesirable event sequences, and use *multi-party computation* to share event details that are needed for detecting violations. Further, through experimental evaluation, we show that our technique reduces the information shared between systems by more than half, and we show that the low performance of multi-party computation can be balanced out with concurrency—demonstrating an event rate acceptable for verification of configuration changes as well as other complex conditions.

1 Introduction

Monitoring of complex systems for configuration errors, security breaches, or regulation compliance requires a large amount of information to be collected (usually in the form of audit logs) and analyzed. In distributed environments like clouds or cloud-of-clouds [2], this monitoring may require logs to be shared across multiple security domains to detect particular security events. However, some of those logs might contain sensitive information about customers or might have commercial value. Without the necessary confidentiality and privacy guarantees, most organizations will be reluctant to share such privileged logs with others.

---

* This material is based on work supported in part by a grant from The Boeing Company, and by a grant from Air Force Research Laboratory and the Air Force Office of Scientific Research under agreement number FA8750-11-2-0084. The U.S. Government is authorized to reproduce and distribute reprints for Governmental purposes notwithstanding any copyright notation thereon.

M. Huth et al. (Eds.): TRUST 2013, LNCS 7904, pp. 65–82, 2013.

Being mindful of such concerns, this paper proposes a solution that facilitates integration of events across multiple security domains while providing the necessary confidentiality guarantees. With our solution, cloud users or cloud providers can detect problems in their own systems (e.g., a virtual machine running in an IaaS cloud), even if some parts of the infrastructure are being controlled by different organizations. We rely on the definition of "invariants," which capture the correct or desirable operations of the systems of interest. *Only* those events that have the potential to identify violations of those invariants are ever shared, minimizing the amount of events that need to be shared in the first place.

Privacy-preserving techniques that rely on data aggregation and anonymization [23,27,17] have been proposed in the past. While those techniques can be effective on policies that use numeric data and thresholds [3,6], many conditions that are of interest to network administrators require the capability to analyze *discrete events* (e.g., configuration changes in servers or network devices, changes in user information, or component failures). To the best of our knowledge, there is no good solution for aggregating or anonymizing discrete events without losing the details necessary for validating policies.

The proposed technique, on the other hand, detects complex, inter-domain policy violations through careful selection of the events to share across the organization boundaries. We introduce a distributed algorithm that coordinates the interaction among a dynamic set of monitoring servers to guarantee the detection of all policy violations, and we use a cryptographic mechanism called *privacy preserving secure two-party computation* [9] to figure out which events are relevant to a violation, and share only them across the domain boundaries.

We show that parallelism in the event correlation problem makes secure two-party computation practical in our case. Additionally, the lack of a central server where information is analyzed makes our technique suitable for multi-cloud systems or cloud-broker-based systems where new resources and security domains are continuously being added at runtime. Our performance evaluation confirms that our technique is indeed capable of significantly reducing the amount of information that needs to be shared, and that it can handle event loads of popular configuration management systems.

The contributions of this paper are summarized as follows:

1. We describe a policy-based algorithm for detecting violations of invariants across multiple security domains, and provide a proof of correctness of that algorithm.
2. We propose a mechanism for generating a policy-dependent implementation of the two-party computation algorithm using an efficient implementation of garbled circuits [10]. This algorithm identifies the information that needs to be shared while preserving privacy.
3. We demonstrate that parallelism of the event correlation problem can lead to a practical deployment of the two-party computation algorithm.
4. Our experimental evaluation shows that our solution is practical and can reduce significantly the amount of information that needs to be shared across multiple domains.

The rest of the paper is structured as follows. Section 2 provides an overview of related work in the area of multi-domain monitoring and secure information sharing. Section 3 discusses our own monitoring architecture and distributed event correlation protocol. Results from the experimental evaluation are presented in Section 4. Finally, Section 5 presents our conclusions and future work.

2 Related Work

Collaboration between organizations for detecting attacks and other security problems has been an important research topic for several years. The interdependencies between systems that we find in today's cloud computing environments increase the need for such collaboration. However, sharing of information presents several security problems. Monitoring data can provide insights into an organization's computing infrastructure which may give a competitive advantage to rival organizations. Such data can also provide attackers with information about possible vulnerabilities. For that reason, a significant amount of work has been focused on reduction of information sharing, while still permitting the detection of complex event patterns.

Several past techniques focus on hiding log information through anonymization [23,27,17]. Lincoln et al. [17], in particular, introduce a technique for removing critical data from network traces. SEPIA [3] provides a threshold-based mechanism for sharing aggregated data about network traffic. Denker et al. [6] use a selective downgrade of GPS data for sharing location data. However, such techniques generally apply to numeric information, and the summarization is strongly dependent on the semantics of the information. Our technique focuses on discrete data that cannot be summarized without loss of the ability to detect policy violations correctly, such as configuration changes, failures of specific machines, or vulnerability information.

Montanari et al. [20] introduce a protocol for the validation of policies across two organizations. The authors use explicit meta-data about the completeness of the information collected from each monitoring system to decide which events to share. Our work does not require explicit metadata, and our approach is applicable to multiple security domains. Additionally, the use of a secure two-party computation protocol further reduces the amount of shared events.

Huh and Lyle [12] propose a trusted computing based approach to enable "blind log analysis," allowing different organizations to freely share raw log data with the guarantees that their raw data will not be revealed to other organizations. A trustworthy log reconciliation service is attested and verified, providing assurance that all the log reconciliation and analysis is performed blindly inside a protected virtual machine. Only the fully processed, privacy-preserving analysis results are made available to other organizations. In contrast, in our approach, only the information required for detecting violations leaves the security domain, reducing the amount of information that need to be shared in the first place. We reduce the reliance on remote software for protecting the confidentiality of data, and we do not rely on the capabilities of remote attestation [5].

Techniques focusing on integrating data in a central server for analysis have also been proposed. Australia's Commonwealth Scientic and Industrial Research Organisation (CSIRO) has developed a Privacy-Preserving Analytics (PPA) software for analyzing sensitive healthcare data with confidentiality guarantees [22]. PPA performs analysis on the original raw data but modifies the output delivered to researchers to ensure that no individual unit record is disclosed. Huh and Martin [13] propose the concept of a "blind analysis server," an attested and verified remote server which allows privileged data analysis to be performed securely and privately. In work closely related to ours, Lee et al. [16] introduce a framework that allows a group of organizations to share encrypted logs with a central auditor. The auditor analyzes the encrypted logs and detects attacks or other policy violations. Our work improves on such approaches in two major ways. First, we remove the need to store centrally the logs collected from all organizations. While having a central authority is feasible in certain situations, in cloud and cloud-of-clouds systems, organizations can integrate resources across multiple providers and provide them to different clients at runtime. Having all entities involved push out their logs to a single central location is impractical and not desirable. Our approach uses a distributed mechanism for correlating data, and security domains interact directly only when they require information about specific external resources.

Other approaches rely on explicit confidentiality policies to define which events to share across organization boundaries. Singh et al. [26] introduce a system defining explicit confidentiality policies on classes of events. Similarly, Evans et al. [7] propose a solution in which access control is enforced by tagging events with labels. Rigid confidentiality policies proposed in those works would not be fully compatible with our multi-domain scenario. As information should be shared only when needed, fixed policies are either too open or too strict. Open policies unnecessarily increase the information shared, while strict policies might make the system unable to guarantee the detection of all policy violations.

3 Multi-domain Event Sharing for Compliance

The increasing complexity of managing and securing large systems has driven the development of policy-based approaches to address the problem [8]. In such approaches, policies or "invariants" identify correct or desirable conditions of the system. Administrators define rules that identify violations of such policies and indicate misconfigurations, vulnerabilities to known attacks, or non-compliance to best-practices that reduce the risk of zero-day attacks. Monitoring systems continuously collect information about the infrastructure to detect violations.

Examples of policy-based approaches can be found in different domains. For example, it is possible to define policies to monitor for compliance with regulatory requirements such as the Payment Card Data Security Standard (PCI-DSS) [24] or the Federal Information Security Management Act (FISMA) [25]. Both regulations mandate a minimum level of security configuration in an infrastructure. PCI-DSS applies to companies handling credit card data, while FISMA

Table 1. Example of a multi-domain policy and events required for the detection of a violation. For each event, we list its source and the information it carries.

Policy example	Events	Source	Res	Description
Not run a critical service on a physical server that is sending malicious traffic	criticalService	Private Infrastructure	P, I	Critical service P is running on instance I
	instanceAssigned	Cloud Provider	I, S	VM Instance I launched on S
	badTraffic	Cloud Provider	S	Malicious traffic detected from S

applies to information systems in the U.S. federal government. Policies define known types of misconfigurations or error situations, and are used to identify quickly the presence of a problem before an attacker can exploit it.

In many modern cloud systems, multiple security domains interact to provide the desired services. For example, in a hybrid cloud environment, services provided by the infrastructure of an organization are integrated with services managed by a cloud provider. In intercloud systems [2], or in systems based on cloud brokers [18], multiple cloud services are integrated to provide a service to cloud users. Such services are provided by a variety of cloud providers, and their selection might depend on dynamic conditions not known beforehand. In such settings, multiple independent monitoring systems acquire information about the infrastructure. Monitoring systems in the private infrastructure acquire application-level information from software running on the local infrastructure and on cloud instances. Monitoring servers managed by the cloud provider acquire information about the physical location of virtual machine instances, the colocation of virtual machines with other customers, and the load of the infrastructure. In these settings, conditions to detect violations can be complex, and analyzing each organization's information independently is not sufficient to detect violations. However, sharing monitoring information outside an organization is often undesirable. Information about the infrastructure configurations provides details about security postures or information about the internals of an organization to competitors.

We can find several examples of policies in enterprise and cloud systems. For example, a policy can specify that a critical service should not depend on services running on machines that process a lot of external traffic; another policy might require a computer joining a private network not to run a certain set of services. In both cases, it might be desirable not to reveal the entire state of a system at once, but only when certain conditions occur. For the purpose of explaining our approach, we use the following example throughout the paper.

Example: An administrator defines a policy requiring that a critical server not be run on a physical server that is sending malicious or unwanted traffic (*e.g.* unexpected port scans). Violation of such a policy can be detected by identifying three events, as shown in Table 1. Such events are generated by different information sources: deployment systems in the cloud provider indicate that a new instance has been created; SNMP agents on virtual machines generate information

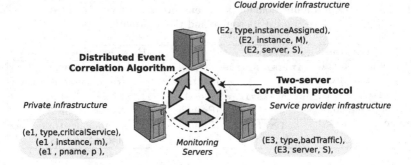

Fig. 1. Architecture of our monitoring system. Multiple monitoring servers are placed in different security domains. Servers communicate to detect violations of policies.

about running programs; and network monitoring systems detect malicious traffic from physical servers. Because information sources are in different organizations, detecting violations requires sharing data across domains.

We design a monitoring architecture (see Fig. 1) that supports such data sharing while minimizing the amount of data shared. The monitoring servers within each organization have a copy of the shared policy and collect information about the local infrastructure. The collected information is used to detect local violations without requiring any communication with other servers. Additionally, each server verifiers if the local information could potentially create a multi-organization policy violation if certain conditions are present in other domains. In such a case, the server uses our distributed event correlation algorithm to check the presence of the condition on remote monitoring servers without revealing information about the local infrastructure, unless a violation is actually detected. We use a distributed naming system to identify monitoring systems potentially containing other portions of the event sequence that could cause a violation. When policies are complex, our policy rewrite algorithm splits the policy into a sequence of simpler conditions that can be checked by communicating with a single monitoring server at each step. The policy rewrite is performed independently on each server, and only local information is used to identify the remote servers with which the local server needs to communicate to continue the processing. We show that, using such local actions, our algorithm identifies the same policy violations found by integrated events in a single server.

3.1 Policy Analysis

Violations of policies are rare events. For that reason, monitoring systems collect a large amount of information that does not contribute to violations. Our correlation algorithm identifies which events might contribute to violation of cross-domain policies and shares only those events with other domains.

To perform such an analysis, we take advantage of the semantic structure of the data in infrastructure monitoring systems. An infrastructure monitoring

Constraint	Description
precedes	$x^+ < y^-$
meets	$x^+ == y^-$
overlaps	$x^- < y^- < x^+ < y^+$
during	$y^- < x^- < x^+ < y^+$
starts	$x^- == y^-, x^+ < y^+$
finishes	$x^+ == y^+, x^- > y^-$
equals	$x^- == y^-, x^+ == y^+$

$1 : (E_1, \text{type}, \texttt{criticalService}),$
$2 : (E_1, \text{instance}, I), (E_1, \text{pname}, P),$
$3 : (E_2, \text{type}, \texttt{instanceAssigned}),$
$4 : (E_2, \text{instance}, I), (E_2, \text{server}, S),$
$5 : (E_3, \text{type}, \texttt{badTraffic}), (E_3, \text{server}, S),$
$6 : [E_1 \text{during} E_2] \wedge$
$7 : ([E_2 \text{overlaps} E_3] \vee [E_2 \text{during} E_3])$
$8 : \rightarrow (v_1, \text{violation}, I)$

Fig. 2. Temporal policy constraints. x^- is the starting time of an event x, and x^+ is its end time.

Fig. 3. Policy requiring that a critical service not be run on a physical server that is sending malicious traffic

system is an event-based system that collects information about the state of a set of entities, such as computer systems, users, software programs, or network connections. We define these entities as "resources." A violation of a policy is the presence of a particular state in a set of related resources (e.g., in Table 1, the resources are a VM instance I, a software P, and a physical machine M). Our system finds violations through the identification of a sequence of events that corresponds to incorrect or invalid changes in the state of such resources.

We represent each event as multiple logic statements. Without loss of generality, we use the Resource Definition Framework (RDF). In RDF, each statement is a tuple $(id, property, value)$ composed of three parts. The first part is an event ID, which identifies uniquely the event throughout the system. The second part indicates the name of an event *property* and represents the type of information provided by the statement (e.g., the property instance indicates id of an virtual instance). The last part contains the value for the given property. An event is composed of multiple statements having the same event ID. In our example, we represent an event with ID e_1 of type criticalService providing information that a VM instance identified with m is running a program p as follows:

$$1 : (e_1, \text{eventType}, \texttt{criticalService}), (e_1, \text{pname}, p), (e_1, \text{instance}, m),$$
$$2 : (e_1, \text{startTime}, t_s), (e_1, \text{endTime}, t_e), \tag{1}$$

A policy identifies a sequence of events by expressing conditions over the logic statements in each event. The condition is represented with a rule expressed using Datalog with negation (we assume typical Datalog stratification and safeness conditions on the rule [4]). In addition, we use seven constraints (and their negation) to represent in interval temporal logic (ITL) all possible temporal relations between events [1]. The constraints are listed in Fig. 2. Using such relations, we can express constraints such as the fact that an event e_1 happens before another event e_2, or that an event e_1 happens while the event e_2 is happening. Using such a language, we represent directly policies expressed as conjunctions and negations of events. We represent disjunctions by creating multiple rules, each representing an alternative in the selection of the events that can occur.

```
1: function SUBPOLICY(V, P, PR)
2:     for all e₁, e₂ ∈ P sharing variable V do
3:         VL = vars(e₁) ∪ vars(e₂) // we select all variables used in the two events
4:         PR = create a rule "e₁ ∧ e₂ ∧ [timec(e₁, e₂)] → partialᵢ(VL)";
5:         // We create P' by removing e₁, e₂ from P and replace them with partialᵢ
6:         P = (P \ e₁ \ e₂) ∪ partialᵢ(VL)
7:         if size of P' is 2 then return P'
8:         else
9:             if P' has no shared variable then
10:                Take two events eₖ, eₙ ∈ P and generate a new random resource r
11:                Add a property to eₖ and eₙ to connect them to r
12:            end if
13:            V' = choose a shared variable
14:            return SubPolicy(V', P, PR)
15:        end if
16:    end for
17: end function
```

Fig. 4. Policy rewrite algorithm pseudocode

Fig. 3 shows the formal representation of the example policy in Table 1. The policy uses the same variable names in the values of the properties `instance` and `server` to define an equality relation between such properties in events E_1, E_2 and E_2, E_3. Temporal conditions are expressed within square brackets, as shown in lines 6-7. The policy is violated if the three events satisfy all conditions.

3.2   Rule Rewrite

Our distributed correlation algorithm splits across multiple servers the process of building subsequences of events that may violate the policy. Each monitoring server *registers* to manage a set of resources in a distributed naming service, and constructs the sequences of events related to them. Servers receive events generated within the security domain about the resources for which they are registered. We use a distributed naming registry based on Zookeeper [14] to maintain an assignment between resources and monitoring servers within each organization, and we expose such an assignment to external organizations through a DNS-based interface: a server obtains the monitoring servers managing a resource through the resolution of a name containing a short hash of the resource.

Monitoring servers identify violations by analyzing events related to the resources they manage and by connecting them with events stored in other monitoring servers. To identify explicitly the relation between resources, we rewrite each policy into an equivalent set of rules called *resource-based rules*.

As resources involved in a policy violation are related to each other, some events contributing to a violation carry information about two or more of the resources involved[1]. Because such a relation between events and resources exists,

---

[1] Such a condition is common among monitoring policies: if no relation exists between events, any occurrence of certain unrelated events could create a violation.

we can split a policy into a set of rules, each composed of two events which carry information about the same resource. As one of the two events also carry information about some additional resource (otherwise the two resources involved would be unrelated to the other resources), we connect resource-based rules together in the following way. The consequence of a resource-based rule is a new logic statement related to the additional resource; such a statement is used in other rules. In the processing of events, the first rule identifies two matching events, and creates a statement indicating that such a match is found. The next rule takes such a statement and integrates it with an additional event; such a process is repeated until all events in the violation sequence are matched.

Fig. 4 describes a greedy version of the algorithm we use in the policy rewrite. Intuitively, the algorithm takes a policy P and selects two events with a resource in common (line 2). A new resource-based rule PR is created (line 4) based on the two events and the time constraints $timec$ involving both of them. We replace the two events in the original policy with the new statement $partial_i$ (line 6). If the resulting policy P is composed of two events, the algorithm is complete (line 7), otherwise the execution continues recursively (line 14). If the remaining policy does not have any common variable (i.e., events are unrelated), a new shared resource is created and added to the events (lines 9-12).

As an example, we apply the rewrite algorithm to our policy of Fig. 3. We consider three resources I, S, and P, where the VM instance I is assigned to the server S, and I runs the program P. Our rewrite splits the policy into two resource-based rules. The first rule integrates the events badTraffic and instanceAssigned related to the physical server S. Because the physical server is managed by the cloud provider, such integration is performed on the cloud provider system. The consequence of such a rule is a statement $partial_1$ that contains a reference to the instance I. We obtained the following resource-based rule, where the variables $E_i sT$ and $E_i eT$ represent the start time and end time of the events.

$$
\begin{aligned}
&1 : (E_2, \text{type}, \text{instanceAssigned}), (E_2, \text{instance}, I), (E_2, \text{server}, S), \\
&2 : (E_2, \text{startTime}, E_2 sT), (E_2, \text{endTime}, E_2 eT), \\
&3 : (E_3, \text{type}, \text{badTraffic}), (E_3, \text{server}, S), \\
&4 : (E_3, \text{startTime}, E_3 sT), (E_3, \text{endTime}, E_3 eT), \\
&5 : ([E_2 \text{overlaps} E_3] \vee [E_2 \text{during} E_3]) \\
&6 : \rightarrow partial_1(I, S, E_2 sT, E_2 eT, E_3 sT, E_3 eT)
\end{aligned} \tag{2}
$$

In the second step, we consider the statement $partial_1$ related to VM instance I, and we integrate the remaining events criticalService generated by the private infrastructure. As the new statement contains all information from the selected events, all temporal constraints and event conditions can still be applied. The result is as follows.

$$
\begin{aligned}
&1 : partial_1(I, S, E_2 sT, E_2 eT, E_3 sT, E_3 eT), \\
&2 : (E_1, \text{type}, \text{criticalService}), (E_1, \text{instance}, I), (E_1, \text{pname}, P), \\
&3 : (E_1, \text{startTime}, sE_1 sT), (E_1, \text{endTime}, sE_1 eT), \\
&4 : [E_1 \text{during} E_2] \rightarrow (v_1, \text{violation}, I)
\end{aligned} \tag{3}
$$

Because part of the information about I is contained in the cloud provider and part in the private infrastructure, the two monitoring servers need to communicate for integrating the two events. The next section describes our mechanism for correlating the two events while revealing information only if a match exists.

The correctness of the rewrite algorithm is shown below in Lemma 1.

Lemma 1. *Given a set of rules R generated through the application of Algorithm 4 to a policy P, a set of events $e_1, \ldots, e_n$ creates a violation of P iff it creates a violation of the set of rules R.*

Proof Sketch. The rewrite of the formula P creates a tree structure. Each rule is a node in the tree. A node A is a child of a node B if the consequence of the rule A (i.e., the *partial$_i$* statement) is a condition in the parent node B. In our example, Eq 2 is a child of Eq 3 because the consequence *partial$_1$* of the first rule appears as a condition in the body of the second rule. We prove by induction on such a tree. If the height of the tree is 1, then the condition is trivially satisfied as we have only one rule and $r = P$. Assuming that the height of the tree is n, we prove that the condition is satisfied for $n + 1$. We consider a node A in the n tree. In the $n + 1$ tree, the node A is replaced with a node A' with a child B. B is obtained by considering two events e_1, e_2 from the rule in A and by creating a new rule r_j having such events as body and a new statement *partial$_i$* as conclusion. The node A' is created by replacing events e_1, e_2 in A with the *partial$_i$* statement. Because the events satisfy all rules at heigh n, the rule r_j is satisfied as the conditions on events e_1, e_2 were satisfied in the tree n. Hence, the statement *partial$_i$* is also satisfied. Because the statement *partial* maintains all the information about matched events, all conditions that were not taken and placed in r_j can still be validated in the original node. Hence, no constraints have been eliminated in this process, and all events that satisfy the rules also satisfy the original policy.

3.3   Event Correlation

The resource-based rules split the identification of the violation in a set of two-event correlations. Such processing is performed independently in each monitoring server: when an event matching a part of the resource-based rule is received, the server triggers a process for identifying the presence of an event matching the remaining part of the rule, even if the event is stored in another domain. The server uses the naming system to identify all servers containing events related to the common resource. For each server, it uses our matching protocol to identify if events matching the remaining portion of the rule are present. If found, the local event is shared. Based on the received event, the remote server repeats the described process and interacts with other servers until a violation is found, or no event matches the resource-based rule.

Because information about a single resource can be spread across multiple domains (e.g., for the same host, a domain might provide network information and another domain provide system information), servers in different domains can be registered for the same resource. Additionally, because events carry information about multiple resources, a server contains information about resources for which it is not registered. Our algorithm uses a *subscription* process to keep track of data about resources for which the server is not registered. When a server s receives an event relevant to resource r that matches a rule, it contacts the registered server for r to search for matching events. Even when matching events are not found, the registered server maintains a reference to s, as it is known that it contains events relevant to r. When new events are received, the registered server contacts s for correlation. Additionally, when another server s' requests a correlation for r, the address of s is shared, so that s' can correlate its events with s directly.

Theorem 1. *If events $e_1, \ldots, e_n$ satisfy all conditions of a policy, the distributed protocol identifies the presence of a violation.*

Proof Sketch: We assume that there exists a sequence of common resources that connects all events, i.e., $r_1, \ldots, r_n$ such that $\forall e_i \exists r_k, e_j : r_k \in e_i, r_k \in e_j$. If such sequence does not exist, our algorithm introduces new common resources to connect all events. Lemma 1 shows the equivalence between the resource-based rules and the policy. Hence, we show that if two events matching a resource-based rule exist, our distributed algorithm identifies them. By construction, such events have a resource r in common. Hence, given an event e, we need to ensure that a server finds all events e' that share the same resource r. We have three cases.

1. Both events e and e' are received by servers registered for the resource r. According to our algorithm, when an event is received, the server interacts with all servers registered for such a resource. As both servers are registered, the last event received would interact with the server storing the first event.
2. Event e is received by a server s registered for r, and event e' is received by a non-registered server s'. If the servers receive the events in the sequence (e, e'), the arrival of e' triggers a lookup on the naming registry, leading to the identification of the server containing e. If the sequence is (e', e), the server of e is identified: however the correlation protocol returns false, as e is not present yet, and the event e' is not shared. In that case, s saves the reference for s'. When the event e is received, s runs the correlation protocol with s' again and identifies the event e'.
3. Both events e and e' are received by two non-registered servers s and s'. In such a case, the first event triggers a lookup in the naming system, leading to the identification of a server s_r registered for the resource r. The correlation process creates the reference to s in the server. Receiving the event e' triggers the same process. This time, s_r saves the reference to s' and returns the reference to s. The correlation process between s and s' identifies the matching events.

3.4   Privacy-Preserving Matching Protocol

The privacy-preserving matching protocol is initiated between two servers. One peer, called the *gc-client*, initiates the process by picking a resource-based rule

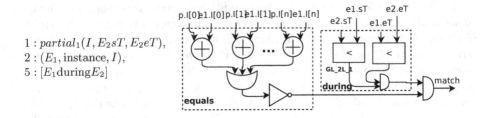

$1 : partial_1(I, E_2sT, E_2eT),$
$2 : (E_1, \text{instance}, I),$
$5 : [E_1 \text{during} E_2]$

Fig. 5. (left) Simplified resource-based rule containing only constraints requiring input from both events; (right) circuit blocks implementing the resource-based rule

and an event e for which it wants to find a match. The other peer, called the *gc-server*, considers all local events satisfying the local condition of the rule and, for each event e', executes a *two-event matching* protocol. To speed up the process, the system executes the two-event matching for all pairs (e, e') in parallel.

We use garbled circuits [9] to implement the two-event matching protocol. Garbled circuits are a cryptographic mechanism for performing secure two-party computation. Without the use of cryptography, one server needs to acquire data about both events to validate all constraints (temporal and others) specified in the rule. However, such an approach would reveal a large amount of information to the other party, as all relevant events need to be stored on one server. Using secure two-party computation, each party provides part of the input data and collaborates with the other party through a distributed protocol to determine if two events satisfy the constraints of the rule. The data provided by each party remains hidden, and only the result of the computation is known to both. In the last several years, garbled circuits have been shown to be one of the most efficient methods for performing secure two-party computation [10].

Garbled circuit protocols require expressing the computation as a binary circuit. Our system encodes events into binary strings and generates a combinatorial circuit based on the conditions of each resource-based rule. Circuits are created through the connection of sub-circuit blocks that depend on the type of constraints specified in the policy. Connections are performed through AND, OR, or NOT gates. We consider only constraints that require input from both events, as other constraints are validated locally.

The sub-circuit blocks in our implementation cover all temporal constraints in Fig. 2, in addition to *equality*, and *less-than* constraints. More circuits can be created for other types of constraints. For the resource-based rule in Eq. 3, the transformation maintains the equality constraint between the values of the variable I used in the event and the statement, and the *during* temporal constraint, as shown in Fig. 5 (left). Fig. 5 (right) also shows the encoding of the policy.

Our system uses a recent implementation of the garbled circuit protocol [10] to execute the circuit. The gc-client sends the ID of the rule to check, and interacts with the server to construct the garbled circuit. The gc-server uses an Oblivious Transfer (OT) protocol [15] to ask the gc-client to encrypt its input, and uses such data to execute the encrypted circuit locally. The encrypted output of the circuit is sent to the client for decryption. If a match is found, the gc-client sends the matched event unencrypted. The gc-server adds the event in its local storage, which might trigger other two-server event correlation protocols.

The system executes the privacy-preserving matching protocol for each pair of events independently from the others. As garbled circuit computation requires several communication round trips for the exchange of data, parallelization can significantly improve throughput because of better utilization of the CPU.

In our interactions, the gc-server returns to the gc-client the number of events satisfying the local conditions to determine the number of times the privacy-preserving matching protocol is executed. If the number reveals information about the state of the infrastructure, the monitoring server can report any number larger than the given value, so that the number of events cannot be used to make any inference. Once the local events are exhausted, additional computations are performed with invalid values to ensure that no matching is possible.

3.5   Privacy Analysis and Limitations

From a privacy perspective, the security property of the two-event matching protocol shows that, for two-event policies, we share only events that create violations. This is the minimum level of information sharing that we can have between two organizations [20]. However, when the complexity of the policy increases and multiple resource-based rules are needed, sequences of events matching a single resource-based rule need to be shared to process the next resource-based rule. In such a situation, we limit information sharing by first selecting, when possible, resource-based rules that are rarely matched.

The interaction between monitoring servers leaks additional information that can be used to make inferences on the state of the remote party, even if no explicit sharing occurs. The request for a two-party correlation reveals the hash of the common resource and the policy involved. The hash is intentionally kept short, so that conflicts and false positives are possible, making the identification of the resource ID hard. The presence of an interaction, even if leads to no matched events, can still reveal that a subsequence of events matching a portion of the policy is present on the server. To counter such an inference, we add spurious requests with random events to ensure that such knowledge cannot be inferred.

The implementation of secure two-party computation used in our system relies on the assumption of an honest-but-curious attacker [9]. Such an attack model assumes that the two parties interact according to the protocol, and do not provide false information about their own systems. In the interaction between organizations, additional mechanisms can ensure that false information is not provided. The periodic auditing currently performed for ensuring compliance to regulations could also validate recoded logs of the interactions. Such logs create an audit trail that could dissuade organizations from providing false information. In addition, techniques have been proposed to validate the received information through independent information sources [21] to ensure its correctness. Moreover, progress has been made in building secure two-party computation that applies to semi-honest adversaries [11]. Such advance can be integrated to our solution.

4   Experimental Evaluation

Our evaluation measured the reduction in the amount of information exchanged when our event-correlation method was used, and the event rate obtained with our two-event matching protocol. We implemented the system in Java and used a garbled circuit protocol implementation by Huang et al. [10], with modifications performed to improve significantly parallelism. We ran our experiments on Amazon EC2 m1.large instances (7.5 Gb memory, 4 compute units), an instance type which computation capabilities fall in the middle of the EC2 spectrum.

4.1   Reduction of Event Sharing

We measured the reduction in the information shared between domains. Resources were partitioned across servers, and events were distributed randomly. Information sharing occurs when events about the same resource are stored in different domains. As the occurrence of such a condition is policy- and event-dependent, we evaluated our solution in different points in the space by changing three critical parameters. The first one is the frequency at which two events in different domains create a partial policy violation. The second parameter is the fraction of the infrastructure under the control of each organization. The third parameter is the number of security domains managing the infrastructure.

We measured the performance of our encrypted communication (`encr`) with rules of different complexity (`2-event rule`, `4-event rule`). We compared it with a clear-text solution (`clear-txt`) that sends events related to a resource to the monitoring servers managing it (even if they are in a different domain) [19], and with the minimum need-to-know information (`min`).

First, we analyzed how the frequency with which events create partial policy violations affects the amount of information shared. We created events so that each pair of events in a policy has a given probability of referring to the same resource, and we randomly distributed them across domains. We show the results in Fig. 6. Our system significantly outperformed the baseline (i.e., `clear-txt`) solution and, for two-event polices, the fraction remained equal to the theoretical minimum (`min`). As we measure events shared over total events, the theoretical minimum number of events for the 4-event rules is smaller than the one for the 2-event rule: in the optimal case, a single interaction can summarize information about multiple events and it is counted as one event.

The distribution of resources across domains affects the fraction of events shared, as shown in Fig. 7. To test the system under less than ideal conditions, we created events that partially matched policies with a probability of 75% and we distributed them randomly to each server. The highest information sharing occurred when each organization had half of the resources, while the amount of event shared is reduced when more resources are managed by a single domain.

We measured the fraction of events stored at each server under different conditions (see Fig. 8). We considered both complete events and events that can be inferred from the presence of partial statements. Increasing the number of

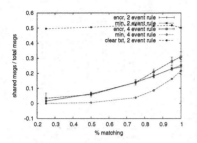

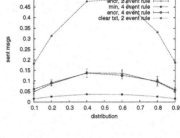

Fig. 6. Probability of matching events affects the fraction of events shared

Fig. 7. Fraction of resources allocated to a monitoring server. 2 servers.

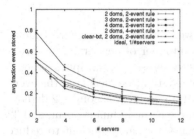

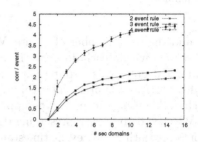

Fig. 8. Average fraction of events known to each server

Fig. 9. Server load, multiple security domains. One server per domain.

security domains reduced the average number of events in each server. In all cases, our system provided a significant improvement over a clear-text solution.

To summarize, our experiment showed that while the performance of the system depends on the conditions of the policy and the frequency of matching events, our solution still outperforms a baseline solution. In many cases, the amount of information shared is close to the minimum possible. Best conditions occur when events in different domains creating a policy violations are not frequent, and when a significant fraction of interacting resources are stored within the same security domains, so that most violations can be found locally.

4.2 Performance Evaluation

To evaluate computation overhead, we measured the average number of secure two-party computations performed by each server, as shown in Fig. 9. We varied the number of domains. We considered the ratio between two-event correlations and events received. We saw that increasing the number of security domains increases the number of two-event correlations performed, as it increases the likelihood that interacting resources are managed by external servers.

We measured the ability of parallelizing and of distributing the computation by measuring the average number of computation per-server, as shown in Fig. 10. We injected a constant number of events into the system and we measured the ratio between the average number of two-event correlations performed on each

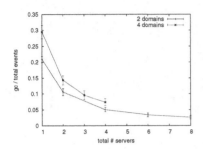

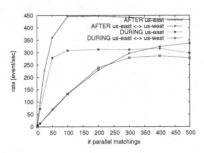

Fig. 10. Distribution of load with the increase of the number of servers within each domain

Fig. 11. Delay in the processing of an event as a function of the level of concurrency in the server

server and the total number of events. When we increase the number of monitoring servers within each domain, the average number of per-server two-event correlations decreases as resources are distributed across the multiple servers.

To demonstrate the practical feasibility of our system, we measured the event rate achievable using our prototype implementation on an Amazon EC2 deployment. We used 64 bits for representing the resource name in binary form, and 32 bits for representing each event timestamp. Such values are sufficient to reduce collisions and to maintain low circuit complexity. Because the performance of garbled circuit protocols depends on the round-trip communication delays, we measured the performance between two servers within the same geographical region, and between servers in different regions. The former represents conditions found when monitoring servers are co-located within the same provider.

We measured the throughput in event correlation per second and we show the results in Fig. 11. The remote dataset was split into groups of 100 events, and the processing of each group occurred in parallel. When using multiple threads, we increased the rate up to 400 correlations per second on a single server.

We evaluated the effects of the policy constraints on the system's throughput. We evaluated two circuits: one checking for an equivalence between properties and for a constraint *after*; and a more complex circuit checking for an equivalence and a constraint *during*. The first one had an input size of 192 bits: 64 bits for each property name and 64 bits for two timestamps. The second circuit used 256 bits: 64 bits for each property name, and 128 bits for the four timestamps. The complex circuit reduced the throughput by about 30%.

We evaluated the effect of colocation of servers on event throughput. We considered servers co-located in the us-east region, and servers placed in us-east and us-west. Without concurrency, co-located servers for the *after* constraints obtained a rate of 9.5 event/s. When servers are located in different regions, the rate was 1.4 event/s. However, increasing the concurrency significantly increased the event rate. With 500 concurrent executions, co-located servers obtained a rate of 435 event/s, while servers in different regions obtained 337 event/s, with a reduction by about 22%. The *before* constraint had similar results.

In summary, our experiments demonstrated that our system is capable of performing hundreds of correlations per second on a single server, and that multiple servers can run in parallel to further improve the performance. This kind of event rate makes our system practical for monitoring system configuration changes and detecting complex attacks. It would scale to, for instance, taking a few seconds to validate the effects of a local configuration change on a remote infrastructure that consists of thousands of servers.

5   Conclusion

This paper introduced a distributed monitoring architecture for detecting violations of policies in multi-domain systems. The system uses secure two-party computation to reduce the amount of confidential information shared outside each security domain: information is shared only after verifying that it can potentially contribute to a violation. Our analysis and experimental evaluation show that the performance of our technique is adequate for configurations and other discrete operational state. Our approach is complementary to techniques that can process a larger amount of numerical data through aggregation and anonymization, such as network traffic information. We show that our technique limits the information shared to a minimal need-to-know for simple policies, and can significantly reduce the amount of information shared for complex policies.

Future work should introduce more optimizations in complex policies by changing the order of correlations so that the frequency of events and the willingness of the organization to share are taken into account. Additionally, reducing information stored in other domains can increase the security of the overall system, as security breaches in one of domains would provide little information to attackers about other systems. However, more work is needed to extended the system beyond the honest-but-curious attack model. For example, redundancy would provide mechanisms for recognizing compromised monitoring servers.

References

1. Allen, J.F.: Maintaining knowledge about temporal intervals. Communications of the ACM 26(11), 832–843 (1983)
2. Bernstein, D., Ludvigson, E., Sankar, K., Diamond, S., Morrow, M.: Blueprint for the intercloud-protocols and formats for cloud computing interoperability. In: ICIW 2009, pp. 328–336. IEEE (2009)
3. Burkhart, M., Strasser, M., Many, D., Dimitropoulos, X.: Sepia: Privacy-preserving aggregation of multi-domain network events and statistics. USENIX Sec (2010)
4. Ceri, S., Gottlob, G., Tanca, L.: What you always wanted to know about Datalog (and never dared to ask). IEEE Transactions on Knowledge and Data Engineering 1(1), 146–166 (1989)
5. Grawrock, D.: The Intel Safer Computing Initiative, ch. 1-2, pp. 3–31. Intel Press (2006)
6. Denker, G., Gehani, A., Kim, M., Hanz, D.: Policy-Based Data Downgrading: Toward a Semantic Framework and Automated Tools to Balance Need-to-Protect and Need-to-Share Policies. In: IEEE POLICY (2010)

7. Evans, D., Eyers, D.: Efficient Policy Checking across Administrative Domains. In: IEEE POLICY (2010)

8. Giblin, C., Müller, S., Pfitzmann, B.: From regulatory policies to event monitoring rules: Towards model-driven compliance automation. IBM Research Zurich, Report RZ, 3662 (2006)

9. Goldreich, O.: Foundations of Cryptography. Basic Applications, vol. 2. Cambridge University Press (2004)

10. Huang, Y., Evans, D., Katz, J., Malka, L.: Faster secure two-party computation using garbled circuits. In: USENIX Security Symposium (2011)

11. Huang, Y., Katz, J., Evans, D.: Quid-pro-quo-tocols: Strengthening semi-honest protocols with dual execution. In: IEEE Symposium on Security and Privacy (2012)

12. Huh, J.H., Lyle, J.: Trustworthy Log Reconciliation for Distributed Virtual Organisations. In: Chen, L., Mitchell, C.J., Martin, A. (eds.) Trust 2009. LNCS, vol. 5471, pp. 169–182. Springer, Heidelberg (2009)

13. Huh, J.H., Martin, A.: Towards a Trustable Virtual Organisation. In: IEEE International Symposium on Parallel and Distributed Processing with Applications, pp. 425–431. IEEE (August 2009)

14. Hunt, P., Konar, M., Junqueira, F.P., Reed, B.: Zookeeper: Wait-free coordination for internet-scale systems. In: USENIX ATC, vol. 10 (2010)

15. Ishai, Y., Kilian, J., Nissim, K., Petrank, E.: Extending oblivious transfers efficiently. In: Boneh, D. (ed.) CRYPTO 2003. LNCS, vol. 2729, pp. 145–161. Springer, Heidelberg (2003)

16. Lee, A.J., Tabriz, P., Borisov, N.: A privacy-preserving interdomain audit framework. In: WPES. ACM (2006)

17. Lincoln, P., Porras, P., Shmatikov, V.: Privacy-preserving sharing and correction of security alerts. In: USENIX Security Symposium (2004)

18. Liu, F., Tong, J., Mao, J., Bohn, R., Messina, J., Badger, L., Leaf, D.: Nist cloud computing reference architecture. NIST Special Publication 500, 292 (2011)

19. Montanari, M., Campbell, R.H.: Confidentiality of event data in policy-based monitoring. In: Dependable Systems and Networks, DSN 2012. IEEE (2012)

20. Montanari, M., Cook, L.T., Campbell, R.H.: Multi-organization policy-based monitoring. In: IEEE POLICY 2012 (2012)

21. Montanari, M., Huh, J.H., Dagit, D., Bobba, R.B., Campbell, R.H.: Evidence of log integrity in policy-based security monitoring. In: Dependable Systems and Networks Workshops, DSN-W 2012. IEEE (2012)

22. O'Keefe, C.M.: Privacy and the use of health data - reducing disclosure risk. In: Health Informatics (2008)

23. Pang, R.: A high-level programming environment for packet trace anonymization and transformation. In: ACM SIGCOMM, Germany (2003)

24. Payment Card Industry (PCI) Security Standard Council. Data security standard version 1.1 (2006)

25. Ross, R., Katzke, S., Johnson, A., Swanson, M., Stoneburner, G., Rogers, G., Lee, A.: Recommended security controls for federal information systems (final public draft; nist sp 800-53) (2005)

26. Singh, J., Vargas, L., Bacon, J., Moody, K.: Policy-Based Information Sharing in Publish/Subscribe Middleware. In: IEEE POLICY (2008)

27. Slagell, A., Lakkaraju, K., Luo, K.: Flaim: A multi-level anonymization framework for computer and network logs. In: LISA (2006)

Towards Trustworthy Network Measurements

Ghassan O. Karame

NEC Laboratories Europe
69115 Heidelberg, Germany
`ghassan.karame@neclab.eu`

Abstract. End-to-end network measurement tools are gaining increasing importance in many Internet services. These tools were designed, however, without prior security consideration which renders their extracted network estimates questionable, given the current adversarial Internet. In this paper, we highlight the major security vulnerabilities of existing end-to-end measurement tools and we sketch possible avenues to counter these threats by leveraging functionality from the OpenFlow protocol. More specifically, we show that the security of bottleneck bandwidth estimation and RTT latency measurements in network coordinate systems can be strengthened when the network deploys a number of OpenFlow-operated switches.

Keywords: Software Defined Networks, OpenFlow protocol, Security, Network Measurements.

1 Introduction

The ability to measure the network performance is an intrinsic component in the design of the current Internet. Network measurements are crucial for the operation and security of the Internet, and of several services including content distribution and peer-to-peer (P2P) systems [23]. Numerous tools for estimating network performance have been proposed (e.g., *bandwidth measurement:* Sprobe [24], *latency:* ping [21], *link quality:* mtr [3], etc.). However, the increasing dependence of current applications and services on network measurement tools is showing the limits of foresight in the design of these tools:

- **End-to-end measurements:** Current measurement tools push the measurement function to the end-hosts, and do not require functionality from intermediate network elements (e.g., switches). By doing so, they implicitly assume that end-hosts are honest and behave "correctly". However, if hosts misbehave and do not obey the measurement protocol (e.g., free-riding [23,27]), the estimated end-to-end metric will not reflect the genuine state of the network.
- **No prior security considerations:** Current network measurement tools were developed without prior security considerations, which makes them vulnerable to a number of security threats. Since the measurements are performed end-to-end, the end-hosts might not be able to distinguish these attacks from "authentic" measurements [15,19].

M. Huth et al. (Eds.): TRUST 2013, LNCS 7904, pp. 83–91, 2013.
© Springer-Verlag Berlin Heidelberg 2013

Till recently, the end-to-end principle [22] has provided a justifiable rationale for moving functions closer to the end-hosts and has shaped the way the current Internet is designed. The true leverage of the end-to-end argument was implicitly a global architecture comprising a "naive" network and "smart" applications that do not require functionality from the switching elements deployed within the network. Given this, the design of network measurements tools equally adopted the end-to-end principle, owing to the unavailability of infrastructural support for measurements and to the absence of viable alternatives. This renders the task of securing network measurements rather challenging in the current Internet.

Nowadays, the emergence of Software Defined Networks (SDNs) suggests a slight departure from the end-to-end principle. These networks separate the "control plane" and the "data plane", and thus achieve a large degree of "network virtualization". OpenFlow [5] is one such protocol that enables the construction of SDNs in practice. OpenFlow is a data link layer communication protocol that enables an *OpenFlow controller* to configure paths, in *software*, through a number of *OpenFlow-operated switches*. Here, the controller issues (routing) rules to the switches using a secure control channel; the switches can then dynamically implement the requested rules on the data plane.

In this paper, we argue that the OpenFlow protocol can strengthen the security of applications that rely on end-to-end network measurements. To that end, we start by highlighting the security vulnerabilities of existing network measurement tools. We then sketch possible avenues that leverage OpenFlow to enhance the security of bottleneck bandwidth estimation and of RTT measurements in network coordinate systems. To the best of our knowledge, the security provisions of OpenFlow-enabled networks (and the resulting division of trust between their hosts) have not been yet analyzed in the context of network measurements.

The remainder of the paper is organized as follows. Section 2 compiles a list of security threats encountered in existing measurement tools. In Section 3, we sketch possible avenues to alleviate attacks against network measurements by leveraging functionality from the OpenFlow protocol. Section 4 overviews related work, and we conclude the paper in Section 5.

2   Threats against Network Measurements

In this section, we start by outlining the major security threats against existing end-to-end network measurement tools.

2.1   Threat Model

While they might be different in purpose and technique, most *active* end-to-end measurement tools share a similar model consisting of a *verifier* and a *prover* connected by a *network*. The verifier wants to *measure* and *verify* the end-to-end performance of the path to the prover. The verifier actively generates probe packets destined to the prover, who appropriately echoes back its reply probe packets to the verifier (the prover *cooperates* with the verifier, otherwise the prover will be denied service by the verifier). The verifier then estimates the performance of the end-to-end path to the prover by extracting and analyzing the probe packets' arrival times depending on the measurement technique.

While an external attacker can *spoof* the IP [11] of the prover and issue back replies on its behalf, *untrusted provers* constitute the core of our *internal* attacker model. Untrusted provers denote those hosts involved in the measurement process, but they are not trusted by the verifier to correctly execute the measurement steps. Untrusted provers can *intentionally* manipulate the sending time of their reply probes and claim a measurement value of their choice.

2.2 Delay Attacks on Network Measurements

Most end-to-end measurement tools rely on ICMP or TCP/UDP implementations at end-hosts or at routers to exchange probe packets along a path.

While rushing attacks (where the adversary predicts the reply packets and sends them ahead of time) and impersonation attacks can be countered by relying on lightweight cryptographic primitives, delay attacks pose a serious challenge to existing network measurements tools. An untrusted prover can intentionally *delay* its reply probes to convince the verifier of a performance value of its choice. Delay attacks can result in both inflated (higher) or deflated (lower) measurement esti-

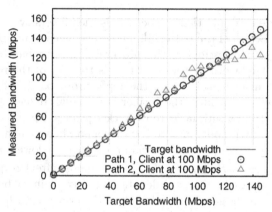

Fig. 1. Delay Attacks on Sprobe [24]. Here, we conducted our measurements on 100 Mbps symmetric physical connections deployed on two paths: **Path1** where both the verifier and the prover are located in the same state, and **Path2** where the verifier is located in Europe and the prover is located in the US.

mates [18,19]. The amount of delay that needs to be introduced depends on the probe size and on the estimation techniques in use.

To perform delay attacks, untrusted provers can "manipulate" their networking interface and introduce appropriate delays that match their desired claims. Alternatively, provers can make use of available software, such as traffic shapers (e.g., NetLimiter [4], HTB [2], etc.) to throttle their outgoing traffic according to a target rate matching their network performance claims.

Example—Delay Attacks on Bandwidth Estimation: The packet-pair technique is a widely adopted technique for measuring the bottleneck bandwidth (the minimum capacity) of an Internet path. To measure the download bandwidth in the packet-pair technique, the verifier sends *two* back-to-back *large* probe packets of equal size to the prover. These packets are likely to queue at the

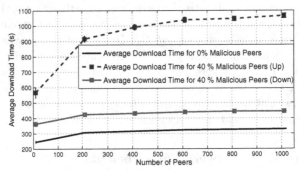

Fig. 2. Impact of bandwidth inflation/deflation attacks on a content distribution network based on multicast binary trees. Each data point is averaged over 1000 runs; where appropriate, we present the corresponding 95% confidence intervals.

bottleneck link; their dispersion is then inversely proportional to the bottleneck bandwidth of the path [24]. The prover then issues back small reply probe-pairs; the verifier estimates the prover's download bandwidth: $B = \frac{S}{T}$, where B is the bandwidth to the prover, S is the size of the request probes, and T is the time dispersion between the reply probe-pair[1] [24]. Similarly, to measure the *upload* bandwidth, the verifier issues small request packet probes; the prover in turn replies with large reply packet probes. The upload bottleneck bandwidth is inversely proportional to the dispersion between the reply packet pairs.

Untrusted provers can claim a higher (or lower) bandwidth by introducing a delay $\Delta = S \cdot |\frac{1}{B_{claimed}} - \frac{1}{B_{auth}}|$ before (after) responding to the first request packet. Here, $B_{claimed}$ denotes the fake claimed bandwidth of the prover and B_{auth} is the genuine bandwidth of the prover [18,19]. We implemented this attack on a popular bandwidth estimation tool based on the packet-pair technique, Sprobe [24]. Our findings are depicted in Figure 1. In the figure, *target bandwidth* refers to the bandwidth that an untrusted prover claims and *measured bandwidth* denotes the bottleneck bandwidth estimate extracted by the verifier. Indeed, the prover can, by appropriately delaying its reply probes, claim a bandwidth of its choice irrespective of its physical bandwidth capability.

Implications of Attacks: We now investigate the impact of the aforementioned attack in a content distribution network (CDN) based on multicast binary trees.

We implemented a C-based simulator that simulates a content distribution network, in which a central verifier measures the bandwidths of peers prior to organizing them in a binary multicast tree. Here, *fast* peers should be located close to the multicast root in order to boost the performance of the network [25]. In our simulations, the nodes' bandwidth were chosen based on the bandwidth distribution in current P2P networks as reported in [23]. Figure 3 shows the detrimental impact of fake bandwidth claims on resource distribution; the average download times over *all* peers in the network *doubles* when 40 % of the

---

[1] Since the reply packets are small in size, their dispersion should reflect the initial dispersion of the large request probes sent by the verifier.

peers claim a lower bandwidth than their own. This effect is more detrimental when those peers claim a higher bandwidth than they actually have; the average download time over all peers almost *quadruples.*

3 Trustworthy Network Measurements Using OpenFlow

In what follows, we analyze the provisions of OpenFlow in strengthening the security of network measurements and their applications. We focus on *bottleneck bandwidth* estimation and on *network coordinate* measurements. Here, we consider the system model outlined in Section 2.1 and we assume a setting where the path between the verifier and the prover traverses a network domain $\mathcal{D}$ that is governed by an OpenFlow controller C. We further assume that C *cooperates* with the verifier in order to ensure the security of the conducted measurements (e.g., cooperation between the CDN and the network operator).

3.1 Bottleneck Bandwidth Estimation

We start by outlining a scheme that leverages the OpenFlow protocol and enables the secure estimation of the upload[2] bottleneck bandwidth of the prover using the packet-pair technique (cf. Section 2.2). Here, we assume that the verifier's download bandwidth is much larger than that of the prover, otherwise, it cannot measure the upload bottleneck bandwidth of the prover.

Our solution unfolds as follows. The verifier crafts request packets that contain pseudo-randomly generated payloads and requires that the reply packet issued by the prover echo the contents of the request packets. This prevents the prover from issuing the reply packets before receiving the corresponding request packets. The verifier also requests that all measurement packets issued by the prover embed within their headers a pre-defined flag (e.g., in the ToS field). This serves to announce to the OpenFlow-operated switches on the path to the verifier that these correspond to bandwidth measurement packets. Finally, the verifier informs the controller C about the IP address of the prover.

C then propagates a rule to the outermost OpenFlow-operated switch that connects to the *prover*, requesting to *queue* all the packets that it receives from the IP addresses of the prover, whose headers contain a measurement flag. This removes any additional delay that the prover may have inserted within the transmission of its packet-pairs. This process is shown in Figure 3(a). In the OpenFlow protocol, this request is defined through a FLOW_MOD message type. For instance, a FLOW_MOD message that requests from a switch to queue packets that originate from IP address "x.y.z.w" and that have the ToS field set to "11111111" looks like:

Match set: All wildcards but (NW_DST that has value "x.y.z.w" AND NW_TOS that has value "11111111")
Action set: ENQUEUE (queue: 1, port: a)

---

[2] A similar analysis equally applies for download bandwidth estimation.

Here, queue 1 must be appropriately defined on the switch in question; the scheduler releases packets from this queue only when it contains at least two packets. In addition, the controller C requests that the switch forwards the packets (that are filtered in the above match set), along with their received timestamps, to C (e.g., in the control plane), who in turn sends them to the verifier. Let $disp$ denote the dispersion between the packet-pair received by the verifier, and let $\delta = (t_2 - t_1)$, where t_1 and t_2 denote the respective reception time of the packet-pair at the switch, as reported by C. Here, two cases emerge:

- $\delta \leq disp$. Here, the bottleneck link is located between the verifier and the OpenFlow switch. Since the latter queued the packet-pair, the verifier is certain that the bandwidth estimate is correct.
- $disp < \delta$. In this case, the bottleneck link is located on the prover's side of the OpenFlow switch and the verifier is certain that the bottleneck bandwidth B of the prover ranges between: $\frac{S}{\delta} \leq B \leq \frac{S}{disp}$, where S is the size of the reply packets of the prover.

The closer is the prover from an OpenFlow-operated switch in $\mathcal{D}$, the more accurate is the estimate acquired by the verifier. That is, the smaller is the number of hops that separate the prover from the outermost OpenFlow-operated switch, the higher is the probability that the bottleneck link is located after the switch, on the path to the verifier. This conforms with recent studies that show that bottleneck links typically co-exist within inter-domains links [12].

3.2   Network Coordinate Measurements

Network coordinate systems provide hosts with the means to easily learn their coordinates (RTT latencies) relative to other hosts in the network. In these systems, hosts compute their "coordinates" in the network by measuring their latency to other nodes [9]. In [15,16], Kaafar *at al.* analyzed the impact of delay attacks on network coordinate systems and propose the reliance on surveyor nodes to counter these threats. In what follows, we show that the reliance on OpenFlow-enabled switches can also alleviate delay attacks on these systems. Here, we assume that the prover wants to claim a coordinate position of its choice relative to the verifier (e.g., to be placed favorably in a CDN).

The verifier measures the coordinate position of the prover as follows. The verifier crafts its echo request packets, by ensuring that their content cannot be predicted (to prevent rushing attacks) and by inserting a pre-defined flag in their headers (e.g., in the ToS field). The verifier also requires that the prover's reply packets *(i)* are correlated in content to the request packets (e.g., echoing the request packets) and *(ii)* embed the flag in their headers. Given the IP address of both the prover and the verifier, the controller C then dynamically configures a random path (across the OpenFlow-operated switches) that the packets (whose headers contain a flag) exchanged among the verifier and the prover traverse (Figure 3(b)). For example, in the OpenFlow protocol version 1.0, this is defined through the following message that is propagated to each switch in $\mathcal{D}$:

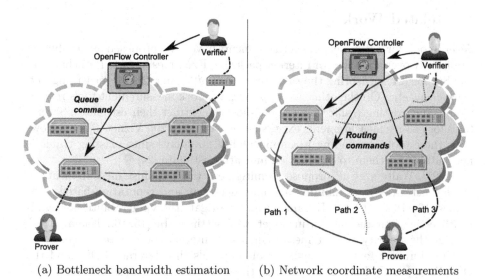

(a) Bottleneck bandwidth estimation   (b) Network coordinate measurements

Fig. 3. Leveraging OpenFlow to strengthen the security of network measurements. The shaded area corresponds to a domain $\mathcal{D}$ that is located on the measured path.

Match set: All wildcards but (NW_DST that has value "x.y.z.w" AND NW_TOS that has value "11111110")
Action set: OUTPUT (port: a)

Here, by defining the output port of the flow, C manages the routing of the filtered packets. C also informs the verifier about the chosen path; the verifier in turn measures the RTT to the prover of the packets traversing the configured path. This process is repeated for a number of independent runs, in which different paths are configured by the controller. Note that these paths need to be chosen such that the same outermost OpenFlow-operated switch does not repeat across different runs. Since the prover cannot predict the path that the packets will follow to the verifier, it is easy to see that the prover cannot insert the accurate amount of delays [16] in order to claim a latency/coordinate of its choice relative to the various OpenFlow-operated switches (and therefore to the verifier, since the latter knows its RTT latency relative to the switches[3]).

Clearly, the bigger is the domain $\mathcal{D}$, the larger is the number of OpenFlow-operated switches, and the harder it is for the prover to predict the path (and the corresponding required delay) to the verifier. We point out that, here, the prover does not have to be located in the proximity of $\mathcal{D}$.[4]

---

[3] These act as hidden landmarks [8] to securely position the prover.
[4] In the case where the prover is located is the close proximity of an OpenFlow switch in $\mathcal{D}$, then the verifier can directly estimate the position of the prover since it knows the relative coordinate of the OpenFlow-operated switch.

4   Related Work

Several tools for *active* network measurements have been proposed and evaluated empirically over a number of Internet paths [1]. Examples include Pathchar [13], and Sprobe [24] measuring the *bottleneck bandwidth*, ping [21] for measuring *network delay*, etc.. On the other hand, *passive* network measurement tools rely on monitoring existing traffic between end-hosts to extract their estimates. Several tools for passive measurements exist, such as Nettimer [20], Viznet [6], etc.. However, these tools are finding less applicability nowadays since existing traffic is not suitable for them to produce an indicative estimate [24].

In [27], Walters *et al.* propose to mitigate attacks against measurements in overlay networks by combining anomaly detection and reputation-based techniques [10, 17]. In [18, 19], Karame *et al.* investigate the vulnerabilities of bandwidth estimation techniques in adversarial settings. In [15, 16], Kaafar *et al.* analyze the security of RTT measurements in Internet coordinate systems.

The literature features a number of proposals that leverage SDNs and the OpenFlow protocol [14, 26]. However, these contributions focus on monitoring the network status, and do not address the security of network measurements.

5   Concluding Remarks

Given the current trends in designing a "clean-slate" future Internet, this paper motivates the need for a *secure* next-generation Internet. Given the importance of network monitoring, *secure* infrastructural support for network measurements becomes rather a necessity [7]. In this respect, we showed that OpenFlow-operated networks can strengthen the security of applications that rely on end-to-end network measurements.

However, even if most switches in the network provide support for network measurements, we still expect other hazards to arise with respect to the security of the overall network. Indeed, the reliance on dedicated measurement components requires the presence of trusted authorities that control and maintain these components. Here, access control to the infrastructure is a crucial design property; any compromise might result in severe performance deterioration throughout the entire network. Overcoming these limitations requires a careful design of the measurement functions in the future Internet.

Acknowledgements. The author would like to thank Srdjan Capkun for the helpful discussions and valuable comments. The author would also like to thank Roberto Bifulco for the various discussions on the OpenFlow protocol.

References

1. CAIDA, tools: taxonomies,
   http://www.caida.org/tools/taxonomy/performance.xml
2. HTB Traffic Shaper, http://luxik.cdi.cz/~devik/qos/htb/
3. mtr, http://www.bitwizard.nl/mtr/

4. NetLimiter, `http://www.netlimiter.com/`
5. OpenFlow–Enabling Innovation in your Network, `http://www.openflow.org/`
6. Viznet, `http://dast.nlanr.net/Projects/Viznet/`
7. Barford, P.: Measurement as a First Class Network Citizen, `http://pages.cs.wisc.edu/~pb/sngi_whitepaper.pdf`
8. Capkun, S., Rasmussen, K.B., Cagalj, M., Srivastava, M.: Secure Location Verification With Hidden and Mobile Base Stations. IEEE Transactions on Mobile Computing (TMC) (2008)
9. Dabek, F., Cox, R., Kaashoek, F., Morris, R.: Vivaldi: A Decentralized Network Coordinate System. In: Proceedings of SIGCOMM (2004)
10. Dimitriou, T., Karame, G., Christou, I.: SuperTrust – A Secure and Efficient Framework for Handling Trust in Super Peer Networks. In: Proceedings of ACM PODC (2007)
11. Harris, B., Hunt, R.: TCP/IP security threats and attack methods. Computer Communications (1999)
12. Hu, N., Li, L., Mao, Z.M., Steenkiste, P., Wang, J.: A Measurement Study of Internet Bottlenecks. In: Proceedings of INFOCOM (2005)
13. Jocobson, V.: Pathchar, `http://www.caida.org/tools/utilities/others/pathchar`
14. Jose, L., Yu, M., Rexford, J.: Online measurement of large traffic aggregates on commodity switches. In: Proceedings of Hot-ICE (2011)
15. Kaafar, M.A., Mathy, L., Barakat, C., Salamatian, K., Turletti, T., Dabbous, W.: Securing Internet Coordinate Embedding Systems. In: Proceedings of ACM SIGCOMM (2007)
16. Kaafar, M.A., Mathy, L., Turletti, T., Dabbous, W.: Virtual Networks under Attack: Disrupting Internet Coordinate Systems. In: Proceedings of CoNext (2006)
17. Karame, G., Christou, I., Dimitriou, T.: A Secure Hybrid Reputation Management System for Super-Peer Networks. In: Proceedings of IEEE CCNC (2008)
18. Karame, G., Gubler, D., Čapkun, S.: On the Security of Bottleneck Bandwidth Estimation Techniques. In: Chen, Y., Dimitriou, T.D., Zhou, J. (eds.) SecureComm 2009. LNICST, vol. 19, pp. 121–141. Springer, Heidelberg (2009)
19. Karame, G., Danev, B., Bannwart, C., Capkun, S.: On the Security of End-to-End Measurements based on Packet-Pair Dispersions. IEEE Transactions on Information Forensics & Security (TIFS) (2013)
20. Lai, K., Baker, M.: Nettimer: A Tool for Measuring Bottleneck Link Bandwidth. In: Proceedings of USITS (2001)
21. Muuss, M.: ping, `ftp://ftp.arl.mil/pub/ping.shar`
22. Saltzer, J.H., Reed, D.P., Clark, D.D.: End-to-End Arguments in System Design. ACM Transactions on Computer Systems (1984)
23. Saroiu, S., Gummadi, P., Gribble, S.: A Measurement Study of Peer-to-Peer File Sharing Systems. In: Proceedings of MMCN (2002)
24. Sariou, S., Gummadi, P., Gribble, S.: SProbe: A Fast Technique for Measuring Bottleneck Bandwidth in Uncooperative Environments. In: INFOCOM (2002)
25. Schiely, M., Renfer, L., Felber, P.: Self-Organization in Cooperative Content Distribution Networks. In: Proceedings of NCA (2005)
26. Tootoonchian, A., Ghobadi, M., Ganjali, Y.: OpenTM: Traffic matrix estimator for OpenFlow networks. In: Krishnamurthy, A., Plattner, B. (eds.) PAM 2010. LNCS, vol. 6032, pp. 201–210. Springer, Heidelberg (2010)
27. Walters, A., Zage, D., Nita-Rotaru, C.: A Framework for Mitigating Attacks Against Measurement-Based Adaptation Mechanisms in Unstructured Multicast Overlay Networks. ACM/IEEE Transactions on Networking (2007)

Stochastic Model of a Metastability-Based True Random Number Generator

Molka Ben-Romdhane[1,2], Tarik Graba[1], and Jean-Luc Danger[1,2]

[1] Institut Mines-Télécom; Télécom ParisTech; CNRS LTCI
[2] Secure-IC S.A.S.
{benromdh,graba,danger}@telecom-paristech.fr

Abstract. True random number generator (TRNG) designers should provide a stochastic model of the target of evaluation to be compliant with the AIS-31 standard evaluation process. In this paper, we present a model of a TRNG that extracts its randomness from the metastable behavior of a D-Latch. Such a model needs to be set up for the TRNG evaluation process. In this work, we describe and analyse the randomness coming from a chain of D-Latches when set near their metastable state. Then, we present a physical model of a metastability-based TRNG. The main novelty of this paper is the stochastic modeling process of a metastability-based TRNG. The presented model is validated on FPGA and a 65nm CMOS technology prototype chip.

Keywords: TRNG, metastability, model, randomness, noise, AIS-31.

1 Introduction

Randomness generation is needed for many applications spanning from Monte Carlo simulations to security communications. Also many cryptographic protocols are contingent to the unpredictability of random variable. A critical part to validate a true random number generator (TRNG) is to satisfy stringent verifications to make sure the function is not biased. For instance, statistical tests have been precisely specified by NIST in [1], BSI in [2] or FIPS in [3]. In the case of AIS-31 evaluation methodology of physical true random number generators [2], TRNG designers should provide a stochastic model of the TRNG behavior besides the compliance with the statistical tests.

On-chip TRNGs extract randomness from the chip ambient noise. There are many noise sources in CMOS circuits. Some of them are deterministic and others are random. Thermal noise, shot noise and $(1/f)$ noise are considered as random noise sources [4]. By applying the central limit theorem, the noise exhibits a Normal probability density distribution [5].

In this paper, a stochastic model of a metastability-based TRNG is presented. This TRNG design is an open-loop structure which extracts the noise entropy by placing a memorizing cell in a metastable state, then observing the stable state which is the consequence of the noise impact. The presented metastability-based

M. Huth et al. (Eds.): TRUST 2013, LNCS 7904, pp. 92–105, 2013.

TRNG output takes advantage of a metastable state, *MSS*, which converges to a final stable state depending on the noise value. Simulations have been performed to estimate the parameters that describe the proposed model. To validate this model, we perform AIS-31 standard statistic tests on acquisitions of both FPGA and ASIC targets.

Stochastic models of a PLL-based TRNG, a noisy diodes physical RNG and a floating-gate-based TRNG were introduced respectively in [6], [7] and [8]. Several analog and digital TRNG designs that extracts randomness from metastability have been proposed in ([9], [10], [11], [12] and [13]). Given our current knowledge, there is no such model for metastability-based TRNG in the literature.

As TRNGs require specific certifications, randomness must be proven first by model then by applying the generated sequence a battery of standard tests. We devote this paper to these two important steps of TRNG design. This paper is organized as follows: In the second section, an introduction to the basics of metastability is given. Then, an analytic expression is established to compute the model parameters. The third section deals with the modeling process and probability computation of the metastability-based TRNG output. In the fourth section, we validate the presented metastability-based TRNG model by comparing simulation results against test-chip measurements.

2   Modeling and Characterisation of Metastability

In storage elements, such as latches and flip–flops, whenever the delay between the clock and data violates the setup or hold time requirements, the normal behavior is not guaranteed. In fact, the input D must be stable for a duration of at least t_{setup} before the active edge of clock and it must remain stable for at least t_{hold} after the same clock edge. If those timing conditions are not met, the output state can go through an intermediate state where its value is not a valid logic value. This intermediate state is called metastable state. The final valid state of the storage element, either 0 or 1, is then not predictable and depends on the circuit ambient noise. The metastability-based TRNG design exploits this phenomenon to generate unpredictable random numbers. The main goal of this work is to try to model the behavior of the TRNG structure and quantify the output entropy.

To characterise this behaviour, let us consider the internal structure of a standard cell D-Latch as shown in Fig. 1a. This D-Latch is designed using tri–state gates controlled by the clock signal G and two back-to-back inverters commonly used in static storage elements. In the following, we consider an active low transparent D-Latch. When the value of the input clock signal G is '0', the D-Latch is said to be transparent, i.e. the output Q is equal to the input D, and when the value of the input clock signal G is '1' the D-Latch is said to be memorizing, i.e., the output Q keeps its value.

Depending on signal arrival times, the three situations are possible as shown in Fig. 1b:

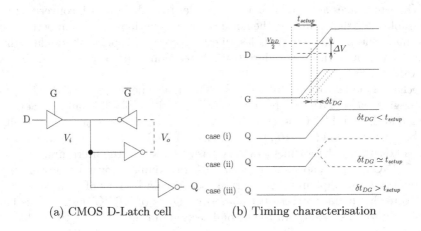

<table>
<tr><td>(a) CMOS D-Latch cell</td><td>(b) Timing characterisation</td></tr>
</table>

Fig. 1. D-Latch internal structure and timing characterisation

(i) The delay between the clock G and the data D, δt_{DG}, is greater than t_{setup}. This implies the Q output goes rapidly to V_{DD}.

(ii) $\delta t_{DG} \simeq t_{setup}$. This means there is a t_{setup} violation and Q may remain stuck around an intermediate voltage level V_{MSS} which is neither a $0V$ nor V_{DD}.

(iii) δt_{DG}, is less than t_{setup} the output Q never leaves $0V$.

Fig. 2 shows the clock-to-output propagation delay T_{GQ} versus the data-to-clock delay δt_{DG}.

When the setup requirements are respected ($\delta t_{DG} < t_{setup}$), the propagation delay is constant and corresponds to the propagation delay of a transparent D-Latch $T_{GQ_{max}}$ given by the manufacturer. When δt_{DG} decreases, the propagation time T_{GQ} increases with a logarithmic shape. This increase is due to the recovery time from metastability. The asymptotic limit defines a minimum setup time for which the propagation delay T_{GQ} becomes infinite. In the following, we refer to this asymptotic value as T_{setup0}.

The metastable state, *MSS*, is a state where the output voltage is neither a valid low nor a high logic state such as depicted in Fig. 3a. In this state the voltage values of both the input and the output of the static storage element, have the same value $V_{MSS} \simeq \frac{V_{DD}}{2}$.

Around this point, the inverters of the static storage element can be modeled as two amplifiers with a negative gain ($-A$) where $A \gg 1$ [14] [15] (we consider equal gains for both inverters for the simplicity of expression). Each inverter drives a resistance R and a capacitive load C (considered equal to simplify the expression) which models the gates and connections at each outputs as represented in Fig. 3b. In the absence of noise, the voltage of the internal node V_o

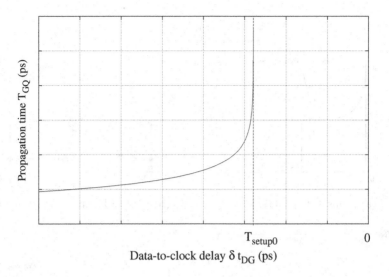

Fig. 2. Behavior of the propagation delay time T_{GQ} vs. δt_{DG} of a CMOS D-Latch.

should remain stuck at this intermediate voltage, around $\frac{V_{DD}}{2}$. The probability to enter a *MSS* whose duration is longer than t_m is expressed as follows [16]:

$$p(t > t_m) = e^{-\frac{(A-1)}{\tau} \cdot t_m} \tag{1}$$

Practically, when the G switches to '1' the node voltage is never exactly $\frac{V_{DD}}{2}$, and even then, ambient noise can shift this position. This bias will condition the final logical value and the time to reach it as shown in Fig. 3c. In fact, ΔV_{DG_0} impacts on the final state of the D-Latch. Fig. 3d shows the behavior of the internal memorizing net at *MSS* state for different data-to-clock delays. The figure (b) is a zoom of (a) around $\frac{V_{DD}}{2}$.

The expression of the voltage difference $V(t) = V_o(t) - V_i(t)$ around *MSS* is given in equation (2) [15]:

$$V(t) = \Delta V_{DG_0} \cdot e^{\frac{A-1}{\tau}t} \tag{2}$$

Where $\Delta V_{DG_0} = (V_o - V_i)(0)$ is the voltage difference at the moment where the D-Latch switches to memorizing mode. $\tau = R \cdot C$ is the time constant.

We introduce a threshold voltage V_{th} around *MSS*. This threshold corresponds to the voltage over which the state goes from *MSS* to a valid logic value.

$$T_r = \frac{\tau}{A-1} \ln\left(\frac{\Delta V_{th}}{\Delta V_{DG_0}}\right) \tag{3}$$

T_r represents the time needed to leave the metastable state or the increase in the propagation delay.

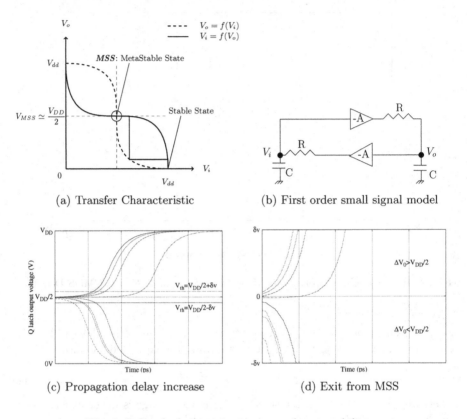

(a) Transfer Characteristic   (b) First order small signal model

(c) Propagation delay increase   (d) Exit from MSS

Fig. 3. D-Latch characterization around metastability

As shown in Fig. 1b, we consider a linear relation between the voltage differences ΔV and the delay in arrival times of the D and G signals such as:

$$\Delta V_{th} = \alpha\, A \cdot \delta t_{th}$$
$$\Delta V_{DG_0} = \alpha\, A \cdot \delta t_{DG} \tag{4}$$

Where α is the slope of the clock and data input and A the gain of inverter.

Thus, by replacing the expression of V_{th} in (3) we can express the resolving time as a function of the time delays as in equation (5).

$$T_r = \frac{\tau}{A-1} \ln\left(\frac{\delta t_{th}}{\delta t_{DG}}\right) \tag{5}$$

Which can be rewritten as:

$$T_r = \gamma(\beta - \ln \delta t_{DG}) \tag{6}$$

Equation (6) shows that the D-Latch propagation delay $T_{GQ} = T_r + T_{GQ_{max}}$ increases as δt_{DG} decreases. And this is what we obtain at simulation as shown in Fig. 2.

The next section provides a detailed analysis of the noise impact on the TRNG and the probability analysis of the output.

3   Stochastic Model of the Metastability-Based TRNG

3.1   Randomness Extraction

To maximize the probability to catch a metastable event at each clock cycle, a high speed metastability-based TRNG structure [10] has been introduced. This structure is illustrated in Fig. 4 and is composed of N latches and a delay structure to assure a race between the clock and data signals. The offset is first adjusted by two coarse chains with two control signals *ctrd* and *ctr* for the data and the clock, respectively.

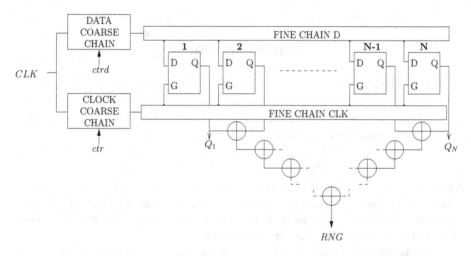

Fig. 4. Structure of the metastability-based TRNG

For the ith D-Latch, δt_{DG_i} represents the delay between D and G signals (G being the clock input of the latch). This delay is incremented between two consecutive latches by a differentiel delay δt, as expressed in equation (7). δt comes from the difference between the two fine delay chains D and CLK.

$$\delta t_{DG_{i+1}} = \delta t + \delta t_{DG_i} \tag{7}$$

Fig. 5 shows the clock-to-data delay at consecutive latches, superposed with the propagation characteristic of a D-Latch. This delay can be expressed,

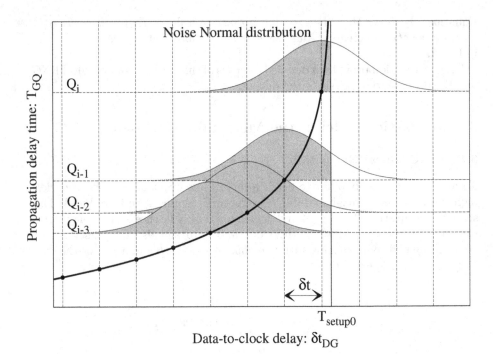

Fig. 5. The probability to correctly sample the input for consecutive latches

as in (8), as the sum of a deterministic delay, which correspond to the signals race and a random delay, which models the noise impact.

$$\delta t_{DG_i} = \Delta D_0 - i \cdot \delta t + \mathcal{N}(\delta t) \tag{8}$$

Where $\mathcal{N}(\sigma)$ is the Normal distribution and ΔD_0 is the initial delay between G and D introduced by the data and clock coarse chains. The incertitude distribution is considered Normal as it models the influence of the multiple noise sources in accordance with the central limit theorem [17].

The D-Latch will sample a high logic value 1 if this delay is smaller than T_{setup0}. We denote $p_{Q_i} = p(Q_i = 1)$ this probability:

$$p_{Q_i} = p(\delta t_{DG_i} < T_{setup0}) \tag{9}$$

This corresponds to the gray colored area of the Normal bell in Fig. 5. This probability can thus be analytically expressed as:

$$p_{Q_i} = \frac{1}{2}\left[1 - \text{erf}(\frac{\delta t_{DG_i} - T_{setup0}}{\sigma\sqrt{2}})\right] \tag{10}$$

Where:

– T_{setup0} is the experimental asymptotic limit such as represented in Fig. 5.
– $\text{erf}(x)$ is the error function.

3.2   Probabilistic Analysis of Metastability-Based TRNG

In the following, we use the notation p_X, representing $p(X = 1)$, where X is a Normal random variable. Since the TRNG output is the XOR of the N D-Latch, as illustrated in Fig. 4, the probability to have TRNG output equal to 1 is the probability parity of having an odd number of the N Q outputs D-Latch settling down to a logic 1. Let $p_{TRNG} = p(TRNG = 1)$ be the probability to have 1 on the TRNG output. Here we distinguish two cases:

(i) Influence of noise on each of the N Latches is independent.
(ii) The value of Q_i of D-Latch i impacts the output value Q_{i+1} of the $(i+1)^{th}$ D-Latch.

In the case (i), computing this probability p_{TRNG} is equivalent to compute the probability of a N-inputs XOR to be equal to 1. Let us consider the first two latches Q_1 and Q_2. Equation (11) represents the probability to obtain '1' at the output of the first stage 2-inputs XOR.

$$\begin{aligned} p_{Q_1 \oplus Q_2} &= p_{Q_1} \cdot \overline{p_{Q_2}} + \overline{p_{Q_1}} \cdot p_{Q_2} \\ &= p_{Q_1} \cdot (1 - p_{Q_2}) + (1 - p_{Q_1}) \cdot p_{Q_2} \\ p_{Q_1 \oplus Q_2} &= p_{Q_1} + p_{Q_2} - 2p_{Q_1}p_{Q_2} \end{aligned} \tag{11}$$

Equation (12) is the factorized expression of (11).

$$\begin{aligned} 1 - 2p_{Q_1 \oplus Q_2} &= 1 - 2p_{Q_1} - 2p_{Q_2} + 4p_{Q_1}p_{Q_2} \\ &= (1 - 2p_{Q_1}) \cdot (1 - 2p_{Q_2}) \end{aligned} \tag{12}$$

Then, by mathematical induction, we can generalize the expression for N-inputs XOR as shown in (13).

$$1 - 2p(\bigoplus_{i=1}^{N} Q_i = 1) = \prod_{i=1}^{N}(1 - 2p_{Q_i}) \tag{13}$$

Thus, from equation (13), the final expression of $p(TRNG = 1)$ is:

$$p_{TRNG} = \frac{1}{2}[1 - \prod_{i=1}^{N}(1 - 2p_{Q_i})] \tag{14}$$

In case (ii) where p_{Q_i} impacts $p_{Q_{i+1}}$ if Q_i equals '1' there is no way that Q_{i+1} equals '0', we can thus eliminate some terms in eq. 14.

For example, for a 3-inputs XOR, only the following input triplets (1,0,0) and (1,1,1) are left. Hence, the probability of the output of XOR $p_{Q_0 \oplus Q_1 \oplus Q_2} = p(Q_0 \oplus Q_1 \oplus Q_2 = 1)$ would be expressed as follows:

$$p_{Q_1 \oplus Q_2 \oplus Q_3} = p_1 \cdot (1 - p_2) \cdot (1 - p_3) + p_1 \cdot p_2 \cdot p_3$$

For a 4-inputs XOR, the product of all p_i does not appear in the final probability, as the XOR of an even number of ones is 0.

$$p_{Q_1 \oplus Q_2 \oplus Q_3 \oplus Q_4} = p_1 \cdot (1 - p_2) \cdot (1 - p_3) \cdot (1 - p_4) + p_1 \cdot p_2 \cdot p_3 \cdot (1 - p_4)$$

By mathematical induction, we can establish a general expression of $p_{TRNG} = p(TRNG = 1)$ for an N-inputs XOR (here N is even). Eq. (15) represents thus the probability p_{TRNG} in case (ii).

$$p_{TRNG} = \sum_{i=1}^{\frac{N}{2}} \prod_{j=1}^{2i-1} p_{Q_j} \cdot \prod_{j=2i}^{N} (1 - p_{Q_j}) \tag{15}$$

In the next section, we present the model verifications by simulation and experimental results on the test-chip. Then, the AIS-31 statistical tests are applied on the random number generated by metastability-based prototypes on both FPGA and ASIC technology targets.

4   Model Verification

TRNG simulations with noise show that the impact of noise on the D-Latch chain is correlated such as explained in case (ii) of the section 3.2.

4.1   Model Validation by Simulation

We plot the increase of T_{GQ} vs. δt_{DG} for a D-Latch standard cell with $1fs$ resolution to estimate the model parameters of equation (10). We find that T_{setup0} is equal to -38.385ps. The differential delay δt introduced by the fine delay chains equals to $1ps$. Then, to extract the parameter σ, standard deviation of the TRNG noise source, transient electrical simulation of a single D-Latch standard cell are held with a noisy data input D for different σ.

Fig. 6 depicts the probability $p(Q = 1)$ as a function of noise standard for two different deterministic delays chosen around T_{setup0}. In Fig. 6a the offset is of -1ps from T_{setup0} and for Fig. 6b it is $1ps$. When the standard deviation of the noise is small, the probability is either 1 or 0 depending on the relative position to T_{setup0}. In this case, no random behaviour will be observed. When the standard deviation is higher than $10ps$, the probability tends to 0.5 making the output final logic value unpredictable.

Fig. 7 represents the simulated probability $p(Q = 1)$ with a noise standard deviation $\sigma = 5ps$ for offsets from T_{setup0} in the interval $[-10,10]ps$. The dashed curve represents, the theoretical $p(Q = 1)$, i.e. the function $f(x) = \frac{1}{2}(1 - erf(\frac{x}{\sqrt{2}\sigma}))$ with $\sigma = 5$ while the plane line curve represents the simulated probability.

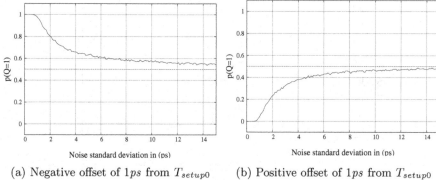

(a) Negative offset of $1ps$ from T_{setup0} (b) Positive offset of $1ps$ from T_{setup0}

Fig. 6. The probability $p(Q = 1)$ *vs.* the noise standard deviation

Then, the same simulation experiment is performed on the TRNG composed of $N = 64$ latches while varying the standard deviation of the noisy data input. Fig. 8 shows side to side the probability p_{TRNG} *vs.* the noise standard deviation obtained from both analytic expression (Eq. (15) and Eq. (14)) and from the spice simulation for one configuration the coarse delay chain ($ctr = 0x00$, $ctrd = 0x00$). We see that for small noise standard deviation both analytic expressions give similar values. This figure also shows that the proposed model matches well the simulation results.

4.2   Silicon Proven Metastability-Based TRNG

In order to validate the TRNG model, we have applied standard statistical tests. FIPS 140-2, AIS-31 and NIST are three evaluation test standards commonly used to validate the randomness quality.

T0-T5 AIS-31 tests are applied on the digitized noise signal after post-processing. FIPS 140-2 [3] are similar to T1-T4 tests with different rejection limits. P2 tests class of AIS-31 (corresponding to T6-T7-T8) are the sole that have to be applied on the raw output of the TRNG, i.e. before any post-processing, as specified in the AIS-31 evaluation methodology [2].

In what follow, we will thus only present the results of the AIS-31 tests. We ran the different AIS-31 statistical tests on $20Mbits$ samples from an ASIC test-chip and for an FPGA implementation. In both FPGA and ASIC prototype, the TRNG structure is composed of N=64 latches.

ASIC Test-Chip Experiments. The test-chips were fabricated in the 65nm CMOS technology process by STMicroelectronics. Two versions of the TRNG have been use, the first one has a δt equals to $5ps$, later referred to as TRNG1, while the second has a δt smaller than a $1ps$, later referred to as TRNG2.

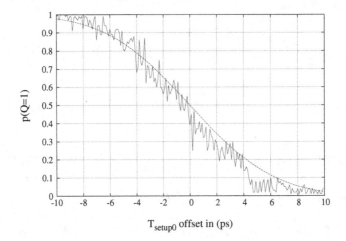

Fig. 7. The probability $p(Q = 1)$ *vs.* the offset from T_{setup0} for a noise standard deviation $\sigma = 5ps$.

The probability $p(TRNG = 1)$ has been measured for different values of the clock to data offset adjusted by $ctrd$ and ctr coarse chain control signals. The values reported in Table 1 for TRNG1 allow to conclude that the noise standard deviation is rather low compared to the diffrential delay δt as most of the probability value are far from 0.5, as shown by the model and simulation probability curves. For exemple, for the coarse chain configuration ($ctr = 0x00$, $ctrd = 0x00$), the probability p_{TRNG} measured on the testchip over 100000 samples as in Table 1 is 84.25%. If we compare this value to the probability obtained for the same configuration from the model and the spice simulation (Fig. 8a and Fig. 8b), we can see that this probability corresponds to a noise standard deviation around $2ps$.

Table 1. $p(TRNG = 1)$ measured on the testchip for TRNG1 and diffrent ctr and $ctrd$ configurations of the coarse delay chains

ctrd \ ctr	0x00	0x01	0x03	0x07	0x0F	0x1F	0x3F	0x7F
0x00	84.25	95.97	77.91	94.13	88.45	4.98	8.11	91.79
0x01	0.14	0.68	21.43	49.65	96.93	100	94.88	55.91
0x03	100	100	74.94	53.8	98.95	99.99	2.16	99.87
0x07	0.11	7.23	98.49	99.73	74.98	0.28	27.95	100
0x0F	0	0	100	97.39	99.7	26.31	49.83	63.27
0x1F	0	0	93.9	44.96	28.17	76.4	94.09	9.37
0x3F	0	0	0	58.84	2.16	40.51	32.82	99.97
0x7F	0	0	0	1.6	38.2	99.98	5.47	66.77

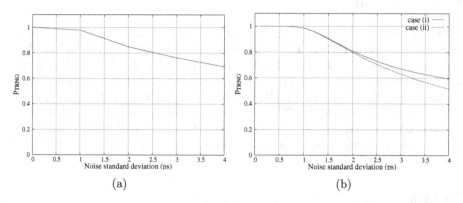

Fig. 8. The probability p_{TRNG} vs. the noise standard deviation (a) simulation (b) analytic expressions.

Table 2. AIS-31 Class P2 Statistical tests results of ASIC (TRNG2 version) and FPGA TRNG

AIS-31 Class P2 Tests	FPGA	ASIC
Uniform distribution test procedure T6a	Pass	Pass
Uniform distribution test procedure T6b	Pass	Pass
Test for homogeneity procedure T7a	Pass	Pass
Test for homogeneity procedure T7b	Pass	Pass
Entropy estimation test T8	Pass	Fail

Results of P2 Class statistical tests on the ASIC TRNG2 without post-processing are reported in Table 2.

P1 class tests have also been run on post-processed samples. Only Von Neumann post-processing have been used here to balance the number of zeros and ones and both TRNGs pass this class of tests.

Results of the TRNG1 version are not presented because more tests fail (3 over 5). This is basically due to a larger δt, which is larger than the exploitable noise standard deviation.

FPGA Experiments. The FPGA implementation has been done on a Xilinx Virtex-5 FPGA device, the delay δt is equal to $6ps$. Random bits acquired on this implementation passes both P1 and P2 classes tests of the AIS-31 statistical tests, without any post-processing as shown in Table 2. This makes us think that in an FPGA exploitable noise has a larger standard deviation than what can be observed in an ASIC implementation. This difference could come from the routing structure of the FPGA which contains more active elements (switch matrices, line buffers ...) that generate more noise.

5   Conclusion

In this paper, we presented a stochastic approach to model and characterize a metastability-based TRNG. The principle is to place a D-Latch in a metastable state, then sample the stable state which is the consequence of the chip ambient noise impact. We discussed and presented the method that allows to compute the parameters of the modeling equation through electrical simulation. The probability expression of the TRNG is computed in terms of the noise standard deviation, the characteristics of the D-Latch T_{setup0}, and the delay δt of the delay chain elements. This stochastic model has been validated on an ST 65nm test-chip and FPGA.

References

1. NIST: Recommendation for the entropy sources used for random bit generation (2012),
   http://csrc.nist.gov/publications/drafts/800-90/draft-sp800-90b.pdf
2. Schindler, W., Killmann, W.: A proposal for: Functionality classes for random number generators1 (September 2011)
3. Federal Information Processing Standards (FIPS) Publication 140-2. Security requirements for cryptographic modules (May 25, 2001),
   http://csrc.nist.gov/publications/fips/fips140-2/fips1402.pdf
4. Mandal, M.K., Sarkar, B.C.: Ring oscillators: Characteristics and applications. Indian Journal of Pure and Applied Physics 48, 136–145 (2010)
5. Korkmaz, P., Akgul, B.E.S., Palem, K.V.: Characterizing the behavior of a probabilistic cmos switch through analytical models and its verification through simulations (2005)
6. Simka, M., Drutarovsky, M., Fischer, V., Fayolle, J.: Model of a true random number generator aimed at cryptographic applications. In: Proceedings of the 2006 IEEE International Symposium on Circuits and Systems, ISCAS 2006, p. 4 (May 2006)
7. Killmann, W., Schindler, W.: A design for a physical RNG with robust entropy estimators. In: Oswald, E., Rohatgi, P. (eds.) CHES 2008. LNCS, vol. 5154, pp. 146–163. Springer, Heidelberg (2008)
8. Xu, P., Horiuchi, T., Abshire, P.: Stochastic model and simulation of a random number generator circuit. In: IEEE International Symposium on Circuits and Systems, ISCAS 2008, pp. 2977–2980 (May 2008)
9. Kinniment, D.J., Chester, E.G.: Design of an on-chip random number generator using metastability. In: Proceedings of the 28th European Solid-State Circuit Conference (2002)
10. Danger, J.-L., Guilley, S., Hoogvorst, P.: High Speed True Random Number Generator based on Open Loop Structures in FPGAs. Microelectronics Journal 40(11), 1650–1656 (2009), doi:10.1016/j.mejo.2009.02.004
11. Suresh, V.B., Burleson, W.P.: Entropy extraction in metastability-based TRNG. In: HOST, pp. 135–140 (2010)
12. Majzoobi, M., Koushanfar, F., Devadas, S.: FPGA-based true random number generation using circuit metastability with adaptive feedback control. In: Preneel, B., Takagi, T. (eds.) CHES 2011. LNCS, vol. 6917, pp. 17–32. Springer, Heidelberg (2011)

13. Hata, H., Ichikawa, S.: Fpga implementation of metastability-based true random number generator. IEICE Transactions 95-D(2), 426–436 (2012)
14. Chen, D., Singh, D., Chromczak, J., Lewis, D., Fung, R., Neto, D., Betz, V.: A comprehensive approach to modeling, characterizing and optimizing for metastability in fpgas. In: Proceedings of the 18th Annual ACM/SIGDA International Symposium on Field Programmable Gate Arrays, FPGA 2010, pp. 167–176. ACM, New York (2010)
15. Ginosar, R.: Metastability and synchronizers: A tutorial. IEEE Design Test of Computers 28(5), 23–35 (2011)
16. Veendrick, H.J.M.: The behaviour of flip-flops used as synchronizers and prediction of their failure rate. IEEE Journal of Solid-State Circuits 15(2), 169–176 (1980)
17. Trotter, H.F.: An elementary proof of the central limit theorem. Archiv der Mathematik 10, 226–234 (1959)

Semi-automated Prototyping of a TPM v2 Software and Hardware Simulation Platform

Martin Pirker and Johannes Winter

Graz University of Technology (TUG),
Institute for Applied Information Processing and Communications (IAIK)
Inffeldgasse 16a, 8010 Graz, Austria
{mpirker,jwinter}@iaik.tugraz.at

Abstract. Recently, the Trusted Computing Group (TCG) released first specification documents on the Trusted Platform Module (TPM) version 2 to the general public. This new TPM specification introduces a novel set of commands and concepts, which in part are fundamentally different to the features found on the previous generation of the Trusted Platform Module. At the time of this writing hardware prototypes and software simulators of the TPM v2 are not available to the general public. In this paper, we explore a semi-automated process to synthesize a TPM v2 software simulator from the published TCG specifications. To demonstrate the feasibility of our approach, we first assemble a prototype TPM v2 software simulator. Further, we show how this prototype TPM v2 software simulator can be hosted on an FPGA platform, which then subsequently can be used as an early hardware simulator for next generation TPMs.

Keywords: Trusted Platform Module, Trusted Computing, TPM v2, Simulator.

1 Introduction

Secure devices and processing nodes grow steadily in complexity, making the security analysis of systems as a whole usually an infeasible hard task. Trusted Computing partly tries to address this problem with a dedicated *secure* hardware root anchor of trust – the Trusted Platform Module (TPM).

The development process of security modules is crucial as one single defect may compromise the security of the whole module, or even worse, of a whole system. Naturally, humans make mistakes. Thus, the development process should aid the human developers wherever possible and provide support for automated toolings. This promises to reduce development complexity and enables detection, understanding and mitigation of issues as early as possible.

Recently, the Trusted Computing Group (TCG) consortium published a first public draft[1] of the new generation "v2" of the TPM. The TPM specification documents are advertised to be suited for automated parsing tools and subsequent automated processing.

---

[1] TPM v2 revision 00.93 was published at the TCG homepage in mid Oct 2012 [10].

M. Huth et al. (Eds.): TRUST 2013, LNCS 7904, pp. 106–114, 2013.

Contribution. In this paper, we follow up on the claim[2] that the TPM v2 specification is written for automated processing. We report on our efforts to process the public TPM v2 specification documents in a semi-automated toolchain. We explore how to extract code fragments, command and response parameters, data structures and constants from the public PDF specification documents.

Based on these results we assemble an (almost) complete software simulator. Only minor manual tweaks and additional implementation efforts are needed to run this software simulator on standard Linux desktop platforms. Further, we show how this software TPM v2 simulator can be hosted on an FPGA hardware platform, which then allows in-system simulation of a hardware TPM on desktop *and* embedded systems.

Outline. Section 2 gives the background on the Trusted Platform Module specification and its use. In Section 3 we first present the specification parser tool used to semi-automatically extract code for the TPM v2 software simulator prototype. Next, we discuss the code generation process and the practical obstacles encountered while converting the extracted code into an executable, standalone TPM v2 software simulator. Based on these results we introduce our prototype TPM hardware simulator in section Section 4. Section 5 concludes the paper.

2   Background

We refer to secondary literature for an introduction to the relevant Trusted Computing terminology and concepts [4], and for an in-depth discussion of state-of-the-art trusted (desktop) platforms [1]. This section gives a short introduction on the Trusted Platform Module specification, its primary user the Trusted Software Stack, and the process from specification to implementation.

2.1   Trusted Platform Module

The Trusted Computing Group (TCG) released the TPM v1.1b specification [8] in February 2002. The specification was continously maintained over the years, up until the current v1.2 revision 116, published March 2011. The TPM v1.2 is in widespread distribution in a variety of platforms, the TCG estimated in 2011 [9] that worldwide more than 500 million TPMs have been shipped. The TCG is a membership-only consortium which requires its members to sign a non-disclosure agreement. Consequently, the development of the TPM v2 was taking place within the TCG, of which the first publicly visible results, in the form of a public draft specification, were finally published in October 2012 [10].

2.2   TPM Support Software Stack

The TPM hardware chip requires a support package of software (libraries). The main component in the trusted platform design is the TCG Software Stack

---

[2] See quote in Section 2.4.

(TSS) [7]. The TSS specification was implemented by two major open-source[3] packages: First, the C language based *TrouSerS* implementation[4]. Further, we (co-)developed *jTSS*[5], a TSS implemented fully in the Java language.

2.3   From Specification to Implementation

The specification of a component such as the TPM is a complex, tedious and fragile process. This is rooted in the complexity of the TPM itself – security functions are hard to get right – as well as the required coordinated process of writing hundreds of pages of specification text. Current TPM specification documents are essentially hundreds of pages of text and tables, which document architectural design decisions, implementation recommendations and data-structures, as well as algorithmic details [8].

For the development of jTSS (Section 2.2) we painstakingly interfaced to every TPM function and data structure in Java. We tried to automate this process, but stopped quite early. While we were able to implement a script which extracts from the TPM v1.2 specification all commands along with their incoming and outgoing data structures, about 50% of the script was related to the handling of special cases to due inconsistencies and bugs in the specification text. In other words, the effort of script implementation was not worth the results obtained.

Consequently, the experience of the manual implementation of 120 TPM commands and the self-observation of human ways to error while doing so leads to two major requirements for TPM specifications: First, specifications should be consistent, accurate and unambigous for easy human comprehension. Next, they should encourage the use of automated support toolings for correctness checking and code generation.

2.4   TPM v2 Specification

The TPM v2 specification consists of four major parts, which describe the high-level architecture, data-structures, commands and support routines. All four parts together comprise almost 1400 pages. To facilitate the use of automated tools the TCG did several format improvements over the TPM v1.2 specification. The new specification [10] prominently states[6] this intention:

> "[...] The information in this document is formatted so that it may be converted to standard computer language formats by an automated process. The purpose of this automated process is to minimize the transcription errors that often occur during the conversion process. [...]"

Further, the support source code included in part 4 documents the inner workings of a TPM and its surrounding environment. This reveals that for v2 a software

---

[3] The history of commercial TSS implementations is not known to the authors.

[4] http://trousers.sourceforge.net/

[5] http://trustedjava.sourceforge.net/

[6] See Part 2, Chapter 4.1 Introduction.

simulation was developed, in parallel to the specification process. Consequently, ideally, the public specification contains enough information and source code to enable construction of a TPM v2 software simulator and support software libraries, with the aid of automated tools.

3   Synthesis of a TPM v2 Software Simulator

To extract a TPM v2 simulator from public TCG specifications, we start with the PDF documents of public revision 00.93 from the TCG homepage [10]. The target runtime environments for the extracted TPM simulator are a Linux-like systems with GNU C compiler and support for the OpenSSL[7] cryptography library. The semi-automated process for assembling a TPM v2 simulator from its specification consists of four major processing steps:

1. Setup and automated input data transformation.
2. Extraction of data-structures and constants from specification part 2.
3. Extraction of source code fragments from specification parts 3 and 4.
4. Manual implementation of missing code fragments and integration with a build process.

To implement the semi-automated extraction process, we use a standard Linux environment, which contains the `LibreOffice` suite, a `Ruby` interpreter, the `Nokogiri` XML parsing library, and the `Makeheaders` tool for C function prototype extraction.[8]

3.1   Setup and Input Data Transformation

In the first step of the TPM simulator extraction process, we transform the PDF print-ready specification documents into a format which is easier to process by automated tools. Our initial idea was to convert the PDF documents to simple plaintext files using a PDF-to-text extractor. Unfortunately, this simplistic approach loses essentially all of the formatting meta-information.

To overcome the limitations of PDF-to-text converters we exploit the non-interactive PDF import function[9] of the LibreOffice suite, to transform the PDF specification documents to the OpenDocument `FODG` format. The XML-based `FODG` document format preserves the layout and formatting of the original input PDF file, which greatly simplifies the further extraction process in later steps.

3.2   Extraction Process

The basis for the further extraction process is a Ruby script, which loads the `FODG` documents using the Nokogiri XML parser and extracts all the raw text

---

[7] http://www.openssl.org/

[8] We used LibreOffice 3.5.6, Ruby 1.9.3p286, Nokogiri 1.5.5 and Makeheaders 0_p4.

[9] `libreoffice --headless --convert-to fodg <pdf-filename>`.

fragments along with their position and text style formatting, ignoring all the remaining markup. Detailed analysis of the extracted text fragments is done by an additional Ruby script, which takes the output of the previous step as input.

The second script searches with regular expression patterns for specific text fragments in combination with their distinctive text style information. This search identifies hooks in the text, from which the following text fragments then can be analysed in more detail. Depending on the nature of the specification part being processed, the Ruby script needs to apply different strategies.

Part 2 of the TPM v2 specification defines data structures and constants. To process this part, the Ruby script scans for the tables which define TPM structures or constants, and constructs a large header file containing appropriate C `#define` directives for constants and type definitions for all TPM data types. As part of this processing step the Ruby script can also auto-generate the marshalling code required to serialize TPM data structures to or from raw byte streams.

Part 3 provides all 110 commands of the TPM v2. The specification of a single TPM command always comprises the input and output data structures, formatted as tables, and C code fragments documenting the command actions. Extraction of the C code fragments is straightforward, as their specific text style and distinct line number at the left page border makes them easy to identify. The extractor script simply dumps the fragments into one C source file per command. The input and output parameter structures of the commands can be handled similarly to the part 2 data types. For each command the script generates a header file which contains the C function signature and the input/output data-structures of the extracted command.

Finally, part 4 of the TPM v2 specification contains support functions and C code. Functions in part 4 are used by the TPM command code fragments in part 3 and by code which provides the proper simulation environment for running a TPM software simulator. Code extraction follows the same strategy as in part 3 and the filenames are provided in the section titles.

In total we are able to directly extract about 6k lines of code from part 3 and 22k lines of code from part 4 of the TPM v2 specification without any need for human intervention. The extracted source code is incomplete, in the sense that most of the header files referenced by C `#include` directives in part 3 and part 4 are missing at this stage. These header files with function prototypes can be easily generated by extending the extractor script, or even simpler by utilizing the well-known *makeheaders* tool.

3.3   Additional Steps

Our proof-of-concept extraction tool demonstrates that a scripted toolchain is capable of automatically creating about 340 source files (`.c` and `.h`), which comprises about 95% of a complete TPM v2 simulator.

At the time of this writing we are currently finalizing scripted support for generation of data structure marshalling code and central command dispatching code as discussed in sections 6.1, 6.3 and 9.11 of part 4 of the TPM v2 draft specification. It is possible to auto-generate these missing parts from the specification PDFs, however implementation of these facilities are not yet fully covered by our toolchain. To allow testing of the extracted simulator we filled the missing parts of the marshalling and command dispatching code with not-autogenerated code.

To successfully compile the extracted code on our Linux build environment a few small patches were necessary. Obviously the TPM v2 specification, and the code snippets contained in the specification, were *not* written with *case-sensitive* file-systems in mind. This problem manifests itself on a Linux build environment, where the sometimes inconsistent upper/lower-case spelling of header files causes build problems. To work around these issues, we simply created symbolic links for inconsistently spelled header files[10] on our Linux build system.

Another issue with the revision 0.93 of the TPM v2 specification is that some fragments of the support routines in part 4 are currently specific to Microsoft Windows platforms, due to their use of Windows-specific system header files such as `winsock.h` and `windows.h` and to their use of Microsoft C compiler specific functions. The affected fragments in part 4 of the TPM v2 specification reside in section "D" which defines a remote-procedure call (RPC) interface for TPM simulation. A simple workaround for these issues is to manually provide "stub" `winsock.h` and `windows.h` header files on the Linux build-system, which emulate the Windows-specific calls using POSIX and BSD socket APIs.

For our further experiments we decided to completely discard the RPC simulation interface discussed in the TPM v2 specification, in favor of a simpler socket based interface: Our Linux TPM 2.0 software simulator exposes one TCP port per TPM locality, which accepts raw TPM command and response blobs, without adding any additional communication protocol overhead[11].

Our work presented in this section produced a Linux executable of a TPM v2 software simulator. Our prototype passes simple TPM initialization and "PCR read" type of use. Unfortunately, as software stacks and demo code for the TPM v2 generation do not exist yet, we have not tested more complex functions, yet. Our Linux software simulator utilizes TCP/IP sockets for communication between the simulated Trusted Platform Module and its users. The communication protocol used by the Linux TPM 2.0 software emulator was intentionally kept extremely simple: Each TPM locality is exposed through a separate TCP port, which accepts raw TPM command and response blobs, without adding an additional communication protocol overhead.

4   Towards a Hardware TPM v2 Simulation Platform

In general hardware TPMs do not expose publicly accessible debug interfaces, such as JTAG ports, due to security reasons. This lack of simple means to debug the TPM itself complicates development and testing of TPM software in its

---

[10] e.g. `tpmError.h` $\rightarrow$ `TpmError.h`.

[11] On transport layer this approach is compatible with IBM's TPM v1.2 software emulator found at `http://ibmswtpm.sourceforge.net/`

native target environment. There is a gap between what can be simulated with an easy to debug TPM software simulator and what can be debugged on an actual hardware platform with a TPM. This gap especially becomes evident when working with trusted bootloaders and similar types of low-level trusted software.

Based upon the results of the TPM v2 software simulator, we started to develop a prototype TPM v2 hardware simulator platform on top of a Xilinx FPGA evaluation board. This hardware simulator platform is intended to be usable as "in-system" substitute for a real hardware TPM, thereby closing the gap between debugging trusted applications with a pure software simulation of the TPM and testing the same programs on a hard-to-debug commercial hardware TPM.

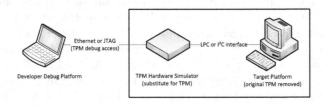

Fig. 1. Setup of the TPM v2 hardware simulator

Figure 1 illustrates the overall system architecture of our in-system TPM simulator prototype. Communication with the target system is established using the target's native TPM communication interface. For current desktop PCs and notebooks this implies that the simulator platform needs to support the Low-Pin-Count (LPC) bus [3] variant of the TPM TIS 1.2 interface [6]. Recent variants of version 1.2 TPMs exist with alternative physical communication interfaces, such as Inter-IC (I^2C) busses or serial peripheral (SPI) busses, which are suitable for use on mobile and embedded devices, like smartphones or even embedded microcontrollers. [12]

Access to the internals of the in-system TPM simulator is possible via an TCP/IP based Ethernet interface as well as via a JTAG debug access port. The Ethernet interface of the in-system simulator is fully compatible with the software TPM simulation platform discussed earlier. The JTAG debug-access port allows remote debugging of the soft-core processor running the TPM firmware, enabling single-stepping of (failing) TPM commands.

4.1 Prototyping Results

The initial prototype implementation of our in-system TPM simulator was done on a Xilinx Spartan 3AN Starter Kit. This development board provides relatively

---

[12] Recent Linux kernels already support I^2C based TPMs from multiple vendors (e.g. [5], [2]).

large volatile and non-volatile memory resources. Due to the large amount of resources available on the FPGA board chosen for our prototype, we decided *not* to focus on accurate modelling of the resource contraints found on a (production) hardware TPM. Instead, our aim was to create an embedded SoC platform, which is able to run the semi-automatically extracted software TPM simulator discussed earlier as debuggable in-system emulation of a TPM v2 module. The hardware design running inside the Xilinx XC3S700AN FPGA is based on a 32-bit Xilinx MicroBlaze soft-core processor, with standard peripherals including a serial UART, an I^2C controller, a DRAM controller and two SPI controllers for interfacing with non-volatile flash memory. Additionally, our SoC includes a PC-compatible Low-Pin-Count (LPC) bus slave controller, based on our earlier work discussed in [11].

On the firmware side, we use the Xilinx Xilkernel microkernel and the open-source lwIP TCP/IP stack to provide basic POSIX-style operating system services and a BSD sockets compatible network API. Cryptography support is realized using a stripped down version of the OpenSSL cryptography library, which just includes the ciphers and hash algorithms used in the TPM v2 simulator. On top of this runtime environment, we reuse the extracted TPM v2 software simulator discussed earlier.

The total uncompressed size of the firmware code for the hardware TPM simulator is currently between 950 KiB and 1 MiB. With simple data-compression the firmware binary can be reduced to approximately 600-650 KiB. This allows us to fit the FPGA bitstream, a small bootloader and the compressed TPM simulator firmware into the on-chip flash of the FPGA. Non-volatile storage is currently held in a small serial EEPROM outside the FPGA, to reduce wear-out of the FPGA's on-chip flash memory.

At the time of this writing, the network and the I^2C interface to our software TPM simulator are fully functional, allowing our in-system simulator to be used as TPM emulator replacement and as model of an embedded TPM v2. The hardware part of the simulator's LPC bus interface is operational and we are in progress of finishing the TPM 1.2 TIS-style protocol implementation.

5 Conclusion and Outlook

In this paper, we showed how information in the TPM v2 specification can be extracted with minimal human intervention. Section 3 outlines the process which was used by us to assemble a working TPM v2 software simulator, using only open source tools. Based on the results of a working software emulator, we contributed a working proof-of-concept prototype of a hardware TPM v2 simulator. Consequently, we conclude that it is possible to discover and experiment with the TPM v2 generation without further delay.

Design and development of a support software stack for the TPM v2 as well as hardware and software simulation of a dynamic root of trust remain interesting open topics and motivate further research.

Acknowledgements. We thank the anonymous reviewers for their helpful feedback on the paper.

This work has been supported by the European Commission through project FP7-ICT-SEPIA, grant agreement number 257433, project FP7-ICT-STANCE, grant agreement number 317753, and project DALIA of the AAL joint programme.

References

1. Grawrock, D.: Dynamics of a Trusted Platform: A Building Block Approach. Intel Press (2009)
2. Huewe, P.: char/tpm: Add new driver for Infineon I2C TIS TPM (February 21, 2011), LKML article archived at:
   http://article.gmane.org/gmane.linux.kernel/1103300
3. Intel: Intel Low Pin Count (LPC) Interface Specification, revision 1.1. (August 2002), http://www.intel.com/design/chipsets/industry/25128901.pdf
4. Martin, A.: The ten page introduction to trusted computing. Tech. Rep. RR-08-11, OUCL (December 2008)
5. Morav, D.: TPM Nuvoton I2C driver, kernel 2.6.35 (August 9, 2010), LKML article archived at: http://article.gmane.org/gmane.linux.kernel/1020890
6. Trusted Computing Group: TCG PC Client Specific TPM Interface Specification (TIS), version 1.2 FINAL. For TPM Family 1.2; Level 2 (July 11, 2005), http://www.trustedcomputinggroup.org/
7. Trusted Computing Group: TCG Software Stack Specification (2007), http://www.trustedcomputinggroup.org/resources/ tcg_software_stack_tss_specification
8. Trusted Computing Group: TCG TPM Specification Version 1.x (2007), http://www.trustedcomputinggroup.org/resources/tpm_main_specification
9. Trusted Computing Group: Do You Know? A Few Notes on Trusted Computing Out in the World (2011),
   http://www.trustedcomputinggroup.org/community/2011/03/ do_you_know_a_few_notes_on_trusted_computing_out_in_the_world
10. Trusted Computing Group: Trusted Platform Module Library Family 2.0, Level 00 Revision 00.93 (2012),
    http://www.trustedcomputinggroup.org/resources/ trusted_platform_module_specifications_in_public_review
11. Winter, J., Dietrich, K.: A hijacker's guide to communication interfaces of the trusted platform module. Comput. Math. Appl. 65(5), 748–761 (2013), http://dx.doi.org/10.1016/j.camwa.2012.06.018

Tapping and Tripping with NFC

Sandeep Tamrakar[1] and Jan-Erik Ekberg[2]

[1] Aalto University School of Science, Finland
sandeep.tamrakar@aalto.fi
[2] Nokia Research Center, Radio Systems Laboratory, Finland
jan-erik.ekberg@nokia.com

Abstract. In public transport ticketing, the tap-in / tap-out user experience is an established metaphor since contactless NFC cards were introduced as travel cards some ten years ago. In our solution fixed smart cards at train station are tapped by NFC-enabled mobile phones of users. By leveraging the phones' communication capabilities, a possible embedded trusted execution environment (TEE) and the user interface, we have constructed a secure solution for so-called non-gated ticketing, where end user devices produce and report ticketing evidence under the threat of inspection. This is technically quite different from the traditional model where a certified, secure reader is tapped by a passive card. Learnings from a public ticketing trial conducted in the Port Washington branch of the LIRR train network in New York is presented along with an overview of the NFC protocols used in that trial. We also discuss extensions to the protocol with the goal to enable ticketing also for NFC phones without TEE support.

1   Introduction

All over the world, transport ticketing has for years been implemented using proximity technologies, increasingly using the ISO / IEC 14443 [12] contactless card standard. Protocols like Mifare[1] developed by NXP semiconductors allow contactless memory cards to be used as secure tokens or travel cards. A travel card used as a ticket can convey the identity of a user, the validity period of the ticket, the balance available in the ticket and other ticketing attributes such as valid region, discount group etc.

Mifare-powered ticketing systems have proven to be very usable in practice, despite some vulnerabilities as mentioned in [9,8,4]. However, Mifare-based schemes do require that the ticket readers which communicate with the travel cards have access to the secret keys of the card issuer, making the readers a security-critical part of the ticketing system setup. Thus, these systems do not easily scale to implementations where the cards are not communicating with the trusted, certified readers.

A more open approach that is applicable to ticketing is defined in the Open Payment initiative from the Smart Card Alliance [15]. In their architecture, each

---

[1] http://mifare.net

M. Huth et al. (Eds.): TRUST 2013, LNCS 7904, pp. 115–132, 2013.
© Springer-Verlag Berlin Heidelberg 2013

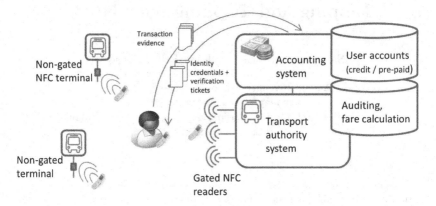

Fig. 1. System architecture

traveler is represented by a travel account in a server cloud. While traveling, only the identity of a user is verified using credentials stored e.g. in a travel card. In this approach, the ticketing and fare calculation operations can be totally separated from the evidence collected at the traveling endpoints. A very tempting variation of this system is to use a contactless credit card for identity verification, possibly allowing the user to travel with his card in many independent transport systems around the world.

An account-based ticketing system is technically easy to arrange in *gated transport*, where the transport end points are controlled via physical gates, e.g. as in the London Underground. We assume that these gates are equipped with a contactless reader that can verify the identity of a user and potentially consult a back-end cloud in real-time to perform all the necessary validation before allowing the user to travel. In our architecture, depicted in Figure 1, we extend this *identity-based ticketing* model[2] to *non-gated transport* such as S-Bahn in Berlin, where the travel tickets are not verified at the station gates. In non-gated transport, travelers are requested to perform certain transport-ticketing related functions on their own accord under the threat of sporadically occurring ticket inspection and system penalties imposed on dishonest travelers. We leverage the mobile phone as an NFC reader as well as its security and communication capabilities towards the back-end cloud in a model where the contactless smart cards are no longer used as end-user credentials, but as proof of location — i.e. identifying where (and partially when) the transport customer enters and exits the transport system.

This paper extends our previous work on non-gated transport [7] which was later publicly trialed with more than 100 participants in New York in 2012. Based on the ticketing data collected in the trial we can now confirm some of

---

[2] The public transport community uses the term *identity-based* for a ticketing system, where a travel account is assigned to each user and the identity of the user is verified at a transport station gate before allowing the user to travel. This does not necessarily imply the use of *identity-based encryption*.

our assumptions regarding system properties, transport user behavior as well as report on some of the data collected in participant interviews. This is the first contribution of this paper.

Additionally, our work on the protocols for the ticketing system has continued with a re-design for NFC-enabled phones where an embedded, programmable trusted execution environment (TEE) is unavailable or practically unaccessible. The design upgrades accommodate such *open devices* in the ticketing system without significantly changing the risk model of fare collection and auditing or inducing unnecessary liability for the travelers. This is a second contribution of this paper.

In Section 2, we explore related work in the general domain of identity verification with NFC-enabled phones. Section 3 outlines the security protocol used in the trial, which is a part of previously published work. Section 4 presents the trial results. The protocol extensions for open devices are presented in Section 5, along with a brief security analysis. Section 6 provides implementation details and measurements for the extended protocol on an Android phone. Section 7 gives the acknowledgments and finally conclusions in Section 8 end the paper.

2   Related Work

A prototype application developed by RFID lab of the University of Rome [10] implements a virtual transport ticket applet stored in a secure environment of an NFC-enabled mobile phone. A ticket can be purchased over SMS using a Java MIDlet application that interacts with the ticket applet running in the secure environment. Before traveling, the ticket information is transmitted over NFC to a ticket reader, which validates the ticket. A similar user-centric ticketing approach is proposed by Chaumette et. al. [3]. They present an architecture for event ticketing using NFC-enabled mobile phones that use SIMs as secure elements. Both of these systems work in online as well as partially offline modes, but require dedicated reading terminals.

A work by Derler et. al. [5] focuses on the anonymity of NFC ticketing in order to protect the privacy of a ticket holder. In their model, a ticket can be verified without divulging the identity of a user. This reduces the risk of an attacker profiling user's travel based on eavesdropped tap events. The Smart Card Alliance promotes an open payment system using an account-based architecture [15] for public transport systems, where the account information is verified by a ticket reader and forwarded to a back-end server. The back-end accumulates these records and later charges the account holder for transport system use.

The abovementioned systems use a secure element on a mobile phone to store the ticketing credentials. Dmitrienko et. al. [6] implement a software-based access token on mobile phones, where the software domains are isolated from each other using TrustDroid [2]. The above contributions neither discuss a complete ticketing system nor consider non-gated ticketing.

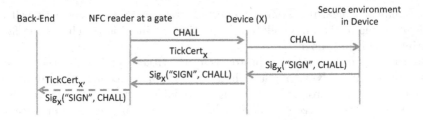

Fig. 2. An overview of gated ticketing protocol

3   Our First Ticketing Protocol

Our public-transport ticketing protocols that form the starting point for this work have been reported in [7]. In short, we built both gated and non-gated transport ticketing for mobile phones with a built-in TEE and NFC communication primitives. The protocol for gated transport, depicted in Figure 2 is a straight-forward challenge-response design. A user touches his device to the reader attached to a transport-station gate. The reader then initiates a session by sending a challenge to the user device. The challenge contains a nonce and the identity of the reader or the station. Upon receiving the challenge, the user device immediately sends back its ticketing certificate issued by the back-end server (or CA) and subsequently signs the challenge with its ticketing keys inside its TEE. The signature over the challenge is also returned to the reader. The reader is equipped with the public key of the back-end server (or CA), and it validates the certificate. From it the reader also extracts the public key information of the user device in order to validate the signature on the challenge. If all the verifications succeed, the station gate is opened.

For non-gated transport, our system is built to satisfy the following goals and user interaction patterns:

R1.   The location, time, identity of a traveler and needed cryptographic evidence shall form a tuple that defines the trip end-points and the traveler in a reliable and non-repudiable manner,

R2.   Trip end-points, e.g. touch points at bus stops, can be equipped with contactless smart cards, but not with gates or contactless devices that require continuous power supply or back-end connectivity.

R3.   The mobile phone cannot be assumed to be connected to a back-end cloud infrastructure in real-time, i.e. the system must be designed to operate in a *partially offline* manner.

R4.   The activity of a traveler with a touch point shall be modeled as 'tap', i.e. a traveler taps his phone to a touch point at a bus stop before begining a trip, and taps another touch point when he ends his trip at another bus stop.

R5.   Travelers might be subjected to random ticket inspection, i.e. protocols must be designed to support this property.

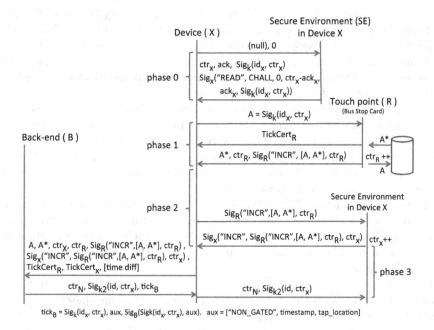

Fig. 3. An overview of non-gated ticketing protocol

Our solution is based on signed challenges produced by the TEEs, where each signature also includes a TEE-specific counter. A *sign and increment* command monotonically increases the counter. Future TEE counter update and signature operations are limited by an authenticated release of the counter window signed by the back-end cloud. This limits the amount of taps that a single user device can perform before being forced to report evidence to the back-end cloud in order to continue tapping. The same TEE logic is used both in the TEE of user devices and in the contactless smart card at touch points. However, the counter window in the contactless cards is not used — touch-point counter values are used to determine the order of tapping that the touch point is involved in, not to enforce reporting.

A complete non-gated ticketing protocol executes in three phases as depicted in the Figure 3. A user device X may enter phase 0 any time after the completion of the last ticketing event. This phase prepares the user device for the next ticketing event. In this phase, the user device X reads the TEE counter state and retrieves a counter commitment $Sig_k(id_X, ctr_X)$, for the latest counter value. The TEE also returns other data which is used as part of ticket inspection.

When the user taps his device X to a touch point R as shown in the Figure 8, the user device enters phase 1. In this phase, the device sends its latest counter commitment $Sig_k(id_x, ctr_x)$ obtained from phase 0 as a challenge to the touch point. In return, the touch point sends back its device certificate $TickCert_R$

as well as a signature Sig_R that binds its own counter ctr_R to the challenge. Additionally, the touch point R also returns some auxiliary data $A*$ that needs to be reported to the back-end server along with the terminal signature for verification. The challenges sent to the touch points are the commitments of the user device. These commitments can be later used by the back-end cloud to statistically infer the device that sent the challenge.

The signature $Sig_k(id_x, ctr_x)$ cannot be resolved without the knowledge of the key k and the value of ctr_x remains fresh each time it is retrieved. Therefore, we can assume that the identity of device X remains unknown to the entities other than the protocol participants. The user device X can determine the identity of a touch point from its certificate and validate the signature in order to protect against the interaction with rogue touch points.

In phase 2, the device X re-invokes its TEE and issues the *sign and increment* command with the response received from the touch point in phase 1 as a challenge. This operation binds the device identity and the current state of its counter to the identity and the counter state of the touch point in a non-repudiable manner.

The user device enters phase 3 immediately after completing phase 2. In phase 3, the device collects all the data generated or gathered from phases 0 - 2 and sends them to the back-end using a server-authenticated TLS channel. Additionally, the device also sends its estimation of the time that has passed between phase 1 and the first message of phase 3. In order to validate a transaction, the back-end identifies both the device X and the touch point R involved in the transaction. After validation, the back-end returns a release commitment for the counter of the device X. Without the release commitment from the back-end, the TEE of the device will eventually exhaust its counter window and refuse to sign any further taps. This mechanism forces the user to report tap evidence in phase 3. Additionally, the back-end will also return to the user device necessary information for ticket inspection.

Phase 3 requires network connectivity to the back-end cloud. In some cases this phase can be significantly delayed e.g. due to poor network coverage. To improve on this delay problem, we also store challenges (i.e. commitments) received from the user devices in the touch-point cards. Each stored challenge is probabilistically selected and cryptographically bound to at least two later invocations of phase 1 interaction (with some other user device). Similarly, every user device that taps a touch point is forced to relay two stored challenges from previous taps back to the back-end cloud in addition to the response for its own challenge. This provides a back channel of tap records, which can be used for security auditing and even fare calculation while waiting for the device that originated the tap to report its evidence.

A discussion on other system features, like enrolment, auditing, ticket verification as well as a protocol security analysis was presented in our previous work [7].

4   MTA/LIRR Mobile-Ticketing Trial

The mobile-ticketing trial was carried out in four phases from December 2011 to June 2012. The duration of the first three trials was about a week, where 20 employees from the Metropolitan Transport Authority (MTA) New York participated. The primary objective of these three trials was to test the system, improve it and add new features based on the feedback received from the participants. The final trial was carried out over a period of four weeks along the Port Washington Branch of Long Island Railway Road (LIRR). A total of 110 registered customers of MTA / LIRR with an annual subscription completed the trial.

The primary objective of the trial was to understand the user acceptance of mobile ticketing in non-gated transport and to learn the pattern of their ticket use. Particularly, we were interested to know the tapping behavior of participants; tap-in begins a trip and tap-out completes the trip. These tap events were reported to our back-end server. We wanted to know exactly how many participants complete their trips by tapping out. If the participants forgot to tap out within 3 hours, from the start of their trip, the application was designed to send a trip expiry message to the back-end server and notify the participants accordingly. We also wanted to learn about the connectivity to the back-end server from the mobile phones used in the trial, e.g. how soon a mobile phone reported a tap.

4.1   Tags in Trial

The final trial was carried out at 14 stations along the Port Washington Branch of LIRR. During initial testing, we found that the NFC operating distance for SmartMX tags with our protocol, using the chosen trial phones, was less than 2 cm whereas the corresponding distance for Mifare Classic tags was 4 cm. The more exact alignment of the antennas needed with the SmartMX tags compared to the Mifare tags was perceived to reduce the user experience. Therefore, Mifare tags were chosen as the primary tags during the trial and the SmartMX tags were left in only for protocol testing and reference.

A total of 105 Mifare classic tags were placed at the stations along with 10 SmartMX tags which were placed at only 5 stations. Each Mifare Classic tag stored a Station ID, corresponding to the station at which the tag was placed, as an NDEF message. During tapping the Station ID along with the Unique Identity (UID) [3] of the tag was collected as a tap record. In case of SmartMX tags, the challenge sent by the phone, the response returned by the tag and other context related information were collected as the tap record. The tap record was then cryptographically signed inside the TEE of the phone before being sent it to the back-end server.

---

[3] UID: a fixed 4 or 7 bytes identity that is assigned to each NFC tag at the time of manufacture.

4.2   Ticketing Application

A ticketing application designed for the trial was integrated as an extension to the Nokia Public transport application [4] and was installed in NFC-enabled Nokia 603 phones used in the trial. The phones were then provided to the participants. An interface to register participants to the back-end server was also included in the application. During registration, necessary ticketing credentials were enrolled into the TEE of the mobile phone. In Nokia 603 phones, we used the On-board Credential (ObC) [13] system to execute the credential algorithms in isolation from the operating system. We enrolled the TEE algorithms and secrets to ObC from the ticketing application using ObC APIs. After successful enrolment, the participants were ready to start their trips by tapping tags installed at the stations. Additionally, a ticket inspection application was provided to the MTA ticket inspectors. The inspection application was capable of interacting with the participants' ticketing applications over peer-to-peer mode of NFC in order to validate the tap-in event of a trip. The protocol used to validate tickets during ticket inspection has been reported in our previous work [7]. The participants were randomly inspected during the trial.

At the request of the MTA, an additional feature termed as *Checkout* was added, which allowed the participants to select any station used in the trial as a manual checkout station. In the ticketing application, a button that allowed manual checkout appeared one hour after the beginning of a trip and the feature was disabled along with the trip-expired event or if the participant selected a checkout station.

Each tap was immediately reported to the back-end server. However, if the network was unavailable at the time of the tap then the ticketing application periodically checked the network status and reported the taps to the server as soon as possible. Using the tap records, we were able to determine the start and the end points of a trip and associate appropriate ticket fare to the trip. However, no actual cost was associated to any trips travelled by trial participants.

4.3   Trial Results

Over the period of four weeks, 3166 complete trips were recorded with an average of around 29 trips per participant. Based on the number of trips made by the participants, we found that 80% of the participants used their ticketing application to make a single trip on a daily basis. 16% of the participants were using the ticketing application actively, i.e. for at least 20 trips. The remaining 4% of the participants were using the ticketing application less frequently, i.e. less than 10 complete trips, during the trial period. We also found that almost 90% of the trips were completed by a proper tapping out at a station. Around 2.4% of the trips were completed using the manual checkout feature and the remaining 7.4% of the trips were automatically expired.

Figure 4, shows that around 67% of the taps were reported immediately and more than 80% of the tap records were reported on the same day. The tap

---

[4] http://store.ovi.com/content/237984

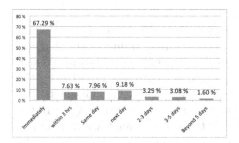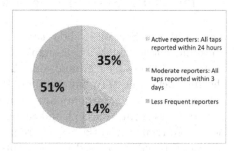

Fig. 4. Tap reporting time   **Fig. 5.** Categorization of the participants based on their tap reporting

reporting allowed the back-end cloud to monitor the transport system with high accuracy. For example, a near real-time system usage statistic as depicted in Figure 6 could be constructed for the non-gated transport.

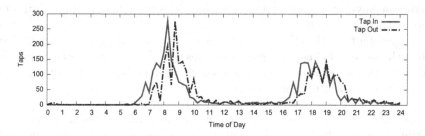

Fig. 6. 24h traveling statistic

We categorized the participants according to their tap reporting behavior as depicted in Figure 5. The median tap reporting time among the travelers in the active category was 109 seconds. As explained in Section 3, we designed the touch-point smart cards / SmartMX tags in such a way that they add old challenges from previous travelers to the currently tapping phone to be returned to the back-end cloud together with the current tap evidence. The impact of this system can be significantly increased if we add the tap reporting activity of travelers to the transport certificate and use this information within a SmartMX tag to assign tap evidences related to the least active travelers to be piggybacked by the most active travelers tapping the tag. Unfortunately, we also learned that trial participants on average had to tap SmartMX tags at least twice to achieve the successful tap event. This may be attributed to the mobile phone antenna not being ideally suited to power up the SmartMX cryptographic operations. In real deployments a 50% failure rate is of course not acceptable, and either the power transfer from phone needs to be improved or the energy consumption of SmartMX cards must be optimized.

5   Ticketing System Upgrade

The results in Section 4 show that the assumption of not having continuous back-end connectivity is reasonable. Even in the LIRR train system that operates completely over ground, only 35% of the devices were well-connected to the Internet while traveling. Around 15% of the evidence was reported by the travelers more than 24 hours after the travel occurred. Another insight is that the travelers seem to accept and remember to tap out after traveling — in the non-gated trial 90% of the trips were properly tapped out even though there was no stated penalty imposed for not tapping out. For non-roaming customers the back-end connectivity cost is likely not an issue. Already in 2010, a published report from mobiThinking [14] indicates that in the U.S. the penetration of flat-rate data plans (29%) was higher than the smartphone penetration (27%), so it is safe to assume that virtually all NFC smartphone are on fixed data plans and reporting the tap evidence back to the server has no marginal monetary cost.

On the other hand, very few NFC-enabled phones today include a programmable secure or trusted environment. Since we must assume that the users cannot be mandated to upgrade their existing NFC-enabled phones in real ticketing deployment, a protocol variant that decreases the dependency on user device security is needed.

The learning from the trial forms the basis of a ticketing system upgrade that enables the use of NFC-enabled mobile phones that do not have a programmable TEE. For this re-design, we revisit the system assumptions of the original non-gated system in the following manner:

1. The user device / mobile phone is not trustworthy. A virus or the traveler himself potentially has access to all the code and secrets in the phone, and may report on these secrets over the Internet.
2. We increase the expectation for the capability of the phone to connect to a back-end cloud. We will design the revised protocol around a time period of t minutes. A traveler must connect his device to the back-end cloud and receive "real-time" tokens at most t minutes before traveling.

Our main incentive for upgrading the ticketing system for open devices is to alleviate the risk of attacks potentially directed against the travelers with open devices. Since our system is Id-based, the main threat is the misuse of identities, i.e. a liability concern for the travelers.

We assume that the main protocols and functions presented in Section 3 still apply to open devices. These devices will still perform the same steps of enrolment, certificate renewal, signing touch-point smart-card responses and receiving authenticated release commitments for the device-specific counter. Compared to a device with a TEE, the trustworthiness of the open device is assumed to be weaker. The only operation that is partially directed against the traveler not reporting taps to the back-end is the requirement for counter release commitments. For open devices, we augment this functionality with a requirement to fetch the challenge for the touch-point smart cards in near-real time from the

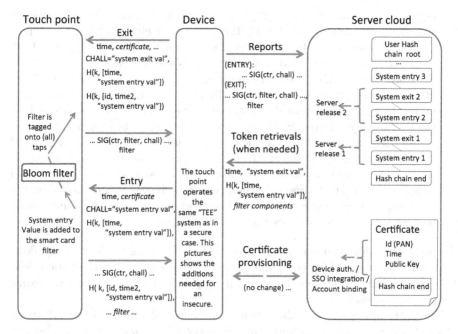

Fig. 7. Ticketing - insecure terminals

back-end cloud. In this manner, we still force the traveler's phone to periodically interact with the back-end cloud in the non-gated transport. This new interaction can also be protected by validating user credentials, e.g. a PIN, to further complicate the system infiltration required to mount any successful attack.

Furthermore, we add some new attributes to the transport certificates issued by the back-end infrastructure to open devices. We augment the touch-point smart card logic with new auditing features that increase the probability of catching identity theft in non-gated transport and we also add a feature to make tail-gating attacks[5] more difficult.

Figure 7 shows the overall additions done to the system. The new data structures are as follows:

1. A reverse hash-chain attribute is added to the transport certificate, signed by the server trust root and bound to an account of a traveler. The reverse hash-chain is split into run lengths of m elements ($m = 2$ in Figure 7). The actual elements (tokens) of the hash chain are retrieved m at a time by the mobile phone of the traveler before traveling. The token retrieval is possibly subject to user authorization for improved end-user protection.
2. A monotonically increasing time value is added to the system, and maintained by the back-end cloud. The time value is updated e.g. once a second,

---

[5] A tailgating attack is where a customer intentionally throws a valid ticket back over the gate to let a friend defeat the physical access control of the gate.

and is consistent across a single transport system. This time value will be signed by the server distributing the hash-chain elements and be cryptographically bound to the last token from the set of m tokens in the hash chain, i.e. the one that is to be spent first, on system entry.

3. All touch-point smart cards are augmented with a time-dependent Bloom filter[1] which is maintained individually by every single smart card. This is in addition to the statistically returned challenges of earlier travelers. Like the statistically selected earlier challenges, the Bloom filter is also returned to the back-end cloud through the tapping client. Cryptographic binding of the filter to the response forces the end-user device that taps the touch-point card to return the filter along with the challenge-response to complete a valid transaction report. A time awareness within each card is built based on the entry tap-time commitments by the back-end, i.e. the reference time may be lagging for touch-point cards that are rarely used.

The extensions for the ticketing system operate according to the message flows outlined in Figure 7. The touch-point smart cards now include distinct operations for entry vs. exit — intermediate taps, if supported, can be modeled according to the exit template.

The entry operation with the touch-point smart card includes the validation of the transport certificate, and that the entry token maps to the hash-chain root. The entry operation will also validate that the time bound to the entry token is e.g. at most $t = 900$ (15 minutes) earlier than the last time seen by the smart card. If all validations succeed, the smart card will return a response to the end-user device that includes not only the signed challenges but also a verification ticket bound to the entry token value. This ticket can later be validated by all other smart cards in the system. Furthermore, the entry token value will be added to a Bloom filter in the card that is periodically emptied, i.e. it contains only entry taps accumulated during a t-minute period. The Bloom filter is a very efficient data structure for this kind of aggregation, since filters for many smart cards can be trivially combined in the server, and a search for possible double-spending of entry taps among all smart cards can be performed efficiently.

During exit, a touch-point smart card does not accept a tap operation without a matching system entry commitment returned by some other smart card in the transport system. An exit token must also be in the same hash chain as the entry token. These mechanisms alleviate identity theft, since an NFC eavesdropper may get the entry tap and the smart card signature, but not the exit token. Whenever tokens are retrieved with NFC eavesdropping or network-based attacks, the extra use of the token will trigger double-spending auditing mechanisms.

The traveler's incentive for reporting back evidence in the revised system is different from the protocols that use TEEs. In the latter case, the phone will force the traveler to report back on the threat of becoming dysfunctional, and all signatures are signed with keys that reside in the TEE. In the former case, the blocking mechanism relies on the conditional reception of the tokens from the server and the assumption that reporting of travel conducted based on those tokens must be performed before the retrieval of the next set of tokens. Token retrieval with missing submitted evidence should by default be considered to represent the maximum fare of any trip that can be made on the system. In this way, the user is always incentivized to report the evidence correctly and promptly. Timely evidence feedback also benefits the user by improving the auditing mechanisms for catching double-spending.

Based on the Bloom-filter contents, and the knowledge of tokens active at a given time (the only condition by which they are accepted at touch-point smart cards), every card returns, on every tap, a statistical representation of the recent entry taps at the touch-point card that is being tapped. This information is channeled by the mobile phones to the back-end cloud. With the assumption that at least 50-70% of phones report back (their own taps) almost immediately, it is easy enough in the back-end cloud to aggregate the Bloom filters and pinpoint double-spending occurring in the transport system - since all tokens are generated in the back-end cloud, full information of their contents and validity (in terms of t) is known to the back-end.

5.1   Brief Security Analysis of the Added Features

A variant of our baseline non-gated ticketing protocol has been formally analyzed in the Ph.D dissertation by Enyang Huang [11]. For this work, we assume that the phones, in addition to the augmentation, operate the default signing scheme already deployed. Thus a replay attack entails both stealing the longer term signature key from a phone, capturing the token over the air (and replaying it) or alternatively mounting a harvesting attack using a real-time virus in the attacked phone. We can identify the following threat categories and corresponding ways the described solution mitigates these issues:

1. An attacker has learned the long-term secrets of a victim. If the attacker copies the entry code off the air, he can likely in a non-gated environment produce a tap and a smart card response that will withstand at least cursory ticket inspection. However, the system will catch double-spending by aggregation and inspection of the touch-point card Bloom filters. In a gated system, entry duplicates are likely caught immediately and even access may be denied for either the attacker or the correct traveler. With token copies retrieved by eavesdropping the NFC interface, the attacker cannot exit a gated system if he does not follow the victim like a shadow.
2. Any copying of the short-lived tokens is valid only for entry during the stated system allowance period t. In a gated transport this is an absolute measure, but old copies will also be caught at ticket verification in a non-gated system and by touch-point cards in case the use of the cards has advanced its notion of time past the time constraint of the token copy.

3. The attacker travels using a complete copy of all ticketing data in the original traveler's phone [6]. This means that the attacker will report all travels to the back-end just like the original traveler would do. Based on the protocol and its secrets, there is no way of differentiating the attacker from the original traveler since we assume that the attacker has full access to the mobile phone of the original traveler. However, double-spending mechanisms will notice parallel usage quickly, and in gated transport one of the two phones may even be denied system access or exit. In any case, the fraud is quickly unearthed, and appropriate measures can be taken. For example, while fetching a fresh token in non-gated transport, the back-end cloud may require additional out-of-band user authentication or verification of one-time-PIN sent to the traveler via a separate channel such as SMS.

4. The attacker travels using the identity of a traveler, but does not report anything to the back-end if ticket verification is not encountered. In this case, the smart card filters will provide information to the auditing server about non-reported taps. Further, tap information becomes available as part of the back-channel from smart cards to the server through other tapping travelers. Using this mechanism, or by the attacker encountering ticket verification, the system will get information of an attacked identity.

5. A traveler may collaborate with an associate and make a copy of his entry tap to his associate. The associate then taps out at a nearby station while the traveler continues his trip. Later, the associate sends the exit-tap information back to the traveler, which the traveler submits to the back-end cloud after he completes his trip. In this way, a traveler pays for only a short distance trip fare while actually traveling a longer distance.

   The probability of spotting such an attack relies on the number of honest travelers who report their tap-evidence immediately. As each reported tap carries evidence of the two earlier taps made at the same touch point, the back-end cloud may receive the information about the dishonest traveler's exit tap made at short distance station before he actually completes his trip. During ticket inspection, such fraud can be identified provided that the inspection device consults the back-end during ticket verification. In case of a TEE implementation the current state of the device's counter commitment will always reveal the early tap out to an inspector.

6. A widespread software attack, where a vast number of phones are infected as a botnet and, for example, one trip from each victim is used by the attacker, will be impossible to protect against with the above assumptions. To alleviate this kind of attack some other reactive security mechanism, for example a virus checker, needs to be deployed.

The protocol additions for open devices put in place several separate mechanisms to protect both the traveler and the system against undue fraud and misplaced liability. Nevertheless, when deployed in a mass-market scenario, there is a clear

---

[6] All needed information is only available for copying at most t seconds before traveling because of the requirement to fetch fresh tokens before traveling, all needed information is only available after the tokens have been fetched.

threat that widespread attacks can cause significant disturbances in the perception of the ticketing system by travelers, since an attacker can easily cause denial-of-service and cases where many kinds of plausible undeniability may surface. Clearly, a system where the traveler's phone is equipped with a TEE is the more user-friendly choice.

6   Implementation and Measurements

We have used Google Nexus S phone running Android 4.1.1, Jelly Bean, to implement our non-gated protocol on the phones without TEE support. Although Google Nexus S has an embedded secure element (SE), an API to access the SE is not included in the publicly available SDK [6]. We have implemented the mobile-ticketing application on the phone using Android SDK with level 14 APIs. The touch-point smart cards implemented using SmartMX tags were upgraded with the protocol addition described in Section 5. Figure 8 shows an example of the touch-point with a SmartMX tag used in the trial. The application on the phone uses NFC reader / writer mode to communicate with the SmartMX tags using Android NFC IsoDep class APIs.

The application reported on in this work retrieves two elements of a hash chain from the server at a time. Therefore the phone can be used twice to interact with the touch-point tags before a new token is required. In other words, a phone can be used for a single journey beginning with a tap-in event and terminating with a tap-out event. Additionally, the token has been generated in such a way that it is valid for the tap-in event only during the first 15 minutes after the token was received. Figure 9 shows the mobile-ticketing application used in the trial running on Nokia 603 phone and the application with the revised protocol for open devices running on Nexus S phone.

Table 1 presents the measurements of average execution times for different SmartMX operations measured from the Nokia 603 with a TEE (as used in the trial) and the Nexus S phone without TEE support. The Nokia 603 and

Fig. 8. touch-point used in the trial

Fig. 9. Mobile-ticketing application running on Nokia 603 and Nexus S

Table 1. Time measurements of SmartMX operations in non-gated protocol

Platform	Initialize and read certificate	Challenge Response	Total
Nokia 603	45 ms	212 ms	305 ms
Nexus S	55 ms	718 ms	820 ms

the SmartMX tag run the baseline protocol intended for devices with a TEE. The Nexus S interacts with the SmartMX tag using the revised protocol for open devices. The measurements do not include the wake-up time taken by the operation systems to indicate the NFC touch event to the application. The new protocol additions increase the amount of SmartMX tag operations which is visible as the 500 milliseconds (ms) increase in the challenge response time. The table also shows that the NFC data exchange speed in Nokia 603 Symbian phone is slightly faster than Android Nexus S phone.

7   Conclusions

The research question how to achieve a workable ticketing solution for NFC phones can be seen as the task to minimize fraud opportunity balancing between networked-based auditing and security mechanisms which can be leveraged in contemporary end-user devices. Requirements stemming from the target transport system and end-user usability must be considered non-negotiable.

In this paper, we studied approaches for using NFC phones with limited platform security in a ticketing system. Likewise, we presented mechanisms by which the fare collection properties of the system can be upheld with insecure devices. We noticed the importance of categorizing users based on their tap reporting behavior and using this information to accelerate the reporting time of tap events to the back-end cloud, thereby improving the auditing accuracy. Speedy identification of misbehavior, such as double-spending attempts, minimizes the liability consequences for the traveler in an identity-based ticketing system.

We also reported on a big-scale trial in a real transport system with more than 100 participants. A user-study conducted at the end of the four-week trial in New York in the summer of 2012 gave very promising feedback and a motivation to continue exploring this field: 42% of the participants felt that a smart phone was the preferred user credential for transport ticketing, compared to only 24% in favor of a smart card or payment card. The perceived comfort level of the participants of this system was also surprisingly high considering that this was a first for most participants — 64% of the travelers were pleased with using the phone as a "travel token" compared to only 11% that were not satisfied with the solution. We believe that this level of user acceptance indicates that ticketing with NFC phones may grow to become a "killer use case" for mobile phone NFC use.

Acknowledgements. The referenced field trial was conducted as a collaboration between MTA in New York and the Nokia Location and Commerce business unit. Without the hard work of Peter Preuss, Justus Brown, Jerome Beaurepaire, Andreas Graf from Nokia L&C, and the technical expertise and contacts of Jukka Virtanen and Jarkko Sevanto the trial would never have seen the light of day.

References

1. Bloom, B.H.: Space/time trade-offs in hash coding with allowable errors. Commun. ACM 13(7), 422–426 (1970)
2. Bugiel, S., Davi, L., Dmitrienko, A., Heuser, S., Sadeghi, A.-R., Shastry, B.: Practical and lightweight domain isolation on android. In: Proceedings of the 1st ACM Workshop on Security and Privacy in Smartphones and Mobile Devices, SPSM 2011, pp. 51–62. ACM, New York (2011)
3. Chaumette, S., Dubernet, D., Ouoba, J., Siira, E., Tuikka, T.: Architecture and comparison of two different user-centric NFC-enabled event ticketing approaches. In: Balandin, S., Koucheryavy, Y., Hu, H. (eds.) NEW2AN 2011 and ruSMART 2011. LNCS, vol. 6869, pp. 165–177. Springer, Heidelberg (2011)
4. de Koning Gans, G., Hoepman, J.-H., Garcia, F.D.: A practical attack on the MIFARE classic. In: Grimaud, G., Standaert, F.-X. (eds.) CARDIS 2008. LNCS, vol. 5189, pp. 267–282. Springer, Heidelberg (2008)
5. Derler, D., Potzmader, K., Winter, J., Dietrich, K.: Anonymous ticketing for NFC-enabled mobile phones. In: Chen, L., Yung, M., Zhu, L. (eds.) INTRUST 2011. LNCS, vol. 7222, pp. 66–83. Springer, Heidelberg (2012)
6. Dmitrienko, A., Sadeghi, A.-R., Tamrakar, S., Wachsmann, C.: SmartTokens: Delegable access control with NFC-enabled smartphones. In: Katzenbeisser, S., Weippl, E., Camp, L.J., Volkamer, M., Reiter, M., Zhang, X. (eds.) Trust 2012. LNCS, vol. 7344, pp. 219–238. Springer, Heidelberg (2012)
7. Ekberg, J.-E., Tamrakar, S.: Mass transit ticketing with NFC mobile phones. In: Chen, L., Yung, M., Zhu, L. (eds.) INTRUST 2011. LNCS, vol. 7222, pp. 48–65. Springer, Heidelberg (2012)
8. Garcia, F.D., de Koning Gans, G., Muijrers, R., van Rossum, P., Verdult, R., Schreur, R.W., Jacobs, B.: Dismantling MIFARE classic. In: Jajodia, S., Lopez, J. (eds.) ESORICS 2008. LNCS, vol. 5283, pp. 97–114. Springer, Heidelberg (2008)
9. Garcia, F., van Rossum, P., Verdult, R., Schreur, R.W.: Wirelessly pickpocketing a mifare classic card. In: IEEE Symposium on Security and Privacy, pp. 3–15 (2009)
10. Ghiron, S.L., Sposato, S., Medaglia, C.M., Moroni, A.: Nfc ticketing: A prototype and usability test of an nfc-based virtual ticketing application. In: First International Workshop on Near Field Communication, NFC 2009, pp. 45–50 (February 2009)
11. Huang, E.: Automated Security Analysis of Payment Protocols. Ph. D. Thesis, Massachusetts Institute of Technology, Dept. of Civil and Environmental Engineering (2012)
12. ISO/IEC 14443: Identification cards – Contactless integrated circuit cards – Proximity cards. ISO, Geneva, Switzerland (2008)
13. Kostiainen, K., Ekberg, J.-E., Asokan, N., Rantala, A.: On-board credentials with open provisioning. In: ASIACCS 2009: Proceedings of the 4th International Symposium on Information, Computer, and Communications Security, pp. 104–115. ACM, New York (2009)

14. mobiThinking: Global mobile statistics 2012 part b: Mobile web; mobile broadband penetration; 3g/4g subscribers and networks, `http://mobithinking.com/mobile-marketing-tools/latest-mobile-stats/b` (accessed: February 2013)

15. Smart Card Alliance: Transit and contactless open payments: An emerging approach for fare collection. A Smart Card Alliance Transportation Council White Paper (November 2011), `http://www.smartcardalliance.org/resources/pdf/Open_Payments_WP_110811.pdf` (accessed: February 2013)

TEEM: A User-Oriented Trusted Mobile Device for Multi-platform Security Applications

Wei Feng[1], Dengguo Feng[1], Ge Wei[2], Yu Qin[1],
Qianying Zhang[1], and Dexian Chang[1,3]

[1] Institute of Software Chinese Academy of Sciences
[2] GUANGDONG KAMFU Information & Technology CO., LTD
[3] Zhengzhou Institute of Information Science and Technology
`vonwaist@gmail.com`

Abstract. Trusted Computing (TC) can improve the security of various computing platforms. However, as new computing devices emerge and application scenarios increase, current trusted computing technology cannot satisfy various new demands. For example, mobile and embedded platforms may lack security components of trusted computing, users may need a portable trusted module[13] for multiple desktop machines, and users may hope to customize their own security features for new applications. This paper presents TEEM, a system that achieves these demands by designing a mobile-based portable TC module. TEEM is built on the general mobile devices of users, and its running environment can be protected by the secure features of embedded CPUs. For desktop machines, the mobile device with TEEM can act as a trusted computing module with USB bus. Finally, we have implemented TEEM using an ARM SoC platform and evaluated the performance of TEEM.

1 Introduction

People are performing safety-critical computations, and collecting or storing confidential data in a wide variety of computing devices, such as the traditional desktop or server machines and the currently popular smartphones or tablets. Unfortunately, these devices are usually not trustworthy, which will compromise users' safety and privacy in many security applications. Trusted computing has been proposed as a promising approach to enhance the security of various computing devices. For desktop PCs, secure chips like Trusted Platform Module (TPM)[1] or Trusted Cryptography Module (TCM)[2–4] can be used. For server machines, it usually isolates a single execution environment using a Virtual Machine Manager. For mobile and embedded devices, many methods are proposed to establish trust, such as TI M-Shield technology[5], ARM TrustZone [6], and TCG's Mobile Trusted Module (MTM) specification[7].

However, to the best of our knowledge, no method supports to provide trusted computing function for multiple computing platforms and meet their security requirements. Firstly, methods designed for desktop machines usually do not fit the needs of mobile devices, and vice versa. There are several reasons for this[22]: (1)Desktop machines are often x86-based, but most mobile devices are

M. Huth et al. (Eds.): TRUST 2013, LNCS 7904, pp. 133–141, 2013.

ARM-based. (2)Mobile devices are usually limited in computing resources and storage spaces compared to desktop machines. Furthermore, even in the desktop platforms, the TC demands are increasing. For instance, a portable TC module is needed to achieve user-based attestation in [13]. Portable Trusted Module (PTM)[13, 14] is proposed to support multiple desktop platforms, but cannot serve mobile devices. To achieve multi-platform property, the TC module is usually bound to a user rather than a device.

Another problem with trusted computing is about flexibility. It needs to add four new TPM commands for TPM chip to support Secure Function Evaluation (SFE) and LBS applications[8]. Aaraj[9] proposes the use of Elliptic Curve Cryptography (ECC) as a replacement for the RSA algorithm in order to reduce the performance overheads without compromising security. Authorisation session protocols (like OIAP and OSAP) of TPM are vulnerable to dictionary attacks and may need be updated to new SKAP protocol[21]. TPM 2.0[10] has just been published, and it includes updates to TPM commands and adds support for new algorithms. Thus it is inevitable for a TC module to support these extension, customization or update needs, but we have no permission to modify an actual hardware TPM/TCM chip which is controlled by its manufacturer.

In this paper, we address these problems by presenting the design and implementation of TEEM, a Trusted Execution Environment Module that can provide flexible trusted computing functions for multiple platforms. TEEM is user-oriented and satisfies various new demands, like the low overheads of mobile platforms and the portability of desktop platforms. TEEM is configurable in TC functions, which supports the extension and update of TC commands, protocols, algorithms and modules. Thus, it can meet various experimental and customization needs. We also implement a prototype of TEEM using a general ARM SoC development board Real210[11]. Finally, we evaluate the overheads imposed by TEEM and compare the performance of TEEM with two actual hardware chips (a TPM 1.2 chip and a TCM chip).

The rest of the paper is organized as follows. First, we present our motivation for TEEM and related work in Section 2. Then, we give the TEEM architecture in Section 3. Next, we present the implementation and evaluation in Section 4. Finally, Section 5 concludes the paper and discusses our future work.

2   Motivation and Related Work

TEEM is inspired by a large body of related work, including portable trusted module (PTM) and trusted computing on mobile and embedded system.

Portable Trusted Module. General TPM/TCM chips (also called Integrated Trusted Module) are attached to the motherboard of a trusted platform via a Low Pin Count (LPC) interface. Intel [12] first introduced PTM in 2002, which can be attached to the system by means of a USB connector. Later, many researchers analyzed the advantages of PTM. The idea of PTM makes the TC module flexible and portable enough to be used in different platforms. In TCG TPM scenario[13], one TPM is bound to one computing device and several users use one TPM. But in PTM scenario[13], one PTM is bound to one user and several computing devices use one PTM. In [13], authors have implemented a PTM based on USB Key. Surya [14] has also successfully designed, built and demonstrated a PTM solution based on an actual TPM chip. Now one user usually has two types of computing platforms: desktop machines and mobile devices. Since we aim to design a general TC module that can serve multiple platforms, PTM is a good choice. However, there are two drawbacks with PTM: (1)It needs user to buy an additional specialized USB device (e.g. a USB key with TPM) and increases user's purchase burden; (2)PTM is mainly designed for desktop machines, and mobile devices may not benefit from PTM. To solve these problems, we design and implement TEEM (our PTM) based on mobile devices rather than specific USB devices. Users often have owned these mobile devices and don't need to buy an additional USB device. Moreover, built on mobile devices, TEEM can also provide TC functions for mobile applications and is really a multiplatform-capable TC module.

Trusted Computing on Mobile and Embedded System. With the success of TPMs/TCMs in desktop computers, the idea of trusted computing has been extended to mobile and embedded devices. The Mobile Trusted Module (MTM)[7] is a specification for mobile platform, which provides APIs for secure storage and attestation, but does not by itself provide an isolated execution environment for secure code. Thus, the implementation of MTMs relies on the security features of mobile CPUs or some onboard smart cards. Winter[18] merged MTMs concepts with ARM TrustZone to build an open Linux-based embedded trusted computing platform. Dietrich[19] gave a MTM design using a JavaCard applet loaded on an on-board smart card. Nokia[20] also implemented a remote owner's MRTM logic on a Nokia N96 platform with the TI M-shield. To enable mobile trusted applications, TEEM includes the secure features of MTM. Its running can be protected by strongly isolation mechanism of ARM TrustZone. Its protected capabilities can be established by implementing the required commands, algorithms, protocols and modules as software components on the mobile device. Only via a software update, TEEM can be ported to any TrustZone-enabled mobile or embedded platforms.

3   TEEM Architecture

TEEM is a user-oriented trusted computing module, which is easy to carry and should be able to serve both the mobile devices and desktop machines. Figure 1 illustrates the deployment of TEEM and its relationship with various computing devices. Each user has two types of computing devices: mobile devices (smartphone, tablet, etc.) and desktop machines(PC, laptop, server, etc.). TEEM is deployed in the secure world (SW) of user's mobile device. The secure world is an isolated execution environment, which can be provided by the secure features of embedded CPUs (e.g. ARM TrustZone). TEEM necessarily relies on and invokes OS code, so a small secure kernel is included in the secure world. The TEEM deployed in the SW contains the necessary protected capabilities of trusted computing. The mobile applications in the normal world (NW) can

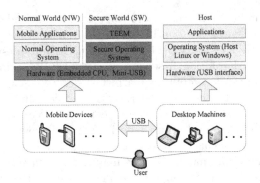

Fig. 1. TEEM deployment and Various Computing Platforms supported by TEEM

use the trusted functions of TEEM. In addition, the mobile device with TEEM can be plugged into any desktop machine via a USB cable. In this case, the mobile device with TEEM can be called *TEEM device*, which is bound to one user and can be used by multiple desktop platforms. Therefore, TEEM device is a Portable Trusted Module (PTM) solution with USB bus.

Though our high-level design is simple, we still need to overcome three main challenges: 1)to make the TC functions of TEEM flexible and configurable, 2)to establish a communication channel between the mobile applications in the NW and the TEEM in the SW, and 3)to establish a communication channel between the host applications and the TEEM device. To address these challenges, we: 1)divide TEEM into several independent functional components and provide a configuration and management GUI interface for it, 2)use the secure monitor call (SMC) instruction and secure procedure call (SPC) method in TLR[22] to enable communication between NW and SW, and 3)adopt the Universal Serial Bus (USB) mechanism to enable communication between the TEEM device and desktop machine. Thus we divide the system into three main parts (Figure 2): TEEM components, the communication components between SW and NW, and the communication components between SW and host.

TEEM Components. The typical functions of TEEM should include cryptographic capacity, communication capacity and TC-processing capacity. Therefore, TEEM itself consists of three independent components:(1)TC-Daemon is used to implement the communication capacity, which is responsible for listening for incoming TC command request, calling a correct TC module to handle the request and sending the replies to the requestor. (2)TC modules implement the TC-processing capacity, which are responsible for handling TC request and producing TC response. TC modules consist of multiple modules and each module follows a certain standard. For each module, it supports to add new commands and use different protocols and cryptographic algorithms. (3)Cryptographic library provides cryptographic capacity. Different TC modules often rely on different algorithms. New algorithms can be added into the library and the algorithm extension also supports localization, like SM2, SM3 and SMS4[2]in China.

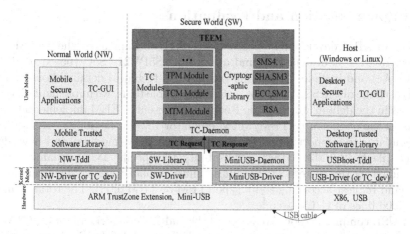

Fig. 2. Three main parts: TEEM components (green background), the communication components between SW and NW (lightgreen background), and the communication components between SW and host (orange background)

Communication Components between SW and NW. We propose to design two kernel-mode drivers: NW-Driver and SW-Driver. The drivers are responsible for implementing the ARM TrustZone context switch in/out of secure mode by using the secure procedure call (SPC) method in TLR[22]. NW-Driver is also responsible for providing a Trusted Computing device driver (TC_dev in Figure 2). SW-Library is used to hand off the appropriate input/output data from/to the SW-Driver, and acts as the bridge between SW-Driver and TC-Daemon. NW-Tddl provides a standardized interface for connecting to TC_dev. Mobile Trusted Software Library is based on NW-Tddl and provides an easy-to-use programming environment for mobile secure applications.

Communication Components between SW and Host. We have designed four components: the MiniUSB-Driver and USB-Driver in the kernel mode, and the MiniUSB-Daemon and USBhost-Tddl in the user mode. The MiniUSB-Driver can talk over a USB cable to the USB-Driver on a host PC and makes the mobile device look like a USB-based TC module. The MiniUSB-Daemon running in the SW is responsible for listening on the MiniUSB-Driver for incoming TC requests, forwarding the requests to TC-Daemon, receiving the corresponding responses from TC-Daemon and returning them to MiniUSB-Driver. The USB-Driver identifies the mobile device and establishes a channel with the MiniUSB-driver, and also provides a TC_dev for host applications. The USBhost-Tddl and Desktop Trusted Software Library have the same functions as the NW-Tddl and Mobile Trusted Software Library, respectively.

Finally, we design a TC-GUI to set (or get) the status of TEEM and test some key TC commands. The TC-GUI is designed to be based on a cross-platform UI development framework, thus it can run on the host and can also be ported to run on the mobile device.

4 Implementation and Evaluation

We use an ARM development board Real210[11] to implement the TEEM prototype. Real210 is designed around a Samsung S5PV210 SoC (based on ARM Cortex-A8) and includes TrustZone support. As technical details about how to use TrustZone of the S5PV210 SoC are not available to us, we implement all components in the default world of the Real210 at present. TEEM implementation is based on the open-source TPM/MTM emulator[15]. For flexibility, we modified the emulator to support more TC modules (like TCM module) and new algorithms (like SM2, SM3, SMS4). For usability, the specific TC commands should be handled by the correct TC modules. Thus, emulator was changed to handle command request according to its type (TPM or TCM ,etc.). The total changes were 4000 lines of C/C++ code.

For USB communication, We adopted the gadget serial driver and CDC/ACM driver[1]. The gadget serial driver talks over USB to a CDC/ACM driver running on a host PC. By designing TDDL library based on these drivers, the host can communicate with the Real210 as if it was using a USB-based TC chip. The USB communication components consisted of 924 lines of C code. To use TEEM, we adopted the libtpm[16], a C/C++ interface to the TPM, developed by IBM. We modified the libtpm to support TCM. We also changed the I/O interfaces of libtpm to use our USB mechanism. The modified version is called libteem, which is used as trusted software library. We used the QT[2] to develop the TC Graphical User Interface (TC-GUI). The modification to libtpm consisted of 1000 lines of C, and TC-GUI was 1300 lines of C/C++.

Figure 3 shows TEEM prototype based on Real210. Figure 4 describes the experimental environment using the prototype. The Windows host is a desktop x86 machine running Windows XP. It is equipped with a 2.4GHz Intel(R) Core(TM)2 Duo CPU, 3GB memory and several USB host interfaces. The Linux host is a VMware Virtual Machine running Ubuntu Linux system, which is assigned with 512MB memory and one-core CPU from the Windows host. The hosts and Real210 are connected via a USB cable.

Using the prototype system, we first evaluate the execution time of TEEM commands when various commands are called respectively by Real210 itself, the Windows host and the Linux host. Table 1 shows the execution time of TEEM commands. Some commands (e.g. Seal, CreateWrapKey, etc.) involve cryptographic operations or keys, and we all adopt 2048-bit RSA algorithm. Then, the performances of TEEM with different algorithms are compared with two actual hardware chips, including an actual TPM 1.2 hardware chip[3], and an actual TCM hardware chip[4]. The results is reported in Table 2. RSA and SM2 are public-key algorithms. SMS4 is a symmetric-key algorithm. For the TPM

---

[1] http://www.thesycon.de/eng/usb_cdcacm.shtml#demo

[2] http://qt.digia.com/Product/

[3] The host for the chip is IBM ThinkCentre M52 81114, and the TPM chip conforms to the TPM 1.2 standard of TCG.

[4] The host for the chip is Lenovo ThinkCentre M4000t, and the TCM chip conforms to the TCM specification of State Cryptography Administration.

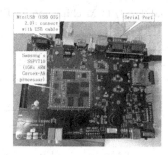

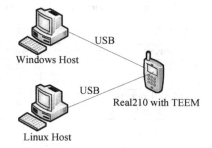

Fig. 3. The Real210 board with USB connected to the host

Fig. 4. Experiment Environment

Table 1. Execution Time of TEEM commands (R: Real210, WH: Windows Host, LH: Linux Host, Req/Resp: data size of Command Request/Response)

TEEM Commands	R (ms)	WH (ms)	LH (ms)	Req (bytes)	Resp (bytes)
Takeownership	3193	3926	3472	624	354
ReadPubEK	31.8	187	20.2-90	30	314
CreateKey	4432	4406	3928	146	610
LoadKey	611	655	439-983	618	55
EvictKey	1.9	62.5	31-547	14	10
GetPubKey	5.7	250	458	59	335
Sign	83	343	217-955	83	311
UnBind	84	375	167	319	66
GetRandom	3.9	78	25-700	14	1038
PcrRead	3.3	62.5	14.2	14	30
PcrExtend	3.2	62.5	15.7	34	30
Quote	86	359	167	84	400
Seal	11	288	116	142	363
Unseal	89	453	169	416	107
MakeIdentity	3240	3593	4337	187	911
ActivateIdentity	111	421	526	364	132

chip and TEEM-RSA, we use 2048-bit RSA algorithm. For the TCM chip and TEEM-SM2, we use 256-bit SM2 algorithm. For TEEM-SMS4, we use 128-bit SMS4 algorithm. All performance measurements for TPM and TCM have been done by calling TSS interface. All measurements for TEEM have been done by calling libteem interface. Therefore, the overheads for the TSS and libteem are included in the execution time.

Analysis. The execution time of TEEM commands is very stable on Real210. Most commands, like Sign, UnBind, Quote, Seal and Unseal, cost only less than 100ms. The Takeownership and CreateKey commands (not frequently used) may take several minutes. However, the execution time for host is not always stable. For example, the GetRandom command for Linux host can take only 25ms sometimes, but may increase to 700ms at other times. We discuss that possible

Table 2. Performance Comparison between actual TPM/TCM chips and TEEM

Commands	TPM	TCM	TEEM-RSA	TEEM-SM2	TEEM-SMS4
CreateKey	407ms	704ms	4432ms	174ms	12ms
LoadKey	781ms	438ms	611ms	170ms	10.7ms
Sign	609ms	625ms	83ms	176ms	n/a
Bind or Encrypt	63ms	15ms	3.5ms	315ms	7.0ms
UnBind or Decrypt	625ms	891ms	84ms	302ms	7.1ms

factors include USB communication, VMware Virtual Machine and kernel modules. Although the time for host is not stable, most commands take only less than 200ms, which is accepted for most secure applications. Thus, TEEM is an efficient solution for multiple platforms. Table 2 shows that TEEM running on Real210 is faster than the actual TPM/TCM chips. This is caused by stronger CPU in Real210 than the coprocessor in TPM/TCM.

5   Conclusion and Future Work

This paper presents a general-purpose trusted computing module TEEM, which can provide flexible trusted computing functions for multiple platforms. For mobile platforms, user can use TEEM only via a software update. For desktop platforms, user can connect the carry-on TEEM device to the desktop host using a USB cable. We have also implemented and evaluated a basic prototype of TEEM based on Real210. For future work, we will experiment with ARM TrustZone on the Real210 development board and further improve the TEEM prototype. We also consider to add and implement TPM 2.0 module based on TEEM prototype. Based on TEEM, we also consider to develop and implement some specific trusted applications.

Acknowledgments. This work has been supported by the National Natural Science Foundation of China (under grants No.91118006 and No.61202414) and the National 973 Program of China (under grants No.2013CB338003). This work has also been supported by Project of "Trusted Terminal System development and Terminal Product Industrialization for Self-help tax service" (under grants No.2011BY100042). We would also like to thank Xiaobo Chu, Li Xi and Bo Yang for their help to develop the prototype system.

References

1. Trusted Computing Group. Trusted platform module main specification. Version 1.2, Revision 103 (2007)
2. State Cryptography Administration. Functionality and Interface Specification of Cryptographic Support Platform for Trusted Computing (2007)
3. Feng, D., Qin, Y.: Research on Attestation Method for Trust Computing Environment. Chinese Journal of Computers (2008)

4. Feng, D., Qin, Y.: A property-based attestation protocol for TCM. Science China Information Sciences (March 2010)

5. Azema, J., Fayad, G.: M-Shield mobile security: Makeing wireless secure. Texas Instruments WhitePaper (June 2008)

6. ARM Limited. ARM Security Technology: Building a Secure System using Trust-Zone Technology. ARM Technical White Paper (2009)

7. TCG Mobile Phone Working Group. TCG mobile trusted module specification. Version 1.0, Revision 7.02 (April 2010)

8. Tate, S.R., Vishwanathan, R.: General Secure Function Evaluation using standard trusted computing hardware. In: PST 2011: International Conference on Privacy, Security and Trust, July 19-21, pp. 221–228 (2011)

9. Aaraj, N., Raghunathan, A., Ravi, S., Jha, A.K.: Energy and Execution Time Analysis of a Software-based Trusted Platform Module. In: Proceedings of the Conference on Design, Automation and Test in Europe. IEEE (2007)

10. Trusted Computing Group. Trusted Platform Module Library Part 1-4, Family "2.0" Level 00 Revision 00.93

11. Real210, http://www.realarm.cn/pic/?78_490.html

12. Intel. Mobile Platform Vision Guide for 2003 (September 2002)

13. Zhang, D., Han, Z., Yan, G.: A Portable TPM Based on USB Key. In: Proceedings of the 17th ACM Conference on Computer and Communications Security, New York, NY, USA (2010)

14. Nepal, S., Zic, J., Liu, D., Jang, J.: Trusted Computing Platform in Your Pocket. In: EUC 2010: Proceedings of the 2010 IEEE/IFIP International Conference on Embedded and Ubiquitous Computing, pp. 812–817. IEEE Computer Society, Washington, DC (2010)

15. Strasser, M.: TPM Emulator, http://tpm-emulator.berlios.de

16. Software TPM Introduction(IBM), http://ibmswtpm.sourceforge.net

17. Vasudevan, A., Owusu, E., Zhou, Z., Newsome, J., McCune, J.M.: Trustworthy Execution on Mobile Devices: What Security Properties Can My Mobile Platform Give Me? In: Katzenbeisser, S., Weippl, E., Camp, L.J., Volkamer, M., Reiter, M., Zhang, X. (eds.) Trust 2012. LNCS, vol. 7344, pp. 159–178. Springer, Heidelberg (2012)

18. Winter, J.: Trusted computing building blocks for embedded linux-based ARM trustzone platforms. In: Proceedings of the 3rd ACM Workshop on Scalable Trusted Computing, Alexandria, Virginia, USA, October 31 (2008)

19. Dietrich, K.: An integrated architecture for trusted computing for java enabled embedded devices. In: Proceedings of the 2007 ACM Workshop on Scalable Trusted Computing, Alexandria, Virginia, USA, November 02 (2007)

20. Ekberg, J.-E., Bugiel, S.: Trust in a small package: minimized MRTM software implementation for mobile secure environments. In: STC 2009: Proceedings of the 2009 ACM Workshop on Scalable Trusted Computing, ACM, NY (2009)

21. Chen, L., Ryan, M.: Attack, solution and verification for shared authorisation data in TCG TPM. In: Degano, P., Guttman, J.D. (eds.) FAST 2009. LNCS, vol. 5983, pp. 201–216. Springer, Heidelberg (2010)

22. Santos, N., Raj, H., Saroiu, S., Wolman, A.: Trusted language runtime (TLR): enabling trusted applications on smartphones. In: HotMobile 2011: Proceedings of the 12th Workshop on Mobile Computing Systems and Applications, pp. 21–26. ACM, New York (2011)

TRUMP: A Trusted Mobile Platform for Self-management of Chronic Illness in Rural Areas

Chris Burnett[1], Peter Edwards[1], Timothy J. Norman[1], Liang Chen[1],
Yogachandran Rahulamathavan[2], Mariesha Jaffray[1], and Edoardo Pignotti[1]

[1] dot.rural Digital Economy Research Hub*, University of Aberdeen, Aberdeen,
United Kingdom
{cburnett,p.edwards,t.j.norman,l.chen,m.jaffray}@abdn.ac.uk
[2] Information Security Group, School of Engineering and Mathematical Science,
City University London, London, U.K.
yogachandran.rahulamathavan.1@city.ac.uk

Abstract. Disease self-management interventions have the potential to greatly benefit both sufferers of chronic illnesses and healthcare providers in rural areas. In this paper, we discuss our vision for a trusted platform for delivering self-management interventions in rural areas of the UK and India using second-generation mobile devices, and outline the key trust and privacy challenges in realising such an infrastructure. We illustrate our discussion with an example depression intervention scenario, highlighting some progress to date, and our plans towards realising this architecture.

1 Introduction

Chronic illnesses, such as diabetes and depression, pose a difficult problem for healthcare providers, requiring a substantial allocation of clinical resources over a prolonged period. This problem is made worse in rural settings, with populations often spread out over large areas, and limited clinical resources situated beyond convenient reach of patients. Unconventional and *ad-hoc* healthcare arrangements, such as mobile clinics, can result in sporadic and inconsistent care. A patient's medical record may be fragmented, with different clinicians and health workers holding different pieces of information relevant to their own areas of expertise.

A growing body of evidence suggest that changes in lifestyle or behaviour can help alleviate symptoms of some chronic conditions [6,14]. This has lead to the development of *self-management behavioural interventions* [13] which can empower patients to conveniently manage their own symptoms, while allowing healthcare providers to allocate their resources more effectively. Rural areas in

---

* This research is supported by the award made by the RCUK Digital Economy and Energy programmes to the TRUMP UK-India project; award reference: EP/J00068X/1.

M. Huth et al. (Eds.): TRUST 2013, LNCS 7904, pp. 142–150, 2013.

particular stand to gain from the deployment of interventions which, for example, reduce the necessity for patients and clinicians to make long and frequent journeys, and allow greater numbers of chronic patients to be easily monitored by fewer clinicians.

In rural India, Internet-enabled mobile phones are becoming more common, making mobile phones an attractive platform for the deployment of such interventions [3]. The TRUMP (TRusted Mobile Platform) project[1] seeks to investigate some of the key issues surrounding the deployment of trustworthy platforms which support self-management interventions on mobile devices, particularly in rural areas of India and the UK. In particular, we are investigating the issues of trust and privacy which arise when medical data is generated and shared among individuals involved in an intervention.

While this paper discusses our vision of a general-purpose trustworthy platform for mobile healthcare interventions, we are also investigating the specific privacy and trust requirements of users in rural UK and India, for both depression and diabetes self-management, which will inform the development and evaluation of a prototype platform. To this end, the TRUMP project comprises clinical experts with experience of the deployment of interventions for depression and diabetes. As privacy and trust attitudes are inherently culturally dependant, the TRUMP project also includes anthropoplogical expertise in order to identify cultural differences in requirements.

In the remainder of this paper, we discuss mobile phone-based interventions for sufferers of depression, with particular focus on trust and privacy issues. We then outline some of our ongoing work towards a trusted platform for these interventions, and potential future directions.

2   Mobile Interventions

Self-management interventions typically comprise sequences of activities, to be carried out at specific times by various parties. For example, an intervention may require the patient to carry out some exercises, and then perform some self-reporting steps to allow progress to be monitored by a clinician. Interventions may employ complex information flows which require (possibly sensitive) information to be shared between participants, such as patients, clinicians, pharmacists, family members and support groups. The effectiveness of these interventions depends not only on the patient's compliance, but also on the acceptance of the intervention's information-sharing requirements by all involved parties.

Mobile phones provide an ideal platform for the delivery of such interventions. Easily carried by a patient, they can display context-relevant advice and prompts, and allow information to be conveniently transferred between patients and clinicians over a network connection, or via SMS[2] messages. Modern mobile phones are often equipped with web browsers, have (limited) on-board storage

---

[1] http://www.trump-india-uk.org/

[2] Short Message Service, allows messages of up to 140 characters to be sent between devices.

and can take often advantage of built-in or external sensors, such as heart-rate monitors, GPS receivers and pedometers, to augment self-reported feedback.

In rural areas however, neither smartphones, nor the infrastructure required to support them, may be particularly widespread. Connectivity and available bandwidth may vary between regions. Therefore, mobile interventions for rural areas must be capable of operating opportunistically in uncertain and changing network environments.

Example Intervention. Studies have shown that exercise can have an anti-depressive effect [6], and can help address the symptoms of depression. It is also known that patients who are prescribed courses of anti-depressive medicine often fail to adhere to or complete the course [9]. Reasons for this may include illness, patient characteristics, side effects and the nature of the doctor-patient relationship. Many healthcare interventions have been designed specifically to improve adherence to anti-depressant medication by improving symptom monitoring, using compliance aids and recently developed combinations of interventions which also encourage physical exercise.

Consider an intervention which aims to: (1) improve compliance with the prescribed medication regime and (2) increase the patient's level of daily exercise activity. The intervention involves a patient and doctor in a sequence of steps (Figure 1). In addition, actions may be performed automatically by the platform itself, according to rules which fire when certain conditions are met. These could include prompts, such as reminding the patient to continue with the course of medication and advising about daily exercise targets, and monitoring activities, such as prompting the patient to complete a mental health questionnaire (e.g. PHQ-9 [5]), and notifying the doctor to review the feedback. Based on the feedback from the patient, the doctor can take a more active role by providing custom messages, or modifying the intervention, for example, by changing the daily exercise targets. In order to help with monitoring compliance, modern mobile devices equipped with GPS technology, could be employed in tracking patients and ensuring that their self-reported feedback is consistent with sensor feedback from the device.

3   Aspects of a Trustworthy Platform

Fostering and maintaining user trust in the platform is crucial in maximising the effectiveness of interventions. Without trust, users may not be willing to provide accurate information to the system, or use it at all. Here, we discuss key trust and privacy issues associated with our platform.

3.1   Security and Privacy

For the platform to operate ethically (for example, to protect patient confidentiality) it must ensure that sensitive data is secured from unauthorised access, both in storage and in transit. In an intervention, a patient may generate and

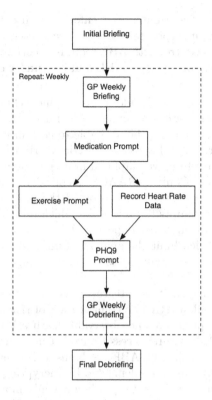

Fig. 1. Example depression intervention workflow

store their own healthcare information in a personally controlled medical record (PCHR) [4], part or all of which may reside on the mobile device at any time, and could be compromised should the phone be lost or stolen. Ensuring timely and appropriate access to sensitive medical information, while preventing malicious access, is therefore a key challenge in the deployment of our platform.

Cryptographic Techniques. To this end, we are investigating lightweight cryptographic protocols capable of providing an appropriate level of security while operating on legacy mobile devices [16]. Attribute-based encryption (ABE) allows data to be encrypted in such a way that it can only be accessed by individuals holding certain *attributes*, or complex combinations thereof. Different parts of a personal medical record can be encrypted according to different privacy policies; for example, a nurse may be able to decrypt general health information, but only a doctor with a given specialisation can decrypt more sensitive information. The existing ABE schemes in healthcare requires highly capable mobile devices at user-end [8]. Hence we are investigating low complexity cryptographic primitives where substantial amount of computational and communication overhead off-loaded to semi-trusted servers [7]. In ABE scheme complexity at user-end increases with number of attributes user enforces with each message, hence it would be appropriate to incorporate risk aware access control within ABE. Combining risk aware access control with ABE requires incorporation of integer comparison protocol within conventional ABE and it is under consideration.

Risk-Aware Access Control. While cryptographic techniques provide a means to protect private information from unauthorised users, they introduce the risk that critical information may not be available to certain key actors (in, for example, a medical emergency) due to overly-strict attribute-based access control or privacy policies. Therefore, we employ a more permissive model in our platform. Risk Aware Access Control (RAAC) [2] considers the *risk* involved when a requestor tries to access some information. If the risk is deemed too high to permit access, RAAC attempts to apply rules which mitigate the risk (*risk mitigation strategies*), for example, by imposing obligations on the requestor. Users are assigned *budgets* which limit the amount of unfulfilled obligations they can take on. Requestors may be required to discharge obligations before, or after, the access is allowed.

Currently, we are investigating integrating computational trust models together with RAAC to allow dynamic computation of risk levels given the trust (i.e. prior behaviour, reputation, and observable features) in the requestor. This TRAAC (Trust and Risk Aware Access Control) can then influence the particular encryption strategy taken by ABE mechanism. For instance, accesses that are considered less risky can be implemented by encrypting the data in question with a general attribute, such as *HospitalStaff*, while more risky accesses can be made to require a specific set of attributes, such as *HospitalStaff, Specialist, Oncologist* to decrypt.

Policies. These techniques require that the platform enable all participants in an intervention to express their privacy preferences in machine-readable formats. *Policies* express the actions that can, must or must not be taken with regards to some information items, expressed in policy *languages* (e.g. OWL-POLAR [12]). While patients may wish to employ strict privacy controls, this has the potential to render interventions infeasible. For example, policies may prohibit the gathering and sharing of information critical to an intervention's success. We consider an intervention *feasible* if it does not require any information transfers which violate the participants' policies. Given a set of policies and a specification of an intervention's information flows, it is possible to automatically determine whether an intervention is feasible. If it is not, a set of *conflict resolutions* can be computed which specify how to modify the policies or information flows so that the intervention is feasible [15]. Participants can then negotiate to find the most acceptable resolution which allows the intervention to proceed.

3.2   Trust and Transparency

Trust, however, is about more than simply securing sensitive information from attackers. Trust in an artefact increases when the artefact behaves as expected.

While the trust that a user places in the system is typically more difficult to define and quantify than purely computational notions of trust, it is critical in our system to maintain user compliance with an intervention. If users do not trust the system, it is unlikely that the intervention will be successful.

Trust in the System. In order to build this trust, it is essential that the behaviour of the system be made as transparent and clear to users as possible. Central to this is the maintenance of rich metadata, or *provenance* [10], about data created and consumed during an intervention. For example, the provenance record for a piece of information may include all the processes and decisions involved in its production, as well as contextual data from sensors, such as time, location, heart rate, weather conditions, and so on. This is necessary to permit all participants to effectively audit the behaviour of the system.

Trust may also be engendered by increasing the perceived *predictability* of the system to the user. Patients may be reluctant to provide accurate information at monitoring points due to uncertainty about the consequences of doing so. For example, consider an intervention where a late response at a particular stage by a patient will generate an automatic obligation on the doctor to investigate. Since our interventions are specified in a workflow language, it is possible to keep users advised about such potential future workflow states the workflow execution may take, in response to their input (or lack thereof). While such functionality would help our platform to appear more transparent to users, these alerting behaviours could also be regulated by policies if required by the intervention.

Trust Assertions. On the other hand, trust is also an important issue for clinicians charged with making critical decisions in an intervention, who must be able to place a degree of trust in the data generated by the patient on a mobile device. To support this, the platform should enable the formation of *trust assertions* about other participants, or the information they produce. Such assertions could take the form $trusts(userA, userB, weeklyReportDeadline, 0.79)$, which states that $userA$ ascribes $userB$ a trust value of 0.79, representing (for example) the probability with which $userA$, in her experience, expects that $userB$ will submit a weekly report by the deadline. However, assertions could also be generalised or *stereotypical* [1]. For example, a particular user $userA$ may have a low degree of trust in any General Practitioner submitting the weekly report on time (e.g. $trusts(userA, GeneralPractitioner, weeklyReportDeadline, 0.2)$). Similarly, a trust assertion could involve two such "stereotypes", representing some biased behaviour in the system. For example, Nurses may be more reliable when completing certain tasks from Specialists than from General Practitioners:

$$trusts(GeneralPractitioner, Nurse, weeklyReportDeadline, 0.7)$$
$$trusts(Specialist, Nurse, weeklyReportDeadline, 0.84)$$

These trust assertions represent the trust placed in users by the *system*, as computed by a computational trust model (see [11] for a comprehensive review), and represent their reliability in fulfilling their roles. These assessments can be formed in a number of ways. For example, reliability of self-reported exercise statistics could be assessed by comparison with heart rate data. Past reporting behaviour, as well as information from other sources, can be used to make assertions about the reliability of information provided by patients in the future. Similarly, trust assertions could be formed about any actor in the intervention. However, these processes must be made transparent to all users

Such assertions are crucial during both instantiation and execution phases of interventions. When an intervention begins, concrete individuals will be assigned to particular roles, and specific details will be added (locations of meetings, deadlines for tasks, etc.). At this stage, these assertions allow the *trustworthiness* of available candidates to be considered when deciding which actors should play which roles, given their past performance. As interventions are executed, a monitoring mechanism updates these trust assertions as new observations are made. Rules can be specified which alert users when the trustworthiness of certain actors changes, or drops below a particular threshold, perhaps indicating that some repair activity may be necessary (e.g. replacing the actor). This is particularly important in dynamic and ad-hoc organisational arrangements frequently found in rural areas with limited access to consistent levels of human or financial resources.

4   Architecture

An overview of our architecture is presented in Figure 2. Since our focus lies with the trust and workflow components, we are investigating off-the-shelf, open-source PCHR software which implements this functionality (Part 1, Figure 2), of which Indivo[3] is a prominent example.

A workflow enactment module (2) is necessary to coordinate execution of the intervention represented in a workflow language [10]. At present, we are investigating the use of the open BPMN[4] language (Business Process Model and Notation). One benefit of adopting this language is the availability of graphical tools for authoring and executing workflows, such as the jBPM (`http://www.jboss.org/jbpm/`) engine. This facilitates mutual understanding of the intervention and its state among its various stakeholders. User and workflow actions are policed by our policy module (2), which enforces user- and system-level policies, and provides conflict-resolution services. A trust module (3) produces trust assertions based on the past behaviours of participants according to the intervention workflow. This is supported by a provenance module (4) which annotates data as required to produce trust assertions. Finally, the security layer (5) provides lightweight authentication and encryption services for the layers below.

---

[3] `http://indivohealth.org/`
[4] `http://www.bpmn.org`

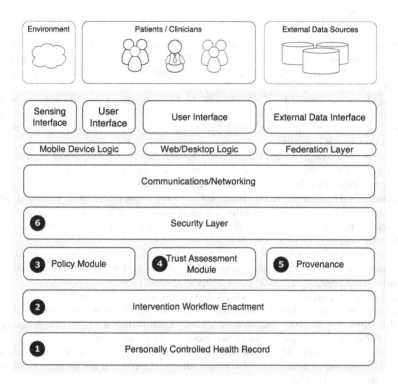

Fig. 2. TRUMP platform architecture overview

5   Conclusion and Future Work

In this paper, we have outlined our vision of a general architecture for the deployment of mobile or web-based self-management interventions for chronic illnesses, giving specific attention to the key trust and privacy issues. Rural environments present a challenging domain for these interventions, but also present an opportunity for positive transformational impact; for example, effective self-management interventions could help to reduce the load and cost placed on already overburdened rural healthcare resources. These platforms must be demonstrably secure, transparent and privacy-preserving. The next phase of the project will bring together clinical, anthropological and computer science expertise, together with various user groups, in a participatory design process. This will gather requirements and attitudes from various user groups (e.g. doctors and patients), informing the design of the mobile intervention and its user-facing aspects, and in turn the kinds of trust-preserving behaviours that the underlying platform will need to support. This will be followed by pilot studies which will investigate the effectiveness of mobile interventions deployed on our platform, for example, in terms of compliance, perceived trustworthiness and improving user attitudes.

References

1. Burnett, C., Norman, T.J., Sycara, K.: Bootstrapping trust evaluations through stereotypes. In: Proc. 9th International Conference on Autonomous Agents and Multiagent Systems, vol. 1, pp. 241–248. International Foundation for Autonomous Agents and Multiagent Systems (2010)

2. Chen, L., Crampton, J., Kollingbaum, M.J., Norman, T.J.: Obligations in risk-aware access control. In: Proc. 2012 Tenth Annual International Conference on Privacy, Security and Trust, PST 2012, pp. 145–152. IEEE Computer Society, Washington, DC (2012)

3. Ganesan, M., Prashant, S., Pushpa, V., Janakiraman, N.: The use of mobile phone as a tool for capturing patient data in southern rural Tamil Nadu, India. J. Health Informatics in Developing Countries, 219–227 (2011)

4. Halamka, J.D., Mandl, K.D., Tang, P.C.: Early experiences with personal health records. J. American Medical Informatics Association 15(1), 1–7 (2008)

5. Kroenke, K., Spitzer, R.L., Williams, J.B.W.: The PHQ-9. J. General Internal Medicine 16(9), 606–613 (2001)

6. Lawlor, D.A., Hopker, S.W.: The effectiveness of exercise as an intervention in the management of depression: systematic review and meta-regression analysis of randomised controlled trials. BMJ 322(7289), 763 (2001)

7. Li, F., Rahulamathavan, Y., Phan, R.C.W., Rajarajan, M.: Low complexity multi-authority attribute based encryption scheme for mobile cloud computing. In: Proc. IEEE Int'l Symposium on Mobile Cloud, Computing and Service Engineering (IEEE MobileCloud 2013), San Francisco. IEEE (March 2013)

8. Narayan, S., Gagne, M., Safavi-Naini, R.: Privacy preserving ehr system using attribute-based infrastructure. In: Proc. 2010 ACM Workshop on Cloud Computing Security Workshop. ACM (2010)

9. Pampallona, S., Bollini, P., Tibaldi, G., Kupelnick, B., Munizza, C.: Patient adherence in the treatment of depression. The British Journal of Psychiatry 180(2), 104–109 (2002)

10. Pignotti, E., Edwards, P., Preece, A., Gotts, N., Polhill, G.: Enhancing workflow with a semantic description of scientific intent. In: Bechhofer, S., Hauswirth, M., Hoffmann, J., Koubarakis, M. (eds.) ESWC 2008. LNCS, vol. 5021, pp. 644–658. Springer, Heidelberg (2008)

11. Pinyol, I., Sabater-Mir, J.: Computational trust and reputation models for open multi-agent systems: a review. Artificial Intelligence Review, 1–25 (2012)

12. Şensoy, M., Norman, T.J., Vasconcelos, W.W., Sycara, K.: OWL-POLAR: Semantic policies for agent reasoning. In: Patel-Schneider, P.F., Pan, Y., Hitzler, P., Mika, P., Zhang, L., Pan, J.Z., Horrocks, I., Glimm, B. (eds.) ISWC 2010, Part I. LNCS, vol. 6496, pp. 679–695. Springer, Heidelberg (2010)

13. Bodenheimer, T., Lorig, K., Holman, H., Grumbach, K.: Patient self-management of chronic disease in primary care. J. American Medical Assoc. 288(19), 2469–2475 (2002)

14. Thomas, C., Day, C.P., Trenell, M.I.: Lifestyle interventions for the treatment of non-alcoholic fatty liver disease in adults: A systematic review. Journal of Hepatology (2011)

15. Vasconcelos, W., Kollingbaum, M.J., Norman, T.J.: Resolving conflict and inconsistency in norm-regulated virtual organizations. In: Proc. of the 6th International Joint Conference on Autonomous Agents and Multiagent Systems, p. 91. ACM (2007)

16. Weerasinghe, D., Muttukrishnan, R.: Secure trust delegation for sharing patient medical records in a mobile environment. In: 2011 7th International Conference on Wireless Communications, Networking and Mobile Computing (WiCOM), pp. 1–4. IEEE (2011)

First-Class Labels:
Using Information Flow to Debug Security Holes*

Eric Hennigan, Christoph Kerschbaumer, Stefan Brunthaler,
Per Larsen, and Michael Franz

University of California, Irvine
{eric.hennigan,ckerschb,s.brunthaler,perl,franz}@uci.edu

Abstract. We present a system of first-class labels that assists web
authors in assessing and diagnosing vulnerabilities in web applications,
focusing their attention on flows of information specific to their application. Using first-class labels, web developers can directly manipulate
labels and express security policies within JavaScript itself, leveraging
their existing knowledge to improve the quality of their applications. Introducing first-class labels incurs no additional overhead over the implementation of information flow in a JavaScript Virtual Machine, making
it suitable for use in a security testing environment even for applications
that execute large amounts of JavaScript code.

1 Motivation

The JavaScript programming language has become indispensable for Web 2.0
applications and powers almost all of today's banking and electronic commerce
sites. These organizations regularly use JavaScript to process sensitive information, such as credit card numbers and user credentials. The ability to perform
client-side processing has facilitated the adoption of interactive pages, while simultaneously introducing a new code injection attack vector known as Cross
Site Scripting (XSS). Within the web browser, the JavaScript execution model
allows objects from different domains to reference each other. This architectural
weakness gives adversaries the ability to gain access to sensitive data held within
the browser and manipulated by a page's code.

Currently, web sites rely on the browser enforced Same Origin Policy [14],
which limits interactions between different domains, with the intent of separating content from different providers. This restriction applies to separate pages

---

* This material is based upon work partially supported by the Defense Advanced Re-
search Projects Agency (DARPA) under contract No. D11PC20024, by the National
Science Foundation (NSF) under grant No. CCF-1117162, and by a gift from Google.
Any opinions, findings, and conclusions or recommendations expressed in this material are those of the authors and do not necessarily reflect the views of the Defense
Advanced Research Projects Agency (DARPA) or its Contracting Agent, the U.S.
Department of the Interior, National Business Center, Acquisition Services Directorate, Sierra Vista Branch, the National Science Foundation, or any other agency
of the U.S. Government.

M. Huth et al. (Eds.): TRUST 2013, LNCS 7904, pp. 151–168, 2013.
© Springer-Verlag Berlin Heidelberg 2013

and `iframe`'s, but does not prevent method and memory access when the host page includes a third party script, such as the JQuery library or a syndicated advertisement. The lack of isolation between scripts from separate origins that execute on the same web page, threatens the privacy of all web users.

Other systems implementing information flow within a web browser [9, 10, 13] attempt to perform fully automatic labeling, with no feedback from the developer. Because privacy concerns are application specific, we present an alternative approach that additionally provides developers with the ability to selectively focus on specific information flows within their web application. Without domain knowledge, fully automatic frameworks detect and report information flows, such as requests from content distribution servers, that application developers would prefer to disregard.

Based on our experience, we think that information flow tracking shows more promise as a web application security debugging tool, if it can help the developer focus only on flows relevant to an XSS vulnerability. We achieve this goal by extending an existing information flow tracking browser with a system of first-class labels that developers can use to inspect their application. By selectively tagging only those variables considered security sensitive, developers can focus their attention on flows of specific information, and avoid sifting through the morass of reports generated by automated tracking systems. We envision web developers using the first-class labeling system as part of a testing environment to answer common auditing questions: "Does this sensitive data ever influence a network request?" and "What values does this object influence?"

After presenting the threat posed by attackers (Section 2), we establish information flow terminology (Section 3) to clarify the capabilities of the underlying tracking engine on which we base our work. We then introduce details of the supporting information flow framework (Section 4) relevant to the following contributions:

- We extend JavaScript's syntax and semantics (Section 5) introducing a reflective `FlowLabelObject` and new `labelof` operator.
- To the best of our knowledge, we are the first to provide a first-class labeling system within JavaScript (Section 6) that allows developers to selectively tag application specific sensitive information from a webpage and compose security policies in JavaScript.
- We demonstrate the utility of the first-class labeling system by showing an attack that aims to exfiltrate sensitive user information and a JavaScript-specified network policy that stops the attack (Section 6.3).

We evaluate (Section 7) our first-class labeling system demonstrating that it maintains performance, resists JavaScript-level attacks against itself while exposing underlying security data structures, and provides a mechanism that the web developer can effectively use to debug security holes in a web application.

2   The Attacker's Threat

Throughout this work, we assume that the attacker has already injected code into the developer's web application. The attacker exploits an XSS vulnerability to inject code in the developer's web application, supplying a JavaScript payload via an included advertisement, mashup content, or library, or via an unsanitized form or URL. Although we limit the attack payload to JavaScript, we assume that its origin does not make it distinguishable from the rest of the web application's JavaScript codebase. The attacker also has publicly-facing knowledge about the application, obtained by visiting and interacting with the application and observing its behavior, which can be used to craft the payload. We also assume that the attacker controls their own web server.

These abilities combine to pose an information leak threat. The code injected into the web application executes with the full abilities of that application. The attacker crafts the payload to exfiltrate application sensitive information, such as personal login credentials, text the user enters into forms, or anything the web application displays to a visitor. The pilfered information leaves the application as part of a resource request submitted to the attacker controlled server, circumventing the Same Origin Policy.

For a typical example, exfiltration code embeds the sensitive data into a URL and attaches that URL to the `src` attribute of a payload generated `img` element. The web browser automatically issues a GET request for the image targeting the attacker controlled server. The attacker then reviews server request logs to harvest the exfiltrated information.

2.1   The Developer's Response

Knowing that the origin of attacker code does *not* reliably distinguish it from the rest of the web application, we focus on the malicious *behavior* of any code within the application. Indeed, an information leak might be the unintended result of a careless or uninformed application developer, rather than an attacker.

In response to this threat, a security-conscious developer tests their application in a web browser that monitors the flows of information within the application. To assist the developer in focusing their debugging attention on specific pieces of sensitive data within the application, we present a labeling system as a first-class language construct. Without leaving JavaScript, the developer creates a label and applies it to the sensitive data, tagging it with a unique identifier. The underlying information flow engine tracks the interaction of application (and injected) code with this sensitive data, ensuring that exfiltration code does not drop the label.

We present a mechanism that allows the developer to write a network monitor using JavaScript, so that they may observe a leak of information tagged as sensitive. The developer implements their own network monitor logic to inspect the labels of all resource requests, enabling the detection and debugging of an information leak.

Table 1. Terminology of Information Flows

Category	Descriptor	Example	Flow	Required Analysis
Explicit	Direct	`b = a`	$a \Rightarrow b$	Dataflow
	Indirect	`b = foo(_, a, _)` `c = bar(_, b, _)`	$a \Rightarrow c$	Dataflow (transitive)

Implicit	Direct	`if (a)`
		`    b = 1`
		`else`
		`    b = 0`
			$a \Rightarrow b$	Control Flow (dynamic)

	Indirect	`c = true`
		`if (a)`
		`    b = false`
		`if (b)`
		`    c = false`
			$a \Rightarrow c$	Control Flow (static)

3   Information Flow Terminology

Previous research in the field of information flow applied to dynamic languages reveals a need for clarifying terminology that goes beyond the basic categories introduced by Denning and Denning [5]. We follow this trend by extending the established categories with easy-to-remember descriptors. We intend for the terminology introduced here to bring clarity and precision to the research describing information flow systems, especially research targeting dynamic languages. The more refined terminology allows us to characterize the capabilities of the information flow tracking engine (Section 4) which supports the first class label system introduced in this paper (Section 6).

3.1   Explicit Information Flows

An *explicit flow* occurs as a result of a dataflow dependence. Table 1 breaks this category down into two descriptors: *direct*, corresponding to an immediate dependence, and *indirect*, corresponding to a transitive dependence.

Explicit Direct Flows occur when a value is influenced as a result of direct data transfer, such as an assignment. A simple single-statement, intra-procedural dataflow analysis can identify these flows. Subexpressions involving more than one argument also have a direct explicit information flow from all argument values to the operator's resulting value. Any labeling or tagging framework that tracks security type information across direct explicit flows includes basic semantic rules for label propagation in each of the language's operators.

Explicit Indirect Flows occur as the transitive closure of direct flows. Identification of indirect flows requires more powerful multi-statement or interprocedural dataflow analysis. The code example for indirect flows in Table 1 shows the transitive nature of this analysis via a functional dependence between values. This paper preserves the use of the term "indirect" as originally defined by Denning and Denning [5].

3.2   Implicit Information Flow

An *implicit flow* occurs as a result of a control-flow dependence. Table 1 breaks this category down into to descriptors: *direct*, corresponding to a runtime dependence, and *indirect*, corresponding to a static dependence.

Implicit Direct Flows occur when a value depends on a previously taken control-flow branch *at runtime*. Identification of this dependence requires a tracked program counter and a recorded history of control-flow branches taken during program execution. Presently, systems that track the program counter to propagate dependence information are known as "dynamic information flow tracking" systems.

Implicit Indirect Flows occur when a value depends on a control-flow branch *not taken* during program execution. Identification of this dependence requires a static analysis prior to program execution. Because the dependence follows code paths not taken at runtime, these flows are notoriously difficult to detect in dynamic programming languages. Unfortunately, even static languages include features, such as object polymorphism and reference returning functions, which make the receiver of an assignment or method call unknown at compile time. Dynamic programming languages, such as JavaScript, include first-class functions, runtime field lookup along prototype chains, and the ability to load additional code at runtime via `eval`. These features prohibit even a runtime analysis from identifying all the values possibly influenced in all alternative control-flow branches.

4   Supporting Framework

The framework which supports the first-class labeling system presented in this paper implements dynamic information flow as part of the JavaScript Virtual Machine (VM). Any viable information flow system within a web browser must support runtime creation and application of labels because security principals represented on a web page do not become known to the browser and JavaScript VM until a user visits the page. Every JavaScript value carries a label representing an element from the finite powerset lattice over principals. The VM conservatively labels the result of every operation with the union (join) of the labels of its inputs, monotonically moving up the lattice of security principals. To prevent attack code from removing or downgrading the labels applied to values tracked by the VM, the labeling framework does not currently provide a mechanism for declassification (i.e., it does not expose an intersection (meet) operation).

4.1   Storage of Security Principals and Labels

The underlying labeling framework allows any JavaScript value to be used as a security principal. Our first-class labeling system merely exposes this ability as

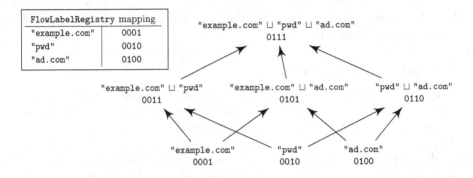

Fig. 1. The `FlowLabelRegistry` mapping three JavaScript strings used as security principals to unique bit positions. These principals form a lattice of security labels, represented as bit vectors.

a concise labeling API to the JavaScript developer. As we shall see (Section 6), the ability to use any JavaScript value as a principal gives web authors enough power to represent security principals as a native part of an application's code.

The supporting information flow VM interns every JavaScript value used as a security principal in the `FlowLabelRegistry`, mapping it to a unique bit position. Figure 1 depicts the interning of three JavaScript string objects, `"example.com"`, `"pwd"`, and `"ad.com"`, each representing a security principal in the `FlowLabelRegistry`. To minimize the attack surface on the system itself, our first-class extensions (Section 5) do not make this data structure accessible to the JavaScript programmer.

As shown in Figure 1, the mapping held by the `FlowLabelRegistry` allows a bit vector to represent each security label. The supporting VM attaches to every JavaScript value a security label, representing an element from a powerset lattice over security principals. Current implementation of the underlying information flow framework does not support more than 64 unique principals. However, we have not found this to be a problem in practice (Section 7).

4.2 Label Propagation

Our labeling system rests atop a pre-existing, JavaScript information flow VM that provides every JavaScript primitive and object reference with a security label. The supporting VM propagates labels through data flows and maintains a shadow stack of labels attached to the program counter [8] that tracks influence through control-flow transfers taken at runtime. These mechanisms allow it to track up to implicit direct information flow (as defined in Section 3).

Performing information flow tracking at the VM level allows the supporting framework to avoid potential attacks on the tracking system itself. This design reduces the attack surface compared to JavaScript rewriting systems [4, 9].

Exposing the underlying framework through our first-class labeling system might create a new attack surface (targeting the underlying label framework itself) meant to be hidden by design. As a result of this concern, we chose not to support declassification through our first-class labeling system. Both the JavaScript developer and any potential JavaScript attack code can only create, apply, and inspect labels, but cannot remove them.

```
1 function sniffPassword(pw) {
2   var spw = "";
3   for (var i = 0; i < pw.length; i++) {
4     switch(pw[i]) {
5     case 'a': spw += 'a'; break;
6     case 'b': spw += 'b'; break;
7     ... // other characters elided
8     }
9   }
10  return spw;
11 }
```

Listing 1.1. Password sniffing via implicit direct information flow.

Listing 1.1 gives an example of an attacker provided function which attempts to drop any label attached to the argument pw. The existing label framework can track the control-flow dependence of the return variable (spw) on the argument (pw) at both the loop condition (pw.length) and the switch condition (pw[i]). By performing such tracking, the returning variable spw subsumes the same set of principals as the incoming function argument pw. The tracking and propagation engine prevents the attacker from dropping labels through implicit direct information leaks in exfiltration code.

4.3   Information Flow in the Browser

Our first-class labeling system resides in a web browser that consists of a hosted JavaScript VM and additional subsystems for information storage, rendering, document description, and network communication. These other subsystems represent covert channels through which an attacker may communicate information. Currently, the supporting framework automatically applies labels to dynamically loaded code and resources according to the site of origin.

In addition to storing visible page elements, the Document Object Model (DOM) allows creation of invisible elements within the document that can be used to store and communicate information. The supporting framework propagates labels to HTML elements and attributes within the DOM so that an attacker cannot use it as a channel to remove labels.

The information flow tracking web browser also contains a network monitor that observes the labels on all network traffic: dynamic requests for remote resources such as images and stylesheets, HTTP GET and POST methods for forms, and XmlHttpRequest for AJAX. Our first-class labeling system presents to the web developer a mechanism for registering JavaScript functions which implements network monitor logic, enabling the developer to inspect labels attached to resource requests and thereby discover information leaks.

5 Design and Implementation of First-Class Labels

Before discussing the first-class label interface that a JavaScript developer uses to hook into the supporting information flow framework, we first give details explaining the extensions and modifications necessary to support labels as first-class JavaScript objects.

5.1 Reflecting Labels into JavaScript

The supporting framework contains a `FlowLabelRegistry` that maps primitive values and JavaScript objects used as principals to a position within a bit vector label. By holding a reference to every JavaScript object (within the standard heap) used as a principal, the `FlowLabelRegistry` keeps it alive during garbage collection. Because of the limited number of principals which can exist within the system (Section 4.1) the `FlowLabelRegistry` does not release any principals.

Our first-class labeling system reflects the underlying labels into the JavaScript language, as native JavaScript objects, via a `FlowLabelObject` wrapper. When reflected into JavaScript as `FlowLabelObject` instances, security labels can themselves be labeled and can also act as security principals, just like any other JavaScript value. Additionally, they are callable objects, providing an interface to apply the internally stored label onto any given argument value. In the interest of clarity, we do not use any examples that exhibit the inherent recursive nature of the first-class labeling system.

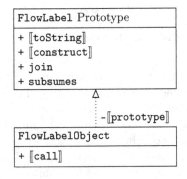

Fig. 2. UML class diagram of the first-class labeling system. Our system introduces the `FlowLabel` prototype constructor, and `FlowLabelObject` instances. As in the ECMA [6] language standard, [[•]] indicates implementation internal methods.

Our first-class labeling system also introduces a singleton `FlowLabel` protototype, which both holds methods common to all `FlowLabelObject` instances and provides an interface through which the JavaScript developer can construct `FlowLabelObjects`. Figure 2 uses UML to depict the relationship between the `FlowLabel` prototype singleton and `FlowLabelObject` instances.

5.2   JavaScript Syntax Extension to Retrieve Labels

Our first-class labeling system implements a small change to the JavaScript language permitting JavaScript code to retrieve a label from a given value. We introduce the keyword `labelof`, as a new case in the *UnaryExpression* grammar rule of the ECMA [6] language standard. Figure 3 presents the entire grammar rule, including our new language keyword.

```
UnaryExpression:
    PostfixExpression
    delete UnaryExpression
    void UnaryExpression
    typeof UnaryExpression
    ++ UnaryExpression
    - UnaryExpression
    + UnaryExpression
    - UnaryExpression
    ~ UnaryExpression
    ! UnaryExpression
    labelof UnaryExpression
```

Fig. 3. Modified JavaScript grammar rule for *UnaryExpression*. Our first-class labeling system introduces the `labelof` keyword.

5.3   Network Hook in the Web Browser

To permit the enforcement of policies written in JavaScript, we make one additional change to the web browser hosted JavaScript environment. Our first class labeling system exposes the underlying network monitor through a function, `registerSendMonitor(fn)` on the hosted `navigator` object. Using this feature, the web developer can phrase application specific security policies concerning allowed network communication as a JavaScript function within the web application itself. Once registered, these functions act as network monitors that inspect the payload of all resource requests before being sent over the network.

6   Using First-Class Labels

We design the first-class labeling system and its JavaScript API according to the functional programming paradigm, with the purpose of making it easier for web developers to adopt. The first-class labeling system contains one minor syntax change to the JavaScript grammar, introducing the new `labelof` operator and keyword. The system also extends the hosted environment (*not* the ECMA specification) with a new built-in `FlowLabel` prototype constructor object that holds methods for label composition (`join`) and comparison (`subsumes`). Labels take the form of native built-in `FlowLabelObject` instances, and behave with the same semantics as any other JavaScript object. Our first-class labeling system makes a minimal set of changes necessary to expose the underlying information flow framework.

We show how our framework detects and prevents information leakage that might occur due to a script injection attack. In the following examples we show output of our system at the JavaScript console. All statements executed by the console begin with a '>'. The console describes the resulting value in two parts: the value itself and the label attached to that value.

6.1 Label Creation

Our system introduces a `FlowLabel` prototype singleton to the JavaScript environment hosted by the web browser. This object implements the internal ⟦construct⟧ method so that JavaScript code may create first-class label objects. The web developer may choose any valid JavaScript value to act as a security principal, and pass that value into the constructor. After interning the provided value in the underlying framework's `FlowLabelRegistry`, the constructor returns a `FlowLabelObject` instance. Interning the principals allows unique identification of labels held by `FlowLabelObject` instances. In the interest of avoiding attacks on the labeling system itself, our system does not provide programmatic access to the `FlowLabelRegistry`.

```
1 > pwdLabel = new FlowLabel("pwd");
2   [FlowLabelObject pwd] [FlowLabel example.com]
```

Listing 1.2. Creating a Label Object.

Listing 1.2 shows a web developer creating a label using the JavaScript string, `"pwd"`, as a security principal. The underlying information flow framework automatically applies a label to every resource representing its domain of origin. Consequently, the resulting `FlowLabelObject` instance returned from the constructor itself carries a label representing the origin of this code snippet: `example.com`.

6.2 Label Application

The `FlowLabelObject` instance acts as a first-class wrapper object around an internal bit-vector representation of a security label. The `FlowLabelObject` instance also implements the internal ⟦call⟧ method, so that the security label may be attached to other JavaScript values, When the `FlowLabelObject` functor is passed a value, it unions that value's current label with its internally stored label and returns the result.

```
3 > pass = "24sk09nk12";
4   24sk09nk12 [FlowLabel example.com]
5 > pass = pwdLabel(pass);
6   24sk09nk12 [FlowLabel pwd, example.com]
```

Listing 1.3. Applying a Label to a JavaScript Value.

Listing 1.3 shows the JavaScript developer applying the password label constructed previously (Listing 1.2), `pwdLabel`, to a string, `pass`. After label application, the resulting password string carries a label describing both the domain of origin, `example.com`, and the password security principal, `"pwd"`.

6.3   Label Retrieval and Comparison

We now assume that the attacker injects code using `sniffPassword` (Listing 1.1) in an attempt to drop the label of the user's password. Because the underlying framework tracks labels inter- and intra-procedurally with respect to both data and implicit direct control flows (Section 4.2), the label on the resulting sniffed password carries both the attacker's principal and the user's password principal. Our first-class labeling system exposes the network object to JavaScript, allowing interception of the information leak at the time of a network request.

```
1 navigator.registerSendMonitor(
2   function(method, url, payload) {
3     if (method == 'GET') {
4       var lab = new FlowLabel("example.com");
5       lab = lab.join(new FlowLabel("pwd"));
6
7       if (!lab.subsumes(labelof url))
8         log(url + " has unexpected label");
9       if (!lab.subsumes(labelof payload))
10        log(payload + " has unexpected label");
11     }
12     // other types of network request elided
13     return true;
14 });
```

Listing 1.4. Developer Provided Network Monitor Function.

Suspecting a possible information leak, the web developer implements a network monitoring logic in a JavaScript method, and registers it through the `navigator.registerSendMonitor` method. When the attack code attempts to communicate the pilfered information over the network, our labeling system first executes all registered monitors (in registration order) to determine if the request conforms to the developer-specified policy.

Listing 1.4 shows an example network monitor that takes advantage of the labels automatically applied by the underlying information flow framework. On Line 4, the developer creates a label representing the security principal, `example.com`. The `FlowLabelRegistry`'s interning of principals ensures that any labels created in this monitor function exactly match the same labels created elsewhere.

Through prototype-based inheritance, all `FlowLabelObject` instances have a `join` method that returns a new `FlowLabelObject` instance representing the union of its argument `FlowLabelObject` instances. On Line 5 of Listing 1.4, the developer `join`s the security principal `example.com` with `"pwd"` to compose together existing labels into a single label representing the union of all principals the developer wishes to allow in an HTTP GET request.

Information flow propagation within the VM labels each new value with the join of the labels of the arguments used to construct that value. Consequently, label propagation naturally results in values labeled with more than one principal, even when the original program only seeded a few values, each with a single principal. In response to this phenomenon, our developer uses the `subsumes` method (Line 7 and Line 9 of Listing 1.4) to check that the label of the request is a subset of all allowed principals. Although our first-class label wrappers also permit strict equality comparison (JavaScript operator `===`) between two `FlowLabelObject` instances, we strongly encourage using the `subsumes` relation for expressing security policy constraints using subsets of principals. This practice allows catching all values with labels below the given upper bound (supremum).

Our labeling extension introduces the `labelof` operator so that JavaScript code can retrieve labels attached to variables for inspection and application. On Line 7 and Line 9 of Listing 1.4, the developer uses this operator to obtain the label attached to the target request `url`, and network `payload`. Because the underlying framework propagates labels following data flows, the resulting `FlowLabelObject` instance returned from `labelof` operator is itself labeled with the union of the provided argument and current program counter. If desired, the developer may use the resulting `FlowLabelObject` instance to label other values.

In the example shown in Listing 1.4, the developer constructs a label over the password principal, `"pwd"`, at two different code locations: once to label the user's input and again in the network monitor. This practice causes no problem for our system, because the `FlowLabelRegistry` interns principals, allowing our system to consider identical, two `FlowLabelObject` instances constructed in different code locations but with equivalent JavaScript values.

7   Evaluation

To evaluate the effectiveness of our system for security debugging we examine four dimensions:

Performance. We show that underlying information flow framework is fast compared to other work and argue that the first-class labeling system introduces negligible overhead.

Completeness. The labeling system inherits the code coverage of the supporting information flow framework.

Security. We argue that the labeling system revealed to the JavaScript programmer does not present a new attack surface in any significant way.

Usability. We demonstrate how developers can use the system to debug security vulnerabilities in their web applications.

We evaluate the effectiveness of our system as a web application security debugging tool. We measure the robustness and performance of the underlying labeling framework, demonstrating that even sites with large libraries of JavaScript code present no execution difficulties. We also use the first-class labeling system to find and debug an XSS vulnerability.

7.1   Performance

The supporting framework, termed FlowCore, modifies WebKit's JavaScript engine JavaScriptCore (version 1.4.2) to attach labels to every value. Additionally, it contains data structures relevant for mapping label bits within a label to domains (the FlowLabelRegistry) and for propagating implicit direct information flow dependencies. To evaluate the costs imposed by FlowCore, we test it against an unmodified JavaScriptCore of the same version.

Because FlowCore implements tracking only in the interpreter, we execute both JavaScript engines with just-in-time compilation disabled. A dual Quad Core Intel Xeon 2.80 GHz with 9.8 GiB RAM running Ubuntu 11.10 executes all benchmarks (at niceness level -20). We choose to use the SunSpider [17] benchmark suite because its status as the standard benchmark suite for JavaScript makes it suitable for comparisons to other work. SunSpider includes test cases that cover common web practices, such as encryption and text manipulation. This benchmark test provides a measure of the baseline overhead involved in maintaining information flow data structures and propagating labels.

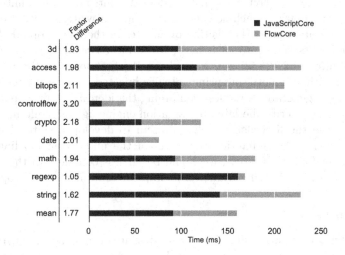

Fig. 4. SunSpider Benchmark results: JavaScriptCore vs. FlowCore.

Figure 4 reveals overall execution speed of JavaScript benchmark results: the mean execution time of FlowCore is 158.33 ms whereas the mean execution time of JavaScriptCore is 89.44 ms. The SunSpider benchmark does not contain first-class labeling operations, so the overall 77% slowdown represents the overhead incurred by the supporting framework's implementation of label propagation. In comparison, other information flow approaches [10] introduce a 150% slowdown making programs two to three times slower.

The VM stores labels as bit vectors attached to values and performs label propagation via bitwise-or. This representation ensures that first-class label objects are only present when explicitly constructed (`new FlowLabel`) or retrieved (`labelof`) by the developer. As a result, the introduction of the first-class labeling system into the hosted environment incurs no additional runtime performance overhead compared to a fully automatic labeling system. We do not evaluate the performance impact of the network hook, because it is insignificant within a debugging environment and the developer has the power to implement any monitor function they desire.

The performance of the underlying labeling framework implies that even sites with large amounts of JavaScript code execute without noticeable slowdown. To test whether the information flow tracking framework causes a noticeable performance decrease, we visited (and logged into) JavaScript intensive sites, such as Facebook, GMail, Google Maps, Bing, GitHub and Cloud9 IDE. These sites do not make use of the first-class labeling system introduced in this paper. However, user interaction proves that the performance overhead of the labeling framework does not introduce any usability issues.

7.2   Completeness

To verify that the underlying framework does not introduce any runtime bugs when interpreting either machine-generated or human-written JavaScript found in the wild, we automated the visiting of all sites in the Alex Top 500 [1]. This webcrawler injects code into each page, to perform two actions: (1) attach a network monitor and (2) fill out and submit the first form on the page using data labeled with an identifying principal. The injected monitor verifies that the submitted form generates a request containing the identifying principal.

Not only do we verify the label propagation engine against code in the wild, but we also use the first-class labeling system to develop a suite of unit test cases for ensuring the semantic correctness of the underlying labeling framework. Without first-class labels, we would be far less confident of the semantic correctness of the underlying framework's implementation of label propagation.

7.3   Security

The underlying framework, FlowCore, generates, at runtime, new security principals for every unique label generated by the developer and new domain encountered by the web browser. Introduction of runtime principals requires mutation of the `FlowLabelRegistry`. By design, FlowCore does not support declassification, preventing a communication channel via the labeling framework itself.

Our first-class labeling system exposes, to the web application and any injected code, a JavaScript API for creating and applying labels to JavaScript values. This exposure represents a new attack surface that might allow an attacker to target the labeling framework. However, we envision the web developer using the first-class labeling system only in a testing environment, where it provides no benefit to the attacker. Nevertheless, the lack of declassification means that the attacker-injected code cannot drop labels applied by the developer for debugging purposes.

Finally, our system allows registration of many monitor functions, through a JavaScript interface accessible by code injected into the web application. Our labeling system evaluates all monitor functions registered, in registration order. The developer-supplied monitor function always executes, even if the attacker's injected code happens to register a different monitor function first.

7.4   Utility as a Debugging Tool

To evaluate our first-class labeling system as a tool for testing web applications and discovering security vulnerabilities, we create a web page that contains a user login form. Acting as a malicious developer, we insert code into the page, which uses the sniffPassword label dropping code prior to exfiltrating the form contents to a second server via both an XmlHttpRequest and as part of an img.src URL. Acting as a security researcher, we mirror the page and add labeling code that applies a tag to the form's DOM node and a network monitor function that checks for the unique tag. Visiting the mirrored page successfully triggers the monitor function, alerting us to the exfiltration. WebKit's developer tools assisted us with finding the portion of the page responsible for generating the image request.

For a more realistic example, we attempt a similar attack using a mirrored ebay.com page obtained from XSSed [11], this time targeting the site's cookie. This page loads content from several different sources, and contains an XSS vulnerability that we exploit to inject the exfiltration code. Because the underlying framework automatically labels the cookie with the domain of origin, we did not need to insert labeling code. Instead, we find it sufficient to implement a network monitor that checks only whether data sent to an origin does not contain third-party principals. This monitor detected the exfiltration of the cookie (labeled with ebay.com) being sent to a server other than ebay.com. Again, WebKit's developer tools assisted us with pinpointing the JavaScript code responsible for the request.

8   Related Work

Developer Accessible Labels: To the best of our knowledge, no other work incorporates a first-class labeling system into a dynamically typed programming language. This feature allows the developer to construct label objects, apply them to label other program values, compose them together, and use them as part of natively programmed policy functions.

Myers et al. [15] introduce a security-type system that allows annotation of Java types with confidentiality labels that refer to variables of the dependent type label [16]. Java does not represent types as first-class entities, but the Jif programmer does have the ability to use the labeling features to program functions with statically type-checked information flow properties. Our work provides a similar, but simpler, labeling system for the dynamically-typed JavaScript.

Li and Zdancewic [12] present a security sublanguage that expresses and enforces information-flow policies in Haskell. Their implementation supports dynamic security lattices, run-time code privileges, and declassification without modifications to Haskell itself. The type-checking proceeds in two stages: (1) checking and compilation of the base language followed by (2) checking of the secure computations at runtime just prior to execution of programs written in the sublanguage. In contrast, our work presents extensions to an existing JavaScript environment and does not require rewriting of existing programs into a secure sublanguage.

JavaScript Information Flow Systems: Other research on language-based information flow specific to JavaScript relies on automatic labeling frameworks that seek to provide end-users with secure browsers and minimize developer. Our system seeks to leverage web developer domain knowledge about their application as part of a security testing environment.

Vogt et al. [18] modify Firefox's JavaScript engine, SpiderMonkey, to monitor the flow of sensitive information using a combination of static and dynamic analysis. Before execution, their modified VM statically analyzes each function via abstract interpretation to detect and mark implicit information flows. Their framework automatically taints objects provided by the browser (e.g., Document, History, Window, and form elements) and enforces information flows according to the Same Origin Policy. Our supporting framework also automatically labels dynamically loaded code according to the Same Origin Policy, but our contribution of first-class labels allows the developer to specify security policies specific to their application in native JavaScript.

Just et al. [10] modify the JavaScriptCore VM in WebKit to perform information flow tracking for `eval`, `break`, `continue`, and other control-flow structures. Our supporting framework achieves the same analysis with better performance due to difference in implementation details. This work moves beyond implementation of an information flow tracking engine to reflect portions of the labeling engine into the JavaScript environment, to enable targeted security debugging.

Chugh et al. [4] attack the problem of dynamically loaded JavaScript by using staged information flow. Their approach statically computes an information flow graph for all available code, leaving *holes* where code might appear at runtime, and subjecting dynamically loaded code to the same analysis as soon as it becomes available. They also introduce a new policy language to the existing babel of languages used for web development. In contrast, our supporting framework avoids delaying code execution and shifts analysis of information flows to runtime and enables the developer to write policies in JavaScript itself.

Jang et al. [9] employ a JavaScript rewriting-based information flow engine to document 43 cases of history sniffing within the Alexa [1] Global Top 50,000 sites. In contrast, our supporting framework performs label propagation in the VM, increasing performance and preventing attackers from subverting the system.

Type-Checking JavaScript for Information Flow: Many researchers give type systems intended to analyze JavaScript programs for information flow security.

Austin and Flannagan, in conjunction with Mozilla, promote sparse labeling techniques intended to decrease memory overhead and increase performance [2] and provide a formal semantics for *partially leaked* information [3]. Hedin and Sabelfeld [7] provide Coq-verified formal rules that cover object semantics, higher-order functions, exceptions, and dynamic code evaluation, powerful enough to support DOM functionality. Efforts along this line of research typically cover a core of the JavaScript specification, and have not seen wide-spread adoption. We forgo formalized verification in a practical effort to target adoption of our work by developers focused on security debugging rather than end users.

JavaScript Language Policies: Meyerovich and Livshits introduce an aspect oriented framework, named CONSCRIPT [13] that supports weaving specific security policies with existing web applications. Using their framework, web authors wrap application code with security monitors specified in JavaScript. Their system supports aspect wrapper functions around arbitrary code, while we focus on monitoring network traffic. An aspect oriented approach cannot detect and prevent information leaks that occur due to control-flow transfers as exhibited in Listing 1.1.

9   Conclusion

We present to the JavaScript developer a first-class labeling system that exposes an underlying information flow framework. Developers can use their domain knowledge to label JavaScript values within their application and construct network monitor policies that selectively ignore automatically applied labels. Our labeling system provides dynamic creation of security principals, supporting the common practice of loading code and resources from many different domains in web applications.

We introduce a new built-in `FlowLabelObject` class, which the developer uses to selectively label JavaScript values. The developer creates `FlowLabelObject` instances using existing JavaScript values as security principals or by composition with other `FlowLabelObject` instances via the lattice `join` method. The `subsumes` method allows comparison of all `FlowLabelObject` instances reporting their subset relation within the label lattice. Together with the ability to retrieve labels attached to values via the new built-in `labelof` operator, our system gives the developer the means to implement security policies in JavaScript.

The first-class labeling system introduces no additional slowdown beyond that of an information flow VM, enabling its use in a testing environment for sites that have large amounts of JavaScript code. By leveraging their domain knowledge and existing JavaScript experience, developers can focus on identifying and debugging application specific information flows. First-class labels allow developers to improve the security of their applications by writing policies in JavaScript that selectively ignore the high quantity of reports produced by automatically attached labels.

References

1. Alexa: Alexa Global Top Sites (2012), http://www.alexa.com/topsites (checked: February 2013)
2. Austin, T.H., Flanagan, C.: Efficient purely-dynamic information flow analysis. In: Proceedings of the ACM SIGPLAN Workshop on Programming Languages and Analysis for Security, pp. 113–124. ACM (2009)
3. Austin, T.H., Flanagan, C.: Permissive dynamic information flow analysis. In: Proceedings of the ACM SIGPLAN Workshop on Programming Languages and Analysis for Security, pp. 1–12. ACM (2010)
4. Chugh, R., Meister, J.A., Jhala, R., Lerner, S.: Staged information flow for JavaScript. In: PLDI 2009: Programming Language Design and Implementation, pp. 50–62. ACM (2009)
5. Denning, D.E.: A lattice model of secure information flow. Communications of the ACM, 236–243 (1976)
6. ECMA International: Standard ECMA-262. The ECMAScript language specification (2009),
   http://www.ecma-international.org/publications/standards/Ecma-262.html
   (checked: February 2013)
7. Hedin, D., Sabelfeld, A.: Information-flow security for a core of JavaScript. In: Proceedings of the Computer Security Foundations Symposium, pp. 3–18 (2012)
8. Hennigan, E., Kerschbaumer, C., Brunthaler, S., Franz, M.: Tracking information flow for dynamically typed programming languages by instruction set extension. Tech. rep., University of California Irvine (2011),
   http://ssllab.org/~nsf/files/tr_instruction_set_extension.pdf
9. Jang, D., Jhala, R., Lerner, S., Shacham, H.: An empirical study of privacy-violating information flows in JavaScript web applications. In: CCS 2010: Computer and Communications Security, pp. 270–283. ACM (2010)
10. Just, S., Cleary, A., Shirley, B., Hammer, C.: Information flow analysis for JavaScript. In: PLASTIC 2011: Programming Language and Systems Technologies for Internet Clients, pp. 9–18. ACM (2011)
11. K.F., D.P.: XSS Attacks Information (2012), http://www.xssed.com/ (checked: February 2013)
12. Li, P., Zdancewic, S.: Encoding information flow in haskell. In: 19th IEEE Computer Security Foundations Workshop, p. 12. IEEE (2006)
13. Meyerovich, L.A., Livshits, B.: ConScript: Specifying and enforcing fine-grained security policies for JavaScript in the browser. In: SSP 2010: Symposium on Security and Privacy, pp. 481–496 (2010)
14. Mozilla Foundation: Same origin policy for JavaScript (2008),
    https://developer.mozilla.org/En/Same_origin_policy_for_JavaScript
    (checked: February 2013)
15. Myers, A.C., Zheng, L., Zdancewic, S., Chong, S., Nystrom, N.: Jif: Java information flow (2001), http://www.cs.cornell.edu/jif (checked: February 2013)
16. Sabelfeld, A., Myers, A.C.: Language-based information-flow security. IEEE Journal on Selected Areas in Communications, 5–19 (2003)
17. SunSpider: SunSpider JavaScript benchmark (2012),
    http://www2.webkit.org/perf/sunspider-1.0/sunspider.html
    (checked: February 2013)
18. Vogt, P., Nentwich, F., Jovanovic, N., Kruegel, C., Kirda, E., Vigna, G.: Cross site scripting prevention with dynamic data tainting and static analysis. In: NDSS 2007: Network and Distributed System Security Symposium (2007)

A Framework for Evaluating Mobile App Repackaging Detection Algorithms

Heqing Huang, Sencun Zhu, Peng Liu, and Dinghao Wu

The Pennsylvania State University
{hhuang,szhu}@cse.psu.edu, {pliu,dwu}@ist.psu.edu

Abstract. Because it is not hard to reverse engineer the Dalvik bytecode used in the Dalvik virtual machine, Android application repackaging has become a serious problem. With repackaging, a plagiarist can simply steal others' code violating the intellectual property of the developers. More seriously, after repackaging, popular apps can become the carriers of malware, adware or spy-ware for wide spreading. To maintain a healthy app market, several detection algorithms have been proposed recently, which can catch some types of repackaged apps in various markets efficiently. However, they are generally lack of valid analysis on their effectiveness. After analyzing these approaches, we find simple obfuscation techniques can potentially cause false negatives, because they change the main characteristics or features of the apps that are used for similarity detections. In practice, more sophisticated obfuscation techniques can be adopted (or have already been performed) in the context of mobile apps. We envision this obfuscation based repackaging will become a phenomenon due to the arms race between repackaging and its detection. To this end, we propose a framework to evaluate the obfuscation resilience of repackaging detection algorithms comprehensively. Our evaluation framework is able to perform a set of obfuscation algorithms in various forms on the Dalvik bytecode. Our results provide insights to help gauge both *broadness* and *depth* of algorithms' obfuscation resilience. We applied our framework to conduct a comprehensive case study on AndroGuard, an Android repackaging detector proposed in Black-hat 2011. Our experimental results have demonstrated the effectiveness and stability of our framework.

Keywords: Mobile apps, reverse engineering, repackaging, obfuscation resilience, malware.

1 Introduction

In the past years, mobile phone sales have grown extremely fast and Android [8] has become the dominant of the mobile device market. This gives a burst of new applications pushed into the Android Market. In the end of 2012, the number of apps reached 700,000; however, Google provides little vetting on these apps to prevent it from plagiarism or malicious repackaging.

There are mainly two motivations for app repackaging. First, dishonest developers may repackage others' apps under their own names or embed different advertisements, and then republish them to the app market to earn monetary profit. Second, malware writers modify a popular app by inserting some malicious payload into the original

M. Huth et al. (Eds.): TRUST 2013, LNCS 7904, pp. 169–186, 2013.

program. The purpose is to take over mobile devices, steal users' private information, send premium SMS text messages stealthily, or purchase apps without users' awareness. They leverage the popularity of the original program to increase the propagation of the malicious one. Both types of repackaging are severe threats to the app markets. Even without consideration of code obfuscation, it has been found that about 5% to 13% of apps in third party app markets are the plagiarism of applications in the official Android market [29]. Besides, according to a recent study [30], among the analyzed 1260 malware samples, the authors found that 1083 of them (or 86.0%) were repackaged versions of legitimate apps with malicious payloads, indicating repackaging is a favorable vehicle for mobile malware propagation. However, as the commercial motivation grows, nothing prevents plagiarizers and repackagers using code obfuscation techniques to evade detection. Moreover, since users can download applications from both official market Google Play and third party markets in different countries (*e.g.*, Anzhi, a big Chinese Android app market), the repackaging problem can appear both inter- and intra- market, which increases the scale and challenge for repackaging detection.

Due to the very large number of applications in the market and easiness for reverse engineering and manipulation of Dalvik bytecode, several researchers have proposed detection schemes based on static analysis on DEX file [29], [19], [23]. Static code analysis based detection is more efficient than the dynamic ones. However, in practice, sophisticated code obfuscations can be easily applied to evade static analysis based detections [28], and such obfuscation techniques can be easily adapted to mobile applications scenario. When applied to mobile applications, they can greatly increase false-negative rates of the existing detection algorithms. Moreover, in these works, manual inspections are often used to check the false positives in their results. In general, all the detection algorithms currently pay more attention to the computational efficiency of their algorithms and are lack of a comprehensive analysis on algorithm accuracy. Hence, they can be very vulnerable against obfuscation based repackaging.

In this work, we propose a framework to automate the evaluation of repackaging detection algorithms against various obfuscation techniques. Our paper makes the following contributions:

1. We perform a survey study on the existing major repackaging detection algorithms, their evaluation methods, and provide insights on their pros and cons;
2. We take the first step in this field to provide an evaluation framework to measure the obfuscation resilience of detection algorithms;
3. We design our framework by gluing seamlessly all the bytecode conversion and obfuscation tools together. The effectiveness and stability of current framework are fully tested and evaluated;
4. To measure the obfuscation resilience of detection algorithms in a comprehensive way, in our framework, we propose the notion of broadness and depth analysis. We perform a case study with our tool on an open source detection algorithm AndroGuard [20] from Blackhat 2011. Our evaluation results show that while Andro-Guard demonstrates reasonable strength against many obfuscation techniques, it is very vulnerable to obfuscation relevant to control flow manipulation performed

on the method granularity, and multiple obfuscations when combined can further decrease its detection capability.

The remainder of the paper is structured as follows. Section 2 provides a study on a number of obfuscation detection algorithms. According to our observation from the study, an evaluation framework on the algorithms' obfuscation resilience has been proposed in Section 3. Section 4 describes the current setup of our framework. Then our experimental result of using the framework to conduct one case study on AndroGuard has been presented. We review related works in Section 5 and conclude with Section 6.

2   Study of Existing Repackaging Detection Algorithms

In this section, we first explain with a toy example how to conduct the Dalvik bytecode manipulation. Then we perform a study on several recently proposed algorithms for Android application repackaging detection, including Fuzzy Hashing based detection [29], Program Dependence Graph (PDG) based detection [19] and Feature Hashing based detection [23].

2.1   Background on Dalvik Bytecode

An Android application package is called *.apk* file, which must contain the program's Dalvik bytecode, resources and a XML manifest file. Each Android application is initially developed as a Java program. It is compiled into Dalvik bytecode, and then packaged into the *classes.dex* file as a Dalvik EXecutable (DEX file) to be executed in

```
----------The original bytecode pattern from Skype classes.dex ------------------
1. invoke-static {v1}, Ljava/lang/Integer;->valueOf(I)Ljava/lang/Integer;
2. move-result-object v1
3. const-string v2, "TYPE"
4. invoke-interface {v0, v1, v2}, Ljava/util/Map;->
     put(Ljava/lang/Object;Ljava/lang/Object;)Ljava/lang/Object;

--------The semantics-preserving bytecode pattern after manipulation--------
1. invoke-static {v1}, Ljava/lang/Integer;->valueOf(I)Ljava/lang/Integer;
2. move-result-object v1
3. move-object v3, v1        <<----- use extra virtual register "v3"
4. const-string v2, "TYPE"
5. move v4, v2              <<----- use extra virtual register "v4"
6. invoke-interface {v0, v3, v4}, Ljava/util/Map;->
     put(Ljava/lang/Object;Ljava/lang/Object;)Ljava/lang/Object;
7. move v2, v4        <<----- update the register "v2" according to register "v4"
8. move-object v1, v3  <<----- update the register "v1" according to register "v3"
```

Fig. 1. An example of Dalvik bytecode manipulation

Dalvik Virtual Machine (DVM) [2]. The whole compiling process includes two phases: (1) Java code compiled into an intermediary representation (IR), the Java bytecode format, which produces a set of *.class* files; (2) the IR code is further compiled into Dalvik bytecode by a utility called *"dx tool"*, which produces *classes.dex*, the DEX file.

During the reverse engineering process, a plagiarist first unpacks the *.apk* file of the downloaded Android application and extracts the *classes.dex* file that includes the actual bytecode for execution. *Classes.dex* can be dissembled by Baksmali [12] into IR format. After manipulation and obfuscation, it is finally assembled back into an updated *classes.dex* by Smali. Dalvik bytecode contains more semantic information and provides a higher programming abstraction for the developer than machine code instructions, (*e.g.*, x86 assembly code). Therefore, it is easy for human analysis, reverse engineering and manipulation.

In Figure 1, we show an example on semantic preserving manipulation of Dalvik bytecode. The dissembled bytecode snippet is from the Skype app for Android platform, and it is a representative function invocation. Similar code patterns can be identified all over the program. We manipulate it by using extra virtual parameter registers $v3$ and $v4$. The corresponding output bytecode is shown in the lower part of Figure 1. This code manipulation is semantic preserving, as the value in registers $v1$ and $v2$ are moved into the two extra registers and restored after the execution of opcode *[invoke-interface]*. The *[invoke-interface]* is executed using the extra virtual registers, instead of $v1$ and $v2$ originally. All these manipulations have no side-effect on the current and following context of the program that might use $v1$ and $v2$. The dissembled Dalvik bytecode contains lots of similar function invocation code patterns, so this type of noise instructions can be inserted with a very high frequency throughout the program.

2.2 Fuzzy Hashing Based Detection

In order to measure the similarity between plaintiff and repackaged applications, Droid-MOSS [29] leverages specialized hashing technique, called fuzzy hashing. Instead of computing a hash over the entire program instruction set, a hashing value is computed for each local unit of opcode sequence of the *classes.dex*. It uses a reset point to split long opcode sequences into small units and then concatenate all the hash values into a whole. In this way, it can localize the modification caused by repackaging. Also, Droid-MOSS focuses on instructions' opcode part in order to be resilient against "oprand string literal" based obfuscation. DroidMOSS can efficiently identify those pieces that were not touched by the repackager and works well when code manipulation was only performed at a few interesting points, *e.g.*, hard coded URLs. For this particular type of repackaging, DroidMOSS has a very high true positive rate.

Among all the detection algorithms we studied, only DroidMOSS has a measurement on its false negative rate through experiments. Two major reasons were reported to lead to potential false negatives. One is that some repackaging cases insert a large chunk of code as noise into the original app and the other fact is that the incomplete white-list of the ad libraries, which produces lots of noise into the opcode sequence. All the noise can result in considerable difference in the final fingerprints.

In Figure 1, we demonstrate that adding extra semantic preserving noise opcodes is not hard. For instance, if one performs the similar code manipulation frequently, the concatenated hashing value in DroidMOSS can be changed dramatically. Since local hashing value of code snippet unit *[invoke-static → move-result-object → const-string → invoke-interface]* and the corresponding manipulated opcode unit *[invoke-static → move-result-object → move-object → const-string → move → invoke-interface → move → move-object]* are very different, by concatenating all the different pieces into a final hash result, the detection can be evaded. The reset points DroidMOSS they uses to split the whole opcode sequence into small opcode units are semantically irrelevant, that is not depending on basic blocks, or other semantic information of the program. Therefore, the detection can be further evaded by carefully crafting the code manipulation pattern and make the inserted opcode hit the predefined reset points. In this way, the overall opcode structure of the fuzzy hashing computation is much modified, but the semantic of the Dalvik bytecode is still preserved.

2.3 PDG Based Detection

In DNADroid [19], the *dex* file of Android application is converted to Jar through a tool called *dex2jar*, so that they can leverage WALA [14] to compute the static data dependency graph (DDG) of every method. DDG is considered as the main characteristic of the apps for similarity comparison. DNADroid compares the DDGs within a pre-computed cluster of Android apps using graph isomorphism based algorithms.

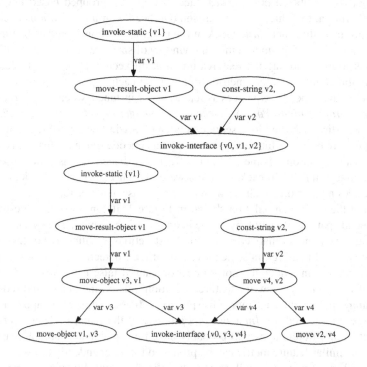

Fig. 2. The example of Data Dependency Graph (Top : original; Below : manipulated)

Specifically, each vertex in a DDG is a bytecode instruction and each edge initiate from one source instruction to one destination instruction. For example in Figure 2, the instruction *[move-object v3, v1]* is considered as the source instruction for both destination instructions *[invoke-interface v0, v3, v4]* and *[move-object v3, v]*. Since the source assignment instruction ($v3 := v1$) has a side effect on a variable $v3$, and also that $v3$ is used later in the following destination instructions, based on their algorithm, we should link the source instruction to both destination instructions by outgoing edges.

In general, static DDG is resilient against several control flow obfuscations and noisy code insertion attacks that do not modify the data dependency. However, the false positive rate is not evaluated. Indeed, some specific data dependency obfuscations can be designed to evade this approach. Figure 1 shows the data dependency graphs of the toy example in Figure 2 before and after code obfuscation. By comparison, we can observe a dramatic change of data dependency relationship between instructions. This side-effect free manipulation has the potential to evade the graph isomorphism algorithm based detection.

2.4 Feature Hashing Based Detection

Juxtapp [23] is a code-reuse detection scheme based on feature hashing. Similar to DNADroid, the unlabeled *classes.dex* files of apps are grouped based upon some predefined criteria, to reduce the comparison overhead. k-grams of various opcode sequence patterns within each basic block of the program are considered as features. For example, they choose 5-gram as a moving window of size 5, which moves within each basic block to map and flag the features into a m bit vector. Then the bit vectors are further combined into a feature metric to fingerprint each app. Juxtapp currently uses various predefined opcode sequences as features. For instance, when *[new-instance → const-string projectSpinnerPos → invoke-direct → iget-object → invoke-static]* appeared in a particular basic block sequentially (with a window size of five), the corresponding feature bit in the bit-vector indicating this opcode sequence feature is flagged with *one*. This detection scheme is able to effectively detect various code reuse cases, including piracy and code repackaging, malware existence, vulnerable code; however, this work does not perform evaluation on the tool's false negative rate.

By using the code manipulation shown in Figure 1, it can potentially destruct the normal opcode pattern of Dalvik bytecode in a very dense fashion. The special features of the program can be normalized by inserted instructions, creating lots of fake feature bits. Both can lead to a high false negative rate of their detection algorithm. Note that although Juxtapp can reduce the noise-injection caused false negatives by decreasing the size of its sliding window for feature definition, this on the other hand reduce the whole feature space and lead to more false positives. To the extreme, Juxtapp can choose window size of one and use *[new-instance]* as one of the features. Then every basic block unit from different apps will probably have this opcode appeared at least once. Thus lots of similar feature metric can be produced for independently developed apps.

In general, we consider it will be very beneficial to tune Juxtapp against various obfuscation techniques and find an optimal way to define the size of its sliding window and the unique feature set.

3   Evaluation Framework

Our study indicates that while each detection algorithm excels at detecting some types of repackaging efficiently and effectively, there is a lack of false negative analysis for all of them. Given the huge number of Android apps in different markets and the easiness in applying obfuscation techniques during repackaging, it becomes a very difficult problem to ensure both efficiency and accuracy of the repackaging detection algorithms. Therefore, we propose a general framework to help comprehensively evaluate the obfuscation resilience of such algorithms. The outcome of evaluation based on our framework can be used as a guidance to enhance the obfuscation-resilience of a detection algorithm through, for example, fine tuning of parameters and adding/removing certain heuristics.

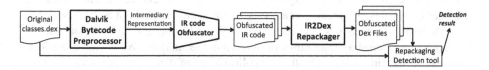

Fig. 3. A Framework for evaluating the obfuscation resilience of repackaging detection algorithms

The proposed framework is illustrated in Figure 3, which contains three major components. The first component is called *Dalvik Bytecode Pre-processor*, which dissembles and transforms the Dalvik EXecutable (DEX) into an intermediary representation (IR) code format. By using an IR format, code manipulation and obfuscation can be performed easily. The second component is an *IR Code Obfuscator*, which works directly on the output IR format of the original program. In the real world scenario, various obfuscators can be applied in different ways by plagiarists to evade the detection. By applying a set of obfuscation algorithms in various ways, the *IR Code Obfuscator* tries to mimic the real-world obfuscation based repackaging process. Hence, this component outputs a set of obfuscated versions from the original input dex file. During this process, we must ensure all the code manipulation and obfuscation actions are semantics-preserving transformations. After the obfuscation, the semantics equivalent IR code is converted back into Dalvik bytecode by *IR2Dex Repackager*, so that it is compatible with most detectors, which take dex files as input.

3.1   Dalvik Bytecode Pre-processor

The preprocessing phase performed on the Dalvik bytecode is to reverse it to an IR code format, so that it can be further manipulated easily and directly. Several intermediary representation candidates can be leveraged, including *smali* format, Java bytecode format or other similar representation, like Jasmin. In our current framework design, we choose Java bytecode format as the IR, since a tool called *Dare* [25] can directly translate the Dalvik bytecode into Java bytecode with a high success rate. In Android platform, the type information for some specific Java bytecode instructions used in Java Virtual Machine is thrown away when *dx tool* compiles Java bytecode down to Dalvik bytecode in Android platform. However, the missed type information is inferred by *Dare* using strong constraint solving and backward slicing. The experiment in *Dare* shows that the information incompleteness between the converted Dalvik bytecode and Java bytecode is reduced to a tolerable rate. It achieves a total of 99% of verifiable code on average for thousands of tested methods from various Android apps. We will elaborate some interesting observations on using *Dare* in our experiments in Section 4.

3.2   IR Code Obfuscator

This component is designed to mimic the real world scenarios where a plagiarist makes basic modifications or uses various obfuscation techniques for repackaging detection evasion. Since our motivation is trying to provide a general evaluation framework, we consider two pieces of information are very important to report. First is the *broadness* analysis result, which shows the general weakness and strength for an evaluated detection algorithm against a broad range of obfuscation techniques. We decide to perform obfuscation algorithms individually and collect a set of detection results for the testing algorithm. This result will provide a wide range of analysis, to reveal the detection algorithm's strength and weakness against each type of obfuscation algorithm. The *broadness* analysis result provides insights to improve the detection algorithm. Second is the *depth* analysis result, which shows the overall obfuscation resilience against deep code manipulation by serializing a set of obfuscation techniques. In this analysis, the detection algorithm is tested against repackaged applications that have been obfuscated multiple times. For example, an application may be obfuscated by variable renaming, followed by noise injection and/or control-flow flattening. With depth analysis, we can test the robustness of detection algorithms against more sophisticated obfuscation attacks.

Specifically, because there already exist some comprehensive obfuscation tools, such as *e.g., SandMarks* [17] and *Zelix KlassMaster* [9], which target at Java bytecode, by leveraging them we can save some engineering effort by avoiding the re-implementation of a large set of obfuscation algorithms. The open source *SandMarks* is a very comprehensive tool, which implements 39 obfuscation algorithms. *Klass- Master* implements some control flow obfuscation techniques, making it a heavy duty obfuscator. We currently take both as our candidate obfuscators. However, our *IR code obfuscator* is not restricted to Java bytecode obfuscation tools. Whenever the obfuscation community provides better tools for Dalvik bytecode obfuscation or other similar IR format obfuscation tools, we will try to include them in our framework. Therefore, our framework can be incrementally updated for more comprehensive obfuscation resilience measurement.

3.3   IR2Dex Repackager

In general, most detection algorithms take Dalvik bytecode of the Android program, namely the dex file, as the initial input, based on the assumption that no availability of source code. Therefore it is necessary to convert the obfuscated IR code back into the dex file by the *IR2Dex Repackager* component. In this way, we can build a standard framework, which is compatible for most detection algorithms that target Dalvik bytecode. For this component, we currently leverage a solid tool named *dx tool* from the Android platform.

An important criteria for the repackager component is that it must preserve the effects of obfuscation performed on our IR code during the conversion. After analyzing the source code [7] of *dx tool*, we find *dx tool* provides very little optimization, except for some dead code removing and a few minor optimizations on register usage. We will further discuss our analysis on the behavior of *dx tool* in Section 4, which indicates that it satisfies the criteria for a repackager component.

3.4 Practical Concern

To the best of our knowledge, currently no repackaging detection algorithm is based on dynamic analysis of Android applications. Due to the requirement of intensive user interactions through the touch-based UI for Android OS, it becomes very hard to automate the input feeding process for dynamic analysis of applications from a large-scale prospective. The other possible reason that static analysis is a better option is that a plagiarist can easily manipulate the GUI of an app and completely defeat dynamic based detection algorithms. Hence, in our current framework we do not aim at guaranteeing that obfuscated applications should be completely runnable. To make a repackaged application completely runnable is only a must requirement for the plagiarists, so that it can be published in the app market again. However, we relax this constraint in our evaluation framework so that we can provide a more comprehensive framework for static analysis based detectors. In other words, our framework indeed offers advantages to the attacker even if in reality he may not be able to apply these obfuscation algorithms easily. We consider the obfuscated *classes.dex* file from our evaluation framework valid as long as it is the valid syntax of Dalvik bytecode, contains the equivalent program semantics of the original one, and can be accepted by Dalvik bytecode dissemblers and other static analysis tools. After all, if needed, our framework can be refined later to produce completely runnable apps for dynamic analysis based repackaging detection algorithms.

4 Experiment

In the framework setup, we choose *SandMarks* as the obfuscator component, which has a comprehensive and powerful collection of obfuscation algorithms for Java bytecode manipulation and all of these obfuscation techniques are well documented. It meets the requirements from both the *broadness* and *depth* analysis aspects. Also, *Dare* and *dx tool* are leveraged for bytecode reverse engineering and repackaging, respectively. To fully automate the experiment, we write shell-scripts to glue the command-line version of *SandMarks* and other components, *Dare* and *dx tool* together. Each component's output is fed into the next component as input and all the tasks in our framework are then pipe-lined. Thereafter, we test the success rate of producing obfuscated dex files under various obfuscations and also conduct one case study with an open source Android application repackaging detection tool, Androguard [20].

4.1 Framework Setup

Preprocessing Android Applications. The preprocessing tool *Dare* that we currently use is one of the most accurate Dex-to-Jar converter, as most of the converted code can be verified by the Oracle Labs Maxine VM verifier [10]; however, some ambiguous type inference problem cannot be completely solved even after performing the constraint solving algorithms for ambiguous type inference. We relieve this problem by two procedures. First, we turn on the -*c* option from *Dare*, which leverages the optimization provided by *Soot* [13] for the reversed Java bytecode. This step can help remove the unnecessary Java bytecode and reduce the possibility of invalid bytecode instructions. Second, we relax the strict type checking performed during the *SandMarks* preprocessing phase by modifying the latest source code of *SandMarks*. After analyzing its source code, we find the strict type checking is performed in *SandMarks* preprocessing phase by using the BCEL libraries [15]. Therefore, after relaxing the type checking from BCEL libraries, we are able to make *SandMarks* accept all the Jar files output from *Dare* and run them through various obfuscation algorithms.

Applying Obfuscation Algorithms. For the *broadness* analysis, we try to perform all the 39 obfuscation algorithms in *SandMarks* separately; however, some obfuscation algorithms can not proceed successfully. For example, *"Array Splitter"*, *"Array Folder"* and *"Integer Array Splitter"* are not able to complete. After further analysis, we find it is because of the missing type information during the backward conversion from Dalvik bytecode to Java bytecode.Dalvik bytecode does not contain the type information for the array relevant instructions. For instance, in DVM, it generally uses *"aget and aput"* for both *int* and *float* arrays and *"aget-wide and aput-wide"* for both *long* and *double* arrays. However, when trying to convert them into Java bytecode, the above opcode *"aget and aput"* need to be type inferred and mapped into *"iaload, iastore, faload and fastore"* strictly. It is the same case for *"aget-wide and aput-wide"*, which should be mapped to *"laload, lastore, daload and dastore"* strictly. Even after *Dare*'s inference of the relevant ambiguous typing from program context by leveraging strong constraint solving and backward slicing, it is still not able to resolve type ambiguity cases completely. In our work we do not solve this problem, as we consider this is one of the fundamental limitation of the conversion from Dalvik bytecode into Java bytecode. Fortunately, this does not hurt other obfuscation algorithms.

Another problem appears when trying to perform the *depth* analysis. Theoretically speaking, it is possible to perform a series of obfuscation algorithms on a program to obtain a deeply obfuscated program. However, some obfuscation algorithms can cause conflicts, due to the limitations of their underlining implementation. Instead of blindingly attempting various permutations of all the algorithms, we first group the obfuscation algorithms into different categories, including *Layout Obfuscation*, *Control Obfuscation* and *Data Obfuscation*, labeled in the score column of Table 4.2 as "L", "C" and "D", respectively. Then based on the result of *broadness* analysis, we try the combination among the most effective individual obfuscation algorithms from each category, so as to maximize the overall effectiveness of multiple obfuscation techniques while minimizing the opportunity of conflicts and the experiment space.

Table 1. The successful output benchmark for the framework

Dare Preprocessor		SandMarks Obfuscator		Android dx tool	
input#	output#	input#	output#	input#	output#
20.dex	20 .jar	20 .jar	720 .jar	720 .jar	720 .dex
100%		92.5%		100%	
Total Successful Rate			92.5% = 100% * 92.5% * 100%		

Framework Stability. Currently, we have comprehensively tested 20 Android applications downloaded from Android Official Market with 36 (out of 39) obfuscation algorithms provided by $SandMarks$ and output 36*20 obfuscated *classes.dex* files. As discussed previously, three obfuscation algorithms that are relevant to array manipulation cannot be performed completely. Both the $Dare$ and *dx tool* components perform well, except for few ambiguous type information cases caused by information loss in the first pre-processing component. By gluing these three components together, we reach a total success rate of 92.5% for the tested apps, which demonstrates the stability of our framework on performing the $broadness$ analysis. On the other hand, when applying blindingly various combinations of the obfuscation algorithms , $SandMarks$ tends to throw errors. After our grouping of relevant obfuscation techniques, we are able to perform four interesting serialization of obfuscation with a high success rate. We will provide detailed observations in Section 4.2.

4.2   Case Study

In order to test the effectiveness of our framework for evaluating obfuscation resilience, we perform a case study with $AndroGuard$ [20], which is an advanced Android application repackaging detection algorithm presented in Blackhat 2011. It can directly perform similarity comparison between a pair of *classes.dex* files from different apps. AndroGuard describes the an Android application as regular expression string, which can capture the control flow structure of the program very efficiently and effectively. Then pair-wise comparisons on the method units between two similar applications are conducted by leveraging the similarity distance computation algorithm based on Normalized Compression Distance (NCD). Then based on the threshold specified in the algorithms, AndroGuard can identify method relevant metric, including *"new method"*, *"diff method"* and *"match method"*. The final similarity score is derived based on the metric.

Applying Single Obfuscation Algorithm. We performed a $Broadness$ analysis on AndroGuard against all the obfuscation algorithms from $SandMarks$ thoroughly using our framework. This analysis is performed in a control way, as each time only one obfuscation is applied and results are collected. Therefore, we can pinpoint the exact weakness of the repackaging detection algorithm. In Table 4.2, the algorithm columns indicate the names of the obfuscation algorithms applied in our framework. For the score column, we first use $AndroGuard$'s detection algorithm to compute the similarity score of a pair of original/obfuscated *classes.dex* files of each Android application.

Table 2. Average Similarity Score by AndroGuard for each Obfuscation Algorithm

Algorithm	Score	Algorithm	Score
Non-obfuscated	1.00 (L)		
Const Pool Reorder	.92 (L)	Split Classes	.94 (L)
Static Method Bodies	.88 (C)	Class Encrypter	.03 (D)
Method Merger	.65 (C)	Reorder Parameters	.92 (D)
Interleave Methods	.56 (C)	Promote Prim Reg	.92 (D)
Opaque Pred Insert	.92 (C)	Promote Prim Types	.93 (D)
Branch Inverter	.77 (C)	Bludgeon Signatures	.96 (D)
Rand Dead Code	.92 (C)	Objectify	.83 (D)
Class Splitter	.87 (C)	Publicize Fields	.91 (D)
Method Madness	.43 (C)	Field Assignment	.86 (D)
Simple Opaque Pred	.92 (C)	Variable Reassign	.85 (D)
Reorder Instructions	.89 (C)	ParamAlias	.92 (D)
Buggy Code	.67 (C)	Boolean Splitter	.85 (D)
Inliner	.89 (C)	String Encoder	.87 (D)
Branch Insert	.87 (C)	Overload Names	.91 (D)
Dynamic Inliner	.84 (C)	Duplicate Registers	.89 (D)
Irreducibility	.86 (C)	Rename Registers	.96 (D)
Opaque Branch Insert	.85 (C)	False Refactor	.95 (D)
Exception Branch	.81 (C)	Merge Local Int	.94 (D)

We then compute an average over all the score of the tested pairs of the 20 applications under the same obfuscation algorithm. Therefore, the average similarity score is a good measurement on the average performance of *AndroGuard* against individual obfuscation attack.

Applying Single Obfuscation Algorithm. In order to check the effect of the Dex2Jar and Jar2Dex conversions on *AndroGuard*, we also use *AndroGuard* to compute the similarity score for the original dex file and the *"non-obfuscated"* dex file that has only been processed by *Dare* and *dx tool*.From Table 4.2, the entry *"Non-obfuscated"* has the corresponding similarity score "1.00" from *AndroGuard*, which means it is 100% similar (the range of the similarity score is [0, 1]). This indicates that the two-way conversions by *Dare* and *dx tool* can keep almost all the semantic information of the code. Based on the classification in Collberg et al. [18], this transformation can be categorized as *Layout Obfuscation*, we tag it as "L" in the corresponding score column, as it touches very little semantic content of the code. All the other scores are below "1.00", which demonstrates that all the other obfuscation algorithms have more or less effect on *AndroGuard*'s detection result.

The algorithms on the left side of the table have "C" tagged on the corresponding scores, because they belong to the *"control transformation"* category, which tries to obscure the control-flow of the code. The ones on the right side and tagged with "D" belong to *"data transformations"*, which obscure the data structure used in the source applications. Generally speaking, *AndroGuard* has better resilience to data structure based obfuscations, since it does not take the detail data dependency or data structure into account. However, the *"Class Encrypter"* obfuscator makes an exception in this category, as this obfuscation reduces the similarity score to ".03". By encrypting class files and decrypting them at runtime, the *"Class Encrypter"* can completely change the semantics of the string structure that *AndroGuard* uses to represent the Dalvik bytecode.

The other obfuscation methods that have big impacts are *"Method Merger"*, *"Interleave Methods"*, *"Method Madness"* and *"Buggy Code"*. To figure out the reason, we analyze the source code of AndroGuard in the similarity comparison part. Basically, the algorithm computes the Control Flow Graph (CFG) within each method, and represents each CFG of each basic block by a predefined regular expression representation and takes this string representation of each method as the core feature. By leveraging Normalized Compression Distance (NCD) algorithm, they can aggregate the final score. Since all the above four obfuscation algorithms are relevant to basic block and control flow manipulation performed on the method granularity, they can reduce the chance of repackaged apps being detected by their similarity measurement algorithm. Actually, these obfuscation algorithms directly obscure the core feature that AndroGuard is trying to extract from the code for comparison and detection. From this result of the *broadness* analysis, our framework is able to comprehensively measure the obfuscation resilience of the detection algorithm and also pinpoints its weakness.

Serializing Multiple Obfuscation Algorithms. Practically, especially when detection algorithms become more powerful, it is very possible that an attacker will try a combination of various obfuscation algorithms. Therefore, our framework also wants to mimic more complicated obfuscation behavior in the real world scenario. Besides the *broadness* analysis performed on AndroGuard, we also perform advanced multiple-obfuscation by serializing several algorithms for *depth* analysis. It is a deeper analysis process on the obfuscation resilience of detection algorithms.

We test various combinations of the effective individual obfuscation based on the result of *broadness* analysis. When trying various permutations, only some of them can be performed successfully for the testing applications and the output obfuscated DEX files can be accepted by *AndroGuard*. We analyze four interesting cases below:

1. *[Method Merger ⇒ Method Madness ⇒ Interleave Methods]*
   Average Similarity Score and Obfuscation Time of 18 apps : 0.33 and 19 min;
2. *[Objectify ⇒ Method Merger ⇒ Method Madness]*
   Average Similarity Score and Obfuscation Time of 19 apps : 0.26 and 16 min;
3. *[Method Madness ⇒ Objectify ⇒ Variable Reassign]*
   Average Similarity Score and Obfuscation Time of 20 apps : 0.35 and 11 min;
4. *[Variable Reassign ⇒ Boolean Splitter ⇒ Objectify]*
   Average Similarity Score and Obfuscation Time of 20 apps : 0.80 and 6 min;

We record the average similarity score computed by AndroGuard and the average total time needed for the whole process of serializing three obfuscation algorithms. All the test cases reduce the average similarity scores to a point which is lower than any the single obfuscation performed individually in the *broadness* analysis. The average total time is the sum of the time for applying each obfuscation algorithm.

Case 1 leverages three heavy control transformation based obfuscations that target specifically at method level manipulations. We choose these top-three obfuscations based on the *broadness* analysis result. This serialization further reduces the similarity score down to a low point 0.33, which results in high false negatives in *AndroGuard*. Generally, for *AndroGuard*, it will cause lots of false positives when setting the threshold below 0.5 for the similarity score. This deep serialized obfuscation process requires more time to perform, about 19 minutes on average for each application. Also there is 5% chance that the output dex file could not be accepted by *AndroGuard*, as 18 out of 20 can be successfully accepted by *AndroGuard*.

Case 2 is a serialization of one data transformation plus two control transformations. Based on the previous *broadness* analysis report, we try several combinations with *"Class Encrypter"* as data transformation, and find no further decrease on the similarity score. As *"Class Encrypter"* already brings the similarity score to a very low level (0.03), the effects of other obfuscation algorithms cannot be directly reflected in the score. Note all other possible obfuscations must be applied before *"Class Encrypter"*, so that the actual effect of these obfuscations can be kept. *"Objectify"* is another top data transformation based obfuscation, and we combine it with two top obfuscation algorithms in the control transformation category, namely *"Method Merger"* and *"Method Madness"*. This combination reduces similarity score to 0.26, which is more effective than the combination of the three top control transformations in Case 1. This is an indication that combining various obfuscations from different categories can potentially produce more powerful obfuscations. Based on further analysis of the result of Case 2, we find that using the obfuscations selected from different categories can increase the number of methods that are considered *not* similar by *AndroGuard* between the original and obfuscated dex files. It is because the manipulations from different obfuscation categories touch different parts of the code and produce the obfuscated methods with less chance of overlapping with the original.

Case 3 serializes one control plus two data transformations, which also indicates that obfuscations from different categories performs better. This two data obfuscations, *"Objectify"* and *"Variable Reassign"* are only at a 0.8 level score when performed separately; however, after our serialization with the *"Method Madness"* on control transformations, it performs well and even approximates the similarity score from case 1. The whole transformation time is reduced to nearly half of the time spent in case 2 for each application and we obtain a 100% success rate for output dex files by this serialized obfuscation. All the 20 heavily obfuscated dex files are accepted by *AndroGuard* successfully. The last case indicates by purely using the data transformation based obfuscations. The average similarity score is further reduced but not as significant as case 2 and 3.

4.3   Discussions

Our experiment and case study demonstrate the effectiveness of our framework for providing a comprehensive and deep measurement on the obfuscation resilience aspect of a proposed repackaging detection algorithms. The *broadness* analysis measures the obfuscation resilience of the detection algorithm comprehensively and points out its exact strength and weakness. On the other hand, *depth* analysis can further attack the detector under an advanced obfuscation scenario, which provides a better understanding of its overall obfuscation resilience. We believe the insight from both analyses is helpful to understand the detection algorithm and can serve as a guidance for its enhancement.

We use AndroGuard to perform the case study because it is currently the only publicly available tool. However, the result from the case study can be applicable to all the other detection algorithms. For example, the *"Class Encrypter"* obfuscation can probably have the same effect on other detection algorithms based on static code analysis. Because it dramatically changes the original bytecode by encryption and only dynamic decryption can help unpack the obfuscation. Hence, without adding special heuristic to prevent this obfuscation, all the static code analysis based detection becomes ineffective. The case study result shows that AndroGuard is not very resilient against control flow manipulation based obfuscation. However, we envision the opposite result will probably be generated when using our framework to test DNADroid.

Since the obfuscation algorithms are performed on the intermediary format, the Java bytecode, which are later converted into *classes.dex* by the *dx tool* on instruction level granularity, one may wonder whether the obfuscation effect has been preserved. We randomly pick and manually analyze outputs of all the 36 obfuscation algorithms and the corresponding serialized ones. According to the corresponding explanations from *SandMarks*, the effect of most control flow obfuscation and data obfuscation algorithms are preserved. The obfuscator is based on semantic preserving obfuscations from *SandMarks*. Moreover, the *dx* tool keeps the program's semantic of the input Java bytecode, and converts the Java bytecode instructions into semantic equivalent Dalvik bytecode instructions based on the predefined transformation rules. Therefore, most of the obfuscation effect on our intermediary representation is preserved in the output *classes.dex* file.

We also confirm that some class level obfuscations, *e.g.*, "Class Splitter" and "Split Classes", need some modifications in the *AndroidManifest.xml* file, so that relevant class information will be updated accordingly. We suggest users to simply turn them off when performing the evaluation, if their detection algorithms try to leverage the information in the *AndroidManifest.xml*. For those which do not need the information from *AndroidManifest.xml*, they can still obfuscate *classes.dex* by using the obfuscations in class level.

5   Related Work

Android Application Reverse Engineering and Code Manipulation. Since Dalvik bytecode contains more semantic information than machine code instructions, its reverse engineering and manipulation are also easier. Several tools, including *Dex2jar* [4], *ded* [24] and *Dare* [25], can transform Dalvik bytecode to Java bytecode. Based on the converted Java bytecode representation of *dex* files, many static analysis tools on Java bytecode can be applied, *e.g.*, *WALA* [14] and *Soot* [13]. In evaluation framework, we also leverage this convenience to deploy *SandMarks* [17] and *KlassMaster* [9] in our obfuscator component. *Smali/baksmali* [12], the assembler/disassembler of *classes.dex* files, not only can reverse engineer Android applications but is able to repackage the modified *smali* code back to Dalvik bytecode. Tools such as *apktools* [1] integrate *Smali/baksmali* to help modify an application, sign with another developer key, and repackage it back into an *apk* file.

To counter reverse engineering, Android developers use obfuscation tools frequently such as ProGuard [11], DexGuard [5] and dasho [3], to prevent the repackaging at the initial stage. These obfuscation techniques rely on Java source code, Our evaluation framework is trying to mimic the obfuscations performed by plagiarists, which is under the assumption that there is no accessibility to Java source code.

Repackaging techniques can be leveraged to provide protection mechanisms, if used in a proper way. Aurasium [27] reverse engineers and repackages the dex files to perform bytecode rewriting, so that protection code can be embedded into the Android apps to specify policy enforcement within user-level sandboxing. In article [6], "Junk byte injection", a x86 architecture well-known obfuscation technique, is proved to be applicable on Dalvik bytecode format to raise the bar of further malicious reverse engineering on Dalvik bytecode.

Repackaging Detection and Evaluation. Paper [30] analyzes the evolution of the Android malware and current status of the repackaging and obfuscation techniques that have been used. We perform study from another prospective, that is trying to analyze and measure the obfuscation resilience of repackaging detection algorithms in [29], [19], [23].

Wang et al., [26] design a system call based software birthmark that represents the unique characteristic of the run time behavior of a program, which can be used for software theft detection. They measure their birthmark against various obfuscations and also with different compiler setups. Jhi et al., [21] design a plagiarism detection technique, which is resilient to various control and data obfuscation techniques. The detection is based on an observation that some critical runtime values are hard to be replaced or eliminated by semantics preserving transformation techniques. They evaluate the obfuscation resilience of the value-based method through SandMark, KlassMaster, Thicket and Loco/Diablo.

The evaluation of the obfuscation techniques has been studied in [16], which assesses how difficulty it is for an attacker to understand and modify obfuscated code through controlled experiments involving human subjects. Karnick et al., [22] propose a standard measurement to analyze and evaluate the strength of obfuscation tools. An analytical metric is developed to quantify the performance of obfuscation in terms of potency, resilience, and cost. Our work provides a general framework to measure the obfuscation resilience of repackaging detection algorithms. We have evaluated our framework using a case study on a real repackaging detection algorithm.

6   Conclusion

Due to the improved code manipulation techniques of code manipulation on Dalvik bytecode, it is very important for repackaging detection algorithms to be obfuscation resilient, so that more stealthy repackaging scenarios can be identified. In this work, we propose a framework to help evaluate the obfuscation resilience of detection algorithms in terms of broadness and depth. The framework provides a uniform obfuscation resilience measurement for all the obfuscation detection algorithms that are based on static analysis of Dalvik bytecode. Our experiments have demonstrated that our framework is stable to create obfuscated *classes.dex* for the *broadness* analysis and also is able to serialize multiple obfuscations together to perform the *depth* analysis. Our study on the serialization of multiple obfuscations from different categories provides some understanding on how to make a stronger obfuscation. Our case study on *Androguard*, shows that our framework can effectively pinpoint the exact strength and weakness of the detection algorithm. The outcome of evaluation based on our framework can be used as a guidance to enhance the obfuscation-resilience of a detection algorithm through, for example, fine tuning of parameters and adding/removing certain heuristics.

Acknowledgments. We would like to give special thanks to Professor Christian Collberg for his help on using the SandMark tool and Damien Octeau's detail clarification on the Dare tool.

This work was partially supported by ARO W911NF-09-1-0525 (MURI), NSF CNS-0905131, NSF CNS-0916469, NSF CNS-1223710, AFOSR W911-NF1210055 from Liu, NSF CAREER 0643906 from Zhu and NSF Grant CNS-1223710 from Wu. Any opinions, findings and conclusions or recommendations expressed in this material are those of the authors and do not necessarily reect the views of the National Science Foundation, Army Research Office or AFOSR.

References

1. Android Apktool: A tool for reengineering android apk files,
   http://code.google.com/p/android-apktool/
2. Dalvik virtual machine: code and documentation,
   http://code.google.com/p/dalvik/
3. Dasho, preemptive solutions, http://www.preemptive.com/products/dasho
4. Dex2jar, http://code.google.com/p/dex2jar/
5. Dexguard, http://www.saikoa.com/dexguard
6. Dexobf, http://dexlabs.org/blog/bytecode-obfuscation
7. Dx tool source code,
   http://grepcode.com/file/repository.grepcode.com/java/
   ext/com.google.android/android/4.1.2_r1/com/android/dx/ssa/
8. Gartner says android to command nearly half of worldwide smartphone operating system market by year-end 2012,
   http://www.gartner.com/it/page.jsp?id=1622614
9. Klassmaster, http://www.zelix.com/klassmaster/docs/index.html
10. Oracle Virtual Machine,
    https://wikis.oracle.com/display/MaxineVM/Home/
11. ProGuard, http://proguard.sourceforge.net/
12. Smali/Baksmali, http://code.google.com/p/smali/
13. Soot: a Java optimization framework, http://www.sable.mcgill.ca/soot/
14. Wala, http://wala.sourceforge.net/wiki/index.php/

15. Byte code engineering library (bcel),
    http://sourceforge.net/projects/javaclass/
16. Ceccato, M., Di Penta, M., Nagra, J., Falcarin, P., Ricca, F., Torchiano, M., Tonella, P.: To-
    wards experimental evaluation of code obfuscation techniques. In: Proceedings of the 4th
    ACM Workshop on Quality of Protection, QoP 2008, pp. 39–46. ACM, New York (2008),
    http://doi.acm.org/10.1145/1456362.1456371
17. Collberg, C., Myles, G., Huntwork, A.: Sandmarks a tool for software protection research.
    IEEE Security and Privacy 1(4), 40–49 (2003)
18. Collberg, C., Thomborson, C., Low, D.: A taxonomy of obfuscating transformations. Tech-
    nical report (1997)
19. Crussell, J., Gibler, C., Chen, H.: Attack of the clones: Detecting cloned applications on
    android markets. In: Foresti, S., Yung, M., Martinelli, F. (eds.) ESORICS 2012. LNCS,
    vol. 7459, pp. 37–54. Springer, Heidelberg (2012)
20. Desnos, A., Gueguen, G.: Android: From reversing to decompilation. In: Black Hat 2011,
    Abu Dhabi (2011)
21. Jhi, Y.-C., Wang, X., Jia, X., Zhu, S., Liu, P., Wu, D.: Value-based program characterization
    and its application to software plagiarism detection. In: Proceedings of the 33rd International
    Conference on Software Engineering, pp. 756–765. ACM (2011)
22. Karnick, M., Macbride, J., Mcginnis, S., Tang, Y., Ramach, R.: A qualitative analysis of Java
    obfuscation
23. Li, S.: Juxtapp: A scalable system for detecting code reuse among android applications.
    Master's thesis, EECS Department, University of California, Berkeley (May 2012),
    http://www.eecs.berkeley.edu/Pubs/TechRpts/
    2012/EECS-2012-111.html
24. Octeau, D., Enck, W., McDaniel, P.: The ded Decompiler. Technical Report NAS-TR-
    0140-2010, Network and Security Research Center, Department of Computer Science and
    Engineering, Pennsylvania State University, University Park, PA, USA (September 2010),
    http://siis.cse.psu.edu/ded/papers/NAS-TR-0140-2010.pdf
25. Octeau, D., Jha, S., McDaniel, P.: Retargeting Android Applications to Java Bytecode. In:
    Proceedings of the 20th International Symposium on the Foundations of Software Engineer-
    ing (November 2012),
    http://siis.cse.psu.edu/dare/papers/octeau-fse12.pdf
26. Wang, X., Jhi, Y.-C., Zhu, S., Liu, P.: Detecting software theft via system call based birth-
    marks. In: Annual Computer Security Applications Conference, ACSAC 2009, pp. 149–158.
    IEEE (2009)
27. Xu, R., Saïdi, H., Anderson, R.: Aurasium: Practical policy enforcement for android appli-
    cations. In: Proceedings of the 21st USENIX Conference on Security (2012)
28. You, I., Yim, K.: Malware obfuscation techniques: A brief survey. In: Proceedings of the 2010
    International Conference on Broadband, Wireless Computing, Communication and Applica-
    tions (2010)
29. Zhou, W., Zhou, Y., Jiang, X., Ning, P.: Detecting repackaged smartphone applications in
    third-party android marketplaces. In: Proceedings of the Second ACM Conference on Data
    and Application Security and Privacy, CODASPY 2012, pp. 317–326. ACM, New York
    (2012)
30. Zhou, Y., Jiang, X.: Dissecting android malware: Characterization and evolution. In: 2012
    IEEE Symposium on Security and Privacy, SP, pp. 95–109. IEEE (2012)

Towards Precise and Efficient Information Flow Control in Web Browsers*

Christoph Kerschbaumer, Eric Hennigan, Per Larsen,
Stefan Brunthaler, and Michael Franz

University of California, Irvine
{ckerschb,eric.hennigan,perl,s.brunthaler,franz}@uci.edu

Abstract. JavaScript (JS) has become the dominant programming language of the Internet and powers virtually every web page. If an adversary manages to inject malicious JS into a web page, confidential user data such as credit card information and keystrokes may be exfiltrated without the users knowledge.

We present a comprehensive approach to information flow security that allows precise labeling of scripting-exposed browser subsystems: the JS engine, the Document Object Model, and user generated events. Our experiments show that our framework is precise and efficient, and detects information exfiltration attempts by monitoring network requests.

1 Motivation

The JS programming language forms a key component in today's web architecture, especially in Web 2.0 applications which regularly use JS to handle sensitive information, such as corporate customer accounts. The current web page architecture allows source and library code from different origins to share the same execution context in a user's browser. Attackers take advantage of this execution model to gain access to a user's private data using Cross Site Scripting (XSS).

XSS is a code injection attack that allows adversaries to execute code without the user's knowledge and consent. Without any observable difference in runtime behavior, a malevolent script can exfiltrate keystrokes, or traverse the Document Object Model (DOM) to exfiltrate all visible data on a web page. Vulnerability studies consistently rank XSS highest in the list of the most mounted attacks on web applications [1, 2]. A recent study [3] confirms the ubiquity of sensitive user data exfiltration currently practiced on the Internet.

* This material is based upon work partially supported by the Defense Advanced Research Projects Agency (DARPA) under contract No. D11PC20024, by the National Science Foundation (NSF) under grant No. CCF-1117162, and by a gift from Google. Any opinions, findings, and conclusions or recommendations expressed in this material are those of the authors and do not necessarily reflect the views of the Defense Advanced Research Projects Agency (DARPA) or its Contracting Agent, the U.S. Department of the Interior, National Business Center, Acquisition Services Directorate, Sierra Vista Branch, the National Science Foundation, or any other agency of the U.S. Government.

M. Huth et al. (Eds.): TRUST 2013, LNCS 7904, pp. 187–195, 2013.

As a first line of defense, browsers implement the same origin policy (SOP) that limits a script's access to information. This policy allows scripts from the same origin to access each other's data and prevents access for scripts of different origins. Regrettably, attackers can bypass the SOP, e.g., by exploiting a XSS vulnerability of a web page, or by providing code, such as a library that is integrated in the same JS execution context as the original page.

Tracking the flow of information in the user's browser seeks to address the limitations of the SOP. Unfortunately, previous work [4–7] either limits tracking to a single bit of information, focuses solely on the JS engine or the DOM, or introduces significant runtime overhead. These limitations make wide browser adoption unlikely. Tracking only one bit of information leads to a high false positive rate in Web 2.0 applications, where pages commonly use Content Distribution Networks (CDNs).

We take inspiration from all of these approaches and present a comprehensive tracking framework (Section 3) that supports precise labeling for the dynamic tracking of information flows within a browser, including: (1) the JS engine, (2) the DOM, and (3) user generated events. We evaluate our system (Section 4) showing that it satisfies the following properties: *a) Secure:* Our system can stop information exfiltration attempts; in particular we show this by injecting malicious code that performs a keylogging attack, and attempts to exfiltrate HTML-form data. *b) Precise:* Our framework makes information flow tracking feasible for Web 2.0 applications by supporting multi-domain label encoding. We confirm this feasibility by visiting the Alexa Top 500 pages using our implemented web crawler. *c) Efficient:* Our approach incurs an average overhead of 82.82% in the JS engine (on SunSpider benchmarks) and 5.43% in the DOM (on Dromaeo benchmarks). Note, that the fastest dynamic information flow tracking frameworks [5, 7] introduce overhead on the order of 200-300%.

2 Threat Model

Throughout this paper, we assume that attackers have two important abilities: (1) attackers can operate their own hosts, and (2) can inject code in other web pages. Code injection into other pages relies either on exploiting a XSS vulnerability of a page, or the ability of attackers to provide content for mashups, advertisements, libraries, etc., which other sites include. The attacker's abilities, however, are limited to JS injection and attackers can neither intercept nor control network traffic. Our framework protects against several threats, including, but not limited to:

Information Exfiltration Attacks: By sending a GET request to a server under the attacker's control, the attacker can exfiltrate information in the URL of an image request: `elem.src = "evil.com/pic.png?"+creditcard_number;`. The attacker uses the request for the image as a channel to exfiltrate a user's credit card number as a payload in the GET request, when loading the image from the server.

Keylogging Attacks: An attacker might also craft code that logs keystrokes by registering an event handler: `document.onkeypress = listenerFunction;`. Our framework can track the flow of information for generated events, and can therefore also detect and prevent keylogging attacks.

3   Design and Implementation

We implement a framework, WIF (WebKit Information Flow), which extends the WebKit browser (version 1.4.2) with support for dynamic tracking of information flows. Several industrial strength desktop and mobile browsers use the WebKit code, e.g., Google's Chrome, or Apple's Safari. To protect the information accessible by an executing script, we use a labeling model that enforces the memory semantics of a non-interference security policy [8].

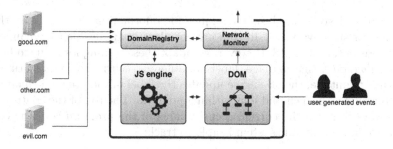

Fig. 1. Architecture of WIF

Our approach extends the browser's JS engine with the ability to tag values with a security label indicating their originating domain. WIF introduces a DomainRegistry (Figure 1) to manage these labels.

A single web page can incorporate data from several different domains, therefore we associate a unique label with each domain. In the JS engine, data and objects originating from different domains may interact, creating values which derive from more than one domain. To model this behavior, we take inspiration from Myers' decentralized label model [9] and represent security labels as a lattice join over domains.

DomainRegistry: When the browser loads HTML or JS, it registers the code's domain of origin in the DomainRegistry before processing. The DomainRegistry maps every domain to a unique bit in a 64 bit label. During execution, our framework attaches these labels to new JS values and HTML-tokens based on the origin. This design allows us to use efficient bit arithmetic for label join (0001|0010=0011) operations that propagate labels.

Information Flow in the JS engine: As a foundation for WIF, we implement information flow tracking within the JS engine using an approach similar to other researchers [4, 3, 5].

We implement security labeling by extending every JS value from 64 to 128 bits, where the upper 64 bits represent the actual JS value and the lower 64 bits indicate the domain of ownership. For example, a simplified example of a binary operation like `c = a + b`, where a comes `a.com` (mapped to 0001) and b originates from `b.com` (mapped to 0010) would cause c to hold the value of a + b in the upper 64 bits, and the labels of both, a and b (0001|0010=0011) in the lower 64 bits.

This design lets us directly encode 63 different domains in one label. We reserve the highest bit in the label to indicate that the direct encoding of 63 domains overflows. The overflow-bit indicates that the page incorporates code from more than 63 different domains. In such a case, our system switches to a slower label propagation mechanism, where the lower 63 bits become an integer index into an array of labels. When visiting the Alexa Top 500 pages with our web crawler, we discovered that pages, on average, include content from 12 different domains.

Conventional static analysis techniques for information flow, such as those developed for the Java-based Jif [10], are not directly applicable to dynamically typed languages, such as JS. However, we adapt these techniques by introducing a *control-flow stack* that manages labels for different security regions of a running program. At runtime, the JS engine updates the label of the *program counter* at every control flow branch and join within a program. The top of the control-flow stack always contains the current security label of the program counter. Using the control-flow stack, our system is able to track:

- *Explicit Information Flows*, which occur when some value explicitly depends on another variable, e.g., `var pub = secret;`.
- *Implicit Direct Information Flows,* which occur when some value can be inferred from the predicate of a branch in control flow, e.g., `if (secret) { pub = true;}`. An attacker can gain information about the secret variable by inspecting the value of the variable `pub` after execution of the `if` statement. The handling of implicit direct information flows therefore requires joining the label of the variable `pub` with the label of `secret`. The latter assignment to `pub` occurs in a labeled (secure) region, which causes `pub` to be tainted with the label of the current program counter.

We refer the reader to an accompanying technical report [11] for further details about maintaining the control-flow stack.

Information Flow in the DOM: The DOM provides an interface that allows JS in a web page to reference and modify HTML elements as if they were JS objects. For example, JS can dynamically change the `src`-attribute of an image so that the image changes whenever the user's cursor hovers over it. Malicious JS can use the DOM as a communication channel to exfiltrate information present within a web page. WIF prevents such exfiltration attempts by labeling DOM objects based on the origin of their elements and attributes. During HTML parsing, browsers build an internal tree representation of the DOM. Our framework uses this phase to attach an initial label, indicating the domain of origin, on all element and attribute nodes in the newly constructed DOM-tree.

JS code that calls `document.write` can force the tokenizer to pause and process new markup content from the script, before continuing parsing the regular page markup. WIF applies labels to HTML tokens so that tokens generated by the call inherit the label of the script, while regular markup inherits the label of the page.

JS can make use of different syntactical variants to assign a value to an HTML attribute in the DOM, e.g., `element.name = value;`. Internally, all the different variants dispatch to a function, `setAttribute`. We extend the argument list to include a label, which supports precise labeling, even for custom attributes available in HTML5. Performing labeling solely on attributes in the DOM, however, does not provide a complete solution. For example, a call to the `innerHTML` property of a `div`-element that returns only plain text of the displayed data without a label. To contain dynamically calculated properties, such as `innerHTML` and `value`, WIF modifies these functions to apply the label of the DOM element to the data before returning it to the JS engine.

User Events: In a web browser, the execution context for every script corresponds to the domain of that document. Whenever JS code triggers an event, WIF handles this event similar to a control-flow branch. It creates a new security region for handling the event, and joins the PC-label (top of the control-flow stack) with the label of the execution context. Once the event handler has finished execution, our framework restores the browser's previous state. Using this technique, our framework attaches a label to user generated JS events.

Network Monitor: At every network request, WIF checks whether the label of the URL-string matches the server domain in the network request. To do so, WIF extracts the domain of the GET request and looks up the corresponding 64-bit label in the DomainRegistry. Then WIF checks whether the 64 bit label of the URL-string matches the 64 bit label of the domain of that URL. Based on the result of an XOR operation on the two labels, our system decides whether the request is allowed.

Policy: We consider inequality of labels ($0011 \neq 0001$) to be a privacy violating information flow. When WIF detects such a violating flow, it records the event and notifies the user.

4   Evaluation

Security Evaluation: To verify that WIF is able to detect information exfiltration attempts, we inject custom exploit code into ten mirrored web pages with known XSS vulnerabilities. To find such web pages, we use XSSed (`xssed.com`), which provides the largest online archive of XSS vulnerable web sites, listing more than 45,000 web pages, including government pages, and pages in the Alexa Top 100 world wide. We inject malicious code that exfiltrates all keys pressed by a user into a mirrored vulnerable web page of `amazon.com`. This mirrored page pulls and integrates code from eight different origins on the Internet. Our framework successfully detects the attempt to exfiltrate logged keys, HTML-form data, and other exfiltration attempts.

Web Crawler Statistics: To perform a quantitative evaluation of our system, we implement a web crawler that automatically visits the Alexa Top 500 (`alexa.com`) web pages and stays on each web page for 60 seconds. To simulate user interaction, we equip this web crawler with the ability to fill out HTML-forms and submit the first available form. We found information flows across domain boundaries on 433 of the 500 visited web pages. This frequency emphasizes the importance of providing an opportunity to retrace the flow of information in a user's browser. The following statistics show a snapshot of consistently changing web pages, taken on December 24th, 2012.

Table 1. Overall findings when browsing the Alexa Top 500 pages

Distinct Content Providers	3,061
Violating Information Flows	8,764
Flows labeled with one domain	5,947
Flows labeled with more than one domain	2,817

Distinct Content Providers: As shown in Table 1, the Alexa Top 500 pages include content from a total of 3,061 distinct domains on the Internet. Verification and proof that all these content suppliers are benign and trustworthy is not available. A recent study [12] shows that web sites expand their "circle of trust" by introducing about 45% new JS inclusions each year. This trend encourages our efforts, because hacking just one of those inclusions gives immediate access to sensitive user data.

Statistics about information flow violations: When visiting the Alexa Top 500 pages we detect a total of 8,764 information flow violations (Table 1) which target a total of 1,384 distinct domains on the Internet. Our precise labeling reveals interacting domains that cause an information flow violation. We found that 2,817 out of the detected 8,764 violating information flows have more than one domain encoded in their label. One such information flow violation was found on `t-online.de`, where information was labeled with domains of `t-online.de`, `stats.t-online.de`, `im.banner.t-online.de`, `imagesrv.adition.com`, `ad2.adfarm1.adition.com`. Using such a multi-domain labeling strategy allows our system to clearly identify CDNs, like e.g., `stats.t-online.de`.

When crawling the Alexa Top 500 pages, our network monitor also reported a flow, where information was labeled with more than one domain, to the hardcoded IP-address `124.17.1.253`. We used the service of `whois.net` and discovered that *China Science & Technology Network* owns the IP-address. Put differently, this IP-address might belong to almost anyone in

China, benign or malicious. Manual inspection of payloads in such network requests is almost impossible, because information is often encoded in a highly obfuscated manner.

This result lets us conclude that only web site authors are able to provide information about permitted flows. Defining a policy of permitted flows and tracking the flow of information in a user's browser therefore seems the most promising approach to prevent information exfiltration attacks.

Performance Evaluation: We execute all benchmarks on a dual Quad Core Intel Xeon E5462 2.80 GHz with 9.8 GB RAM running Ubuntu 11.10 (kernel 3.2.0) using gcc-4.6.3, where we use `nice -n -20` to minimize operating system scheduler effects.

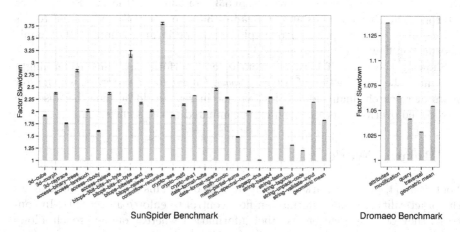

Fig. 2. left: Detailed JS engine performance impact per SunSpider benchmark, **right:** Detailed DOM performance impact per Dromaeo benchmark (both normalized by WebKit's JS interpreter, `JavaScriptCore`).

Figure 2 (left) shows the results for executing the SunSpider benchmarks using WIF. Our system has an average slowdown factor of 1.8×, or 82.82% when normalized to WebKit's original JS interpreter, `JavaScriptCore`. WIF introduces this overhead in the JS engine because it propagates labels for all created and modified JS values during execution of an application. To the best of our knowledge, the fastest information flow tracking systems run two to three times slower with tracking enabled [5, 7], which indicates that our implementation is substantially faster.

The results of the DOM benchmarks in Figure 2 (right) show that WIF introduces an average overhead of 5.43%, on Dromaeo benchmarks. This overhead is due to WIF managing not only the attribute value in the DOM, but also the corresponding label.

Current Limitations, Discussion and Future Work: Our system does not yet handle *implicit indirect information flows*, where information can be inferred by inspecting values in the non-executed path. The efficient handling of such flows still remains an open research question.

Currently, consumer browsers do not support any kind of information flow control to provide security against information exfiltration attacks. We believe that the introduced overhead for tracking the flow of information is the major obstacle for widespread adoption. We have shown that labeling the DOM introduces only around 5% overhead. To the best of our knowledge there is no just-in-time (JIT) compiler that performs information flow tracking for interpreted languages, such as JS. Other information flow tracking systems also integrate their tracking mechanisms in the JS interpreter (cf. [4, 7, 5]). Comparing the performance of our tracking framework against WebKit's JIT compiler reveals that our system introduces a slowdown of $6.3\times$, or 536.48% (the `JavaScriptCore` interpreter itself introduces an overhead of $3.5\times$, or 248.14%, compared to it's JIT compiler). We are planning on exploring the performance impact of dynamic information flow tracking using a JIT.

Showing the tradeoff between security and performance, the reader might remember the introduction of *Address Space Layout Randomization*, which after years of research finally found deployment in real world systems because the introduced overhead became negligible compared to the security gain.

5   Related Work

Vogt et al. [4] presents work closely related to ours. This pioneering work shows the practicality of using information flow control to enforce JS security. In contrast, they only use one bit as label information whereas our approach allows multi-domain labeling. Unfortunately they do not provide performance numbers which would make comparison to other work more comprehensive. Just et al. [5] presents an information flow framework improving on the results of Vogt et al [4]. They also use a stack for labeling secure regions of a program, but solely focus on the JS engine. Russo et al. [6] provides a mechanism for tracking information flow within dynamic tree structures. This work, in contrast, solely discusses information flow tracking in the DOM.

De Groef et al. [7] presents a system that uses secure multi-execution to enforce information control security in web browsers. Even though their approach presents a general mechanism for enforcing information flow control, their approach introduces substantial overhead. This is due to the nature of secure-multi-execution, which requires them to execute JS up to 2^n times, for n domains.

Hedin and Sabelfeld [13] present a dynamic type system that ensures information flow control for a core of JS. They do not provide an implementation but address the challenge of tracking the flow of information for objects, higher-order functions, exceptions, arrays as well as JS's API to the DOM.

6   Conclusion

We have presented a framework for the dynamic tracking of information flows across scripting exposed subsystems of a browser that allows precise labeling of values. To achieve this objective we added a DomainRegistry to the browser, modified the underlying JS engine and APIs to handle DOM and user events. We demonstrated that our framework is (1) able to detect information exfiltration attempts, (2) allows precise statistics about domains involved in an information flow violation, and (3) lowers performance overhead down to 83%. Thus, our system provides a major step towards precise and efficient information flow control in web browsers.

References

1. OWASP: The open web application security project, https://www.owasp.org/
2. Microsoft: Microsoft security intelligence report, vol. 13 (2012),
   http://www.microsoft.com/security/sir/default.aspx
3. Jang, D., Jhala, R., Lerner, S., Shacham, H.: An empirical study of privacy-violating information flows in JavaScript web applications. In: Proceedings of the Conference on Computer and Communications Security, pp. 270–283. ACM (2010)
4. Vogt, P., Nentwich, F., Jovanovic, N., Kruegel, C., Kirda, E., Vigna, G.: Cross site scripting prevention with dynamic data tainting and static analysis. In: Proceedings of Annual Network and Distributed System Security Symposium (2007)
5. Just, S., Cleary, A., Shirley, B., Hammer, C.: Information flow analysis for JavaScript. In: Proceedings of the ACM International Workshop on Programming Language and Systems Technologies for Internet Clients, pp. 9–18. ACM (2011)
6. Russo, A., Sabelfeld, A., Chudnov, A.: Tracking information flow in dynamic tree structures. In: Backes, M., Ning, P. (eds.) ESORICS 2009. LNCS, vol. 5789, pp. 86–103. Springer, Heidelberg (2009)
7. Groef, W.D., Devriese, D., Nikiforakis, N., Piessens, F.: FlowFox: a web browser with flexible and precise information flow control. In: Proceedings of the ACM Conference on Computer and Communications Security. ACM (2012)
8. Goguen, J., Meseguer, J.: Security policies and security models. In: Proceedings of IEEE Symposium on Security and Privacy. IEEE (1982)
9. Myers, A.C., Liskov, B.: Protecting privacy using the decentralized label model. ACM Transactions on Software Engineering and Methodology 9, 410–442 (2000)
10. Myers, A.C., Zheng, L., Zdancewic, S., Chong, S., Nystrom, N.: Jif: Java information flow (2001), http://www.cs.cornell.edu/jif
11. Hennigan, E., Kerschbaumer, C., Brunthaler, S., Franz, M.: Tracking information flow for dynamically typed programming languages by instruction set extension. Technical report, University of California Irvine (2011)
12. Nikiforakis, N., Invernizzi, L., Kapravelos, A., Van Acker, S., Joosen, W., Kruegel, C., Piessens, F., Vigna, G.: You are what you include: Large-scale evaluation of remote javascript inclusions. In: Proceedings of the Conference on Computer and Communications Security. ACM (2012)
13. Hedin, D., Sabelfeld, A.: Information-flow security for a core of JavaScript. In: Proceedings of the Computer Security Foundations Symposium, pp. 3–18 (2012)

Granddaughter Beware! An Intergenerational Case Study of Managing Trust Issues in the Use of Facebook

Ann Light[1] and Lizzie Coles-Kemp[2,*]

[1] Northumbria University School of Design, Newcastle upon Tyne, NE1 8ST, UK
ann.light@northumbria.ac.uk
[2] Royal Holloway University of London, Egham, TW200EX
lizzie.coles-kemp@rhul.ac.uk

Abstract. We offer a qualitative analysis of on-line safety practices and expectations in a community setting to look at trust practices that contribute to the complexity of information behaviors in the use of social media. Staging an encounter between local families by bringing together grandmothers and granddaughters at a workshop, we interrogate resulting discussions to understand how information practices are deployed to perform and interpret social identity. The analysis reveals the importance of trust practices and in particular, shows the tension between inward-looking and outward-looking behavior and how different perspectives on trust influence the manner in which communities work to protect members and police alternative uses of Facebook. In doing so, we add to knowledge about on-line safety and trust practices and the roles that families and tools play in supporting, enforcing and augmenting these practices.

Keywords: identity, norms, Facebook, social media, privacy, trust practices.

1 Introduction

The workshop discussed below forms part of the VOME research project, which uses qualitative social research to ground the development of tools to support informational privacy and consent decision-making [5]. The workshop was set up to explore how a community of internet users regards social media as part of their identity and how this influences their actions with respect to trust, safety and privacy online.

The workshop ran in northern England in July 2011 and brought together grandmothers and granddaughters through a community center that sits at the heart of activity in an area classified as economically deprived. Barnard-Wills and Ashenden [1] had shown there are tensions between generational perspectives on identity which come to the fore in institutional settings, including the family. Previous work on the project had also influenced the research: some of the user experience evaluations of on-line registration had found grandmothers influencing grand-daughters in their internet use, in particular over personal information disclosure practices and social networking.

---

* Corresponding author.

M. Huth et al. (Eds.): TRUST 2013, LNCS 7904, pp. 196–204, 2013.
© Springer-Verlag Berlin Heidelberg 2013

During these studies, stories emerged of grandmothers using social networking sites together with granddaughters as a social activity and supporting granddaughters in relationship problems that cropped up in using social networking. (The same pattern, however, did not emerge with other intergenerational pairings.) In designing the next stage of the research, the team sought room for differing views and interpretations of technology to emerge and gave a chance for these family members to show each other - and reflect upon - how they mediate their relationships using technology.

1.1   Related Work

Information practices are situated phenomena, shaped by their contexts. Nissenbaum [14] highlights the need for the consideration of privacy contexts in privacy-enhancing technology design. Dourish and Anderson [6] and Stutzman and Kramer-Duffield [19] have written on 'contextual information practice' [19], following Dourish and Anderson's insights that security and privacy practices, which contribute to the creation and maintenance of social identities, are culturally informed, performative and collectively achieved (see also [7]). Further, the ways that identity is performed and interpreted (and our beliefs about the way that identity is constituted) have become significant in the design of digital tools as we design more tools that directly impact on identity and our sense of self [11]. This is not to say that issues of social identity were not relevant to design before (e.g. Reeves and Nass [17]), but new trends are bringing complex identity issues to the fore, which go beyond technical data protection and which require an understanding of the complex range of information practices [5, 13, 16,] that are deployed to perform and interpret our identities.

Digital technology is moving into intimate spaces of domestic life and mediates many of our relationships as well as providing means to represent our lives and organize our personal business: Odom, Zimmerman, and Forlizzi [15] describe how digital objects in family homes help children of divorcees achieve a sense of belonging; Hodkinson and Lincoln [8] discuss young people's individually owned and controlled territory online, equating it with the privacy of the bedroom; Miller [12] shows a diversifying use of Facebook, noting how Facebook can work to make up for a restricted social life. This takes us beyond the notion of identity as a credential for controlling access to data and links it to an emotional and representative side that can inform discussions of trust and safety more fully. In this paper, we examine one social system for what it can tell us about trust and safety perceptions and practices in a tight-knit community with sharply demarcated uses of social media such as Facebook.

2   Details of the Identity Workshop

This paper draws on analysis of experiences of a workshop set up to explore dynamics between granddaughters and grandmothers using social media in a tight community setting.

The workshop involved six granddaughters (GDs) and six grandmothers (GMs). It was staged in a northern English town where local granddaughter/grandmother pairs were recruited through a community center. Preliminary work had already identified that there were close family pairings and internet active family members. Participants self-selected on criteria given to the center leaders, with a stress on relations not individual characteristics. Given the personal nature of perceptions of identity and the practices that are used to perform and interpret identity, it was important that the group was small enough for participants to feel comfortable to speak about sensitive issues. To support this aspect, the workshop was run at the community center, which was familiar to all participants.

As it turned out, the participants were all known to each other from daily life in the community, coming from a small area where social mobility is low. For instance, all the GDs had been to the same school. Each pair was part of what would be classed as a "close" family unit; while the GDs defined themselves as very fond of their GMs and identified as part of the community. All the GDs (16-24) used social networking sites; they were immersed internet users.

The GMs were aged 55+ and four of the six GMs were great-grandmothers. They included a mix of active social networkers and those without accounts for any social networks. One GM used social networking to keep contact with relatives in Australia. Two of the others used the Internet for email and on-line shopping. Those who did not use Facebook directly had experience of family who uses social networks. Each was interested in interaction with their GDs and her friends. The relationships with their granddaughters varied, although all took an active role in their GDs' lives and could report acting as a "safety valve" when GD relations with her mother became tense.

2.1   Planned Interactions

Only a small amount of formal intervention was planned into the workshop so that emphasis would be on emergent discussion and reflection. The event was facilitated by a community leader and a VOME researcher. The workshop began with an introduction to VOME research and the process for the day. This explained that VOME's work is on personal information control, but didn't develop the theme. Events were videoed by someone from the community group who was known to the majority of the participants. Before lunch, individuals and pairs from the group showed each other how they used social networking; after lunch they worked in pairs.

A few specific structuring elements were included, to focus the work and initiate discussion. During the morning's "show and tell" sessions, while someone used the big screen in the room to show their activities, the group was encouraged to discuss issues that arose and write down thoughts and reflections. Then a summary session was run before lunch and objectives were set for the afternoon. In the afternoon, the GD/GM pairs were mixed up. Each GD was tasked with showing their "new" GM what they did on-line and also to show GMs how to search on the internet, find information and look at websites of interest. During all these activities, there was little direction given from the facilitation team. However, the facilitators did pick up on issues, press participants to develop points and widen the discussion to hear others' voices on a topic. In other words, with some focusing, the topics spoken about and the way that discussion developed emerged from the activities of sharing and showing.

2.2   Designing the Methodology

Drawing on traditions of emergent investigation (e.g. [2],[10]), an open-ended process was used in the workshop to allow identity to be performed. We sought to encourage participants to express themselves in their own language and allow themes to come and go. But, further, room for sensitive and controversial issues to arise was built in (and made 'safe' as possible by the presence of a familiar community worker, a familiar space and so on). Indeed, the device of putting members of close families together for so long with so much freedom of topic in a reflective mode was to stimulate encounters – with ideas and with each other. Tensions that arose were explored reflectively: neither cultivated, nor ignored.

The form contrasts with most design research workshops, where a purpose is explicit, more activity is scheduled and relations between participants are less important than focus on an outcome. Instead, here, the motive was to explore issues the group found important *when together*. The approach did not seek to simulate the situatedness of ethnography, yet it is situated in existing relations. In one respect, it is naturally occurring: the event took place in the lives of six families in a center they use; they showed each other normal activities; normal relations were lived out. In another, it is contrived: a staging that fueled reflection and encouraged debate [3]. In other words, the research team deliberately under-determined the process, and, in *assembling a carefully chosen set of social roles* (though not selecting the people stepping into them), issues of identity and relations played out, while shared activity and community processes joined the topic of media use for contemplation.

The team took the recorded video of the day and watched it repeatedly, as advocated by Knoblauch et al [9]. We looked particularly for tensions – in our expectations, in the use of tools, in group relations, in family pairs – and how they were managed. Were they new or well worn? Was there friction, working around the issue, or acceptance? How did actions and attitudes bear on what was happening with the tools?

This search for friction points is distinct from looking for problems to solve or design opportunities, but it may be a precursor. We put emphasis on this earlier phase as it is the point where we formed an analysis of identity issues that challenged traditional thinking about trust, privacy and online safety practices and attitudes.

In the next sections, we give a flavor of the insights that emerged, though, for the sake of clarity and brevity, we only share our most relevant findings.

3   Emergent Interactions

Facebook (FB) dominated: in the morning, one GD/GM pair showed how they used it and then further GDs showed their presence on it. Later, one GM who did not use it was set up with an account and 'friend' requests were sent. In general, the GMs were less digitally literate, but more socially skilled and led commentary and questioning of social media uses by the GDs. Two striking behaviors will be raised here.

1) The interaction between GMs and GDs suggests that using FB may be a communal activity *offline* as well as across cyberspace. One GD/GM pair showed how they play online games, using FB together in the same physical space, often sharing

the computer. Interestingly, the GD has access to and uses the GM's username and password for both FB and email. However, this is not reciprocal; the GM has chosen to give control to the GD. The GM informed the group that she shares her details with her GD, not out of ignorance but out of feelings of intimacy; her GD, however, does not share her log-on details because of feelings of identity and autonomy. This is counter to expected use but cannot be linked to simple lack of understanding or digital literacy as the GM displays both. Instead, we observed a social space where GM and GD play together with their own rules of access and where co-use and users who are traditionally classified as "non-users" influence trust, privacy and safety practices.

2) From the "show and tell" sessions, it was evident that five of the six GDs populated their FB 'friends' primarily with family and people they knew from the immediate community. This pattern was replicated when setting up a FB account for one of the GMs: all the 'friend' requests (22) that popped up during the day came from members of the family or from families connected to the family in the near locality. When undertaking paired activities later, further examples emerged of how social media acts as entertainment for co-located and/or hardly separated friends. As one GD said: "It means I can keep in touch with my mates without going out" and another: "I am really shy, but using social networking gives me the chance to be able to talk to anyone.... I don't know what else we would do if we didn't have the internet." (However, by 'anyone' she meant people she already knows in the neighborhood.) FB was seen as something to do, offering a range of pastime activities. Key to use was socializing with 'friends' on FB who were also friends in the locality, i.e. already part of the community in which the GDs lived. It was clear that the networks they used online reproduced the social network around them, remained fairly homogenous and reflected a lifestyle centered on home and surrounding area, where trust relationships are primarily built off-line and those relationships are mirrored on-line.

However, for one GD, the patterns of engagement were very different. For her, going online and using FB was a means to meet people outside the community. This woman is classed as a 'vulnerable' young adult and whilst holding down a job and being an active member of the community, she is not part of the set who socialize as the other five do. In fact, she sees FB as her chance to engage with people from outside the tight networks in which she lives and in which her status as different is played back to her. This very different use led to conflicting views.

We will describe this encounter in detail since it illustrates well the relationship between design, identity, trust, social relations and peer pressure. (For ease of description in the following narrative, we call this GD 'Lisa'.)

3.1   An Open and Shut Case

During Lisa's description of her social practices, a tension emerged regarding the interpretation of her privacy settings. FB provides the means to set choices of who can see your profile and your postings: it can be 'friends', 'friends of friends', chosen networks or 'everyone'. (Between the workshop and writing this paper, FB changed the label for "Everyone" to "Public"). For those who regarded FB as entertainment within the community in which they lived, setting the privacy to 'friends' or other selected groups was regarded as a sensible safety measure. With this inward-looking behavior, trust is a prerequisite for disclosing personal information. They might not all follow this policy, but they nevertheless viewed it as reasonable and wise. Everyone they talked to on FB was known to them and knew more about them than they ever posted on FB, so FB privacy was seen as irrelevant locally. But strangers were unwelcome and 'everyone' represented strangers. For Lisa, who used FB as a means to reach beyond the community in which she lived, the 'everyone' setting was necessary and Lisa's outward-looking behavior demonstrates that trust is not a prerequisite for disclosing personal information. Her day routinely involved checking to see if she had been 'friended' by anyone new and her 'friends' were not known to her before such an approach. She saw the 'everyone' setting as entirely reasonable.

When people heard her privacy settings, the social pressure on Lisa to change them was evident and she was lectured by another GD. Even though not all the other FB users in the group had restricted access to their FB postings, it was an expectation that the privacy settings would be understood in a particular way (i.e. a local norm). It was the insistence by Lisa that, for her purposes, the 'everyone' setting was most desirable, which caused the tension. This tension was illuminating as an example of how Lisa resists norms in the group and puts herself outside what is deemed acceptable behavior, possibly motivating her search for company who accepts different values.

It also offers an example of how a group may operate with expected stances in social networking, even if they do not always act on them, and how this carries through into their information practices - trust and safety management can be situated offline as well as in the online interactions this offline network supports. By working with such a closed circle, the researchers were able to see this play out as a dominant subset of connections. In a more heterogeneous set of 'friends', such stances would be less apparent and have less purchase (as Stutzman and Kramer-Duffield [19] note about reach and expectation).

And, more particularly of interest here, it points to the different understandings of trust and the varying privacy and security-related needs among the young women.

The five GDs were primarily using FB to connect with people in their community and as a social and entertainment outlet. It could be argued that their needs and values put them at less risk socially because the *lack of* privacy at community level – both on and off FB – works to keep them accounted for. Everyone in the community knows their business; no one outside it cares to know it – trust is a local phenomenon that does not reach into a wider world. Nonetheless, aspects of privacy do emerge: the GD who does not reciprocally share log-in details with her GM (behavior which is customarily about security and protection of ID data) refuses to share as a matter of autonomy, not because she distrusts her GM.

It is concern for safety that comes up as the principal drawback with Lisa's behavior. This throws the focus back on the technology, rather than social mechanisms, largely because Lisa's position in the group has already violated the protective norms that operate within it and so people do not know her business. This is apparent - they are dismayed at her use of FB as well as her privacy settings, though the two revelations emerge together and are related. Lisa, the isolated granddaughter, uses FB as her route out of the community; the need for privacy is different; the support from the community, more fragile. In her case, using FB is about hiding certain aspects of her identity and accentuating others, which cannot be performed within her geographical community. Using the 'everyone' setting and exposing information to others is part of interacting online and she wants strangers to see her news updates and other postings. If there is risk in this disclosure, she is unmoved, explaining it as a trade-off for greater virtual mobility, and if there is a risk to her person, which is the far more severe threat that the rest of the group has begun to consider, then it only becomes real if she contemplates meeting the strangers she 'friends'. In this way she reconciles risks - and the greatest risk for her remains that social isolation, which use of FB mitigates. This moment of conflict in the group reflects the different values in using FB:

1. as a tool within a co-located community, and
2. as a tool for an individual wanting to move beyond a co-located community.

Using the tool within the community, there is support provided at community level for users' wellbeing and the tools' controls are subverted to be replaced, or augmented, by social gatekeeping practices at another point in the negotiation of appropriate behavior. This provides a set of very different priorities to those of someone who uses FB to reach out of their immediate community, where privacy, security and safety are screen-based choices, though not necessarily informed by the factors that motivated the design of the controls. For instance, Lisa does not see broadcasting to public channels in FB as related to privacy. It is the potential to make new friends that motivates her and that inevitably entails some information disclosure and exchange.

4   Learning about Social Media Use

By taking a performative view of identity [4, 11], the research team was able to conceive of a workshop in which making space for roles and identities to play out was more important than setting specific goal-directed activities and so designed an event to stress social and dynamic aspects. Room was given over for people to question themselves and others about what they do, making good use of existing social relations in the group. This 'spaceful' technique did not rule that tensions should occur, but gave a chance for the questioning of practices and motivations. Focusing on identity as a shared emergent phenomenon allowed us to consider the information practices and values in the group. It helped reveal that not only were understandings of privacy, security and safety different from those embedded in most privacy and security management systems, but that two different social systems were operating at odds with each other. In fact, there were signs that the presence of the tightly knit group, dealing socially with eventualities, actually made the risks greater for Lisa as she operated alone, outside the social support system and divergently from it.

4.1   Different Priorities Require Different Designs

Though the incident with Lisa was brief, it gave insight into using social media and the expectations operating in the group. In Lisa, the team was reminded of Miller's [11] study of a person using FB to compensate for a restricted social world; thereby troubling relations with her physically close community and invoking strong reactions in those upholding 'normal' behavior. However, Lisa was not trying to violate norms or navigate privacy. She was trying to perform her chosen identity with the tools available to her, clearly showing that, for her, trust was not a precursor to disclosing personal information. No amount of education about privacy, cautioning about strangers or designing out disclosure will alter her position, unless it also meets her need for friends *and* safety. Therefore, interventions to support Lisa in performing her identity require a different shape to those used to support the rest of the group.

4.2   The Challenges for Designing in Trust

As we have already indicated, identifying the principal zone of gatekeeping and information negotiation as diffused through the community, rather than at the interface to the software, destabilizes models of privacy. This opens the way to think about personal information control, not as an off-line or on-line concept but as socially negotiated[1]. The practices we witnessed are not based on misconception of privacy or a cheating of the rules (such as the use of lying [7]). The concept of protecting data is clearly second to concerns about trusting strangers in other matters.

More significantly, as the group explored its priorities it revealed two quite polar contexts of use, both of which trouble conventional wisdom. In one, a tight-knit world, non-users co-manage tools and information flows. Much of the group's thinking about FB and how to behave on it emanates from off-line grandmothers who are worldlier than their granddaughters. These women are abreast of new trends, but choose their relation to them. This is most intriguingly captured in the GM who uses FB only to play with her GD as a co-user. With the insight that experience of use does not necessarily come from using (see also Sambasivan et al [18]), it offers a new slant on digital inclusion and our understanding of older people's use of technology. At the moment, these co-users are in the shadows and invisible to the technology, but perhaps one day they will have their own side-cars to travel in.

The other narrative considered here leads straight to matters of identity, belonging and beyond. We had played out before us the tension between privacy and expression and the way that social norms about protection and 'right' behavior can be oppressive for individuals who must travel virtually to find their kin. Although we analyzed this here through exploring a tension in one small group, it points to a far wider issue that most of us instinctively acknowledge. This trade-off is implicit in much usage but not so apparent in the design of the technologies we use.

5   Conclusion and Future Work

As the examples here show, designing to support social networking practices requires technologies for users with different trust perceptions and needs. Online sociality may be based on trust, but it is an interaction of trust and self-expression, problematizing existing discourses around information disclosure. A further insight is the amount of interaction taking place off-line within social groups around the tools. This points to

---

[1] [19] and [6] point to other aspects of the social negotiations that manage disclosure.

potential to develop technologies that support co-use and make space for the role and influence of the non-user. As governments move to a service delivery position of "digital by default", future work will use these insights to research non- and co-use and to inform the design of spaceful software interfaces that can incorporate different on- and off-line interventions designed to support trust practices.

References

1. Barnard-Wills, D., Ashenden, D.: Public sector engagement with online identity management. Identity in the Information Society, 1–18 (2010)
2. Belk, R., Wallendorf, M., Sherry Jnr, J.F.: The Sacred and the Profane in Consumer Behavior: Theodicy on the Odyssey. J. Consumer Research 16(1), 1–38 (1989)
3. Binder, T.: Why Design:Labs? In: NORDES 2007, 2nd Nordic Design Research Conference, Konstfack, Stockholm (May 2007)
4. Butler, J.: Gender Trouble: Feminism and the Subversion of Identity. Routledge, NY (1990)
5. Coles-Kemp, L., Kani-Zabihi, E.: Practice Makes Perfect: Motivating confident on-line privacy protection practices. In: IEEE International Conference on Social Computing (2011)
6. Dourish, P., Anderson, K.: Collective Information Practice: Exploring Privacy and Security as Social and Cultural Phenomena. J. HCI 21(3), 319–342 (2006)
7. Dourish, P., Bell, G.: Divining a Digital Future: Mess and Mythology in Ubiquitous Computing. MIT (2011)
8. Hodkinson, P., Lincoln, S.: Online Journals as Virtual Bedrooms?' In Young: Nordic Journal of Youth Research (2008)
9. Knoblauch, H., Schnettler, B., Raab, J., Soeffner, H. (eds.): Video Analysis: Methodology and Methods. Peter Lang (2006)
10. Light, A.: Adding Method to Meaning: a technique for exploring peoples' experience with digital products. Behaviour & Information Technology 25(2), 175–187 (2006)
11. Light, A.: HCI as heterodoxy: Technologies of Identity and the Queering of Interaction Design. IwC 23(5) (2011)
12. Miller, D.: Tales from Facebook. Polity Press (2011)
13. NISA: To Log or Not to Log? – Risk and Benefits of Life-Logging Applications (2011), http://www.enisa.europa.eu/activities/risk-management/emerging-and-future-risk/deliverables/life-logging-risk-assessment (retrieved)
14. Nissenbaum, H.: Privacy in context: Technology, policy, and the integrity of social life. Stanford Law Books (2009)
15. Odom, W., Zimmerman, J., Forlizzi, J.: Designing for Dynamic Family Structures: Divorced Families and Interactive Systems. In: Proc. DIS 2010, pp. 151–160 (2010)
16. O'Hara, K.: Transparent government, not transparent citizens: a report on privacy and transparency for the Cabinet Office. London, GB, Cabinet Office (2011)
17. Reeves, B., Nass, C.: The Media Equation: How People Treat Computers, Television, and New Media Like Real People and Places. CUP, Cambridge (1996)
18. Sambasivan, N., Cutrell, E., Toyama, K., Nardi, B.A.: Intermediated technology use in developing communities. In: Proc. CHI 2010 (2010)
19. Stutzman, F., Kramer-Duffield, J.: Friends Only: Examining a Privacy-Enhancing Behavior in Facebook. In: Proc. CHI 2010 (2010)

Contextualized Web Warnings, and How They Cause Distrust

Steffen Bartsch[1], Melanie Volkamer[1],
Heike Theuerling[2], and Fatih Karayumak[3]

[1] CASED, TU Darmstadt
Hochschulstraße 10, 64289 Darmstadt, Germany
{steffen.bartsch,melanie.volkamer}@cased.de
[2] IAD, TU Darmstadt
Petersenstr. 30, 64287 Darmstadt, Germany
h.theuerling@iad.tu-darmstadt.de
[3] Cyber Security Institute, TUBITAK BILGEM
41470 Gebze / Kocaeli, Turkey
fatih.karayumak@tubitak.gov.tr

Abstract. Current warnings in Web browsers are difficult to understand for lay users. We address this problem through more concrete warning content by contextualizing the warning – for example, taking the user's current intention into account in order to name concrete consequences. To explore the practical value of contextualization and potential obstacles, we conduct a behavioral study with 36 participants who we either confront with contextualized or with standard warning content while they solve Web browsing tasks. We also collect exploratory data in a posterior card-sorting exercise and interview. We deduce a higher understanding of the risks of proceeding from the exploratory data. Moreover, we identify conflicting effects from contextualization, including distrust in the content, and formulate recommendations for effective contextualized warning content.

1 Introduction

Warnings in Web browsing are an example of how difficult it is to craft effective security interventions. A plethora of studies (e.g. on certificate warnings: Sunshine et al. [19]) have shown that current warnings are ineffective at influencing the behavior of users for two main reasons: First, because of habituation effects from the frequent unhelpful warnings in non-critical situations [2]. Second, because of the technical language that prevents users from understanding the risks of proceeding – that is, how likely it is that an adverse event occurs and what the personal consequences are [6,8,13]. We thus not only need to prevent the occurrence of warnings in uncritical situations, but also make the warnings understandable so that the infrequent warnings will enable users to take informed decisions about proceeding based on the actual risks involved.

One proposal to solve the problem with the understanding of the risks is to move away from traditional approaches to warnings as described by Wogalter

M. Huth et al. (Eds.): TRUST 2013, LNCS 7904, pp. 205–222, 2013.

[20]: generic hazard warnings with static texts and symbols for a broad audience. Instead, we follow earlier proposals to *contextualize* security interventions and thereby increase their *concreteness* [7,4]. The idea is to employ additional information on the context (e.g. user intention) so as to generate more concrete warnings – for example, by mentioning specific consequences, such as credit-card fraud in case of online shopping – and therefore make it easier for users to relate to and understand the risk of proceeding.

Since contextualization has been primarily studied technically for warnings up to now – for example, on how to acquire the available context information [7] –, we address the practical value of contextualization in this paper. The goal of this work is to test whether contextualization is more effective in increasing the understanding of the risks and in influencing behavior than traditional content, and to explore how to craft effective contextualized warning content. We developed contextualized warning content based on a pre-study with lay and expert users. We then conducted a between-subject study with 36 participants who were confronted with warnings either showing the contextualized content or content from existing warnings while solving realistic tasks in a lab environment. In addition to the participants' reaction to the warnings, we also collected qualitative data from a posterior card sorting of the warnings and a posterior interview. Our main contributions are:

1. We show a positive effect from contextualization on how concretely participants assess the risks of proceeding;
2. We demonstrate how confounding factors, such as visual stimuli that imply severity, can dominate the effect of contextualization in real-world settings;
3. We identify complexities related to contextualization, including distrust in the warning content due to its concreteness;
4. We derive recommendations of how to craft effective contextualized content.

2 Prior Research on the Content of Web Browser Warnings

Bravo-Lillo et al. [6] showed empirically that warnings are not understood – for example, due to technical terminology. Improved warning content may help, though: Biddle et al. [5] found that their reformulated warnings made users more responsive to different levels of connection security. More specifically, Downs et al. [8] showed that phishing warnings are more often ignored if the threats and consequences are unknown. Furthermore, Kauer et al. [13] found that individuals are more likely to heed warnings if they perceive personal consequences. However, when Krol et al. [14] confronted users with either a very generic warning or one with more specific consequences, they found no significant difference in behavior.

To warn in an adequate form and achieve the necessary impact, De Keukelaere et al. [7] proposed to adapt the intervention to the context; they found improvements from considering the security risk and prior actions of the user. In this paper, we follow a related approach, the Framework for Contextualized Interventions (FOCI), which supports the systematic development of contextualized security interventions [4]. The framework targets two aspects: first, whether, when, and in which form the intervention appears (intervention strategy, e.g. active as a warning or passive as a symbol), and, second, what content it conveys (e.g. technical threats or personal consequences). This paper focuses on the content aspect.

3   Pre-study: How Expert and Lay Users Assess Web Risks

From prior work, it remains unclear, *what* contextualized content helps users in understanding the risks of proceeding. To guide our choice of content in the main study of this paper, we explored what is missing for users to understand the risks. Prior literature showed that expert and lay users differ in how they assess risks and that experts are more likely to have a sufficient understanding [3]. Thus, we analyzed the difference between expert and lay users in how they assess risks of Web browsing.

3.1   Study Design

We recruited seven lay and seven expert users from personal contacts for a card-sorting exercise. Their task was to sort Web site screenshots into stacks of similarly perceived consequences if their personal account was compromised. Our goal was to motivate participants to talk about factors that influence their categorization. We asked expert and lay users to imagine that they have user accounts at 67 Web sites (selected from the Alexa.com Top-500 most-visited Web sites in Germany for diversity), which were presented to them as the cards to be sorted in the form of printed DIN-A5 screenshots of the pages ("picture sorting": giving visual clues [17, p. 83]). Expert users (age avg. 37 yrs., min 28, max 52) covered a broad span of participants professionally related to security, including at least two each of system administrators, security researchers, and security consultants. Lay users (age avg. 23 yrs., min 22, max 25) were without professional relation to security, but covered a broad span of self-assessed PC expertise from receiving help with computer problems to providing help, even with difficult problems.

3.2   Analysis

We qualitatively analyzed the transcribed recordings of the card-sorting exercise. We inductively developed codes for the risk concepts that participants used to assess risks. These concepts differed between arguments based on the type or function of the page (e.g. activity "Shopping", institution "Bank", content "Information") and risk-related factors (affected data "Contacts", Consequence "Financial loss", adversary activity "Hacker accesses my account"). We also found a difference in how concrete these arguments were (e.g. for consequences "I'll lose money from my account" vs. "This somehow affects my finances").

Table 1. Primary concepts used in the categorization of Web sites

Argument	Examples	Lay	Expert	$p < 0.05$
Type of page	Activity "Shopping"	225 **58%**	134 **38%**	Yes
Risk factor	Consequence "Financial loss"	172 **45%**	236 **67%**	Yes
Total		385	354	

3.3 Experts Focus More on Consequences and Adversary Activities

Expert and lay users significantly differ in their argumentation as shown in Table 1[1]. Experts more frequently used the risk-factor arguments, particularly the specific consequence and the adversary activity, than lay users. Lay users, in contrast, more often relied on the Type-of-page factors of a Web site without explicitly considering risk factors – for example, only the possible activities ("Eventim, that's where one may buy, order tickets"). Table 2 shows how the risk factors break down into different risk concepts. When lay users discussed risks, they less often mentioned consequences and adversary activities. Our hypothesis for warning content thus is to emphasize these factors for lay users to help them to better understand the risks of proceeding.

Table 2. Frequency of different risk concepts and their concreteness

Risk concept	Lay	Expert	$p < 0.05$
Data-related	101 59%	126 53%	No
Concrete data	41 24%	86 36%	No
Consequence	63 37%	148 63%	Yes
Concrete consequence	34 20%	112 47%	Yes
Adversary activity	75 44%	148 63%	Yes
Concrete activity	22 13%	114 48%	Yes
Further risk factors	90 52%	142 60%	No
Concrete risk factor	3 2%	65 28%	Yes

3.4 Experts Are More Concrete

Not only did lay users less often discuss risk factors than experts; when they did, they did so less concretely. Experts rather formulated concrete adversary activities ("modifies my preferences") and named the concrete consequence or affected personal data ("bank account data put there"), and the concrete evaluation of specific risk factors ("I will find out quickly"), instead of only mentioning solely a general risk level such as "I'd classify it as comparatively bad" when categorizing Web sites (cf. concreteness in Table 2).

---

[1] We applied a Welch Two Sample t-test on the individuals' proportions and noted in the last column for which proportion the differences between expert and lay users are significant, i.e. the null hypothesis was rejected because of $p < 0.05$.

4   Research Hypotheses

The findings from the pre-study indicate that it is helpful for lay users if we emphasize adversary activities and consequences, and we are thereby more concrete with respect to the current situation. This is further supported by literature on risk communication: According to Rothman and Kiviniemi [16] concrete risks are more successful in creating awareness and influencing behavior in health risk communication: Consequences (symptoms) that are easier to picture increase the awareness, as do testimonials of affected individuals when there is an identification with those. Cognitive psychology indicates that it is important that people are able to "simulate" or imagine the antecedents and consequences of risks [12]. As previously noted, Kauer et al. [13] found that individuals are less likely to ignore warnings when they perceive personal risks, corresponding to the experience from medical risk communication. Overall, as depicted in Figure 1, we thus expect that *contextualization* of the content and thereby including *concrete risks* according to the situation will increase the *understanding of risks* and thus the *motivation to behave securely*.

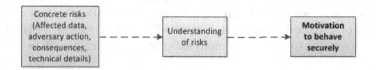

Fig. 1. Model underlying the research hypothesis

In this paper, we apply this model to study the behavior of participants when confronted with different warnings, that is, whether they follow the recommendation of the warning and leave the Web site (comply) or whether they proceed with their task on the Web site. While prior studies [14] have found that the habituation effect dominates the effect of different content, we assume that our more intensively improved content should influence the behavior of the participants. Accordingly, our first hypothesis is:

> *H1 The participants who are confronted with the contextualized content more frequently comply with warnings than those with standard content*

When the change in behavior is due to better understanding of the risks, we expect that this change in whether to comply (the warning effect) occurs differently depending on the objective risk of the individual situation [13], despite potential confounds, such as additional visual stimuli:

> *H2 The relation between the* warning effect *and the objective risk is stronger for warnings with contextualized content than for standard content*

Moreover, the difference in understanding should not only show in the behavior, but also when asked to consciously assess the criticality of the situation (warning perception):

> *H3 The relation between the* warning perception *and the objective risk is stronger for warnings with contextualized content than for standard content*

Lastly, since we hypothesize that better understanding is related to perceiving risks concretely, we expect participants to also emphasize concrete aspects in their risk assessment depending on the type of warning:

> *H4 Participants who are confronted with the contextualized content assess the risks of proceeding more concretely than those with standard content*

5   Research Method

Our study has two goals: first, testing the effectiveness of contextualized content in warnings in behavior (H1–2) and in conscious assessment (H3–4), and, second, exploring how to optimally contextualize content. To generate realistic behavioral results, we confront 36 participants either with warnings with contextualized or standard content while they solve twelve realistic Web-browsing tasks. Moreover, we collected and analyzed posterior qualitative data.

5.1   Study Design Overview

The between-subjects study on warnings with contextualized or standard content consisted of two main parts. In the first, behavioral, part, participants solved twelve tasks and were interrupted with warnings in five of these, representing situations of different levels of objective risks. Due to the technical complexity of integrating the different warnings in the Web browsing tasks, the study was conducted in our usability lab on a study laptop. In the second, explanatory, part, participants conducted a card-sorting exercise of screenshots of the warning scenarios, explaining their reasoning, and were interviewed on the risks of proceeding in each situation.

No IRB consent was required as all university criteria for studies without explicit IRB consent were met. For privacy reasons, the screening data that included personal identification (name was optional, but an email address was required for experiment logistics) was separated from the screening data used later for demographics. After the end of the first part of the study, the participants were informed about the actual goal of the study.

5.2   Instruments: Warnings with Contextualized and Standard Content

We created prototypes of warnings with contextualized and standard content for five scenarios of different objective risk levels for the study. We redesigned both

Table 3. Scenarios with technical threat, estimated likelihood of attack (L), and the estimated severity of likely consequences (S)

Scenario	Activity	Technical threat	Data at risk	Highlighted properties	L	S
Bank	Log in to online banking	Self-signed certificate	Banking credentials	Identity	High	High
Shop	Pay with credit card	Unprotected connection	Payment credentials	Identity, confidentiality	Med	High
OSN	Register for OSN	Unprotected connection, negative reputation	Personal data	Identity, confidentiality, trustworthiness	Med	Med
Insurance	Request quote for insurance	Self-signed certificate	Health data	Identity, confidentiality	Med	Med
Information	Find flight cost	Negative reputation	Travel destination	Trustworthiness	Med	Low

types of warnings to have the same "newness" effect for both types of warnings [18]. For standard content, we reused and adapted the content from warnings from Mozilla Firefox 3 and Web of trust 1.4.8. For the contextualized content, we followed the insights of how lay and expert users differ in risk assessment (cf. Section 3). Since we recruited only lay users, we included concrete information on the risks of proceeding.

We crafted the scenarios with warnings to represent a wide range of objective risks to enable a within-subject comparison of participants' behavior regarding different levels of risks. The scenarios, listed in Table 3, include self-signed certificates, unencrypted connections, and negative reputation for the activities banking, shopping, social networking (OSN), requesting an insurance quote, and information seeking for flights.

A translated version of the warning with contextualized content for the banking scenario is shown in Figure 2. The warning with the contextualized content was developed in an iterative process that included eliciting the concrete risk aspects to mention, expert consultations, and user feedback on the warning design and content. The version employed in the study included:

1. the user intention – "entering account number and PIN" in the banking scenario;
2. a warning headline with an indication of the attack probability – "probably an attack";
3. the potential personal consequences from proceeding – "attackers could plunder your account". From the potential consequences to name, we selected those appropriate for the situation that were most often mentioned in the pre-study;
4. boxes with concrete and transparent indications whether and how three main security properties of the situation (identity of Web site provider,

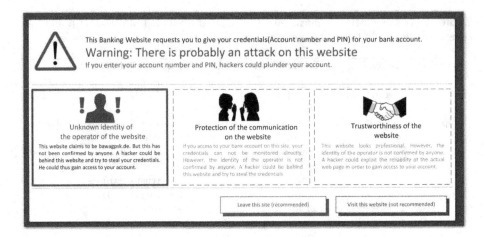

Fig. 2. Translated example warning with contextualized content

confidentiality of connection, trustworthiness of Web site provider)[2] are upheld. Each box included a short description of how the security property affects the user when proceeding. The boxes with threatened properties are highlighted (shown in Table 3) as a confound to explore how such visual stimuli interact with the effects of contextualization.

5.3   Procedure

After an initial introduction that included the priming as a Web-browsing usability study – to counter a potential unrealistic focus on the warnings –, the experimenter informed the participants that they would need to complete twelve tasks (cf. Section 5.2). To counter the effect that participants may feel an unrealistic urge to complete the given task in the lab setting [18], we offered an alternative: filling out a "usability problems" form for the study, which required the participants to enter a carefully selected amount (3 lines) of information on a separate sheet of paper. In this way, participants would not perceive the alternative as an easy way to get around the tasks.

Each task described a problem related to the overarching theme of travelling and gave instructions, including an address of a Web site, to solve it. Where it was necessary to enter data, such as credentials, the instructions also included these. To reduce the confounding effects of using a stranger's laptop and personal data, the experimenter presented himself as student whose personal credentials and laptop were used in the study. As part of completing the task, each task either caused a warning to appear or not (warning or dummy task, respectively). To prevent the participant from noticing the actual intent of the study early on,

---

[2] We identified these properties by analyzing an extensive list of threats in Web browsing and how these can be addressed through security properties. This approach to content presentation follows Biddle et al. [5].

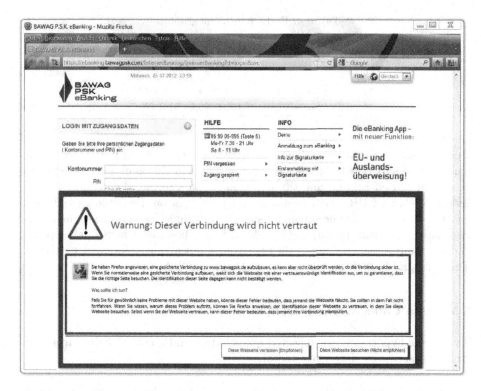

Fig. 3. Example warning with standard content as screenshot (original German content)

one to three dummy tasks occurred between the warning tasks. We organized the warning tasks in one of two fixed orders to cancel out effects from the order, either starting with the most or least critical scenario, banking or flight information, respectively.

In the second part of the study, the experimenter revealed the actual goal of the study to the participants and instructed them to read the warnings again. To further explore their perception of the risks in the warning tasks, participants were asked to carry out a card-sorting exercise with printouts of the warning scenarios (Web site screenshot with warning overlayed, as shown in Figure 3), sorting them by criticality and commenting on their reasoning. The experimenter further asked the participants to explain for each warning what they thought why the warning appeared and what the potential consequences of proceeding would have been.

The audio was recorded for the entire study.

5.4   Participant Recruitment

We targeted lay users with the warning content so that we excluded participants with security-related professional or study background. We advertised for the

Table 4. Participant demographics

Group	Contextualized	Standard
Female	11	11
Male	7	7
Mean age (stddev)	26.3 (4.1)	24.8 (2.6)
Mean PC knowledge	63.9 (20.0)	51.0 (22.5)

study as one on usability problems with Web browsing using posters at public places (local supermarkets, bus stops), direct dissemination of a similar flyer to people on and off-campus and through email to non-technical students' mailing lists. We offered EUR 10 compensation for participation. Potential participants had to complete an online screening survey, including demographics, their professional/study background, and PC skills. From those, we selected participants and randomly assigned them to the two groups, but arranged for gender balance. The demographics of the two groups are shown in Table 4.

5.5   Data Collection and Analysis

To test the hypotheses, we collected quantitative and qualitative data from the study. Quantitative data consisted of:

1. Which warnings participants complied with from the experimenter's notes (for H1–2)
2. The order of the warnings from the card-sorting exercise (H3)

Qualitative data was collected through the audio recordings, which were transcribed for analysis. In particular, we analyzed the qualitative data for

1. How participants reasoned about risks while conducting the card-sorting exercise and while answering the interview questions (H4)
2. Further comments on the appearance and content of the warnings

For both aspects, we coded the qualitative data, a method that has been successfully employed in HCI research [1]. We inductively developed codes by first applying "open coding", then "selective coding" from Grounded Theory [11]. To analyze the participants' reasoning about risks, we identified different risk concepts that participants used – for example, whether they referred to the affected data, consequences, technical threats, adversary activities, or abstractly as "this is a dangerous situation". For comments on the warning, we identified the categories design, content, understanding, and doubts. One researcher assigned a total of 823 codes (625 on risks, 198 on warnings) to 733 quotes in the transcripts. For coding reliability, a second researcher independently coded six of the transcripts as suggested by [15], showing a good overlap.

Table 5. Overview of average compliance with warnings relative to all warnings for both groups

Group	Contextualized		Standard	
	n		n	
Average compliance	18	**46%**	18	**17%**
Female	11	35%	11	15%
Male	7	63%	7	20%
Low PC knowledge	2	40%	4	30%
Med. PC knowledge	10	50%	9	18%
High PC knowledge	6	40%	5	4%

6 Results

6.1 H1–3: The Effectiveness of Contextualization

We recorded the compliance of the participants with each warning while completing the tasks to test H1:

H1 The participants who are confronted with the contextualized content more frequently comply with warnings than those with standard content

H1 was confirmed, since the participants with contextualized content significantly (Fisher's exact test for the distribution of compliance count, $p = 0.04$) more often complied with the warnings than the group with the standard warning (shown in Table 5 as overall relative compliance). We saw similar trends for different demographic groups. Since the self-reported PC knowledge should represent the self-confidence of participants with respect to interacting with PCs and people feeling insecure tend to comply with warnings [14], it is not surprising that lower knowledge scores seem to correlate with higher compliance, particularly for the standard warnings.

We further hypothesized that participants can better differentiate between the different risk levels by measuring their compliance to the warning as the warning effect:

H2 The relation between the warning effect and the objective risk is stronger for warnings with contextualized content than for standard content

This hypothesis cannot be confirmed by our results. We even see a contrary effect as shown in Figure 4: The participants with the standard warnings, who needed to deduce the risk level from the scenario and the technical threat, showed a general trend that corresponds to the objective risk level (supporting the findings from Kauer et al. [13]). However, this was not the case for the contextual-warning group. If the group with the contextualized warnings had better understood the situation, the trend should have been more pronounced. Instead, the shop and OSN scenarios caused more compliance than expected from the relative risk level.

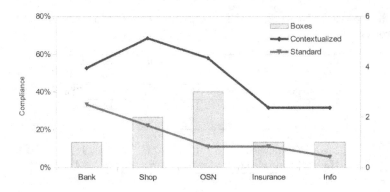

Fig. 4. Average compliance by scenario for both groups, with the number of highlighted boxes in contextualized warnings

A likely explanation is that our implanted confound, the number of highlighted boxes, strongly influenced the decision to comply. This result shows that content can be easily dominated by other factors, in line with the results of Krol et al. [14].

We not only expected the behavior to more closely correspond to the objective risk levels, but also tested how participants perceived the warnings when instructed to read them carefully. We conducted the posterior card-sorting exercise for this hypothesis:

> *H3 The relation between the* warning perception *and the objective risk is stronger for warnings with contextualized content than for standard content*

In the card-sorting exercise, the order of the contextual group corresponded only slightly better with the objective risk than the control group (particularly for the bank and flight scenarios; see Table 6 that shows the mean sort order). This is supported by the lower standard deviation (in brackets in the table) for the most and least critical scenarios; the contextual group produced less spread in the sorting than the standard-content group. Moreover, the bump from the highlighted threats is not present in the card-sorting results, where users were instructed to actually read the warning, further supporting the notion that the bump in the behavior was caused by the implanted confound.

6.2   H4: Participants' Assessment of the Risks

We instructed the participants to think aloud while sorting the warnings after completing the tasks, and, in addition, asked them to state the reasons for each warning's occurrence and what could have been the consequences of proceeding in each situation.

> *H4 Participants who are confronted with the contextualized content assess the risks of proceeding more concretely than those with standard content*

Table 6. Average sorting position for the warning scenarios, 1 being most, 5 least risky (with standard deviation)

Group	Contextualized		Standard	
Bank	**1.3**	**(1.1)**	**1.7**	**(1.8)**
Shop	2.1	**(0.9)**	2.1	**(1.9)**
Insurance	3.2	(1.9)	2.9	(1.8)
OSN	3.8	(1.7)	3.9	(1.6)
Information	4.6	(1.8)	4.3	(2.3)

We coded how participants mentioned or reasoned about risk in the transcripts, differentiating between different concepts of risks. In Table 7[3], we report the occurrence of the different concepts relative to the total quantity of risk-related codes for the two groups in the study. While the contextualized and the standard-content groups similarly often mentioned the affected data as a risk consideration, the context group more often mentioned consequences (in particular, concrete consequences, such as property-related, like losing money) and adversary activities, such as how an adversary would access their account[4]. In contrast, the standard-content group more often resorted to problematic consequence concepts, such as abstract "something bad will happen"; more technical aspects, such as the missing encryption; and more abstract reasoning, such as "this is a dangerous situation"[5]. As elaborated in Section 4, we expect that more concrete concepts are more "natural" and thus more understandable for lay users that we recruited the participants for. Accordingly, we conclude from the reported frequencies of risk concepts that the contextual warnings were more understandable. We will verify this aspect in future work.

6.3 Further Findings on the Contextualization.

The participants mentioned further aspects on the warnings that relate to the content of the warning and its contextualization.

"Too Much Text". Five participants who were confronted with the contextualized warnings mentioned in the posterior interview that there was too much content or too small text in the warning. However, several also stated that all the information given was necessary.

---

[3] p values of a Welch Two Sample t-test on the participants' proportions for each risk concept are noted in the last column.

[4] We also checked whether participants only directly reproduced (reading aloud) the content of the warning. This was not the case. Due to the interview situation, all participants formulated their own statements. Moreover, the majority at least paraphrased the content – for example, for property-related consequences, participants used different terms in 77% of the cases.

[5] In contrast to abstract consequences, abstract risk reasoning does not point to any consequences at all.

Table 7. Risk concepts mentioned by participants relative to the total number of mentioned risks, including different types of consequences mentioned

Group		Contextualized		Standard		p
	Example	n		n		
Risk		354		271		
Data	Payment credentials	81	23%	61	23%	0.98
Adversary activity	"Accesses account"	79	**22%**	25	**9%**	< 0.001
Consequences	Financial loss	120	34%	75	28%	0.065
Mitigation	Enter fake data	9	3%	8	3%	0.77
Technical	"Missing encryption"	33	**9%**	65	**24%**	< 0.001
Context	"Unknown site"	9	3%	12	4%	0.28
Abstract	"Seems dangerous"	10	**3%**	24	**9%**	< 0.01
Other		13	4%	1	0%	
Consequences		120	34%	75	28%	
Annoyance	Spam	5	1%	11	4%	0.049
Property	Loose money	78	**22%**	28	**10%**	< 0.001
Problematic	Unknown, misconception...	11	**3%**	32	**12%**	< 0.001
Other		26	7%	4	1%	

Prior Partial Knowledge and Experiences. Due to our recruitment strategy, none of the participants was a security expert. However, eleven participants referred to their prior partial knowledge on risks or prior adverse experiences at some point in the risk assessment. While this knowledge helped in the assessment of the risks, its absence in the majority of cases also demonstrated the lack of reliability of warnings if their understanding requires prior knowledge to deduce consequences. Moreover, prior general knowledge also caused the speculation on and misconceptions of consequences as seen in the above analysis of mentioned risk concepts. One effect was that the availability heuristic led participants to assume less severe consequences.

Risk Attitudes. Participants differed in what consequences they considered relevant for them. For example, one participant mentioned that it would be more interesting to mention that pictures from the OSN account would be reused than id theft.

Trust in the Warning. In several cases, statements of the participants revealed distrust in the warning, particularly for the contextualized warnings. For example:

> "But I found this strange because an employer must not access my data, really... because everything would need to be passed on and registered and that cannot be true!" (T2)

The distrust either related to whether the described attack could take place, as in this quote (4 cases); to the stated consequences (8); or to the basis of the risk assessment, such as user ratings (13). All of these aspects were originally included in the warning content to increase the warning's concreteness.

7 Discussion

7.1 Challenges of Drawing Attention to Warning Content

While we show that the contextualized warnings significantly more often caused participants to comply with the warning, our findings also support the notion that it is difficult to draw people's attention to the content of warnings in real-world scenarios (cf. [14]). We assume that habituation, lack of helpful information, and time pressure provide strong incentives for people not to expend enough cognitive effort on a warning to completely grasp its content. Having a combined behavioral/explanatory study allowed us to underscore the previously reported discrepancies between near-practice situations and offline consideration of warnings [18], furthering the point that warnings always need to be tested in carefully crafted, realistic study designs as ours.

7.2 Contextualization Helps in Risk Assessment – and in Understanding the Risk

However, independent of the problems with creating attention for the warning content and with motivating users to consider the content, the content needs to be optimally understandable. Concerning this goal, we find, based on the qualitative data, that participants reasoned about risks more concretely and less technically or abstractly than the control group (cf. Section 6.2). In particular, the reasoning depended to a lesser degree on the prior knowledge about threats or prior personal experiences of adverse events. Since experts in our pre-study were similarly more concrete in their risk assessments than lay users, we see the changed reasoning as an indication that contextualized content caused a better understanding of the risk of proceeding. Our findings thus extend prior research – for example, by Kauer et al. [13] – that showed personal consequences as more effective in warnings.

7.3 Building Trust in Contextualized Warnings

Moreover, we identified problems that participants encountered due to the contextualization of the content in Section 6.3, particularly related to trust in the warning. The complex interrelation between user characteristics (such as expertise), the concreteness of content, understanding, and trust in the warning warrants a closer look at the problems and how we can address them. Focusing on the results from the explanatory part of the study (card sorting and interview), we need to extend the model from Section 4 that our hypotheses were based upon. The extension of the model in Figure 5 shows how the concreteness of the warning content has – for some participants – negative effects. One such effect is distrust as shown in the quote in Section 6.3.

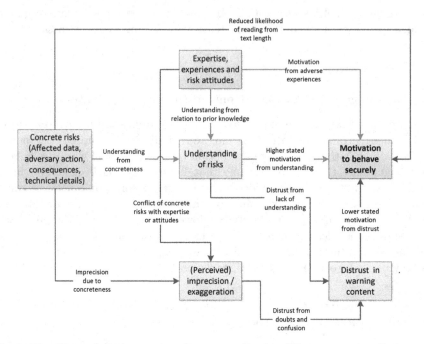

Fig. 5. The effects of concreteness and contextualization (edges represent effects; green for positive, red negative)

Specifically, the extended model still describes how mentioning concrete risks (affected data, consequences, ...) leads to a higher level of *understanding of the risks* from proceeding and thereby motivate users to follow the recommendation laid out in the warning content (*Motivation to behave securely*). Our results indicate that the *expertise, prior experiences, and risk attitudes* of the user play an important role in the understanding and the motivation. However, the extended model now also shows that concreteness leads to *distrust of the warning content* if the more concrete information is not understood (*Understanding of risks*) or if *(perceived) imprecision or exaggeration* in the content raises doubts. For example, depending on which risks are considered problematic by the participant (*risk attitudes*; e.g. only financial consequences, not so much social-privacy consequences), mentioned consequences were considered exaggerated. Conflicts of the content with the user's expertise can have similar effects. From the participant's comments in the study, we expect that distrust will also reduce the motivation to follow the recommendation from the warning content.

Thus, our results indicate several negative side effects from the content's concreteness. We conclude that to realize the positive effects of increased concreteness without compromising on other factors (e.g. the trust in the warning content), individualization for the user is necessary: For instance, people with higher expertise need different content – for example, less concrete consequences, so as to not raise doubts about the given information – than people with lower expertise.

While it has been found before that trust plays an important role in the behavior of users when confronted with security-critical situations, prior research has focused on the trust in the Web site [10,21,9]. Krol et al. [14] also mentioned as one conclusion of their study that the trust in the warning needs to be restored, but they addressed the habituation effects from over-frequent warnings in non-critical situations. Our results and the derived model go beyond those findings by addressing the trust in the warning as affected by the warning content.

The extended model is foremost based on the qualitative and subjective data from a relatively small sample of 36 participants. Therefore, the extended model should primarily serve as a hypothesis for further studies on the contextualization of content with larger and more representative samples that we are planning as future work, particularly on the individualization of warnings between lay users.

Acknowledgments. We thank Michaela Kauer and Christoph Seikel for their support on designing and conducting the pre-study. The work presented in this paper is supported by funds of the Federal Ministry of Food, Agriculture and Consumer Protection (BMELV) based on a decision of the Parliament of the Federal Republic of Germany via the Federal Office for Agriculture and Food (BLE) under the innovation support programme.

References

1. Adams, A., Lunt, P., Cairns, P.: A qualitative approach to HCI research. Cambridge Univ. Press, Cambridge (2008)
2. Amer, T., Maris, J.: Signal Words and Signal Icons in Application Control and Information Technology Exception Messages – Hazard Matching and Habituation Effects. Tech. Rep. 06-05, Nothern Arizona University (2006)
3. Asgharpour, F., Liu, D., Camp, L.J.: Mental Models of Computer Security Risks. In: WEIS 2007: Workshop on the Economics of Information Security (2007)
4. Bartsch, S., Volkamer, M.: Towards the Systematic Development of Contextualised Security Interventions. In: Proceedings of Designing Interactive Secure Systems, BCS HCI 2012. BLIC (2012)
5. Biddle, R., van Oorschot, P.C., Patrick, A.S., Sobey, J., Whalen, T.: Browser interfaces and extended validation SSL certificates: an empirical study. In: Proceedings of the 2009 ACM Workshop on Cloud Computing Security, CCSW 2009, pp. 19–30. ACM, New York (2009)
6. Bravo-Lillo, C., Cranor, L.F., Downs, J., Komanduri, S., Sleeper, M.: Improving Computer Security Dialogs. In: Campos, P., Graham, N., Jorge, J., Nunes, N., Palanque, P., Winckler, M. (eds.) INTERACT 2011, Part IV. LNCS, vol. 6949, pp. 18–35. Springer, Heidelberg (2011),
http://www.springerlink.com/content/q551210n08h16970
7. De Keukelaere, F., Yoshihama, S., Trent, S., Zhang, Y., Luo, L., Zurko, M.E.: Adaptive Security Dialogs for Improved Security Behavior of Users. In: Gross, T., Gulliksen, J., Kotzé, P., Oestreicher, L., Palanque, P., Prates, R.O., Winckler, M. (eds.) INTERACT 2009. LNCS, vol. 5726, pp. 510–523. Springer, Heidelberg (2009)

8. Downs, J.S., Holbrook, M.B., Cranor, L.F.: Decision strategies and susceptibility to phishing. In: SOUPS 2006: Proceedings of the Second Symposium on Usable Privacy and Security, pp. 79–90. ACM, New York (2006)

9. Egelman, S., Cranor, L.F., Hong, J.: You've been warned: an empirical study of the effectiveness of web browser phishing warnings. In: CHI 2008: Proceeding of the Twenty-Sixth Annual SIGCHI Conference on Human Factors in Computing Systems (2008)

10. Fogg, B.J., Marshall, J., Laraki, O., Osipovich, A., Varma, C., Fang, N., Paul, J., Rangnekar, A., Shon, J., Swani, P., Treinen, M.: What makes Web sites credible?: a report on a large quantitative study. In: CHI 2001. ACM, New York (2001)

11. Glaser, B.G., Strauss, A.L.: The Discovery of Grounded Theory: Strategies for Qualitative Research. Aldine Transaction (1967)

12. Kahneman, D., Tversky, A.: The simulation heuristic. Cambridge University Press, Cambridge (1982)

13. Kauer, M., Pfeiffer, T., Volkamer, M., Theuerling, H., Bruder, R.: It is not about the design – it is about the content! Making warnings more efficient by communicating risks appropriately. In: GI SICHERHEIT 2012 Sicherheit – Schutz und Zuverlässigkeit (2012)

14. Krol, K., Moroz, M., Sasse, M.: Don't work. Can't work? Why it's time to rethink security warnings. In: 7th International Conference on Risk and Security of Internet and Systems (CRiSIS), pp. 1–8 (October 2012)

15. Lazar, J., Feng, J.H., Hochheiser, H.: Research methods in human-computer interaction. Wiley (2010)

16. Rothman, A.J., Kiviniemi, M.T.: Treating People With Information: an Analysis and Review of Approaches to Communicating Health Risk Information. J. Natl. Cancer Inst. Monogr. (25) (1999)

17. Rugg, G., McGeorge, P.: The sorting techniques: a tutorial paper on card sorts, picture sorts and item sorts. Expert Systems 14(2), 80–93 (1997)

18. Sotirakopoulos, A., Hawkey, K., Beznosov, K.: On the challenges in usable security lab studies: lessons learned from replicating a study on SSL warnings. In: SOUPS 2011: Proceedings of the 7th Symposium on Usable Privacy and Security. ACM, New York (2011)

19. Sunshine, J., Egelman, S., Almuhimedi, H., Atri, N., Cranor, L.F.: Crying Wolf: An Empirical Study of SSL Warning Effectiveness. In: USENIX Security 2009 (2009)

20. Wogalter, M.S.: Handbook of warnings. Routledge (2006)

21. Wu, M., Miller, R.C., Garfinkel, S.L.: Do security toolbars actually prevent phishing attacks? In: CHI 2006: Proceedings of the SIGCHI Conference on Human Factors in Computing Systems, pp. 601–610. ACM, New York (2006)

All In: Targeting Trustworthiness for Special Needs User Groups in the Internet of Things

Marc Busch[1], Christina Hochleitner[1], Mario Lorenz[2], Trenton Schulz[3], Manfred Tscheligi[1,4], and Eckhart Wittstock[2]

[1] CURE—Center for Usability Research & Engineering, Businesspark MARXIMUM, Modecenterstraße 17 / Gebäude 2, 1110 Vienna, Austria
[2] Chemnitz University of Technology, 09107 Chemnitz, Germany
[3] Norwegian Computing Center, P.O. Box 114 Blindern, NO-0314, Oslo Norway
[4] ICT&S Center, University of Salzburg, Sigmund-Haffner-Gasse 18, 5020 Salzburg, Austria
http://www.cure.at, http://www.tu-chemnitz.de, http://www.nr.no, http://www.icts.sbg.ac.at

Abstract. We showcase how privacy, security, and trust requirements of people with mental and physical disabilities can be integrated in the development of smart home applications and devices. We present our chosen process leading to trustworthy design of a smart medicine cabinet that informs about potential privacy and security risks along with helping users manage their life.

1 Introduction

The Internet of Things (IoT) is an umbrella term describing the integration of ubiquitous technology in the users' environments [1], e.g., in form of sensors or embedded computing systems. Our research on IoT particularly focuses on the inclusion of technologies in the users' homes. Many IoT applications target persons with special needs or older adults living at home independently through the usage of assistive technologies [2] or welfare technology, such as intelligent medicine cabinets. Although the design of these applications often caters to the needs of these particular user groups, significant aspects, such as security, privacy and trust are not in the center of research yet. Nevertheless, these topics are important when looking at users with limited physical and mental capacities, such as patients with dementia. These patients depend on reliable information systems that facilitate their daily life. Therefore this paper will describe the creation process of a smart medicine cabinet designed for older adults that respects and informs about potential privacy and security issues. We enhance the user-centered design process by using method triangulation (focus groups, personas, quantitative, and qualitative evaluations) tailored to the factors privacy and trust in an Internet of Things-context.

The paper is arranged as follows: in Section 2, we examine current literature on the development of smart medicine cabinets and lack of inclusion of trust in the process and the final product. Section 3 documents the devolpment and evaluation of our intelligent medicine cabinet that is hypothesized to be trustworthy. This includes requirements engineering, designing the prototypes, and evaluating them in a virtual reality (VR) environment. Section 4 describes the further development to the final prototype. Finally, Section 5 concludes our described design approach for trustworthy interfaces and presents opportunities for future work.

M. Huth et al. (Eds.): TRUST 2013, LNCS 7904, pp. 223–231, 2013.

2　Smart Medicine Cabinet and Trust

Since 2000, several applications and devices have been introduced that answer requirements of users with special needs for medical assistance remotely and through caregivers [3–5]. These applications rely on similar principles: the information needs to be understandable for older adults [6], the application should prevent incorrect intake [6], and remind older adults of scheduled medicine intake [6–8]. With the tendency to network these devices and applications and to connect them to the pharmacy or doctor's office [5], concerns of privacy and security arise. Literature mainly focuses on privacy in ubiquitous environments [9] and information needs of older users [10, 11], but few approaches include the factors needed to safeguard the user's privacy and evoke trust [12]. We have incorporated existing literature and research to create and evaluate a trustworthy medicine cabinet for older adults. This information is modified and adapted from literature and user-centered design to iteratively target the particular needs of older adults.

We see trust as a consequence of provided privacy and security information, it is important to create a unified understanding of trust within the development and design team. Trust has different definitions depending on the field of study (e.g., interpersonal trust or system trust). In our case, we are conducting research on the users' perceived trust in a system (i.e., system trust). That is, whether a user trusts the objects in the IoT environment. To aid in examining user trust in the IoT, we use the definition proposed by Dobelt et al. [13]: *A user's confidence in an entity's reliability, including that user's acceptance of vulnerability in a potentially risky situation.*

3　Development and Evaluation

Our research goal is to examine the development of trustworthy systems and trustworthiness feedback for informing users about threats and providing information about security and privacy. Our approach is to provide a usable and intuitive solution that caters to the requirements of users with special needs in IoT environments. The developed and described intelligent medicine cabinet is part of a smart home scenario that contains different objects that communicate and help to make certain tasks simpler. One of these functions is to remind the person in the home about other tasks. The smart home can also be helpful for caregivers as it allows them to know if something is wrong and provides a better overview to support the person in the home. The medicine cabinet helps older adults with their day-to-day lives by reminding them to take their medicine and ordering new prescriptions. This raises trust issues for both, the caregivers and the older adults in the home. Below, we outline our special needs groups-centered design process leading to a trustworthy medicine cabinet. The process itself follows a user-centered design approach and includes methods such as personas, end-user research and iterative design and evaluation phases. To particularly target older adults as well as trust in IoT systems, the methods have been adapted to focus especially on the chosen target group. Therefore all activities brought a main focus to older users, ranging from focus groups with participation of older persons and caretakers to evaluations with older adults. Therefore the used methods and material, as well as instructions and information provided had to be useful and understandable by this particular target group.

3.1 Personas

We followed the method outlined by Pruitt and Adlin [14] for constructing personas in order to approach the design of the medicine cabinet with the main focus on the user. Therefore we collected relevant literature as well as statistics and user opinions in regards to medicine cabinets, IoT and the users' understanding and needs towards privacy, security and trust. To make sure that our personas included people with disabilities, we specifically targeted people with vision impairment and dyslexia, but also included the needs of an older adult, who was beginning to suffer from dementia [15]. Among our personas, the first one is Paul, our older persona who has started developing early dementia. Paul's grandson, Fredrik, sometimes helps him. Fredrik is a technology early adopter, but has dyslexia and normally skips reading manuals. Paul's son, David, is very concerned that the smart house works properly and that Paul receives good care, even when he cannot be there. Another persona is Anna, who works in customer support and has 20% normal vision. During development and evaluation, we ensured the focus on the target groups by recruiting participants that fit into the representative personas profiles. This is an advancement from the normal use of personas to ensure inclusion of our target groups' requirements.

In addition, we applied tactics similar to Pruitt and Grudin [16] for keeping the personas active throughout the process. Each partner took control of one persona for providing that persona's perspective. Each month, a persona would send a story to let us know about some issue in their daily life and keep us aware of the persona's needs. We would also receive small gifts (e.g., candy and memory sticks with pictures of the personas on them) that would remind us to keep the personas in our thoughts.

3.2 Understanding Trust in the IoT

In addition to the literature-based research, we conducted focus groups with samples that have been chosen according to the features of the personas to understand privacy and security practices in an IoT-context. This led to a deeper understanding of how trust can be incorporated into the design of a medicine cabinet. It also helped to check if our personas and real users have similar issues.

We conducted five two-hour focus groups with six to eight participants each in two different countries. Two of the focus groups involved people with different levels of visual impairment. The other focus groups involved older adults and persons taking care of people with disabilities (e.g., caregivers or family members). Besides the discussion from the groups, each focus group also included a questionnaire gathering participants' demographics and their general privacy concerns.

One of the first issues was explaining the concept of the IoT to the focus group participants. Even though the concept has been around for a while in the research community, we found it not to be very mainstream. After giving examples of items that can be considered *things* in the IoT and how they communicate, we pointed out that one thing that needs to be considered is that many of the objects would act independently and potentially transfer information without a user knowing about it. Once participants understood the IoT concept, they were able to focus on the trust issues.

In particular, older users as well as caretakers were asked about their or the person in their care's opinion on security and trust issues in connection to new technology and issues they encounter when using technology. Thus, they provided input and concerns for our target groups, e.g., concerning secure transmission or mental and physical capabilities of users to interact with the cabinet.

Participants were concerned about what information would be disclosed and who would have access to their data. There was also skepticism to the medical cabinet in and of itself. How would it know which medicine should be taken at which time? How would it know that someone had actually taken their medicine and not cheated somehow? Some also felt that the whole concept of identifying themselves to the cabinet seemed too complicated. Some participants were also concerned about practical issues addressing trust in the system's functionality, e.g., how the cabinet would work if there were no electricity. Another participant pointed out that a smart medicine cabinet may reduce uncertainty of some of the issues that exist now: for example, a doctor's bad handwriting can have a real effect on a prescription and not remembering to take medicine or taking too much medicine can be a fatal mistake.

When discussing the impact of security and privacy violations for the cabinet, participants mentioned consequences connected to targeted advertisements, image loss, tampering with their medication, and loss or increase of insurance. It was desirable to restrict access to the participants' medical records. At the same time, a system conveying privacy and security information seemed helpful to them. This system should allow the participants to know what was going on (system transparency) and make the cabinet more trustworthy. One of the participants pointed out that for people who have dementia it is important to have routines and not change things much, so a new medicine cabinet, as well as the feedback provided needs to be learned beforehand.

The focus groups led to the definition of privacy and trust issues participants discovered for the medicine cabinet. These issues were then summarized in end-user-based requirements that formed the basis for the development of the interaction workflows, the software, and hardware prototypes.

3.3 The Interface Approach

The interfaces for the medicine cabinet were designed based on the requirements elicited in the focus groups and with the end-users in form of personas (mainly, Paul) in mind. Furthermore, relevant literature on trustworthy interface design [17] and existing literature in this field was taken into account [6]. For example, we considered the principles outlined by Siegemund et al. [1] and adopted similar ones. Additionally, the interfaces are based on principles from the Android Design Guidelines [18]. Thus, we have included the needs of older adults in regards to trust and respected requirements towards usable and intuitive interfaces.

We addressed three interface design issues to create a trustworthy medical cabinet: (a) *Screen elements and screen estate to answer the needs of older adults* [17]—clear and self-explanatory interface elements, readable font size, clear visual design. (b) *Transparent privacy and security information, including interpretations of the information* [12]—understandable, non-technical and brief explanations, clear statements of consequences and recommendations, known paradigms. (c) *Multimodal feedback*

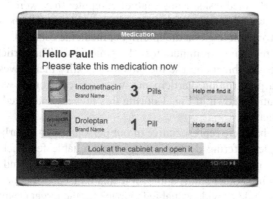

Fig. 1. Prototype user interfaces for the medicine cabinet *(left)* and smartphone *(right)*

(audio, visual, and tactile) for better recognition of feedback by different target groups (older adults, dyslexic, and visually impaired) [2]—acoustic reminder for taking medicine, haptic feedback for communicating the system's trustworthiness state, using text-to-speech functionalities.

A detailed explanation of the trustworthy interface prototyping approach, in particular issue (a), is described by Hochleitner et al. [17] and comprises clear instructions as well as information on what data is being disclosed, to whom, and for what purpose. In addition, the initial prototypes made use of icons to convey this information (see examples in Fig. 1).

3.4 Simulation and Evaluation in Virtual Reality Environments

As part of our iterative process, the scenarios and initial prototypes of the medicine cabinet were evaluated before we invested the cost in creating fully functional prototypes. We did this by using virtual reality to create a simulated smart home that included the smart medicine cabinet [19]. Participants navigated through the environment using

Fig. 2. A user evaluating the medicine cabinet in VR

a Wii Balance Board and performed tasks using a tablet computer they were holding (Fig. 2). The tablet computer would present information that would normally be shown on touch-screens in the environment (e.g., on the intelligent medicine cabinet).

One of the tasks involved receiving a reminder for taking medicine. The participants would navigate to the medicine cabinet and use the tablet to identify themselves, take their medicine, and renew a prescription. Participants were also confronted with the privacy and security information shown in Fig. 1 during this process and asked about the perceived trust in this situation.

We recruited participants that were representative of our personas, particularly Paul. Since it is difficult for people suffering dementia to provide reliable feedback (e.g., dementia-induced short-term memory loss during the repeated recognition and usage of the system), we again recruited older adults and people that took care of people with dementia. These participants could provide valuable feedback for the target group since they take care of older adults or people with dementia and had detailed knowledge of older adults' physical and mental capabilities in terms of new technologies.

Older persons that were recruited for the evaluation mostly thought that the smart home setting was a good idea and appreciated the support given by the medical cabinet. Some were reluctant in relying on a machine for medication, being afraid of system failures and power outages. The provided feedback was rated to be trust inducing because of information provided about the medicine, the functionality of the medical cabinet, the availability of security information and the efficient interaction. Generally, the trustworthiness feedback was consciously noticed by less than half of the participants, who valued the information on the process, especially about the drug store where the medicine was purchased. Furthermore participants indicated to be more alert to feedback on positive aspects to foster trust, not on negative aspects (risks, warnings).

Apart from the trust and privacy issues, the design of the user interfaces posed an issue. Many found the smaller displays difficult to read or to concentrate on the reading. The people who substituted for the target group with dementia stated that their patients would not be able to concentrate enough to go through the whole information. Further, most of the older adults had only limited understanding of the underlying technical procedures and consequently had problems interpreting the technical information that was given. They were also missing a history-function to see what medicine they have taken within the last few days. Yet, some of the participants realized that they should be thinking about security and privacy issues once they were presented with such information when refilling the prescription. More information about security parameters seemed to cause more concern. Generally, the possibilities to configure the transmitted information was appreciated. Further and more detailed information can be found in [20].

4   The Final Prototype

As the VR evaluations revealed several weaknesses in feedback, the interfaces were further developed to fulfill Paul's need for privacy and security information. To create a coherent physical setup, we decided to convert the displayed information from landscape (Fig. 1) to portrait mode (Fig. 3). This also made it possible to arrange larger lists of information (e.g., medicine to be taken) on the screen and employ larger font styles.

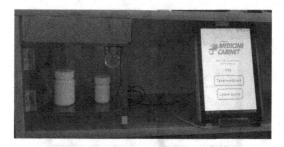

Fig. 3. The final prototype of the medicine cabinet

The final medicine cabinet guides Paul through three scenarios: taking medicine as scheduled, unscheduled medicine intake, and taking along needed medicine when he leaves his house. Paul can also reorder medicine directly from the cabinet when medicine begins to get low. With this task, privacy—what data and who receives the data—and security information—how the data is sent—are displayed to Paul.

As part of the feedback from the VR evaluations, we eliminated the icons, as they showed no positive effect on the perceived trust of the target group. Instead, we focused on providing clear instructions and recommendations based on known interface paradigms, such as progress bars. This information is color-coded (green for high security and privacy to red for low security and privacy) for better recognition. We also provide positional information so that people with red-green colorblindness can see at a glance the information as well, and have included text-to-speech information that can be picked up by screen readers on tablets and smart phones. These changes are targeted at assisting users with special needs to make decisions about their privacy and security. Therefore, Paul is able to decide on either trusting the system and the perscriptions (based on the displayed information and provided recommendations) or not to trust the medicine cabinet (implying that he will get the medicine by himself or through caretakers). An example of the newer user interface on the smartphone is shown in Fig. 4. In addition, we developed hardware prototypes of the medicine cabinet (Fig. 3). These prototypes will be tested in the next round of real world and VR evaluations.

5   Conclusion and Future Work

We have adapted a user-centered design process focusing on the needs of users with disabilities to design a medicine cabinet that they can trust. To do so, we have applied and adapted user-centered design methods such as personas and iterative development to target the particular requirements of users with disabilities. The process ensured that the focus on the users (i.e., older adults) was kept and their advice was frequently consulted. The result of this process is a trustworthy interface for a medicine cabinet with design elements particularly targeted at users with beginning dementia. The medicine cabinet as well as its components have been subject to evaluations and have been considered understandable and usable during preliminary evaluations.

Fig. 4. Near final prototype of color-coded feedback and security bar on a mobile screen

Our adapted user-centered design process worked well for this development and showed how important it was to include users with special needs in the design process. It also shows some challenges when using this process. For example, it is very difficult to directly include people with dementia in activities like focus groups. It is important in that case to either find people that understand the needs of people with dementia or organizations that help people who have dementia. User organizations that represent people with different disabilities are also a valuable place to recruit people to inform the design of a system or evaluate it.

In our next evaluation, we plan to include people with dyslexia or impaired vision to see how well they can use the cabinet and how trustworthy it is perceived by them. We plan on using the results to publish guidelines about how best to present security information to people regardless of their disabilities. That way everyone can have a trustworthy experience in the IoT.

Acknowledgments. This research is funded as part of the uTRUSTit project. The uTRUSTit project is funded by the EU FP7 program (Grant agreement no: 258360).

References

1. Siegemund, F., Floerkemeier, C., Vogt, H.: The value of handhelds in smart environments. Personal and Ubiquitous Computing 9(2), 69–80 (2004)
2. Salces, F.J.S., Baskett, M., Llewellyn-Jones, D., England, D.: Ambient Interfaces for Elderly People at Home. In: Cai, Y., Abascal, J. (eds.) Ambient Intelligence in Everyday Life. LNCS (LNAI), vol. 3864, pp. 256–284. Springer, Heidelberg (2006)
3. Wan, D.: Magic Medicine Cabinet: A Situated Portal for Consumer Healthcare. In: Gellersen, H.-W. (ed.) HUC 1999. LNCS, vol. 1707, pp. 352–355. Springer, Heidelberg (1999)
4. Calabretto, J.P., Warren, J., Darzanos, K., Fry, B.: Building Common Ground for Communication Between Patients and Community Pharmacists with an Internet Medicine Cabinet. In: Proceedings of the 35th Annual Hawaii International Conference on System Sciences, pp. 2087–2094. IEEE Comput. Soc.

5. Palen, L., Aaløkke, S.: Of pill boxes and piano benches. In: Proceedings of the 2006 20th Anniversary Conference on Computer Supported Cooperative Work - CSCW 2006, p. 79. ACM Press, New York (2006)

6. Khan, D.U., Siek, K.A., Meyers, J., Haverhals, L.M., Cali, S., Ross, S.E.: Designing a personal health application for older adults to manage medications. In: Proceedings of the ACM International Conference on Health Informatics - IHI 2010, p. 849. ACM Press, New York (2010)

7. López-Nores, M., Blanco-Fernández, Y., Pazos-Arias, J.J., García-Duque, J.: The iCabiNET system: Harnessing Electronic Health Record standards from domestic and mobile devices to support better medication adherence. Computer Standards & Interfaces 34(1), 109–116 (2012)

8. Tsai, P.-H., Shih, C.-S., Liu, J.W.-S.: Mobile Reminder for Flexible and Safe Medication Schedule for Home Users. In: Jacko, J.A. (ed.) Human-Computer Interaction, Part III, HCII 2011. LNCS, vol. 6763, pp. 107–116. Springer, Heidelberg (2011)

9. Konomi, S., Nam, C.S.: Supporting Collaborative Privacy-Observant Information Sharing Using RFID-Tagged Objects. Advances in Human-Computer Interaction 2009, 1–13 (2009)

10. Godfrey, M., Johnson, O.: Digital circles of support: Meeting the information needs of older people. Computers in Human Behavior 25, 633–642 (2009)

11. Liao, Q.V., Fu, W.T.: Age differences in credibility judgment of online health information. In: Proceedings of the 2nd ACM SIGHIT Symposium on International Health Informatics - IHI 2012, p. 353. ACM Press, New York (2012)

12. Ho, G., Wheatley, D., Scialfa, C.T.: Age differences in trust and reliance of a medication management system. Interacting with Computers 17, 690–710 (2005)

13. Döbelt, S., Busch, M., Hochleitner, C.: Defining, Understanding, Explaining TRUST within the uTRUSTit Project. Technical report, CURE, Vienna, Austria (2012)

14. Pruitt, J., Adlin, T.: The Persona Lifecycle. Morgan Kaufmann, San Francisco (2006)

15. Schulz, T., Skeide Fuglerud, K.: Creating Personas with Disabilities. In: Miesenberger, K., Karshmer, A., Penaz, P., Zagler, W. (eds.) ICCHP 2012, Part II. LNCS, vol. 7383, pp. 145–152. Springer, Heidelberg (2012)

16. Pruitt, J., Grudin, J.: Personas: practice and theory. In: Proc. of the 2003 Conference on Designing for User Experiences. ACM, San Francisco (2003)

17. Hochleitner, C., Graf, C., Unger, D., Tscheligi, M.: Making Devices Trustworthy: Security and Trust Feedback in the Internet of Things. In: Fourth International Workshop on Security and Privacy in Spontaneous Interaction and Mobile Phone Use (IWSSI/SPMU), Newcastle, UK (2012)

18. The Android Open Source Project: Android Developer Guidelines (2013)

19. Wittstock, V., Lorenz, M., Wittstock, E., Pürzel, F.: A Framework for User Tests in a Virtual Environment. In: Bebis, G., et al. (eds.) ISVC 2012, Part II. LNCS, vol. 7432, pp. 358–367. Springer, Heidelberg (2012)

20. Busch, M., Döbelt, S., Hochleitner, C., Wolkerstorfer, P., Schulz, T., Fuglerud, K.S., Tjøstheim, I., Pürzel, F., Wittstock, E., Dumortier, J., Vandezande, N.: uTRUSTit Deliverable D6.2. Design Iteration I: Evaluation Report. Technical report, CURE–Center for Usability Research and Engineering (2012)

Trust Domains: An Algebraic, Logical, and Utility-Theoretic Approach

Gabrielle Anderson, Matthew Collinson, and David Pym

University of Aberdeen
Scotland, U.K.
{g.a.anderson,matthew.collinson,d.j.pym}@abdn.ac.uk

Abstract. Complex systems of interacting agents are ubiquitous in the highly interconnected, information-rich ecosystems upon which the world is more-or-less wholly dependent. Within these systems, it is often necessary for an agent, or a group of agents, such as a business, to establish within a given ecosystem a trusted group, or a region of trust. Building on an established mathematical systems modelling framework — based on process algebra, logic, and stochastic methods — we give a characterization of such 'trust domains' that employs logical assertions of the properties required for trust and utility-theoretic constraints on the cost of establishing compliance with those properties. We develop the essential meta-theory and give a range of examples.

1 Introduction

Complex systems of interacting agents are ubiquitous in the highly interconnected, information-rich ecosystems upon which the world is more-or-less wholly dependent. Within these systems, it is often necessary for an agent, or a group of agents, such as a business, to establish within a given ecosystem a trusted group, or a region of trust.

In this paper, we are concerned with characterizing such 'trust domains' within a mathematical systems modelling framework. Developing the modelling framework developed in [6], and initial ideas about trust domains presented in [3], we provide a characterization that employs logic — in order to determine the properties that an agent, or group of agents, must satisfy in order to be trusted — and utility — in order to determine and limit the cost of establishing compliance with these properties.

The key components of the framework are the following: first, a resource-sensitive process algebra, within which the decision-theoretic notion of utility is used to establish the relative cost of different choices; second, a corresponding, resource-sensitive modal logic of processes; and third, a conceptual notion of trust domain, characterized using our algebraic, logical, and utility-theoretic tools, that encapsulates the intuitions described above.

In Section 2, we discuss our motivation in modelling 'trust domains', giving a precise, but informal, introduction to the concept. In Section 3, we provide the necessary conceptual background to our systems modelling approach and, in Section 4, we give a mathematical formulation of a weighted (costed) process algebra that provides a suitable basis for modelling systems and decision-making about choices within them.

M. Huth et al. (Eds.): TRUST 2013, LNCS 7904, pp. 232–249, 2013.

In Section 5, we describe the associated modal, substructural logic. Cost modalities play a key role in describing trust domains. In Section 6, we return first, in the light of our mathematical set-up, to the definition of trust domains, and proceed to discuss a range of examples. In Section 7, we discuss some directions for further research.

2 Trust Domains

In systems of interacting agents, an individual or group of agents may establish a part of the system, or a collection of agents within the system, that it trusts. Similarly, a system's designer or manager might establish a collection of parts of the system such that, within any given part, the agents trust one another. We shall refer to such a part of the system, or such a collection of agents, as a 'trust domain'. This term is used in the Trusted Computing Project (www. trustedcomputing.org.uk), the Open Trusted Computing consortium

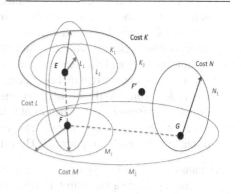

Fig. 1. Iso-utilities and Trust Domains

(www.opentc.net), and the 'Trust Domains' project (www.hpl.hp.com/ research/cloud_security/TrustDomains.eps). The literature on models of trust is very large and cannot be surveyed in this short article, but a good survey with a relevant perspective for us is [18].

In this section, we consider informally how an agent might decide which part of its system, or which agents within the system, to trust. We propose a characterization of a trust domain for a given agent within a given system that has two components. First, a logical assertion that expresses the properties that must be possessed by any trusted agent. Second, a cost bound that limits the extent to which the system around the agent can be trusted; that is, the agent will trust only those parts of the system that can be reached or observed within a given expenditure of resource. The intended situation is depicted schematically in Figure 1. This picture is intended to be understood in the context of the classical model of distributed systems (see, for example, [7,6]) in which processes (here, agents) execute relative to collections of resources, located at specified places within the system. The system is understood as residing within an environment from which events are incident upon it and to which it exports events [7,6].

Here the agent, E, may be given one of two different choices of cost function, K_E. If $K_E = K$, then F is not within E's trust domain at either the K_1 or K_2 levels. If, however, $K_E = L$, then F is within E's trust domain at the L_2, but not at the L_1 level. Agent F's cost function, M, includes agent G at the M_2 level, but not at the M_1 level $(M_1 < M_2)$. F' is in no-one's domain at any of the given levels of cost.

Examples of the propositions that might be associated with a trust domain include access control assertions, such those as described in [2,1,6] (and references therein).

We make use of logical *cost modalities*, that place bounds on the cost that is acceptable for a given agent. This formalizes the above notion of levels of trust.

In Section 6, we consider three examples of trust domains, illustrating different aspects of their form and use. Our focus here is on modelling decision-making about trust in situations inspired by corporate environments.

1. *Establishing Boundaries.* In a dock, the harbour master and the captain of an inbound ship must determine at what point responsibility for navigating the ship should pass between them: The captain must trust the harbour master with the care of the ship and the harbour master must trust the captain to navigate the dock safely.
2. *Contract Choices.* In the management of mergers & acquisitions, the deal team must establish valuations of the principals. This requires access to highly confidential information, and the deal team may need to outsource specialized parts of the valuation, so that is a risk that confidential data may be lost. Who should be trusted by the deal team? And with what information?
3. *Information Provenance.* When establishing data-sharing arrangements, the provenance of the evidence used to assess, say, the reliability of the outsourced service provider is of critical importance. How does an agent decide to trust that evidence?

The examples are not intended to cover all of the interesting issues: they are illustrative.

We aim to provide a modelling framework within which this notion of trust domain can be established and shown capable of handling substantial examples, encompassing a variety of situations. We begin with a mathematical treatment of distributed systems, including an account of how agents' choices are modelled.

3   Systems Modelling and Decision-Making

The classical model of distributed systems, such as described in [7], provides the conceptual inspiration for our modelling framework, which builds on [6,3]. First, a model resides within an environment; that is, the part of the system not modelled in explicit structural detailed. The interaction between the model of interest and its environment is captured mathematically using stochastic processes to provide occurrences of events. Second, the structural components of a model can be described as follows:

- Location: locations are the places within (and, indeed, outwith) the system at which resources reside; locations can be logical or physical;
- Resource: resources are the building blocks of the system's services; they can, for example, be consumed, created, and moved between locations by processes;
- Process: processes deliver services within and outwith the system, manipulating the resources that are distributed around the system's logical and physical locations; they interact with the system's environment.

Mathematically, our treatment of process is based on Milner's synchronous calculus of communicating systems (SCCS) [15], as developed as a basis for systems modelling in [6]; note that asynchronous calculi can be encoded within synchronous calculi [15]. The key idea is that locations, resources, and processes co-evolve, according to a judgement $L, R, E \xrightarrow{a} L', R', E'$, which is read as 'the process E, using resources R at locations L, performs action a and so becomes the process E' that is able to evolve using resources R' at locations L''. For simplicity of presentation, and with little loss of generality for our present purposes, we suppress locations in the remainder of this presentation, though make informal use of them in our examples, in Section 6. The reader might think of them either as implicitly present, or consider them to be rolled up into the definition of resources (see [6] for relevant technical support).

This judgement is defined using a structural operational semantics, such as in the definition of SCCS [15,6]. Three mathematical details are important. First, actions are required to form a commutative monoid (a and b combine to form ab). Second, resources are assumed to form a preordered partial commutative *resource monoid*, $\mathbf{R} = (\mathbf{R}, \sqsubseteq, \circ, e)$, in which resource elements $R_1, R_2 \in \mathbf{R}$ can be combined, using the monoid operation to form $R_1 \circ R_2$ (with unit e) or compared, $R_1 \sqsubseteq R_2$, say, using the preorder. The structure of the monoid is subject to some coherence conditions [17,6]. A key example of a monoid of resources is given by the natural numbers (with 0), with addition as the monoid operation and less-than-or-equals as the order: $(\mathbb{N}, \leq, +, 0)$. Third, the relationship between actions and resources must be specified using a *modification function* that specifies the effect of performing an action a on a resource element R: that is, $\mu : (a, R) \mapsto R'$. Modification functions must satisfy some (mild) coherence conditions relating the monoid structure of actions and the monoidal structure of resources (details may be found in [6]). This treatment of resource just as in bunched logic [17] and in various versions of separation logic [19] and, for brevity, we refrain from further rehearsing its justification here.

With this set-up, the operational semantics, in its basic form, admits rules such as

$$\frac{R, E \xrightarrow{a} R', E' \quad S, F \xrightarrow{b} S', F'}{R \circ S, E \times F \xrightarrow{ab} R' \circ S', E' \times F'} \quad \text{and} \quad \frac{R, E_i \xrightarrow{a} R', E'_i}{R, E_1 + E_2 \xrightarrow{a} R', E'_i} \quad (i = 1, 2)$$

giving, respectively, concurrent product and simple non-deterministic choice.

In determining the extent of trust domains, agents do not, however, make simple non-deterministic choices. Rather, they make choices according to their (situated, or located) preferences. Accordingly, we must set up a version of the approach sketch above that captures a suitable representation of preference-driven choice.

Many process calculi include a form of prioritized sum, for example [20]. In prioritized sums, say $w \cdot a : E + w' \cdot b : F$, with $w > w'$, the option $a : E$ is always preferred in any context in which both a and b are available (which they may not be, because of restriction operations). By contrast, we argue that an agent, even with the same potential choice of actions, should be permitted to associate different costs to the same options, dependent on its situation and the properties of the agents with which it is interacting. To this end we make use of *cost-dependent choice* (or simply *sum*) $\sum_u E_i$, in which an agent has a choice between alternatives E_i, and its preference is codified by the cost function u. Cost is used as in utility theory to encompass uplift for revenue; that is, as in loss. Cost functions map from a resource-process pair to rational numbers.

As we wish to model agents whose preferences differ dependent on their situation, the cost ascribed to the different possible choices at a choice point must not rely on those potential choices alone. For example, if the choice $R, a : E +_u b : F$ (here we use an infix notation) occurs within a wider context $R \circ S, (a : E +_u b : F) \times G$, then the preferences in the given context are determined by the cost calculations $o = u(R \circ S, a : E \times G)$ and $p = u(R \circ S, b : F \times G)$. If the first summand is chosen then we annotate the cost o on the evolution arrow and, if the second is chosen, then we annotate p on the evolution arrow. An occurrence of the same choice $R, a : E +_u b : F$ within a different context, such as $R \circ T, (a : E +_u b : F) \times H$ with $G \neq H$ or $S \neq T$, may have different cost calculations and associated costs.

Along with the concept of a process algebra with costs comes an associated modal logic. Just as in [3,6], the logic admits the usual classical (or, if preferred, intuitionistic) propositional connectives, as well as thus usual 'separating' or 'resource-sensitive' multiplicatives from bunched logic [17], as in [6], and action modalities, as in Hennessy–Milner logic [10,9,16].

Critically in our present setting, it also admits weighted, or cost, modalities. Utility-based decision-making for ordinal preferences can be incorporated into a process-theoretic setting [3]. Standard economic reasons (particularly moves towards uncertain outcomes) require the further development of this to cardinal utility, and we embark upon such a task in this paper. The possibility connectives $\langle \leq n \rangle \phi$ and $\langle > n \rangle \phi$ denote that there exists an evolution whose cost m is, respectively, less than or equal to, or greater than, n, where the resulting state (or continuation) satisfies ϕ. The necessity connectives $[\leq n]$ and $[> n]$ denote, respectively, that in all evolutions whose cost m is less than or equal to, or greater than, n, where the resulting state satisfies ϕ. Thus, a logical property of a trust domain that is guarded by a sequence of choices has an associated cost capturing the associated agent's preferences and determining which choice is made.

4 A Process Algebra with Contextual Costs

Section 3 describes our conceptual formulation of system models and the associated model of decision-making. We now establish the necessary mathematical set-up. Related work, based on Milner's π-calculus, is in [8].

In order to consider the different situations or contexts that a given process trusts, we wish to consider how a process values its options dependent on the context in which it occurs. As such, the sub-evolutions of a composite process may not be independent of each other. This is in contrast with typical process calculi, where the behaviour of a composite process is usually defined in terms of the behaviours of its sub-processes alone.

To see how this works, consider a choice $R, a : E +_u b : F$ that occurs as part of a wider model $R \circ S, (a : E +_u b : F) \times G$. When a choice is made we annotate the cost n of the chosen summand on the evolution (e.g., $R, a : E +_u b : F \Longrightarrow^n R', a : E$). As these costs depend on the context, then the evolution needs to know what this context is. We henceforth annotate the context in which a process is evolved on the underside of the evolution arrow (e.g., $R, a : E +_u b : F \xRightarrow[S, [] \times G]{} {}^n R', a : E$), where $[]$ denotes the hole into which $a : E +_u b : F$ may be substituted to regain the complete system $(a : E +_u b : F) \times G$, and S are the resources allocated to G. In addition, any choices in $[] \times G$ will make use of the process that is substituted into the hole $[]$. We therefore annotate the process that is substituted, into the process being evolved, on top of the evolution arrow; for example, $S, [] \times G \xRightarrow{R, a : E +_u b : F} {}^m S', [] \times G'$.

In essence, the judgement for evolution for processes with cost of the form

$$C \underset{C_1}{\overset{C_2}{\Longrightarrow}}{}^{n} C' \tag{1}$$

denotes how a context C, that exists in a system that can be decomposed as $C_1(C(C_2))$, evolves in terms of its choices. We refer to C as the *(primary) context*, C_1 as the *outer context*, and C_2 as the *substituted*, or *inner context*. Intuitively this denotes the evolution of one part, C, of an entire system, $C_1(C(C_2))$. In order to reason compositionally, we wish to be able to describe the evolution of C independently and structurally. As choices take account of context, this is not possible. The semantics of choice, however, makes use of just the definition of the inner and outer context, disregarding their structure. So we do not need to make use of the structure of C_1 and C_2, as we do with C, but need only record their definitions, for reference at choice points. They are therefore annotated on the evolution arrow, but are not evolved in that relation.

We now describe the theoretical set-up in detail. Assume a set U of symbols, called *formal costs*, with a distinguished element 0_U, called the *neutral cost*. Processes are generated by the grammar

$$E ::= 1 \mid [\,] \mid a : E \mid \sum_{i \in I}{}_u E_i \mid E \times E. \tag{2}$$

These are really process contexts: the term $[\,]$ is a *hole* into which other processes may be substituted. For this work, it turns out to be convenient to develop contexts as first-class citizens rather than merely meta-theoretic tools.

The *choice* $\sum_{i \in I}{}_u E_i$ is the key construct: it describes situations in which an agent has a choice between alternatives E_i indexed by a $i \in I$, and its preference (in a larger context) is codified by the cost $u \in U$. The infix operator $E +_u F$ may be used for binary sums, and the subscript u may be dropped when $u = 0_U$. The *zero* process $\mathbf{0}$ is defined to be the sum indexed by the empty set and the neutral cost. The zero process, *unit* process $\mathbf{1}$, and *synchronous products* $E \times F$ are well-known in process calculus, as are *prefixes* $a : E$, where $a \in Act$. Assume, for each formal cost $u \in U$, an associated, real-valued *cost function* $u : Cont \longrightarrow \mathbb{R}$ [13] that fixes an interpretation for each formal symbol $u \in U$. The identically zero function is associated with 0_U. Henceforth, we do not distinguish between formal costs and their costs functions.

A process E is *well-formed* if it contains at most one hole and that hole is not guarded by action prefixes. The process E is *closed* if it has no holes and *open* otherwise. Let $PCont$ be the set of all well-formed processes, $PCCont$ be the set of all closed well formed processes, and $POCont$ be the set of all open well-formed processes. Let $\mathbf{R}$ be a resource monoid and μ be a fixed modification function, as defined in Section 3. Define the products of sets $Cont = \mathbf{R} \times PCont$, $CCont = \mathbf{R} \times PCCont$ and $OCont = \mathbf{R} \times POCont$. The letter C is reserved for contexts. Define $C_\emptyset = e, [\,]$. Brackets will be freely used to disambiguate both processes and contexts. For $C = R, E$, the notational abuses $C \times F = R, (E \times F)$ and $C +_u F = R, (E +_u F)$ will sometimes be used. Substitution in processes, $E(F)$, replaces all occurrences of $[\,]$ in E with F; for example, $(([\,] +_u E) \times G)(F) = (F +_u E) \times G$. Substitution of contexts $C_1(C_2)$, where $C_1 = R, E$ and $C_2 = S, F$, is defined as follows: if E is open,

$$\frac{}{R,1 \xrightarrow[C_1]{C_2} R,1}(\text{TICK}) \quad \frac{}{R,a:E \xrightarrow[C_1]{C_2} a \mu(a,R),E}(\text{PREFIX}) \quad \frac{C_2 \xrightarrow[C_1]{(e,1)} a C_2'}{e,[] \xrightarrow[C_1]{C_2} 1 e,[]}(\text{HOLE})$$

$$(S\times)\frac{R,E \xrightarrow[C_3]{C_2} a R',E' \quad S,F \xrightarrow[C_4]{C_2} b S',F'}{R \circ S, E \times F \xrightarrow[C_1]{C_2} ab R' \circ S', E' \times F'}(\text{PROD})$$

Fig. 2. Action Operational Semantics

$$\frac{}{R,1 \xRightarrow[C_1]{C_2} 0 R,1}(\text{TICKW}) \quad \frac{}{R,a:E \xRightarrow[C_1]{C_2} 0 R,a:E}(\text{PREFIXW}) \quad \frac{C_2 \xRightarrow[C_1]{(e,1)} n C_2'}{e,[] \xRightarrow[C_1]{C_2} 0 e,[]}(\text{HOLEW})$$

$$\frac{n = u(C_1(R,E_i(C_2)))}{R,\sum_u E_i \xRightarrow[C_1]{C_2} n R,E_i}(\text{SUMW}) \quad (S\times)\frac{R,E \xRightarrow[C_3]{C_2} o R,E' \quad S,F \xRightarrow[C_4]{C_2} p S,F'}{R \circ S, E \times F \xRightarrow[C_1]{C_2} o+p R \circ S, E' \times F'}(\text{PRODW})$$

Fig. 3. Operational Semantics of Cost

then $C_1(C_2) = R \circ S, E(F)$, where $E(F)$ is process substitution; if E is closed, then $C_1(C_2) = C_1$.

Developing the formulation sketched above, we separate the operational semantics into two dimensions: the evolution system for performing actions (Figure 2) and the evolution system for determining the cost of possible choices (Figure 3), as in [20], and building on [3]. Overall, the evolution sequences for the calculus are interleavings of the two dimensions. The operational semantics for performing actions is defined in Figure 2. The unit process always ticks, effecting no change. The prefix process evolves via its head action. The hole rule is a technical one used to terminate evolution derivations of open contexts. An important feature of this system is that contextual information about conclusions is propagated up to premises. In the product case, information about each premiss is propagated up from the conclusion to the other premiss, so that derivations of transitions occur in context. This is effected by the side-condition $(S\times)$ is which states that $C_3 = C_1((S,F(C_2)) \times [])$ and $C_4 = C_1((R,E(C_2)) \times [])$.

The operational semantics for determining the cost of possible choices, as defined in Figure 3, is used to determine the cost of a given set of choices of a process. A neutral cost is given to tick, prefix, and hole processes, as they contain no choices. The sum process $\sum_u E_i$ represents a preference-based choice by the agent: it evolves to one of its summands, annotating the value of that summand in the wider context on the evolution arrow, according to its cost function u. A special case of the sum is for the zero process $\mathbf{0}$, which never evolves. The product evolves two processes synchronously in parallel, according to the decomposition of the associated resources, and annotates the sum of the sub-processes' costs on the evolution arrow. This approach to combining costs, and the value given to tick or prefix processes, is one possible design decision, and will be considered more fully in future work. We make use of the abbreviation $C \stackrel{n}{\Longrightarrow} C'$ and $C \stackrel{a}{\rightarrow} C'$ to denote $C \stackrel{e,1}{\underset{e,[]}{\Longrightarrow}}^{n} C'$ and $C \stackrel{e,1}{\underset{e,[]}{\longrightarrow}}^{a} C'$, respectively.

To demonstrate how contextual decisions can be utilized in modelling, we give a simple example (inspired by [5]). Consider a banker who has a presentation (for a client, that includes confidential business data) on a USB drive. The banker may chose to access the drive or not, depending on the situation. The banker is modelled as a process

$$Banker = present : Banker' +_{u_B} idle_B : Banker', \qquad (3)$$

where u_B represents its costs. The banker may be willing to access the presentation when visiting a client, on the assumption that the client's network is firewalled, so making the document safe from attack. In order to do so, however, the banker must be given access to a computer by the client. The client is modelled as

$$Client = logIn : Client' + idle_C : Client', \qquad (4)$$

which, for simplicity, makes a non-deterministic choice between logging the guest in and idling. The interaction between the banker and the client is a form of joint access control (i.e., both agents must grant access), in which the banker cannot show the presentation without having been logged in, and the client cannot see the presentation unless the banker accesses it. If the banker's cost function is u_B, then we have

$$u_B(C_C(R, idle_B : Banker')) = 0.3 \qquad u_B(C_C(R, present : Banker')) = 0.1. \quad (5)$$

and the banker would prefer to present the work. Here, where C_C is the client context, the banker can access the presentation with a low cost

$$R, Banker \stackrel{e,1}{\underset{C_C}{\Longrightarrow}}^{0.1} R, present : Banker' \stackrel{present}{\longrightarrow} R, Banker'. \qquad (6)$$

In a different situation — here, a different context — the banker may have different costs associated with the possible choices. Consider a home computer, compromised by an attacker who wants to steal the presentation, but cannot do so unless the banker accesses it from the USB stick. The attacker is modelled as

$$Attacker = steal : Attacker' + idle_A : Attacker' \qquad (7)$$

In this situation, the banker prefers to idle than to work on the presentation.

$$u_B(C_A(R, idle_B : Banker')) = 0.2 \quad u_B(C_A(R, present : Banker')) = 0.6. \quad (8)$$

and the banker has a much higher cost, due to the increased risk of the data being stolen, when performing the *present* action

$$R, Banker \underset{C_A}{\overset{e,1}{\Longrightarrow}}{}^{0.6} R, present : Banker' \xrightarrow{present} R, Banker'. \qquad (9)$$

Were we reasoning about the decisions that the banker would make, we could easily argue that the document would not be accessed from home, as the banker's cost for doing so is so high. Indeed, we could straightforwardly implement this by introducing a restriction operator to the language to filter choices above/below a given cost bound.

A fundamental aspect of process calculus is the ability to reason equationally about behavioural equivalence of processes [15]. We now adapt these notions to suit the calculus above, which incorporates ideas from [6].

The *bisimilarity (or bisimulation) relation* $\sim \subseteq PCont \times PCont$ is the largest binary relation such that, if $E \sim F$, then for all $a \in Act$, for all $R, R', S, T \in \mathbf{R}$, and for all $G, H, I, J \in PCont$ with $G \sim I$ and $H \sim J$, then

1. for all $E' \in PCont$, if $R, E \xrightarrow[S,G]{T,H}{}^{a} R', E'$, then there is F' such that $R, F \xrightarrow[S,I]{T,J}{}^{a}$
   R', F' and $E' \sim F'$, and if $R, E \underset{S,G}{\overset{T,H}{\Longrightarrow}}{}^{n} R, E$, then there is F' such that $R, F \underset{S,I}{\overset{T,J}{\Longrightarrow}}{}^{n}$
   R, F' and $E' \sim F'$, and
2. for all $F' \in PCont$, if $R, F \xrightarrow[S,I]{T,J}{}^{a} R', F'$, then there is E' such that $R, E \xrightarrow[S,G]{T,H}{}^{a}$
   R', E' and $E' \sim F'$, and if $R, F \Longrightarrow [S,I]T, J^n R, F'$, then there is E' such that
   $R, E \underset{S,G}{\overset{T,H}{\Longrightarrow}}{}^{n} R, E'$ and $E' \sim F'$.

The union of any set of relations that satisfy these two conditions also satisfies these conditions, so the largest such relation is well-defined. Define $\sim \subseteq Cont \times Cont$ by: if $E \sim F$ then $R, E \sim R, F$ for all $R \in \mathbf{R}$ and $E, F \in Cont$.

Definition 1. *A cost function, u, respects bisimilarity if, for all $C_1, C_2 \in Cont$, $C_1 \sim C_2$ implies $u(C_1) = u(C_2)$.*

That is, behaviourally equivalent (bisimilar) states are required to be indistinguishable by u. Note that the cost reductions $\Rightarrow^n$ used in the definition of bisimulation do not necessarily use cost functions to determine the cost n, as the base case reduction rules for tick, prefix, and hole processes all output a constant zero cost. The set U of utilities respects bisimilarity if every $u \in U$ respects bisimilarity. Any real-valued function defined on the quotient $Cont/\sim$ defines a cost that respects bisimilarity. Henceforth cost functions are assumed to respect bisimilarity. We can show that if bisimilar contexts are substituted into each other, then the result is bisimilar:

Proposition 1. *If $E \sim G$ and $F \sim H$ then $E(F) \sim G(H)$.*

All proofs are omitted in this short paper.

With this result, we can obtain a key property for reasoning compositionally.

Theorem 1 (Bisimulation Congruence). *The relation $\sim$ is a congruence. It is reflexive, symmetric and transitive, and for all a, E, F, G with $E \sim F$, and all families $(E_i)_{i \in I}, (F_{i \in I})_I$ with $E_i \sim F_i$ for all $i \in I$, $a : E \sim a : F$, $E \times G \sim F \times G$, and $\sum_{i \in I}{}_u E_i \sim \sum_{i \in I}{}_u F_i$.*

In order to reason equationally about processes, it is also useful to establish various algebraic properties concerning parallel composition and choice. We derive these below, for our calculus. We use the binary version of sum here in order to aid comprehension, but finite choices between sets of processes work straightforwardly.

Proposition 2 (Algebraic Properties). *(1)* $E +_u F \sim F +_u E$; *(2)* $E \times 0 \sim 0$; *(3)* $E \times 1 \sim E$; *(4)* $E \times F \sim F \times E$; and *(5)* $E \times (F \times G) \sim (E \times F) \times G$.

5   A Cost-Sensitive Modal Logic

We now introduce a cost-sensitive modal logic of system properties. The semantics is given using a satisfaction relation

$$C \models_{C'} \phi, \tag{10}$$

where C is a closed context, C' is an open context, and ϕ is a formula of a (Hennessy–Milner-style) modal logic of processes: this may be read 'the *primary context* C satisfies ϕ in the *surrounding context* C'' (cf. (1)). The context C may satisfy different logical propositions, perhaps even negations of each other, when placed in different surrounding contexts; an example of this is below. Context-sensitive logics have been studied previously [14,4]. The structural nature of processes and resources provides a semantic framework in which such logics seem particularly natural.

The propositions of the logic are defined by the grammar

$$\phi ::= p \mid \bot \mid \top \mid \neg\phi \mid \phi \wedge \phi \mid \phi \vee \phi \mid \phi \rightarrow \phi \mid \langle a \rangle \phi \mid [a]\phi \mid I \mid \phi * \phi \mid \phi \rightarrow\!\!\!* \phi \mid$$
$$\langle \leq n \rangle \phi \mid [\leq n]\phi \mid \langle > n \rangle \phi \mid [> n]\phi, \tag{11}$$

where p ranges over atomic propositions, a over actions, and n over rational numbers. The symbols for propositions for *truth, falsehood, negation* and *(additive) conjunction, disjunction,* and *implication* are standard. The *(additive) modal connectives* are $\langle a \rangle$ and $[a]$. The connectives I, $*$, and $\rightarrow\!\!\!*$ are the *multiplicative unit, conjunction,* and *implication*, respectively. The *(cost) modal connectives* are $\langle \leq n \rangle$, $[\leq n]$, $\langle > n \rangle$, $[> n]$, and denote possible and necessary modal bounds on costed evolutions.

The interpretation of cost modalities is straightforward. The possibility connectives $\langle \leq n \rangle \phi$ and $\langle > n \rangle \phi$ denote that there exists an evolution whose cost m is less than or equal to, or greater than, n, respectively, where the resulting state satisfies ϕ. The necessity connectives $[\leq n]$ and $[> n]$ denote that in all evolutions whose cost m is less than or equal to, or greater than, n, respectively, where the resulting state satisfies ϕ. The satisfaction relation for cost modalities is specified in Figure 4, with the satisfaction relation for additive formulae specified in Figure 5, and that for multiplicative formulae specified in Figure 6.

We describe the interpretation with an example: recall the model of the banker's context dependent preferences and choices (cf. (3-9)). In the client context, the banker has a low-cost choice of 0.1 (cf. 6), but in the attacker context all its possible evolutions

$$C_1 \models_{C_2} \langle \leq n \rangle \phi \quad \text{iff} \quad \text{there are } C_1', C_2', m, o \text{ such that } C_1 \overset{e,1}{\underset{C_2}{\Longrightarrow}}^m C_1'$$

$$\text{and } C_2 \overset{C_1}{\underset{C_\emptyset}{\Longrightarrow}}^o C_2', \text{ and } m \leq n \text{ and } C_1' \models_{C_2'} \phi$$

$$C_1 \models_{C_2} [\leq n] \phi \quad \text{iff} \quad \text{for all } C_1', C_2', m, o \text{ such that if } C_1 \overset{e,1}{\underset{C_2}{\Longrightarrow}}^m C_1' \text{ and}$$

$$C_2 \overset{C_1}{\underset{C_\emptyset}{\Longrightarrow}}^o C_2' \text{ and } m \leq n, \text{ then } C_1' \models_{C_2'} \phi$$

$$C_1 \models_{C_2} \langle > n \rangle \phi \quad \text{iff} \quad \text{there are } C_1', C_2', m, o \text{ such that } C_1 \overset{e,1}{\underset{C_2}{\Longrightarrow}}^m C_1'$$

$$\text{and } C_2 \overset{C_1}{\underset{C_\emptyset}{\Longrightarrow}}^o C_2', \text{ and } m > n \text{ and } C_1' \models_{C_2'} \phi$$

$$C_1 \models_{C_2} [> n] \phi \quad \text{iff} \quad \text{for all } C_1', C_2', m, o \text{ such that if } C_1 \overset{e,1}{\underset{C_2}{\Longrightarrow}}^m C_1' \text{ and}$$

$$C_2 \overset{C_1}{\underset{C_\emptyset}{\Longrightarrow}}^o C_2' \text{ and } m > n, \text{ then } C_1' \models_{C_2'} \phi$$

Fig. 4. Interpretation of Propositional Cost Modalities

are of higher cost of 0.2 and 0.6, respectively (cf. 9). Hence we can show that the banker process has different logical properties in different contexts

$$R, Banker \models_{C_C} \langle \leq 0.1 \rangle \top \qquad R, Banker \models_{C_A} \neg (\langle \leq 0.1 \rangle \top), \qquad (12)$$

where $\top$ is a formula that is true for all processes in all contexts.

The standard interpretation of Hennessy–Milner logics uses the relation specified by the operational semantics as a Kripke structure to support the modal connectives. In our work, the operational semantics is more complex: a context occurs, and evolves alongside an outer context. Therefore, when we consider whether $C_1 \models_{C_2} \langle \leq n \rangle \phi$ holds, we have to consider whether there are evolutions of the form $C_1 \overset{e,1}{\underset{C_2}{\Longrightarrow}}^m C_1'$ and $C_2 \overset{C_1}{\underset{C_\emptyset}{\Longrightarrow}}^o C_2'$ such that $C_1' \models_{C_2'} \phi$ and $m \leq n$. The occurrence of the tick process and the empty context ensure that no extraneous contextual information is introduced into the evolutions of interest. Other modal operators are interpreted similarly.

A *valuation*, $\mathcal{V}$, is a function that maps each atomic proposition to a $\sim$-closed set of closed contexts. In the interpretation of atoms, the surrounding context is wrapped around the primary context, and the valuation of the atom consulted to see if it contains this compound context. This is what makes our logic context-sensitive. $\top, \bot, \neg, \wedge, \vee$, and $\rightarrow$ are all interpreted (essentially) classically. The interpretation of the multiplicative connectives here is similar to that for the logic MBI in [6].

Recall again the example of the banker who decides which actions to take in different contexts (3-9). In a situation that consists of a client (context C_C), the banker can access the presentation with low cost, but in a situation that consists of an attacker (context C_A) the banker accessing the presentation has a high cost; that is,

$$R_B, Banker \models_{C_C} \langle \leq 0.3 \rangle \langle present \rangle \top \text{ and } R_B, Banker \models_{C_A} \neg (\langle \leq 0.3 \rangle \langle present \rangle \top). \qquad (13)$$

$$C \models_{C'} p \qquad \text{iff} \quad C'(C) \in \mathcal{V}(p)$$
$$C \models_{C'} \bot \qquad \qquad \text{never}$$
$$C \models_{C'} \top \qquad \qquad \text{always}$$
$$C \models_{C'} \neg\phi \qquad \text{iff} \quad C \not\models_{C'} \phi$$
$$C \models_{C'} \phi \wedge \psi \qquad \text{iff} \quad C \models_{C'} \phi \text{ and } C \models_{C'} \psi$$
$$C \models_{C'} \phi \vee \psi \qquad \text{iff} \quad C \models_{C'} \phi \text{ or } C \models_{C'} \psi$$
$$C \models_{C'} \phi \to \psi \qquad \text{iff} \quad C \models_{C'} \phi \text{ implies } C \models_{C'} \psi$$

$$C_1 \models_{C_2} \langle a \rangle \phi \qquad \text{iff} \quad \text{there are } C'_1, C'_2, b \text{ such that if } C_1 \xrightarrow[C_2]{e,1}{}^{a} C'_1 \text{ and } C_2 \xrightarrow[C_0]{C_1}{}^{b} C'_2,$$
$$\text{then } C'_1 \models_{C'_2} \phi$$

$$C_1 \models_{C_2} [a] \phi \qquad \text{iff} \quad \text{for all } C'_1, C'_2, b \text{ such that if } C_1 \xrightarrow[C_2]{e,1}{}^{a} C'_1 \text{ and } C_2 \xrightarrow[C_0]{C_1}{}^{b} C'_2,$$
$$\text{then } C'_1 \models_{C'_2} \phi$$

Fig. 5. Interpretation of Additive Propositional Formulae

$$R, E \models_{C'} I \qquad \text{iff} \quad R = e \text{ and } E \sim 1$$
$$R, E \models_{C'} \phi * \psi \qquad \text{iff} \quad \text{there are } S, T, F, G \text{ such that } R = S \circ T, E \sim F \times G, \text{ and}$$
$$S, F \models_{C'(T, [] \times G)} \phi \text{ and } T, G \models_{C'(S, F \times [])} \psi$$
$$R, E \models_{C'} \phi \mathbin{-\!*} \psi \text{ iff} \quad \text{for all } S, F \text{ such that } R \circ S \text{ is defined and } S, F \models_{C'} \phi,$$
$$R \circ S, E \times F \models_{C'} \psi$$

Fig. 6. Interpretation of Multiplicative Propositional Formulae

Hence, in different contexts the process satisfies different propositions that, moreover, would be inconsistent over the same context.

If we make use of real value quantification we can recover optimality properties about the least or most costly choices, as in [3]. For example, we could state that the most costly option has logical property ϕ as $\exists x. [> x] \bot \wedge \langle \le x \rangle \phi \wedge \neg [> x] \neg\phi$, using standard techniques to define equality with inequalities and negation. This could be used to reason about a scheduler's possible options.

Behaviourally equivalent processes are also logically equivalent (they satisfy the same logical properties). This is half of the Hennessy–Milner property [10,9].

Theorem 2. *If* $C_1 \models_{C_2} \phi$, *and* $C_1 \sim C_3$, *and* $C_2 \sim C_4$, *then* $C_3 \models_{C_4} \phi$.

Hence, bisimilar processes can be used interchangeably within a larger system, without changing the logical properties of the larger system.

It is unclear whether a useful converse can be obtained, for the given bisimulation relation. With restrictions on the available fragments of the logic, and a different (*local*) equivalence relation, however, it is possible to obtain a converse [3]. The local equivalence, however, fails to be a congruence, and as such its usefulness is limited. It is a strictly local reasoning tool.

The logic might also be enriched to handle expected cost [13]. Quantitative path-based logical properties of Markov Chains are studied in [11]: they support reasoning about complex notions such as average utility with a given time discount, but do not provide compositionality results over model structures. A more extensive study of such extensions is future work.

In game-theoretic approaches to security, the notion of a level of security is important. That is, if a defender chooses to perform some defensive action: then all possible attacks have a high cost for the attacker. With preference modalities we can make statements relevant to security levels. To see this, consider the proposition

$$\phi \rightarrow\!\!\ast [< n][d](\neg \langle a \rangle \top), \tag{14}$$

This proposition states that any attacker that is characterized by ϕ, when a defensive action is effected, there is no possible choice to attack that incurs a cost less than bound n (we hold the costs of the defender constant). The multiplicative implication operator permits us to reason about composition within arbitrary processes, and hence of the efficacy of defensive measures relative to an arbitrary (partially) described attacker. The interaction between multiplicative implication and cost operators is surprisingly powerful, and can be used to describe the intuitive description of trust domains [3].

6   Trust Domains Revisited

In Section 2, Given different preference functions and different bounds, a given agent may decide to trust different agents. We now formalize that definition, and provide a selection of examples that demonstrate how trust domains can model natural problems.

In [3], trust domains are defined relatively informally, in terms of an agent E that is considering what to trust, a logical property ψ that denotes some *goal property* for the agent, and a cost bound n. A trust domain then consists of the set of contexts into which the agent can be substituted, where the entire system can evolve to some other system that satisfies the goal property, and the cost of the evaluation, is within the cost bound n.

Here, using a cost modality, we define a trust domain as

$$TD((R, E), \phi, \psi, n) = \{S, F \mid S, F \vDash_{C_\emptyset} \phi \text{ and } R \circ S, E \times F \vDash_{C_\emptyset} \langle \leq n \rangle \psi \}, \tag{15}$$

where ϕ limits the agents being considered with, for example, some locality condition.

Recall that multiplicative implication is valid when, for any context that fulfils the left hand side of the implication, if it is composed with the current agent, then the joint system fulfils the right hand side of the implication. In essence, a trust domain is the collection of such contexts, for the logical property $\phi \rightarrow\!\!\ast \langle \leq n \rangle \psi$ interpreted with respect to the agent R, E that is doing the trusting.

We now turn to the three examples from Section 2 in order to illustrate these ideas.

Establishing Boundaries. We consider how a harbour master and a ship's captain establish an appropriate point at which to transfer control of the ship between them. In attempting to establish a boundary between the parts of a system controlled by co-evolving agents, use must be made of the agents' preferences. We must consider both agents with 'fixed' preferences, which do depend on the context structure, such as heavy seas, but not on the cost functions of other agents in the system, and agents with 'variable' preferences, depending on the cost functions of other agents in the system.

Upon approach the harbour, the process $Capt$ can either move forward under the ship's own propulsion, wait out at sea, or transfer control to a tug (operated by the harbour master). The forward action takes a token representing the ship one location closer to the port. The wait action idles. The transfer action transfers control to a tug. The process $Capt'$ then defers to the tug (idles).

$$Capt = \text{forw} : Capt +_u 1.Capt +_u \text{transf\_contr} : 1. \tag{16}$$

The cost function u encodes the captain's preferences with respect to the environment. The captain wants to hand over to the harbour master as soon as possible (e.g., for insurance reasons) and will transfer control as soon as the harbour master is willing

$$\text{for all } R, C.u(C(R, \text{transf\_contr} : 1)) = 0.1. \tag{17}$$

In each location, from the high seas onwards, the captain will have a preference as to whether to continue moving forwards or to wait at that location for a tug. This preference will depend on the context; in heavier seas, the captain will wait for a tug further out. Consider a sequence of locations: $Ocean \to L_1 \to L_2 \to Harbour$. Let s_{loc} refer to the presence of the ship at location loc. We define that in calm seas that the captain is willing to take the ship as far as L_2 and then will wait; that is, for all R, E,

$$\begin{array}{ll} u((R, s_{L_1}), \text{forw} : Capt \times E) = 0.3 & u((R, s_{L_2}), \text{forw} : Capt \times E) = 0.7 \\ u((R, s_{L_1}), 1 : Capt \times E) \quad = 0.7 & u((R, s_{L_2}), 1 : Capt \times E) \quad = 0.3, \end{array} \tag{18}$$

where R doesn't include $rough$. However, in rough seas the captain prefers to wait at both L_1 and L_2; that is, for all E, R and all $loc \in \{L_1, L_2\}$

$$\begin{array}{l} u((R, s_{loc}, rough), \text{forw} : Capt \times E) = 0.7 \\ u((R, s_{loc}, rough), 1 : Capt \times E) \quad = 0.3. \end{array} \tag{19}$$

The harbour master may then choose to wait or to have the tug take control of the ship:

$$Master = 1 : Master +_v \text{acpt\_contr} : Master' \quad Master' = \text{tow} : Master' \tag{20}$$

The harbour master wants to take control of incoming ships as late as possible so as to have the highest throughput (less time spent on each ship means the same number of tugs can get more ships through), but no later than location L_2. If the captain refuses to come further in, the harbour master will compromise and send a tug further out. This calls for a more complex cost function, one that depends on the decisions of the captain

$$v(R, E) = 0.3 \text{ if } u(R, E) < u(R, F) \quad v(R, E) = 0.7 \text{ if } u(R, E) \geq u(R, F) \tag{21}$$

$$v(R, \text{acpt\_contr} : Master \times Capt) = 0.5, \tag{22}$$

for all R, where $E = \text{wait} : Master \times Capt$ and $F = \text{forw} : Capt \times Master$. The harbour master chooses to wait control if the captain is willing to continue forwards, and accepts control over waiting if the captain is not. Evidently there is game theoretic analysis to be done here, which will be considered in future work.

The trust domain can be evidenced as follows below (using location informally). The goal property is for the tug to attach to the ship (and thereafter to pull it into the harbour). This can be done at either position L_1 or position L_2. In calm seas, the captain's cost judgement will permit the making of the connection at either position L_1 or position L_2, while the harbour master will only permit it at L_2. In stormy seas, however, the captain's cost judgement permits the connection only at L_1, and the harbour master will apply different preferences in order to make the connection at L_1. Note the combination of logical properties (tug connection) and cost properties (intersection of cost boundaries of two different actors).

Contract Choices. We consider a mergers and acquisitions (M&A) deal team. One goal of such a team is to provide valuations of companies that are under consideration for mergers or acquisitions. The task requires access to very confidential details of the company being valued. Often the deal team will contract out specialized aspects of the valuation to external specialists. These contractors may have varying level of security infrastructure. One of the key risks in company valuation is data loss, and the risk is exacerbated when information is shared outside the deal group to external contractors.

Consider a scenario in which the M&A deal team has two potential contractors. The first contractor is a smaller firm that is more specialized, but as it is smaller has a less secure IT infrastructure. The M&A deal team could get a better service (e.g., more efficient, with more accurate valuation, etc.) from using this firm, but incurs more risk of data loss. The second contractor is a large firm that is more generalized, and has a more secure IT infrastructure.

We model each contractor as a process that can provide a valuation (either specialized or general) or idle. The specialized contractor, in addition, has the possibility of leaking information. We make use of the resource $data_{gen}$ to denote data when it is sent to the general contractor, and $data_{spec}$ to denote data when it is sent to the specialized contractor. Both the valuation actions and the leak action require the appropriate data resource, and are not enabled when the resource is absent. These actions ensure mutual exclusion. The general and specific contractors, respectively, are modelled as

$$Contr_{gen} = \text{gen\_val} : Contr'_{gen} + 1 : Contr_{gen}$$
$$Contr_{spec} = \text{spec\_val} : Contr'_{spec} + \text{leak} : Contr_{spec} + 1 : Contr_{spec}. \tag{23}$$

In this example, we are concerned with the choices that the deal team can make and are more interested in *what* the respective contractors can do, rather than *why* they do.

We model the deal team as a process that chooses between the two firms (or idles), and then proceeds to receive a valuation from the chosen contractor.

$$Deal = \text{enbl\_spec} : Deal' +_u \text{enbl\_gen} : Deal' +_u 1 : Deal. \tag{24}$$

The enbl_spec action produces the $data_{spec}$ resource, which enables the specialized contractor to produce a valuation, and the enbl_gen action produces the $data_{gen}$

resource, which enables the generalized contractor to produce a valuation. The whole system is then defined as

$$e, Deal \times Contr_{gen} \times Contr_{spec}. \tag{25}$$

We define the deal team's cost function u as:

$$\begin{aligned}
u(e, Contr_{gen} \times Contr_{spec} \times \text{enbl\_spec} : Deal') &= 0.7 \\
u(e, Contr_{gen} \times Contr_{spec} \times \text{enbl\_gen} : Deal') &= 0.3 \\
u(e, Contr_{gen} \times Contr_{spec} \times 1 : Deal) &= 0.
\end{aligned} \tag{26}$$

We can consider a trust domain based on the logical property $\langle \text{gen\_val} \rangle \top \vee \langle \text{spec\_val} \rangle \top$, which denotes that an evaluation (specialized or general) is provided. If we were to define a cost bound of 0.5, for example, then the general contractor would be chosen but not the specialized one, as they both provide the required service, but there is too much risk associated with the specialized contractor.

Information Provenance. One issue of particular importance, when making decisions about data sharing arrangements, is the provenance of the evidence used by the contracting company. In particular, the evidence can be categorized as verifiable, or can be taken 'on trust' (perhaps due to a history of positive interaction). The level of evidence required by a decision-maker can be mitigated using technical and social mechanisms, such as use of virtual machines (as in Contract Choices) and external certification (e.g., ISO27000 security certification). We can then consider what risks and costs can occur, given a choice of how much verifiable evidence will be required, and how much can be taken on trust (in the presence of some mitigating mechanisms).

Consider two different contractors, which a bank can choose to employ. Contractor A is safer, and can leaks can only occur in one way; we model this by saying that the $leak_A$ action is only enabled by resource r_1. Contractor D is a little less safe, and its leaks can occur in one of two ways; we model this by saying that the $leak_D$ action is enabled by either of the leak pathways, modelled as resources p_1 and p_2. We then make use of different pieces evidence, which provide different guarantees. We consider two pieces of 'trust' evidence, the first (t_1) that rules out the first type of leaks (modelled by the fact that $p_1 \circ t_1 \uparrow$), and the second (t_2) that rules out the second type of leaks (modelled by the fact that $p_2 \circ t_2 \uparrow$). We also consider a piece of 'verifiable' evidence v, that rules out both types of leaks (modelled by the fact that $p_1 \circ v \uparrow$ and $p_2 \circ v \uparrow$).

We model the bank as a process that chooses between two contractors

$$Bank = B_A +_u B_D \quad B_A = \text{chooseA} : 1 \quad B_D = \text{chooseD} : 1. \tag{27}$$

the 'chooseA' (resp. 'chooseD') action creates a token c_A (resp. c_D) that enables contractor A (resp. D) to proceed. We model the contractors as processes that can accept a contract token and then proceed to either provide a leak or possibly leak some data

$$A = \text{acpt}_A.(\text{report} : A' +_0 \text{leak}_A : A') \quad D = \text{acpt}_D.(\text{report} : D' +_0 \text{leak}_D : D'). \tag{28}$$

The report actions are the same in both cases, but 'leak' actions are different for each process. In contractor A the leak can only occur by the first pathway, which is modelled by the 'leak$_A$' action being enabled only by the resource p_1. In contractor D, however, the leak can occur by either of the pathways, which is modelled by the 'leak$_D$' action being enabled both by the resource p_1 and by the resource p_2.

We then consider different ways the the bank can value, and make use of, the evidence to which it has access. Consider one possible valuation

$$u(v, B_A \times A) = u(v, B_D \times D) = 0.1$$
$$u(t_1, B_A \times A) = u(t_1, B_D \times D) = 0.4 \qquad u(t_2, B_A \times A) = u(t_2, B_D \times D) = 0.6.$$

(29)

Here, the scenario where verifiable evidence can be obtained, to the effect that no leaks will occur (modelled as the fact that the resource v is present), has the least risk, with a cost of 0.1. The scenario where trusted evidence can be obtained to the effect that the first type of leak will not occur (modelled as the fact that the resource t_1 is present) is the next most risky, with a cost of 0.4. The scenario in which trusted evidence can be obtained that the second type of leak will not occur (modelled as the fact that the resource t_2 is present) is most risky, with a cost of 0.6.

Given this valuation we can show that errors can occur, even below the rather generous cost bound of 0.5. As the banker expects the cost of company D at 0.4, in the presence of trust guarantee t_1, it is possible to show that at least one of the two leak actions occurs within the cost bounds

$$e, B_A +_u B_D \nvDash_{C_\emptyset} (p \wedge \phi) \twoheadrightarrow ([\text{chooseA}] \, [< 0.5][\text{leak}_A]\bot \wedge [\text{chooseD}] \, [< 0.5][\text{leak}_D]\bot),$$

(30)

where p is a proposition that denotes the presence of resource t_1 and ϕ limits the processes under consideration, to be put in parallel with, to either contractor A or contractor D, modulo bisimulation.

Consider a slightly more nuanced valuation of the provenance of pieces of evidence. Perhaps, through experience, the bank comes to realize that the first trusted property t_1 is not quite so effective an indicator with respect to the second contractor. We can then define a different cost function, v, which assigns more risk to t_1 for the contractor D

$$v(v, B_D \times A) = u'(v, B_D \times D) = 0.1 \qquad v(t_1, B_D \times A) = 0.4$$
$$v(t_1, B_D \times D) = 0.5 \qquad v(t_2, B_D \times A) = u'(t_2, B_D \times D) = 0.6.$$

(31)

With this new costing, no leaks can occur within the given cost bounds:

$$e, B_A +_v B_D \vDash_{C_\emptyset} (p \wedge \phi) \twoheadrightarrow ([\text{chooseA}] \, [< 0.5][\text{leak}_A]\bot \wedge [\text{chooseD}] \, [< 0.5][\text{leak}_D]\bot).$$

(32)

7 Further Work

Further work includes extending the calculus to include probabilistic evolution and expected cost [13], thereby enriching the notion of trust domain with the ability to accommodate stochastic environments. Although we have given some quite rich examples, it remains for us to explore a meta-theoretically more systematic collection of compositional and structural properties. This work begins with an exploration of the transitivity of trust domains — suppose that agent B is within agent A's trust domain, and that agent C is within B's trust domain: how does A decide whether to trust C (e.g., in supply chains, or in outsourcing)? — and would also include a more careful distinction between intensional (as in the harbour) and extensional (as in M&A) formulations of trust domains. This work would also consider how to do substitution within trust domains in a way that preserved the selected set of contexts. One approach would be to make use of Theorem 2, which would permit us to substitute bisimilar agents and preserve the goal properties that define the trust domain.

It would also be interesting to consider whether the (pre)sheaf-theoretic semantics considered by Winskel [12] can be adapted to our calculus.

References

1. Abadi, M.: Logic in access control. In: Proc. LICS 2003, pp. 228–233. IEEE (2003)
2. Abadi, M., Burrows, M., Lampson, B., Plotkin, G.: A calculus for access control in distributed systems. ACM Trans. Prog. Langs. Sys. 15(4), 706–734 (1993)
3. Anderson, G., Collinson, M., Pym, D.: Utility-based Decision-making in Distributed Systems Modelling. In: Schipper, B.C. (ed.) Proc. 14th TARK, Chennai (2013), Computing Research Repository (CoRR): http://arxiv.org/corr/home ISBN: 978-0-615-74716-3
4. Barwise, J., Seligman, J.: Information Flow: The Logic of Distributed Systems. CUP (1997)
5. Beautement, A., Coles, R., Griffin, J., Ioannidis, C., Monahan, B., Pym, D., Sasse, A., Wonham, M.: Modelling the Human and Technological Costs and Benefits of USB Memory Stick Security. In: Johnson, M.E. (ed.) Managing Information Risk and the Economics of Security, pp. 141–163. Springer (2008)
6. Collinson, M., Monahan, B., Pym, D.: A Discipline of Mathematical Systems Modelling. College Publications (2012)
7. Coulouris, G., Dollimore, J., Kindberg, T.: Distributed Systems: Concepts and Design, 3rd edn. Addison Wesley (2000)
8. Hennessy, M.: A calculus for costed computations. Logical Methods in Computer Science 7(1), paper 9 (2011), doi:10.2168/LMCS-7(1:7)2011
9. Hennessy, M., Milner, R.: Algebraic laws for nondeterminism and concurrency. Journal of the ACM 32(1), 137–161 (1985)
10. Hennessy, M., Plotkin, G.: On observing nondeterminism and concurrency. In: de Bakker, J.W., van Leeuwen, J. (eds.) ICALP 1980. LNCS, vol. 85, pp. 299–308. Springer, Heidelberg (1980)
11. Jamroga, W.: A temporal logic for Markov chains. In: Proc. AAMAS 2008, pp. 607–704. ACM Digital Library (2008)
12. Joyal, A., Nielsen, M., Winskel, G.: Bisimulation from open maps. Information and Computation 127(2), 164–185 (1996)
13. Keeney, R., Raiffa, H.: Decisions with multiple objectives: Preferences and value tradeoffs. Wiley (1976)
14. McCarthy, J.: Formalizing context. In: IJCAI, pp. 555–562 (1993)
15. Milner, R.: Calculi for synchrony and asynchrony. Theoret. Comp. Sci. 25(3), 267–310 (1983)
16. Milner, R.: Communication and Concurrency. Prentice Hall, New York (1989)
17. O'Hearn, P., Pym, D.: The logic of bunched implications. Bulletin of Symbolic Logic 5(2), 215–244 (1999)
18. Ramchurn, S., Huynh, D., Jennings, N.: Trust in multi-agent systems. The Knowledge Engineering Review 19(1), 1–25 (2004)
19. Reynolds, J.: Separation logic: A logic for shared mutable data structures. In: Proc. 17th LICS, pp. 55–74. IEEE (2002)
20. Tofts, C.: Processes with probability, priority and time. Formal Aspects of Computing 6(5), 536–564 (1994)

"Fairly Truthful": The Impact of Perceived Effort, Fairness, Relevance, and Sensitivity on Personal Data Disclosure

Miguel Malheiros[1], Sören Preibusch[2], and M. Angela Sasse[1]

[1] University College London, Information Security Research Group
Gower Street, WC1E 6BT, London, UK
{m.malheiros,a.sasse}@cs.ucl.ac.uk
[2] Microsoft Research, 21 Station Road, CB1 2FB, Cambridge, UK
spr@microsoft.com

Abstract. While personal data is a source of competitive advantage, businesses should consider the potential reaction of individuals to certain types of data requests. Privacy research has identified some factors that impact privacy perceptions, but these have not yet been linked to actual disclosure behaviour. We describe a field-experiment investigating the effect of different factors on online disclosure behaviour. 2720 US participants were invited to participate in an Amazon Mechanical Turk survey advertised as a marketing study for a credit card company. Participants were asked to disclose several items of personal data. In a follow-up UCL branded survey, a subset (N=1851) of the same participants rated how they perceived the effort, fairness, relevance, and sensitivity of the first phase personal data requests and how truthful their answers had been. Findings show that fairness has a consistent and significant effect on the disclosure and truthfulness of data items such as weekly spending or occupation. Partial support was found for the effect of effort and sensitivity. Privacy researchers are advised to take into account the under-investigated fairness construct in their research. Businesses should focus on non-sensitive data items which are perceived as fair in the context they are collected; otherwise they risk obtaining low-quality or incomplete data from their customers.

Keywords: personal data disclosure, privacy, effort, fairness, relevance, sensitivity.

1 Managing Disclosure of Personal Data

Customers' personal data is seen as a source of competitive advantage by businesses in the information society. The low-cost of storage technologies and the increased efficiency with which large quantities of data can be transferred between systems and analysed have removed most economic disincentives for widespread data gathering efforts. At the same time, the potential benefits realisable through the processing of these data, such as better customer targeting, personalised service, or risk management, contribute to create a seemingly very attractive value

M. Huth et al. (Eds.): TRUST 2013, LNCS 7904, pp. 250–266, 2013.
© Springer-Verlag Berlin Heidelberg 2013

proposition for companies. Left out of this equation, however, is the potential negative impact of customers' behaviour when dealing with requests for their personal data that, for some reason, are deemed too unappealing to comply with. Individuals value their personal data and, if they do not consider truthful disclosure advantageous to them, they may engage in privacy protection behaviours such as withdrawal from the data collection interaction or omission or falsification of data. These behaviours can thus represent lost business opportunities or a lowering of the quality of customer data held, both of which constitute adverse economic effects for the business.

When individuals disclose their personal data to an organisation in exchange for some product or service they are engaging in a social contract; while the benefits of this contract are higher then the costs they will continue engaged [9,27]. Thus, even interactions that pose privacy risks may be accepted by individuals looking to realise a gain bigger than the perceived privacy cost [12]. In particular, several studies have shown that individuals are willing to trade their personal data for economic benefits such as money rewards (e.g., [4,11,14,15,19]). If the rewards are not considered worth the cost of disclosure, individuals may engage in privacy protection behaviours by either withholding [32] or falsifying personal data [10,22]. This can be interpreted as an attempt to minimise the costs of disclosure while still obtaining the reward. However, it is unclear how prevalent privacy protection behaviours are, or what combination of factors trigger them.

Previous privacy research has identified several factors that affect how individuals perceive the collection and use of their personal data.

Sensitivity. Individuals do not see all personal data as equally sensitive. Typically, more personally defining or identifying items, such as social security number [26], financial data [29] or medical data [1] are perceived as more sensitive; however, sensitivity assessments can vary with the situation [2]. Collection, storage, and use of more sensitive items are associated with feelings of discomfort [1] and perceptions of privacy invasion [35,36]. Consequently, individuals are more likely to omit or falsify [23,26] data they consider sensitive.

Perceived Relevance. The same data request can seem more or less acceptable, depending on the context where disclosure occurs. Being asked about cases of cancer in the family during a doctor's appointment is considered relevant, but if one was asked the same question when applying for a store's loyalty card it would be considered irrelevant and inappropriate. Relevance of a data request is related to the perceived data needs of the receiver in that context and whether the expected usage of the data is perceived as legitimate [17,24]. Lower relevance or legitimacy of a data request is associated with a higher privacy cost [3] and feelings of privacy invasion [8,36]. Lower perceived relevance of a data request has not been associated with privacy protection behaviours.

Perceived Fairness. Perceived fairness of a data requests describes the individual's belief that data being collected will be used for the purpose communicated by the data receiver, and in an ethical manner [9]. Past research has shown that when individuals believe that their personal data will be processed fairly they perceive data practices in a more positive manner [23]. Beyond privacy, perceived fairness has been associated with customer satisfaction and higher perceived service quality [9]. No research has been done on the effect of perceived fairness of data requests on disclosure behaviour. Horne et al. [18] explored the impact of the perceived difference between the value obtained by an individual and the data receiver and lying and found no effect.

Data Receiver. It is widely accepted that individuals' perceptions of data practices involving their personal details depend on the organisation with whom they are interacting [34]. However, this relationship between comfort with the data practice and organisation is not linear. While individuals usually feel more comfortable disclosing personal data to organisations with whom they have an existing and trusted relationship [1], such as an employer [35, 36], such is not the case when the data portrays the individual in a bad light. Negative data increases sensitivity when shared with close data receivers [2, 25].

Data Usage. The purpose of the data collection and the perceived use that organisation will make of their data affects individuals' privacy perceptions [1, 29]. One of the main concerns refers to secondary data use, where data that was collected in one context and for one purpose is then used to achieve a completely different goal [2, 8]. Another concern is that data is used in a way that harms the individual who disclosed it. The potential negative consequences of a disclosure can make individuals reticent to part with their personal data or make them perceive a data practice as invasive [25, 29, 35].

Effort. In addition to privacy costs there are other costs associated with disclosure, such as the effort involved in answering data requests. If a data request is difficult to answer [3] or a larger number of data items are requested [19, 28], individuals will perceive the interaction as more costly. The higher the perceived effort the more likely an individual is to withhold data [19].

Privacy Protection Behaviours in Web Forms. Previous work has shown that consumers resist to data collection via forms: Among German Web users, 25% state they have entered false data into forms [6], half of whom have faked their name or age. Unease with the amount of data collected is the main driver for users to falsify their information, followed by the attempt to escape unsolicited advertising. Faking is also observed on online social networks, in particular for younger users, although with overall lower prevalence [5]. In a survey among active social media US consumers, 88% indicated to intentionally have left information out or entered incorrect information when creating a new account at a Website—an increase by 12 percentage points compared to the previous year [21].

Contribution. While some of the factors above have been linked to privacy concerns, not all have been linked to actual privacy behaviour. Making the connection to privacy behaviour is important because past research has shown that stated privacy concern may not correspond to privacy behaviour [23, 33]. Individuals taking part in research often exhibit a social desirability bias when answering questions about personal data collection manifesting higher concerns than what their behaviour suggests. Thus, observation of actual disclosure behaviour in contextualised scenarios is a more reliable indicator than self-reported privacy attitudes. In this paper, we describe an online field-experiment on the impact of perceived effort, fairness, relevance, and sensitivity of a data request on the decision to answer the request and truthfulness of answer. We believe this is the first large-scale experimental study to quantify the impact of four factors on disclosure decision and disclosure truthfulness. We also test the impact of reciprocity, materialism, and privacy concern on amount of data disclosed.

Paper Structure. We outline our experimental hypotheses in Section 2. In Section 3 we describe our 2-phase experimental design and provide reliability statistics for the scales used. We report and discuss our sample composition, item disclosure rates by treatment, and the effect of the different factors on disclosure and truthfulness in Section 4. Section 5 presents our conclusions on the implications of our study for research and practice, limitations of our work, and directions for future research.

2   Experimental Hypotheses

Based on the analysis of past research on privacy perceptions (see Section 1), we hypothesise that some factors related to how individuals perceive data requests will influence the way they chose to respond to them. For our analysis we chose two factors which have been linked to disclosure behaviour: sensitivity and effort; and two which, to our knowledge, have only been linked to privacy attitudes: perceived relevance and fairness. We measure two different variables regarding disclosure: disclosure decision (binary variable) and self-reported truthfulness of answer (4-level scale).

We predict sensitivity and effort will have a negative effect on disclosure and truthfulness and that perceived relevance and fairness will have a positive effect on disclosure and truthfulness:

H1a: Perceived effort of a request for a data item has a negative effect on decision to disclose that item.

H1b: Perceived fairness of a request for a data item has a positive effect on decision to disclose that item.

H1c: Perceived relevance of a request for a data item has a positive effect on decision to disclose that item.

H1d: Perceived sensitivity of a request for a data item has a negative effect on decision to disclose that item.

H2a: Perceived effort of a request for a data item has a negative effect on the truthfulness of the corresponding answer.

H2b: Perceived fairness of a request for a data item has a positive effect on the truthfulness of the corresponding answer.

H2c: Perceived relevance of a request for a data item has a positive effect on the truthfulness of the corresponding answer.

H2d: Perceived sensitivity of a request for a data item has a negative effect on the truthfulness of the corresponding answer.

We further hypothesise that reciprocity and materialism will affect amount of disclosure, but not privacy concern as measured by Westin's index:

H3a: Reciprocal individuals disclose more data than non-reciprocal individuals.

H3b: Individuals more concerned about privacy do not disclose less data than individuals less concerned about privacy.

H3c: More materialistic individuals disclose less data to minimise privacy cost and maximise value of answering.

3   Experiment Methodology

3.1   Phase 1: The Platixx Web Form

In early 2013, 2720 US participants were invited through the crowdsourcing platform Amazon Mechanical Turk (mTurk) to participate in a "short survey [with] fast approval". The term "survey", commonly found on mTurk, was used although the study is indeed an experiment: participants had to disclose items of personal data rather that stating their willingness to do so. The experiment therefore uncovers actual willingness to disclose rather than self-professed preferences.

The experiment design closely follows an earlier study on voluntary data disclosure [30]. The materials were also pre-tested on 20 participants before the main deployment. A Web form with 5, 10, or 15 questions was given to the participants, depending on treatment. Some of the questions clearly relate to a banking context (e.g., income, debt situation, spending, number of credit cards), others are plausible indicators of social and demographic status (e.g., age, gender, marital status, health, education). Some questions are uncommon in banking context, such as the number of relatives who died during the childhood or the duration of the longest relationship. However, these factors have been found to be potentially good predictors of credit-worthiness [20].

In accordance with the mTurk guidelines, highly sensitive questions or questions asking for identifying personal details were not included. The order of the questions was not randomised but constant; treatments with fewer questions were truncated not to include all the items.

Across all treatments, there were also two extra mandatory check questions (6 and 7) which tested whether participants had read the instructions properly. The mandatoriness of the other questions varied by treatment, with the other 5, 10, or 15 questions being mandatory as well. If there were mandatory questions, these were always at the beginning of the form and any optional ones towards the end. The instructions, displayed at the top of the form, were adjusted accordingly. There was no visual indicator of mandatoriness (such as starring or highlighting) and the blocks of questions were not separated. All questions were answered using free text fields. There was no warning if some mandatory items had been omitted or if the answer did not match the required format (e.g., no input validation for date of birth).

In total, a 3×4 full triangular design with 9 treatments was run, covering all combinations of question count ($X = 5, 10, 15$) and subset cardinality of mandatory items ($Y = 0, 5, 10, 15$)—excluding the check questions from now onwards. Throughout the remainder of the paper, the following short-hand will be used to refer to the different treatments: qXmY, where X is the total number of questions and Y is the number of mandatory questions amongst those.[1]

The Web form was framed as a preparation for the launch of a new credit card product—the Platixx Card. To gauge the potential interest in this new scheme, Platixx would ask participants to complete a one-page online survey. Using a professionally designed logo and colour scheme, all materials, including the Website URL, were prominently branded as Platixx, a fictitious banking provider.

Participants received 20, 40 or 60 US cents for submitting the form in treatments q5, q10 and q15 respectively. This payment acts as a show-up fee and increased linearly in question count. All participants were paid regardless of whether or not they had complied with the instructions or answered the check questions correctly. As stated in the instructions, no extra payments were made for voluntary over-disclosure. Multiple participation was prevented.

3.2   Phase 2: The UCL Follow-Up Questionnaire

After submitting their Web form, participants were invited to a follow-up questionnaire to investigate personality traits, demographics and privacy preferences. Checks were in place to make sure that this questionnaire could only be taken

---

[1] For instance, treatment q5m0 said: "Please provide some information about yourself. Questions 6 to 7 are mandatory. All other fields are optional. There is no bonus for this HIT." whereas treatment q10m10 said: "Please provide some information about yourself. Questions 1 to 12 are mandatory. There is no bonus for this HIT.".

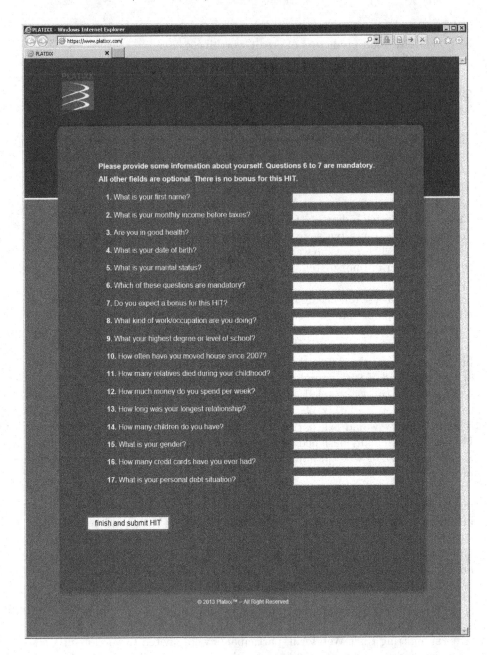

Fig. 1. Screenshot of the Platixx Web form in phase 1, treatment q15m0

by those who had participated in the first phase (Section 3.1). Two days after
the initial invitation, one reminder was sent to those who had not yet taken the
follow-up. Across all treatments, a 79% of all phase 1 participants also completed
the follow-up survey.

The follow-up was soliciting critical feedback regarding phase 1, including participants' admission to have lied on some questions. To avoid participants giving socially desirable answers, there was a break in the administering party: the follow-up questionnaire was branded as a research study by UCL. The colour scheme and logo differed markedly from the first phase. The purpose was to build trust to induce respondents to answer truthfully. Furthermore, participants were assured that their answers would be kept confidential, and not shared with Platixx. This assurance was re-iterated during the questionnaire whenever sensitive demographic details were solicited, including income, age and gender.

For each question participants had been asked in phase 1 they were asked to rate the perceived effort involved in answering (Cronbach's alpha across all items was $\alpha = 0.91$), its fairness ($\alpha = 0.88$), its relevance ($\alpha = 0.84$), and how truthfully they had answered the question ($\alpha = 0.95$). For 36 general items sensitivity ratings (i.e.: level of comfort with disclosure) were collected ($\alpha = 0.84$). Out of these 36 items, 8 closely matched items collected in phase 1 of the study. An average of the perceived sensitivity of these 36 items was used as a measure of privacy concern, with higher sensitivity averages corresponding to higher levels of concern.

Personality traits were investigated using instruments with established reliability. For measuring materialistic values, the validated 18-item Richins-Dawson scale was used [31]. Reliability was good (Cronbach's alpha $\alpha = 0.89$). Reciprocity was measured on a 6-item, 7-point Likert scale [13] ($\alpha = 0.60$). Privacy attitudes were assessed using the 3-item Westin scale [16], which binned participants into three groups ($\alpha = 0.70$). Using the original terminology, 41% were classified as "privacy fundamentalists", 48% as "privacy pragmatists" and 11% as "privacy unconcerned". According to this segmentation, the participants would have been much more concerned about data protection issues than the general public. Owing to its brevity and its prior use in similar studies, the Westin scale was chosen despite its methodological shortcomings.

3.3 Ethical Approval

Both phases of this study were granted permission to be conducted after going through the university's ethical review process.

3.4 Data Processing and Coding

All answers were manually coded by a single skilled rater into three categories: provided, not provided or refusal. Examples of refusals are: "A lady doesn't reveal her age" or simply nonsense text. Additional data coding was done for some input fields, such as date of birth. In the following analysis, only participants who answered both check questions correctly will be included.

4 Results and Discussion

Across all treatments, there are 2360 valid participants, 1851 of whom also completed the follow-up questionnaire. Table 1 summarises the sub-sample sizes for the different treatments. Explicit refusals to answer and omissions were coded together, so that, for each participant, an item was considered either disclosed or not-disclosed. Based on the information provided in the follow-up, the mean age of participants was 30 years (range from 17 to 80). For 1477 participants, both date of birth from the first phase and age from the follow-up were disclosed and were compared. For 1164 participants (78.8%) there was no discrepancy between the two. Mean discrepancy was 3.43 years. 41% of respondents were women, 59% men according to the follow-up. Less than 1% refused to reveal their gender. For 641 participants there was also gender data available from the first phase questionnaire. When comparing the two gender disclosures only 17 participants (2.7%) disclosed different genders in the first phase and follow-up

4.1   Focus on q15 Treatments

As shown in the top half of Table 1, there is an overriding effect of items being mandatory on disclosure rates. While we plan to explore the mandatory vs. optional relationship with disclosure behaviour in a future publication, in this paper we focus on the effect of perceived fairness, relevance, sensitivity, and effort. Our disclosure analysis here is of the q15m0 treatment, where answers to all data requests are optional. We focus on q15m0 as opposed to q5m0 or q10m0 because it offers a wider range of data items to analyse and identify differences. When investigating the effect of the different factors on truthfulness (Section 4.5), we use all q15 treatments as we do not expect mandatory vs. optional to have an overriding effect. When reporting descriptive statistics for the ratings of perceived fairness, relevance, effort, and sensitivity of data items (Section 4.3) we use data from all nine treatments for the same reason.

4.2   Effect of Personality Traits on Disclosure

We regressed the number of items disclosed by participant on their normalised scores for reciprocity and materialism and Westin category (coded as two dummy binary variables: fundamentalist and pragmatist). We found that only reciprocity was a significant predictor ($\beta = 0.175$, $p < 0.05$) of number of items disclosed. Whether the participant was a fundamentalist ($\beta = 0.014$, n.s.) or pragmatist ($\beta = 0.053$, n.s.), and level of materialism ($\beta = 0.048$, n.s.) were not significant predictors. The overall model fit was $R^2 = 0.042$.

Reciprocity did have a significant and positive effect on disclosure with more reciprocal participants disclosing more data. Since all the data requests were optional and a reward would be offered unconditionally, it is possible more reciprocal participants felt more obliged to disclose data. The absence of effect of Westin category on behaviour was expected, as there is little evidence that this scale is a good predictor of privacy behaviour and attitudes (see, for example, [7]). The data supports both **H3a** and **H3b**. It was expected that participants who scored higher in the materialism scale would be less likely to disclose data to maximise the value of answering the survey (they would have received a full payment even if no personal data was disclosed), but that was not the case. **H3c** was not supported.

We also regressed number of items disclosed on age and gender but found no significant effect of either variable. Finally, we also regressed the same outcome variable on the average perceived sensitivity across 36 items measured on a 5 level scale by itself. We found it to be a significant predictor ($\beta = -3.212$, $p < 0.01$). The overall fit of this model was $R^2 = 0.056$. This finding suggests that gathering perceived sensitivity ratings across a range of personal data items is a better measure of privacy concern and a better predictor of disclosure behaviour than privacy indices such as Westin's.

4.3 Perceived Effort, Fairness, Relevance, and Sensitivity of Data Requests

The bottom half of Table 1 summarises the average perceived effort, fairness, and relavance ratings for all questions across all treatments. All items have negative effort ratings, indicating a perceived low level of effort when answering the questions. Gender, children count, and marital status were considered the easiest questions to answer, which makes intuitive sense since these questions do not seem to imply any calculations or memory effort. Weekly spending, childhood deaths, and monthly income were considered the hardest questions to answer. While weekly spending and childhood deaths do require participants to recall past events and make some calculations, monthly income should, in theory, be easy to recall. It is possible that some participants do not receive their salaries monthly, so have to compute the value to answer the question. In any case, no questions were considered difficult to answer.

Childhood deaths, relationship max length, and good health were perceived as the most unfair questions. The first two, in particular, were perceived quite negatively. One possible explanation is that it may be difficult for participants to understand how these items will be used, and to imagine a fair use of such data. First name, occupation, and monthly income were considered the fairest questions. Both first name and occupation are common questions in surveys. Monthly income is not commonly asked, but possibly due to its also high perceived relevance participant thought it fair to ask in this context.

The items considered most unfair were also the ones considered most irrelevant in the context of a credit card company survey. It seems legitimate to believe participants saw no connection between these questions and the specified purpose of the survey. The items perceived as most relevant were monthly income, debt situation, and credit card count. These are all questions related to financial matters and, therefore, aligned with the context of data collection.

Sensitivity ratings were collected for 36 items, of which 8 closely match items collected in phase 1 of the study. *Annual income* was considered to be an acceptable proxy of *monthly income* and *illnesses* as an acceptable proxy of *good health*.

Unsurprisingly, illness and annual income were considered the most sensitive items. Past research has shown that medical and financial data are usually considered sensitive by individuals. The least sensitive items were gender and education. Both of these questions are commonly asked in surveys for demographics purposes, so it is likely participants are used to them and consider them not sensitive.

4.4 Effect of Fairness, Relevance, Sensitivity, and Effort on Disclosure

The top section of Table 2 shows the models obtained by regressing disclosure of each data item (as a binary variable) on perceived effort, fairness, relevance, and sensitivity (when applicable) of that data item. The models explain between 7% and 20% of the variability in disclosure decision.

Fairness is clearly the most powerful predictor of disclosure decision, with a significant positive effect on the outcome in 11 out of 15 cases, supporting **H1b**. For four data items, fairness has no significant effect: monthly income, health, credit-card count and debt situation. With the exception of health, these are all items with high perceived relevance to the context of credit cards. We suspect fairness may be more important when data requests are considered irrelevant. Perceived fairness of a data request is an under-researched factor in privacy research and has never been linked to disclosure behaviour. Here it emerges as a promising predictor of privacy decision making.

Sensitivity is a significant negative predictor of disclosure for 3 out 8 items: first name, date of birth, and occupation. **H1d** is thus partially supported. The effect of data sensitivity on disclosure decision has been previously observed in the literature [23, 26].

Relevance has a significant effect on the disclosure of 3 data items, but this effect is unexpectedly negative. Similarly, effort coefficients are significant for 3 data items, but positive contrary to out predictions. It is possible that participants who did not answer a question rated it as requiring low effort precisely because they did not answer it. Meanwhile, participants who disclosed the data may have reported a higher effort. Both **H1c** and **H1a** are rejected.

4.5 Effect of Fairness, Relevance, Sensitivity, and Effort on Truthfulness

Truthfulness ratings of each item (a 4-level scale ranging from -2=Completely disagree my answer was truthful to +2=Completely agree my answer was truthful) were regressed on perceived effort, fairness, relevance, and sensitivity (when applicable) of that item. The resulting regression models for each item can be seen in the bottom section of Table 2. The models explain between 10% and 26% of the variability in truthfulness.

Fairness is once again the best predictor, with a significant positive effect on truthfulness on the same 11 items as in the disclosure regressions, supporting **H2b**. Fairness has a particular and significant strong effect in items with low relevance such as relationship max length or childhood deaths, again suggesting that fairness has bigger important when data requests are seen as irrelavant.

Table 1. Sample sizes by treatment, as the total number of participants (N) and the number of those who answered the check questions correctly (N_{valid}); amongst the latter, proportions of participants who provided the given data item. Bold numbers indicate that the question was mandatory in this treatment. The lower part of the table gives the feedback descriptives across all treatments (valid cases only) for item effort, fairness, relevance and sensitivity. Effort, fairness, and relevance were measured on a 4-level agreement scale ranging from -2 (strongly disagree that the question was hard, fair, and relevant) to $+2$ (strongly agree that the question was hard, fair, and relevant). Sensitivity was measured on a 4-level scale ranging from 1 (very happy to disclose) to 4 (very unhappy to disclose). Thus, higher ratings correspond to higher sensitivity. Ratings are only available for a subset of data items; for income and health, happiness to provide annual income and illnesses was asked for, respectively.

treatment	N	N_{valid}	first name	monthly income	good health	date of birth	marital status	occupation	education	times moved	childhood deaths	weekly spending	relationship max length	children count	gender	credit-card count	debt situation
q5m0	300	258	61.6	57.8	74.0	58.1	72.5										
q5m5	300	271	**99.3**	**99.3**	**100.0**	**99.6**	**99.6**										
q10m0	300	262	69.5	60.3	77.1	59.9	76.7	70.2	71.0	69.1	61.8	53.1					
q10m5	300	254	**99.2**	**98.8**	**100.0**	**100.0**	**100.0**	64.6	66.5	62.6	57.9	53.5					
q10m10	300	257	**99.2**	**98.1**	**100.0**	**98.4**	**99.6**	**98.8**	**99.6**	**98.8**	**98.1**	**96.9**					
q15m0	320	279	64.5	64.9	75.3	57.0	74.2	67.0	71.0	67.0	60.2	54.5	61.3	67.4	72.4	65.9	56.6
q15m5	300	253	**99.2**	**98.0**	**99.2**	**98.8**	**99.2**	69.2	70.4	67.2	62.1	51.4	61.3	66.0	67.6	63.2	53.4
q15m10	300	258	**98.4**	**100.0**	**100.0**	**100.0**	**100.0**	**100.0**	**100.0**	**100.0**	**99.6**	**95.0**	71.3	77.5	78.3	76.7	66.7
q15m15	300	268	**97.0**	**98.5**	**100.0**	**100.0**	**100.0**	**99.3**	**99.6**	**99.3**	**99.6**	**95.1**	**93.3**	**99.3**	**98.9**	**97.8**	**95.9**

feedback

		first name	monthly income	good health	date of birth	marital status	occupation	education	times moved	childhood deaths	weekly spending	relationship max length	children count	gender	credit-card count	debt situation
Effort	mean	-1.47	-0.81	-1.29	-1.27	-1.50	-1.43	-1.49	-1.19	-0.70	-0.56	-1.13	-1.56	-1.65	-1.19	-0.96
	s	0.99	1.29	1.06	1.18	0.91	0.97	0.93	1.17	1.46	1.43	1.26	0.90	0.82	1.23	1.37
Fairness	mean	1.37	1.15	0.29	1.14	1.00	1.22	0.86	0.57	-0.98	0.51	-0.81	0.39	0.91	1.04	0.92
	s	0.93	1.02	1.44	1.09	1.16	0.99	1.23	1.34	1.31	1.35	1.42	1.43	1.35	1.19	1.28
Relevance	mean	0.92	1.35	-0.52	1.09	0.64	1.08	0.39	-0.01	-1.58	0.58	-1.42	0.05	0.44	1.11	1.16
	s	1.35	0.92	1.42	1.14	1.35	1.13	1.41	1.44	0.94	1.39	1.08	1.50	1.55	1.20	1.18
Sensitivity	mean	2.12	2.62	2.70	2.52	1.84	1.98	1.77						1.63		
	s	0.89	0.86	0.97	0.94	0.74	0.78	0.70						0.66		

Table 2. Item disclosure (upper part) and item truthfulness rating (lower part) regressed on item perceived effort, fairness, relevance, and sensitivity ratings. Sensitivity is only included in the regression model when applicable to that data item. Nagelkerke's R^2 was used to assess model fit. *significant at $p = 0.05$; **significant at $p = 0.01$; ***significant at $p = 0.005$

Item	R^2	Effort	Fairness	Relevance	Sensitivity	Constant
			item disclosure			
first name	0.174	0.056	0.624**	−0.342*	−0.655***	1.407
monthly income	0.085	0.051	0.063	0.398	−0.193	0.517
good health	0.069	0.188	0.217	−0.132	−0.331	1.736
date of birth	0.206	−0.049	0.586*	−0.304	−0.723***	1.896
marital status	0.101	0.330*	0.388*	−0.032	−0.103	0.510
occupation	0.149	0.129	0.728***	−0.448*	−0.597***	1.326
education	0.125	0.296*	0.484**	−0.173	−0.359	0.789
times moved	0.099	0.022	0.565***	−0.296*	n/a	0.317
childhood deaths	0.153	−0.178	0.685***	−0.312	n/a	0.750
weekly spending	0.108	−0.154	0.381*	0.012	n/a	0.101
relationship max length	0.135	−0.067	0.588***	−0.060	n/a	1.090
children count	0.089	0.175	0.400*	−0.071	n/a	0.403
gender	0.121	0.344*	0.497**	−0.297	−0.329	0.720
credit-card count	0.089	0.027	0.423	0.006	n/a	0.163
debt situation	0.063	−0.047	0.375	−0.028	n/a	−0.008
			item truthfulness			
first name	0.096	0.005	0.384**	−0.189*	−0.355***	1.416
monthly income	0.097	−0.082	−0.082	0.475***	−0.181	0.921
good health	0.096	0.013	0.098	0.124	−0.244**	1.817
date of birth	0.259	−0.032	0.431***	−0.048	−0.613***	1.910
marital status	0.153	0.118	0.361***	0.003	−0.229	1.096
occupation	0.209	−0.034	0.442***	0.077	−0.285**	1.192
education	0.149	0.020	0.339***	−0.010	−0.301**	1.469
times moved	0.188	0.028	0.580***	−0.183*	n/a	0.636
childhood deaths	0.137	−0.146*	0.487***	−0.188	n/a	1.030
weekly spending	0.140	−0.141*	0.285*	0.120	n/a	0.472
relationship max length	0.154	−0.057	0.500***	−0.065	n/a	1.215
children count	0.118	0.032	0.413***	−0.074	n/a	0.885
gender	0.139	0.095	0.307***	−0.013	−0.267*	1.335
credit card count	0.147	−0.050	0.312	0.192	n/a	0.457
debt situation	0.105	−0.032	0.066	0.368*	n/a	0.309

The truthfulness regressions support the idea that fairness is a strong predictor of privacy decision-making.

Sensitivity is a significant negative predictor of disclosure for 6 items out 8 where it is applicable, supporting **H2d**. Effort coefficients are significant and negative for 2 data items, offering partial support to **H2a**. Taking into account past research, the negative effects of sensitivity and effort (partially supported by the data) were expected [23, 26].

Relevance coefficients are significant in 3 models, but unexpectedly negative in two of them. Only for monthly income truthfulness is the effect positive. Thus, **H2c** is rejected.

5   Conclusions

Detailed personal data from their customers can help companies to gain insights to improve their services, differentiate their products or adapt their pricing regimes. These competitive advantages have to be weighed against consumers' concern for privacy. Previous research has shown that web users are put off by websites asking personal information that they are unwilling to provide. Many web users admit having provided deliberately wrong data on a web form. Conversely, high prevalence of voluntary over-disclosure has been observed in experimental studies with up to 2/3 of online users volunteering sensitive information, such as date of birth. So far, little has been known about the drivers and inhibitors that make users disclose, respectively withhold or falsify personal data on Web forms.

Our large-scale experiment now provides first insights into the determinants of consumers' willingness to disclose personal data on the web. Four factors were hypothesised to influence user behaviour: perceived effort, relevance, fairness and sensitivity. These factors were tested in administering a web form to 2720 web users, who were asked to provide 15 personal details including financial and health information in preparation for the launch of a new credit-card scheme. The visual appearance of the form provided a highly realistic framing. Participants' disclosure behaviour was then contrasted with their judgements of each of the questions on the form, as collected through a follow-up questionnaire.

Unless a field is mandatory, fairness has a significant, consistent positive effect on the disclosure and truthfulness of the response. Fairness is crucial in driving disclosure for all data items, except for those that are obviously relevant for the purpose of the form (in this case of a credit-card scheme: monthly income, health, credit-card count and debt situation). In parallel, there is a significant positive effect of perceived fairness on the truthfulness of the responses. Perceived fairness is particularly influential and very highly significant for seemingly irrelevant data items such as the length of the longest relationship or the number of deaths during one's childhood. No significant support was found for the effect of relevance on disclosure or truthfulness. Perceived effort had a positive effect on disclosure for three items, possibly due to participants who disclosed an item rating it as requiring more effort than the ones who did not. A negative effect of effort on truthfulness was expected, but only found in three items. Partial support was found for the effect of sensitivity: first name, date of birth and occupation disclosure was significantly affected by their sensitivity. For 6 out of 8 data items, lower sensitivity was significantly associated with more truthful answers.

The managerial implications of this experiment are two-fold. First, website operators should capitalise on the positive impact of perceived fairness. If users are convinced it is fair for a web form to ask for certain information, they will be less likely to withhold these details or give false information. This holds regardless of the sensitivity of a data item. Second, past research may over-estimated the importance of perceived relevance. A positive effect on disclosure was only observed for a few data items. In parallel, fairness has not received the attention it deserves in privacy research and offers strong and consistent predictive power of privacy decision-making.

This study opens several new research avenues. In particular, the interplay between optional and mandatory fields in a web form warrants further investigation. It would also be helpful to test the robustness of the results across different contexts. The current study was set in a financial context which is familiar to most consumers. Individuals also have a more or less accurate perception of what information is relevant to the financial industry. Studying disclosure in more hedonistic applications, such as gaming or social networking, would provide a different perspective. Future work should also remedy the limitations of this work. Although mTurk has been found to feature diverse socio-economic backgrounds, users of this platform may be more inclined to volunteer personal data. There may also be a bias from the research-like character of the study, although efforts were made to create a realistic, commercial framing. One way of overcoming these biases may be field observations of user behaviour on popular web forms in the wild.

References

1. Ackerman, M.S., Cranor, L.F., Reagle, J.: Privacy in e-commerce: examining user scenarios and privacy preferences. In: Proceedings of the 1st ACM Conference on Electronic Commerce, EC 1999, pp. 1–8. ACM, New York (1999)
2. Adams, A., Angela Sasse, M.: Privacy in multimedia communications: Protecting users, not just data. In: Blandford, A., Vanderdonckt, J., Gray, P. (eds.) People and Computers XV: Interaction without Frontiers, pp. 49–64. Springer, London (2001)
3. Annacker, D., Spiekermann, S., Strobel, M.: E-privacy: Evaluating a new search cost in online environments. SFB 373 Discussion Papers 2001,80, Humboldt University of Berlin, Interdisciplinary Research Project 373: Quantification and Simulation of Economic Processes (2001)
4. Beresford, A.R., Kübler, D., Preibusch, S.: Unwillingness to pay for privacy: A field experiment. Economics Letters 117(1), 25–27 (2012)
5. BITKOM: 12 Millionen Deutsche machen Falschangaben im Web (2010), http://www.bitkom.org/62107_62102.aspx
6. BITKOM: Jedes vierte Mitglied flunkert in sozialen Netzwerken (2011), http://www.bitkom.org/de/presse/70864_67989.aspx
7. Consolvo, S., Smith, I.E., Matthews, T., LaMarca, A., Tabert, J., Powledge, P.: Location disclosure to social relations: why, when, & what people want to share. In: Proceedings of the SIGCHI Conference on Human Factors in Computing Systems, CHI 2005, pp. 81–90. ACM, New York (2005)

8. Culnan, M.J.: "How did they get my name?": An exploratory investigation of consumer attitudes toward secondary information use. MIS Quarterly 17(3), 341–363 (1993)
9. Culnan, M.J., Armstrong, P.K.: Information privacy concerns, procedural fairness, and impersonal trust: An empirical investigation. Organization Science 10(1), 104–115 (1999)
10. Culnan, M.J., Milne, G.R.: The Culnan-Milne survey on consumers & online privacy notices (2001)
11. Cvrcek, D., Kumpost, M., Matyas, V., Danezis, G.: A study on the value of location privacy. In: Proceedings of the 5th ACM Workshop on Privacy in Electronic Society, WPES 2006, pp. 109–118. ACM, New York (2006)
12. Dinev, T., Hart, P.: An extended privacy calculus model for e-commerce transactions. Information Systems Research 17(1), 61–80 (2006)
13. Gerlitz, J.Y., Schupp, J.: Zur Erhebung der Big-Five-basierten Persönlichkeitsmerkmale im SOEP. Research notes, DIW Berlin (2005)
14. Grossklags, J., Acquisti, A.: When 25 cents is too much: An experiment on willingness-to-sell and willingness-to-protect personal information. In: Proceedings of the Sixth Workshop on the Economics of Information Security (WEIS 2007) (2007)
15. Hann, I.H., Hui, K.L., Lee, T., Png, I.: Online information privacy: Measuring the cost-benefit trade-off. In: Applegate, L., Galliers, R.D., DeGross, J.I. (eds.) Proceedings of the Twenty-Third International Conference on Information Systems, p. paper 1 (2002)
16. Harris, Associates Inc., Westin, A.: E-commerce and privacy: What net users want. Privacy and American Business and Pricewaterhouse Coopers LLP (1998)
17. Hine, C.: Privacy in the marketplace. The Information Society 14(4), 253–262 (1998)
18. Horne, D.R., Norberg, P.A., Ekin, A.C.: Exploring consumer lying in information-based exchanges. Journal of Consumer Marketing 24(2), 90–99 (2007)
19. Hui, K.L., Teo, H.H., Lee, S.Y.T.: The value of privacy assurance: An exploratory field experiment. MIS Quarterly 31(1), 19–33 (2007)
20. Hunt, J., Fry, B.: Spendsmart. Piatkus Books (2009)
21. Janrain: Research study: Consumer perceptions of online registration and social sign-in (2011)
22. Lwin, M., Williams, J.: A model integrating the multidimensional developmental theory of privacy and theory of planned behavior to examine fabrication of information online. Marketing Letters 14(4), 257–272 (2003)
23. Malheiros, M., Brostoff, S., Jennett, C., Sasse, M.A.: Would you sell your mother's data? personal data disclosure in a simulated credit card application. In: 11th Annual Workshop on the Economic of Information Security (WEIS 2012) (2012)
24. Malheiros, M., Jennett, C., Patel, S., Brostoff, S., Sasse, M.A.: Too close for comfort: A study of the effectiveness and acceptability of rich-media personalized advertising. In: Proceedings of the SIGCHI Conference on Human Factors in Computing Systems, CHI 2012, pp. 579–588. ACM, New York (2012)
25. Malheiros, M., Jennett, C., Seager, W., Sasse, M.A.: Trusting to learn: Trust and privacy issues in serious games. In: McCune, J.M., Balacheff, B., Perrig, A., Sadeghi, A.-R., Sasse, A., Beres, Y. (eds.) Trust 2011. LNCS, vol. 6740, pp. 116–130. Springer, Heidelberg (2011)
26. Metzger, M.J.: Communication privacy management in electronic commerce. Journal of Computer-Mediated Communication 12(2), 335–361 (2007)

27. Milne, G.R., Gordon, M.E.: Direct mail privacy-efficiency trade-offs within an implied social contract framework. Journal of Public Policy & Marketing 12(2), 206–215 (1993)
28. Miltgen, C.: Customers' privacy concerns and responses toward a request for personal data on the internet: an experimental study. Tech. Rep. 369 (2007)
29. Phelps, J., Nowak, G., Ferrell, E.: Privacy concerns and consumer willingness to provide personal information. Journal of Public Policy & Marketing 19(1), 27–41 (2000)
30. Preibusch, S., Krol, K., Beresford, A.R.: The privacy economics of voluntary over-disclosure in web forms. In: The Eleventh Workshop on the Economics of Information Security (WEIS) (2012)
31. Richins, M.L., Dawson, S.: A consumer values orientation for materialism and its measurement: Scale development and validation. Journal of Consumer Research: An Interdisciplinary Quarterly 19(3), 303–316 (1992)
32. Sheehan, K.B., Hoy, M.G.: Flaming, complaining, abstaining: How online users respond to privacy concerns. Journal of Advertising 28(3), 37–51 (1999)
33. Spiekermann, S., Grossklags, J., Berendt, B.: E-privacy in 2nd generation e-commerce: Privacy preferences versus actual behavior. In: Proceedings of the 3rd ACM Conference on Electronic Commerce, EC 2001, pp. 38–47. ACM, New York (2001)
34. Stone, E.F., Gueutal, H.G., Gardner, D.G., McClure, S.: A field experiment comparing information-privacy values, beliefs, and attitudes across several types of organizations. Journal of Applied Psychology 68, 459–468 (1983)
35. Tolchinsky, P.D., McCuddy, M.K., Adams, J., Ganster, D.C., Woodman, R.W., Fromkin, H.L.: Employee perceptions of invasion of privacy: A field simulation experiment. Journal of Applied Psychology 66(3), 308–313 (1981)
36. Woodman, R.W., Ganster, D.C., Adams, J., McCuddy, M.K., Tolchinsky, P.D., Fromkin, H.: A survey of employee perceptions of information privacy in organizations. Academy of Management Journal 25(3), 647–663 (1982)

Formal Evaluation of Persona Trustworthiness with EUSTACE

(Extended Abstract)

Shamal Faily, David Power, Philip Armstrong, and Ivan Fléchais

Department of Computer Science, University of Oxford
Oxford UK OX1 3QD
firstname.lastname@cs.ox.ac.uk

Abstract. Personas are useful for considering how users of a system might behave, but problematic when accounting for hidden behaviours not obvious from their descriptions alone. Formal methods can potentially identify such subtleties in interactive systems, but we lack methods for eliciting models from qualitative persona descriptions. We present a framework for eliciting and specifying formal models of persona behaviour that a persona might, in certain circumstances, engage in. We also summarise our preliminary work to date evaluating this framework.

1 Motivation

Personas —narrative descriptions of fictional users based on archetypical user behaviour — are commonly used when building interactive systems [1]. However, many insights about these personas may be hidden in these description or related qualitiative data. When properly identified and analysed, this data might suggest untrustworthy behaviour that personas might engage in. Unfortunately, the volume of data underpinning personas means we cannot rely on casual inspection alone to find such behaviour. Moreover, given that personas are grounded in qualitative data, devising formal models of interactive behaviour that software tools can verify is difficult.

Although usually used as a verification technique, Communicating Sequential Processes (CSP) [2] has also been used for modelling patterns of interaction at higher levels of abstraction. It is precise enough for its specifications to be formally checked, yet also expressive enough to deal with the nuances of human interactions. Jirotka and Luff [3] have demonstrated how CSP can be used for modelling and reasoning about interactions and behavioural norms associated with multiple people. Using model checking technology, it is possible to verify such interactional specifications modelled in CSP to determine whether these are valid refinements of a secure system specification. Deriving behavioural characteristics of personas using such refinements should allow us to investigate whether their behaviour satisfies a system's safety and liveness properties, or are free from divergent behaviour; this may indicate behaviour that betrays the trust placed by the system on the user.

M. Huth et al. (Eds.): TRUST 2013, LNCS 7904, pp. 267–268, 2013.

2   Approach and Preliminary Results

We devised the EUSTACE (Evaluating the Usability, Security, and Trustworthiness of Ad-hoc Collaborative Environments) framework to formally identify untrustworthy behaviour hidden in persona descriptions. This entails checking whether CSP descriptions of persona behaviour are valid refinements of a CSP system specification. To apply the EUSTACE framework, we carry out four steps. First, we create an initial CSP system specification satisfying an agreed requirements of interest. Second, using the Persona Case framework [4], we code persona data based on the specified events, and elicit new events that personas might engage in. Coding is guided by Riegelsberger's trusted interaction framework[5], which provides sensitising questions about intrinsic and contextual trust properties. We also draw relationships between codes which, in turn, may lead to the elicitation of new codes in addition to relationships between existing ones. Third, cogent fragments of persona behaviour elicited from these relationships are annotated using CSP process descriptions. Finally, to evaluate whether persona behaviour in a specific context diverges from the system's intended behaviour, these implied descriptions are refinement checked against the system specification. These disparate CSP descriptions are combined based on specific context events of interest present in the individual implied specifications.

We extended the open-source Computer Aided Integration of Requirements and Information Security (CAIRIS) requirements management tool to support the first three steps of the EUSTACE framework. We have also built an interface to the FDR model checker to automate refinement checking against the implied specifications generated by CAIRIS. We have validated the feasibility of the framework by analysing personas of application developers and end-users to identify ways installing apps on mobile phones might be exploited.

Acknowledgements. The research was funded by the EPSRC *EUSTACE* project (R24401/GA001).

References

1. Cooper, A.: The Inmates Are Running the Asylum: Why High Tech Products Drive Us Crazy and How to Restore the Sanity, 2nd edn. Pearson (1999)
2. Hoare, C.A.R.: Communicating sequential processes. Prentice-Hall, Inc. (1985)
3. Jirotka, M., Luff, P.: Representing and modeling collaborative practices for systems development. In: Social Thinking–Software Practice. MIT Press (2002)
4. Faily, S., Fléchais, I.: Persona cases: a technique for grounding personas. In: Proceedings of the 29th International Conference on Human Factors in Computing Systems, pp. 2267–2270. ACM (2011)
5. Riegelsberger, J., Sasse, M.A., McCarthy, J.D.: The mechanics of trust: A framework for research and design. International Journal of Human Computer Studies 62, 381–422 (2005)

Identity Implies Trust in Distributed Systems – A Novel Approach

(Extended Abstract)

Lyzgeo Merin Koshy, Marc Conrad, Mitul Shukla, and Tim French

University of Bedfordshire, Computer Science Department
Park square, Luton, Bedfordshire, LU1 3JU, UK
firstname.lastname@beds.ac.uk

Abstract. Distributed software systems comprise a decentralized network topography wherein a collection of autonomous computers communicate with each other by exchanging messages [1]. The internet (Web 2.0) and social networks and immersive virtual worlds (VW) are the focus of our research. Distributed systems embed a variety of applications that seek to disclose, partially or fully obfuscate an individual's identity ranging from "role play" VW, social networking to various forms of B2C, B2B, on-line auctions (EBay) and ubiquitous B2B e-commerce transaction via electronic payment. Trust and identity management are inherent phenomena of most if not all forms of such distributed web-based systems. This research seeks to investigate how the role of identity impacts upon trust and e-trust in distributed systems.

Trust is seen as a heterogeous phenomenon affecting users in such environments. According to Taddeo [2], e-trust is understood as a relation that holds when the trustor relies on the trustee to perform a given action to a given level of quality. This research will help to comprehend how trust is formed between two strangers from the identity portrayed in distributed systems. Preliminary results show that there is a relationship between an individual's identity and their trustworthiness with another user. Should users trust each other? In the context of cyber-stalking (June 2008), a middle aged woman was charged for cyber bullying a 13 year old girl who later went on and took her own life [3]. Could this have been avoided? Other types of cyber criminal activity commonly operating within in such environment includes: pedophilia, identity theft, blackmailing and many more. This shows that individuals are abusing web 2.0 social networks, hence raises issues of serious concern in relation to trust and identity misuse.

To fully explicate the relationship between identity and trust, we need to thoroughly understand the nature of identity, self-perceptions and expression in a world increasingly dominated by human-computer-device communication of many kinds. Indeed a world in which a hybrid form of reality and virtual reality is emerging (Google glasses, Second Life avatars, social networks). Identity and identity management can be split into two broad categories, "Self" and "social identity". Self identity is how one perceives themselves and social identity is seen as others perception of us. Misinterpretation of identity and trustworthiness is seen as a serious concern. Communication between strangers is common

M. Huth et al. (Eds.): TRUST 2013, LNCS 7904, pp. 269–270, 2013.

even in real life. However, in distributed systems, limited controls are in place. Does having better controls contribute towards the establishment of trust?

By taking all the mentioned risks into consideration, it is important to find a solution. The main purpose of this research is to provide a framework on identity management in Distributed Software Systems and to provide practical guidelines and processes for managing identity and trust based on a philosophical and ethical underpinning.

Experiments were designed to investigate the relationship between identity and trust on social networking websites (Facebook) and VW (such as Second Life). An OpenSim based experiment comprised of participants being interrogated on the portrayed identity in the avatar created. Questions such as, "Are you portraying yourself?" or "Why have you chosen this avatar?" were asked. The results were analyzed and show the privacy concerns in these VW's. This experiment also shows the % of fabricated identities is higher than replicated identities. Another experiment will be conducted using Facebook profiles to investigate how identity and trust are related as the first experiment was inconclusive in this matter. This experiment should also investigate the main attributes that formulate an individual's identity and show how those attributes help to form trust.

References

1. Li, H., Singal, M.: Trust Management in Distributed Systems (2007)
2. Taddeo, M.: Modelling Trust In Artificial Agents, A First Step Toward The Analysis of E-trust. (2), UK (July 2010)
3. Computer Fraud: Woman accused of bullying teen on MySpace. Computer Fraud and Security, 1–2 (June 2008)

Non-intrusive and Transparent Authentication on Smart Phones

(Extended Abstract)

Nicholas Micallef, Mike Just, Lynne Baillie, and Gunes Kayacik

Interactive and Trustworthy Technologies Research Group
Glasgow Caledonian University
name.surname@gcu.ac.uk

1 Introduction

This work aims to contribute to the field of non-intrusive and transparent authentication on smart phones by defining an implicit authentication model consisting of a set of distinguishable recurring features extracted from a combination of different sources of inbuilt sensors which have not yet been previously combined for this purpose. The research goals of this work are (1) define a robust methodology for accurate and transparent sensor data collection (2) identify sets of distinguishable and recurring features to define an implicit authentication model and (3) evaluate the usability and security threats of this authentication model so that a smart phone could be trained for a brief period of time after which it will be capable of authenticating users in a non-intrusive and transparent manner.

2 Context and Motivation

By 2013 smart phones are expected to overtake PCs as the main way to access the Web [1]. This means that robust and efficient authentication and access control systems are required. Traditional authentication techniques (e.g., passwords) which are being deployed on smart phones require active user involvement, are not considered user-friendly [1], and take users away from their main task [2]. Methods that attempt to improve usability (e.g., Android pattern) do so at the detriment of security [3]. Implicit techniques that rely upon a users transparent interaction with the phone (e.g., how users hold or use a phone) offer a promising alternative or enhancement to the currently deployed authentication techniques since they do not require any explicit user involvement [4].

Therefore, this work evaluates a combination of in-built low level sensor data to find recurring distinguishable features to build an authentication model which would implicitly authenticate users. The sensor data is being obtained from motion sensors (i.e. accelerometer), environment sensors (i.e. Sound, Light, Magnetic field), location sensors (i.e. Wi-Fi and cell tower) and usage information (i.e. duration of sessions, etc). This authentication model will be evaluated from a usability perspective and through different levels of security attacks.

---

[1] Gartner forecast: http://news.cnet.com/8301-1001_3-10434760-92.html

M. Huth et al. (Eds.): TRUST 2013, LNCS 7904, pp. 271–272, 2013.
© Springer-Verlag Berlin Heidelberg 2013

3   Research Goals, Methods and Status

The first research goal has been accomplished with the definition of the methodology and development of a robust application that collects sensor data through an in the wild study. The second research goal defines an implicit authentication model. A 2 week pilot experiment with 4 users helped in defining the optimal sampling rates together with defining which sensors should be excluded from further experiments. A 2 week experiment with 14 users is currently in progress. The collected sensor data is being distributed in a number of different buckets (i.e. location, physical activity, time of the day, etc) in order to determine the optimal sets of recurring distinguishable features which when applied to machine learning algorithms will define the implicit authentication model.

Table 1. shows how physical activity is being used to assign weights to sensor data. These weights give higher weight to motion sensors when the user is moving and higher weight to usage data when the user is stationary. In the third research goal an implicit authentication framework consisting of features extracted during the second goal will be evaluated from both a usability and security attack perspective. Security attacks will be evaluated through three different attacking models (i.e. naive, partially informed and fully informed attackers). A naive attacker would know some of the locations of the user and would occasionally guess some usage information. In contrast, a fully informed attacker would be well informed about the user's actions,i.e. he would know the user's exact locations and most of the applications used.

Table 1. Weight distribution of sensor data according to physical activity

	Motion		Location		User		Environment		
	Acceleration	Rotation	Wi-Fi	Cell Tower	Usage	Orientation	Sound	Light	Magnetic Field
Stationary	Low	Low	Med	Low	High	High	Med	Med	Low
Moving	High	High	Med	Med	Med	Med	High	Med	Low
Moving Fast	High	High	High	High	Low	Low	High	Low	Low

References

1. Jakobsson, M., Shi, E., Golle, P., Chow, R.: Implicit authentication for mobile devices. In: HotSec 2009 (2009)
2. Mantyjarvi, J., Lindholm, M., Vildjiounaite, E., Makela, S., Ailisto, H.: Identifying users of portable devices from gait pattern with accelerometers. In: IEEE ICASSP 2005, vol. 2, p. ii/973 (2005)
3. De Luca, A., Hang, A., Brudy, F., Lindner, C., Hussmann, H.: Touch me once and i know it's you!: implicit authentication based on touch screen patterns. In: CHI 2012, pp. 987–996. ACM (2012)
4. Shi, W., Yang, J., Jiang, Y., Yang, F., Xiong, Y.: Senguard: Passive user identification on smartphones using multiple sensors. In: WiMob, p. 141. IEEE (2011)

Quaestio-it.com: From Debates Towards Trustworthy Answers
(Extended Abstract)

Valentinos Evripidou and Francesca Toni

Department of Computing, Imperial College London,
London, SW7 2AZ, United Kingdom
{ve10,ft}@imperial.ac.uk

Abstract. Information sharing between online users has altered the way we seek and find information. Users have at their disposal a wide range of tools for exchanging opinions and engaging into discussions. This creates a large amount of user generated information that can often be misleading, false or even malicious. We demonstrate a question-and-answer web application, based on Computational Argumentation, that offers debating infrastructure for opinion exchanges. It empowers users to organically determine trustworthy answers through their feedback which takes the form of voting and posting attacking or supporting arguments.

Social networks, discussion platforms and forums have changed the way we interact on the web. Users can easily share and express their opinions, views and thoughts over a plethora of topics, as well as initiate conversations. This creates an overwhelming amount of user generated information in the form of discussions and debates that can include misleading, false or even malicious information. A sub-category of these platforms are question-and-answer (Q&A) websites where users turn to for asking questions and receiving answers.. These platforms depend entirely on user contributions and therefore need strong mechanisms for controlling the quality of their content. We demonstrate *quaestio-it*, a prototype Q&A web application which provides an intelligent way for evaluating answers to questions, using Computational Argumentation, a method that has proven its importance in a number of application areas such as medicine, law, robotics and decision tools [1]. Quaestio-it can be used to provide a way for users to give their feedback and identify the most trustworthy answers on any question. It takes a novel approach on Q&A functionality and offers the infrastructure for discussing each answer to any user posted question. It imposes a basic structure for posting answers and comments and offers an interactive visualised way for browsing through conversations. Posted answers are open for debate and users can vote or post their attacking/supporting comments as arguments either on the answers or on other comments. The answers are then evaluated using techniques from Computational Argumentation, taking arguments and votes into account, with the best answers being identified and highlighted.

Figure 1 shows a screenshot of a debate about a question on quaestio-it.com. On the right, the debate is represented as a tree with the root node being the

M. Huth et al. (Eds.): TRUST 2013, LNCS 7904, pp. 273–274, 2013.
© Springer-Verlag Berlin Heidelberg 2013

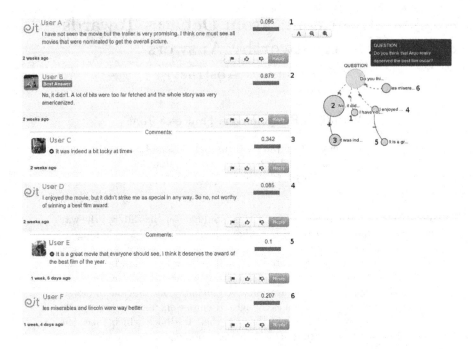

Fig. 1. Visualisation of debates in quaestio-it.com

question, its immediate children being the answers and all subsequent level nodes being comments (posted by users as attacking or supporting arguments). The edges between the nodes illustrate the relations between the question, the answers and the comments; dotted edges indicate direct answers to the question, while straight, red (-) or green (+) edges show attacking or supporting arguments on the answers or on other arguments. Nodes vary in size depending on the strength evaluation from the underlying algorithm, offering a quick insight about the dominant, most trusted (by other users) answers for a particular question. On the left of Figure 1 a linear representation of the answers and comments is shown, corresponding to the nodes of the tree as indicated by the numbers 1–6. It includes further information such as the positive/negative votes ratio, strength evaluations and all available actions to the user.

Future developments include: (i) adapting the algorithm and argumentation framework to implement reputation mechanisms for determining a user's trustworthiness, and (ii) including spam detection techniques to prevent the manipulation of the system or the underlying algorithm.

Acknowledgements. This research was supported by an EPSRC Pathways to Impact project.

Reference

1. Bench-Capon, T.J.M., Dunne, P.E.: Argumentation in artificial intelligence. Artif. Intell. 171(10-15), 619–641 (2007)

Towards Verifiable Trust Management
for Software Execution
(Extended Abstract)

Michael Huth and Jim Huan-Pu Kuo

Department of Computing, Imperial College London
London, SW7 2AZ, United Kingdom
{m.huth,jimhkuo}@imperial.ac.uk

Abstract. In the near future, computing devices will be present in most artefacts, will considerably outnumber the number of people on this planet, and will host software the executes in a potentially hostile and only partially known environment. This suggests the need for bringing trust management into running software itself, so that executing software be guard-railed by policies that reflect risk postures deemed to be appropriate for software and its deployment context. We sketch here an implementation of a prototype that realizes, in part, such a vision.

The technical work described below relies on the concept of *Trust Evidence*. By this we mean any source of information (credentials, reputation, system state, past or present behavior, etc.) that can be used in order to assess the trustworthiness of running a unit of code. The variety of sources for Trust Evidence suggest the need for an extensible language in which such evidence can be combined. The quantitative (e.g. reputation) and qualitative (e.g. a claimed credential) nature of such evidence means that such a language has to consistently compose qualitative as well as quantitative notions of Trust Evidence.

We here present an exploratory case study (whose usability issues are discussed in [1]) where Scala [2] methods are the units of software that guard rails are meant to control. Guard rails use heterogeneous Trust Evidence sources to decide the circumstances in which methods may be invoked. The data-flow diagram of our case study, in Figure 1, has a three-layered guard rail architecture.

Annotation blocks @Expects, @Policy, and @Switch precede each method declaration and, roughly, correspond to a *context-sensitive access request*, a *policy decision point* (where the contextualized request is evaluated), and a *policy enforcement point* (where the evaluated decision is realized) – as familiar from access-control architectures. Atomic expectations (expressed in @Expects) may be predicates associated with a certain trust score. Intuitively, truth of the predicate secures this trust score in isolation. For example, an atomic expectation may assign trust score 0.2 if the method is not called by a specific caller method. Atomic trust scores would then be composed within sub-blocks based on a specified composition operator (e.g. a pessimistic min operator). Sub-block scores may be accumulative, pessimistic, etc. and are themselves combined into a local trust score that is referred to in the second level (@Policy), which specifies

M. Huth et al. (Eds.): TRUST 2013, LNCS 7904, pp. 275–276, 2013.

a *rule-based policy* for whether or not to execute the method body. The third level (`@Switch`) then implements the *enforcement of the guard rails* specified in the expectation and policy levels. We implemented this as a switch statement that ranges over possible policy decisions and that specifies, for each possible decision, whether and if so how the "payload" method body should execute.

The proof of concept framework was implemented in the Scala programming language [2]. One reason for choosing a JVM based language such as Scala is that there exist frameworks to extend the language and inject behaviours/aspects at various points of the source code, allowing us to deliver more refined, future prototype implementations. The two frameworks we use in our first implementation are: ANTLR [3] and AspectJ [4].

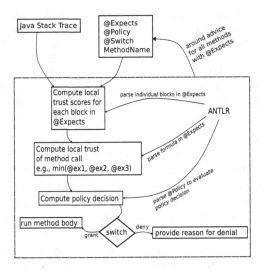

Fig. 1. Dataflow of our trust-management implementation for method guard railing

Acknowledgment. Intel® Corporation kindly funded a sub-project within its *Trust Evidence* project. Work reported here is an outcome of said sub-project.

References

1. Huth, M., Kuo, J.H.-P., Sasse, A., Kirlappos, I.: Towards usable generation and enforcement of trust evidence from programmers' intent. In: Proc. of 15th Int'l Conf. on Human-Computer Interaction. LNCS. Springer (to appear, 2013)
2. Odersky, M.: The Scala Language Specification Version 2.9. Programming Methods Laboratory, EPFL, Switzerland (May 24, 2011) (draft)
3. Parr, T.: The Definitive ANTLR 4 Reference. The Pragmatic Programmer (2013)
4. Lopes, C.V., Kiczales, G.: Improving design and source code modularity using AspectJ (tutorial session). In: ICSE, p. 825 (2000)

Author Index

Aigner, Ronald   37
Anderson, Gabrielle   232
Armstrong, Philip   267

Baillie, Lynne   271
Bartsch, Steffen   205
Ben-Romdhane, Molka   92
Bobba, Rakesh B.   65
Brunthaler, Stefan   151, 187
Burnett, Chris   142
Busch, Marc   223

Campbell, Roy H.   65
Chang, Dexian   133
Chen, Liang   142
Chen, Liqun   47
Cheng, Yueqiang   19
Coles-Kemp, Lizzie   196
Collinson, Matthew   232
Conrad, Marc   269

Danger, Jean-Luc   92
Ding, Xuhua   19

Edwards, Peter   142
Ekberg, Jan-Erik   115
England, Paul   37
Evripidou, Valentinos   273

Faily, Shamal   267
Feng, Dengguo   133
Feng, Wei   133
Fléchais, Ivan   267
Franz, Michael   151, 187
French, Tim   269

Gligor, Virgil   1
Graba, Tarik   92

Han, Jun   1
Hanser, Christian   47
Hein, Daniel   47
Hennigan, Eric   151, 187

Hochleitner, Christina   223
Huang, Heqing   169
Huh, Jun Ho   65
Huth, Michael   275

Jaffray, Mariesha   142
Just, Mike   271

Karame, Ghassan O.   83
Karayumak, Fatih   205
Kayacik, Gunes   271
Kerschbaumer, Christoph   151, 187
Koshy, Lyzgeo Merin   269
Kuo, Jim Huan-Pu   275

Larsen, Per   151, 187
Light, Ann   196
Lin, Yue-Hsun   1
Liu, Peng   169
Lorenz, Mario   223

Malheiros, Miguel   250
Micallef, Nicholas   271
Montanari, Mirko   65

Nordholz, Jan   37
Norman, Timothy J.   142

Perrig, Adrian   1
Pignotti, Edoardo   142
Pirker, Martin   106
Potzmader, Klaus   47
Power, David   267
Preibusch, Sören   250
Pym, David   232

Qin, Yu   133

Rahulamathavan, Yogachandran   142

Sasse, M. Angela   250
Schulz, Trenton   223
Shukla, Mitul   269

Tamrakar, Sandeep   115
Teufl, Peter   47
Theuerling, Heike   205
Toni, Francesca   273
Tscheligi, Manfred   223

Volkamer, Melanie   205

Wei, Ge   133
Winter, Johannes   47, 106
Wittstock, Eckhart   223
Wu, Dinghao   169

Zhang, Qianying   133
Zhou, Zongwei   1
Zhu, Sencun   169